It's been a year since I started working on *Dragon Ball Super*. The more I work on it, the more I realize how far away Toriyama Sensei is from where I stand right now. However, people say that being able to recognize someone else's strength is proof that you've improved too. In that sense, perhaps I can assume that I've gone from Hercule-level to Yamcha-level. You may find some things in this manga that seem odd to you, but I truly appreciate you reading this series with an open mind.

—Toyotarou, 2016

Toyotarou

Toyotarou created the manga adaptation for the *Dragon Ball Z* anime's 2015 film, *Dragon Ball Z: Resurrection F*. He is also the author of the spin-off series *Dragon Ball Heroes: Victory Mission*, which debuted in *V-Jump* in Japan in November 2012.

Akira Toriyama

Renowned worldwide for his playful, innovative storytelling and humorous, distinctive art style, Akira Toriyama burst onto the manga scene in 1980 with the wildly popular *Dr. Slump*. His hit series *Dragon Ball* (published in the U.S. as *Dragon Ball* and *Dragon Ball Z*) ran from 1984 to 1995 in Shueisha's *Weekly Shonen Jump* magazine. He is also known for his design work on video games such as *Dragon Quest*, *Chrono Trigger*, *Tobal No. 1* and *Blue Dragon*. His recent manga works include *COWA!*, *Kajika*, *Sand Land*, *Neko Majin*, *Jaco the Galactic Patrolman* and a children's book, *Toccio the Angel*. He lives with his family in Japan.

DRAGON BALL SUPER 1

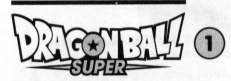

SHONEN JUMP Manga Edition

STORY BY **Akira Toriyama**
ART BY **Toyotarou**

TRANSLATION **Toshikazu Aizawa**
TOUCH-UP ART & LETTERING **Paolo Gattone and Chiara Antonelli**
DESIGN **Shawn Carrico**
EDITOR **Rae First**

Printed in Italy

Published by VIZ Media, LLC
P.O. Box 77010
San Francisco, CA 94107

10
First printing, May 2017
Tenth printing, April 2022

VIZ MEDIA
viz.com

SHONEN JUMP

ratings.viz.com RATED T TEEN

PARENTAL ADVISORY
DRAGON BALL SUPER is rated T for Teen and is recommended for ages 13 and up. This volume contains fantasy violence.

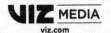

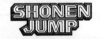

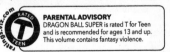

DRAGON BALL SUPER

WARRIORS FROM UNIVERSE 6!

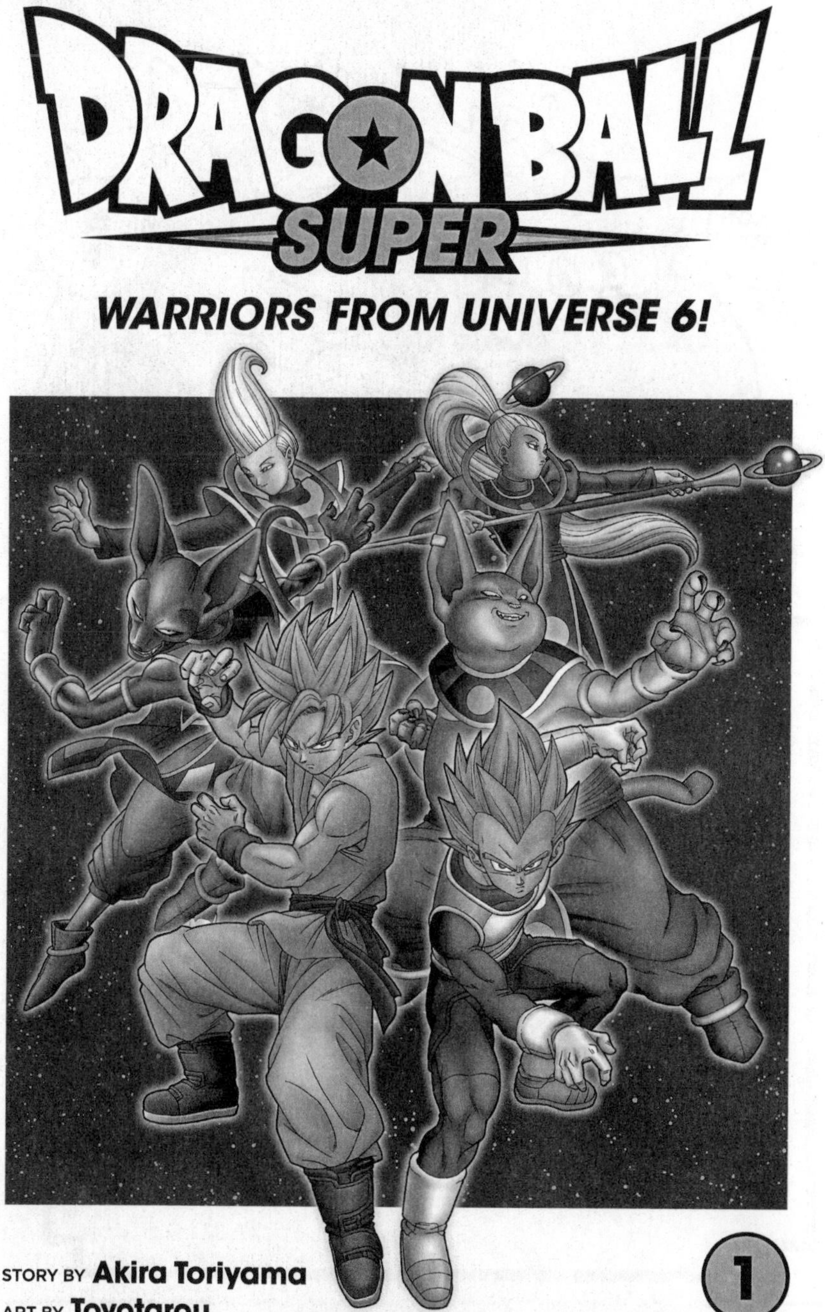

STORY BY **Akira Toriyama**

ART BY **Toyotarou**

1

DRAGON BALL

SUPER

1

CONTENTS

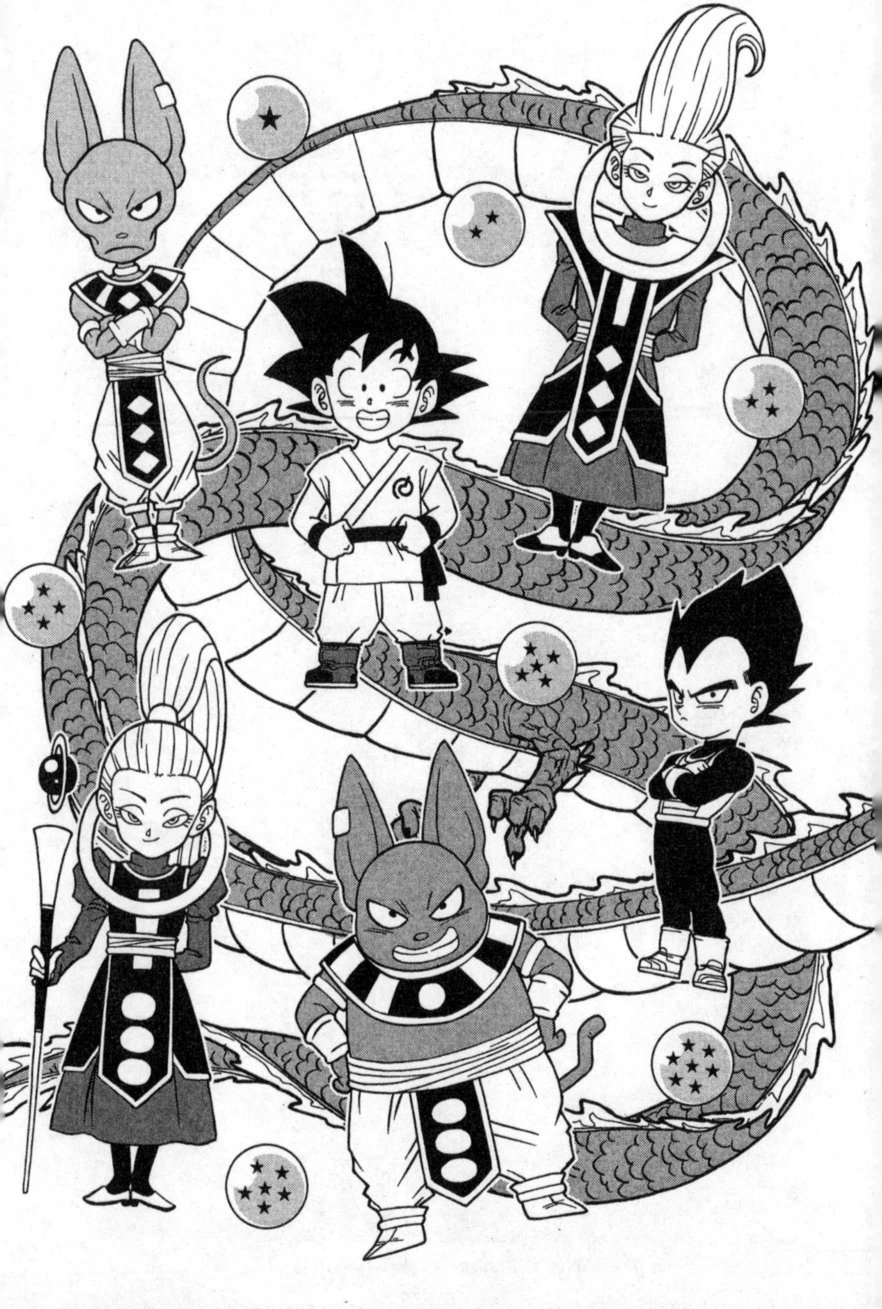

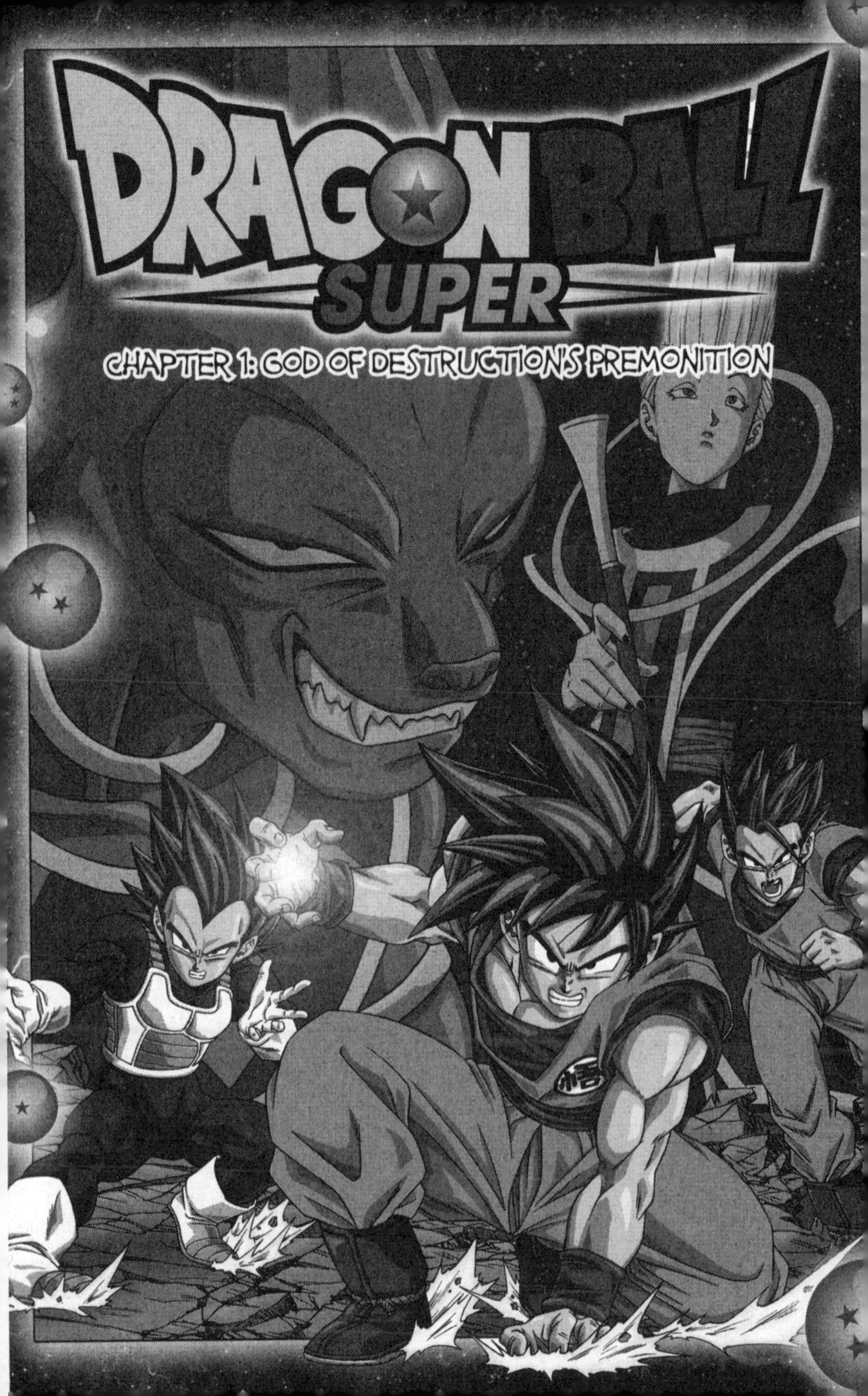
DRAGON BALL
SUPER
CHAPTER 1: GOD OF DESTRUCTION'S PREMONITION

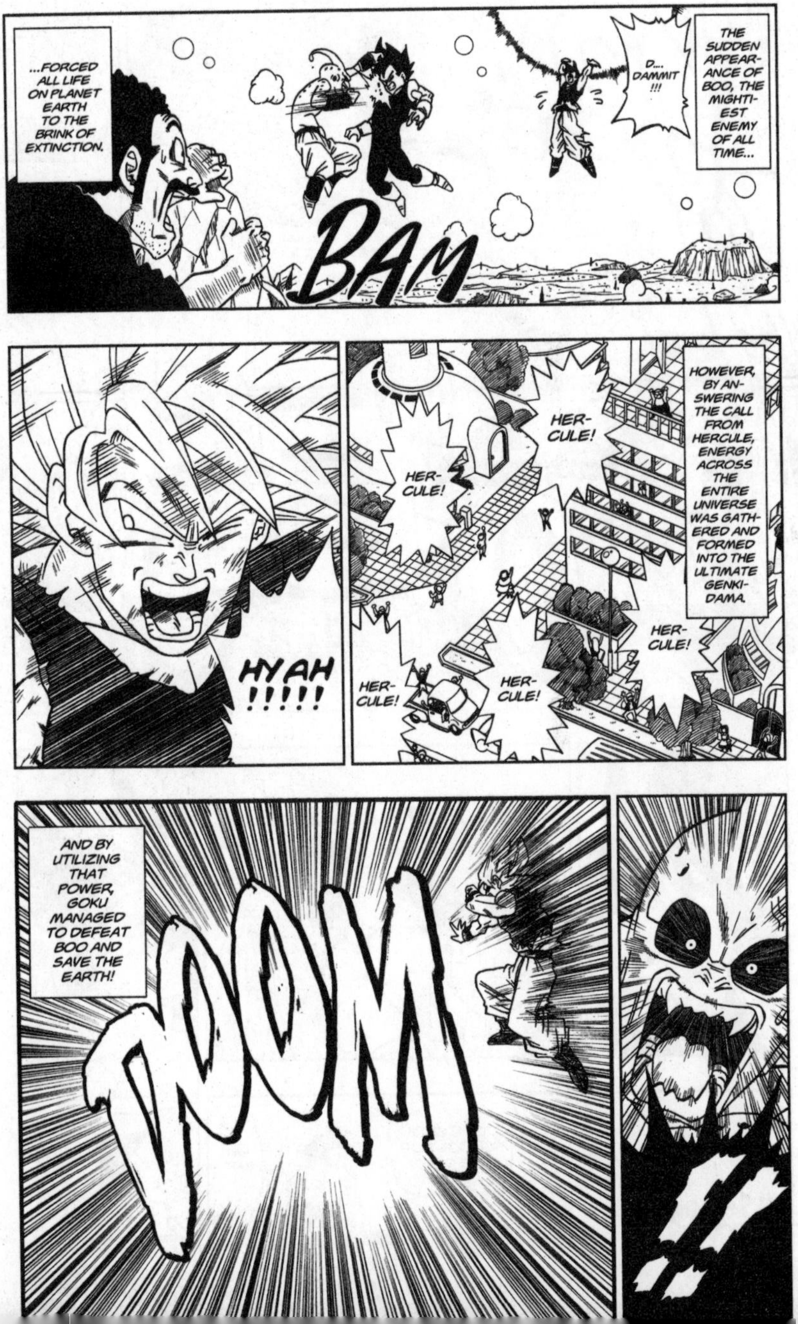

THE SUDDEN APPEARANCE OF BOO, THE MIGHTIEST ENEMY OF ALL TIME...
D... DAMMIT!!!
...FORCED ALL LIFE ON PLANET EARTH TO THE BRINK OF EXTINCTION.
BAM
HOWEVER, BY ANSWERING THE CALL FROM HERCULE, ENERGY ACROSS THE ENTIRE UNIVERSE WAS GATHERED AND FORMED INTO THE ULTIMATE GENKI-DAMA.
HERCULE!
HERCULE!
HERCULE!
HERCULE!
HERCULE!
HYAH!!!!!
!!
AND BY UTILIZING THAT POWER, GOKU MANAGED TO DEFEAT BOO AND SAVE THE EARTH!
DOOM

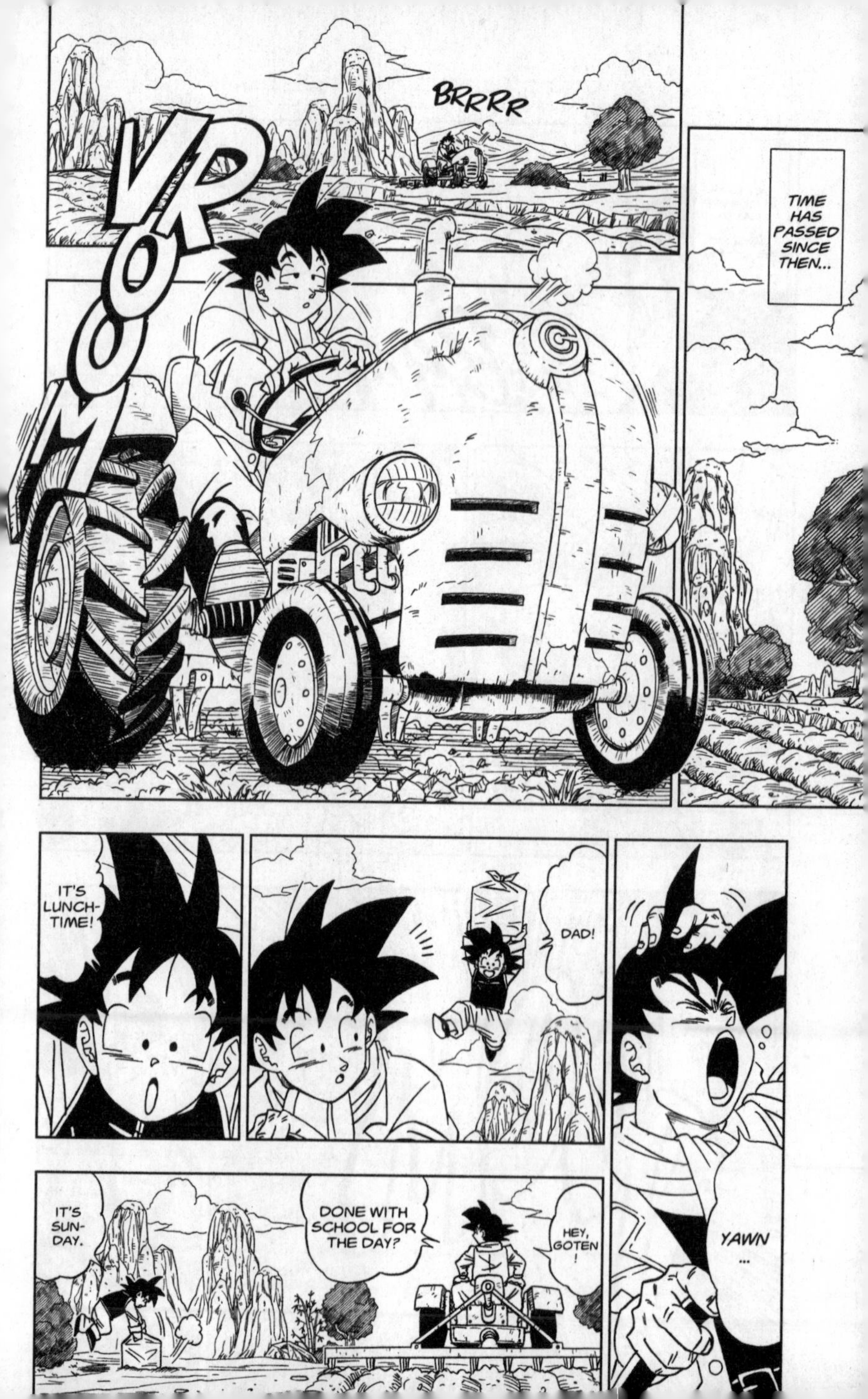

TIME HAS PASSED SINCE THEN...
BRRRR
VROOOM
YAWN ...
DAD!
IT'S LUNCH-TIME!
HEY, GOTEN!
DONE WITH SCHOOL FOR THE DAY?
IT'S SUN-DAY.

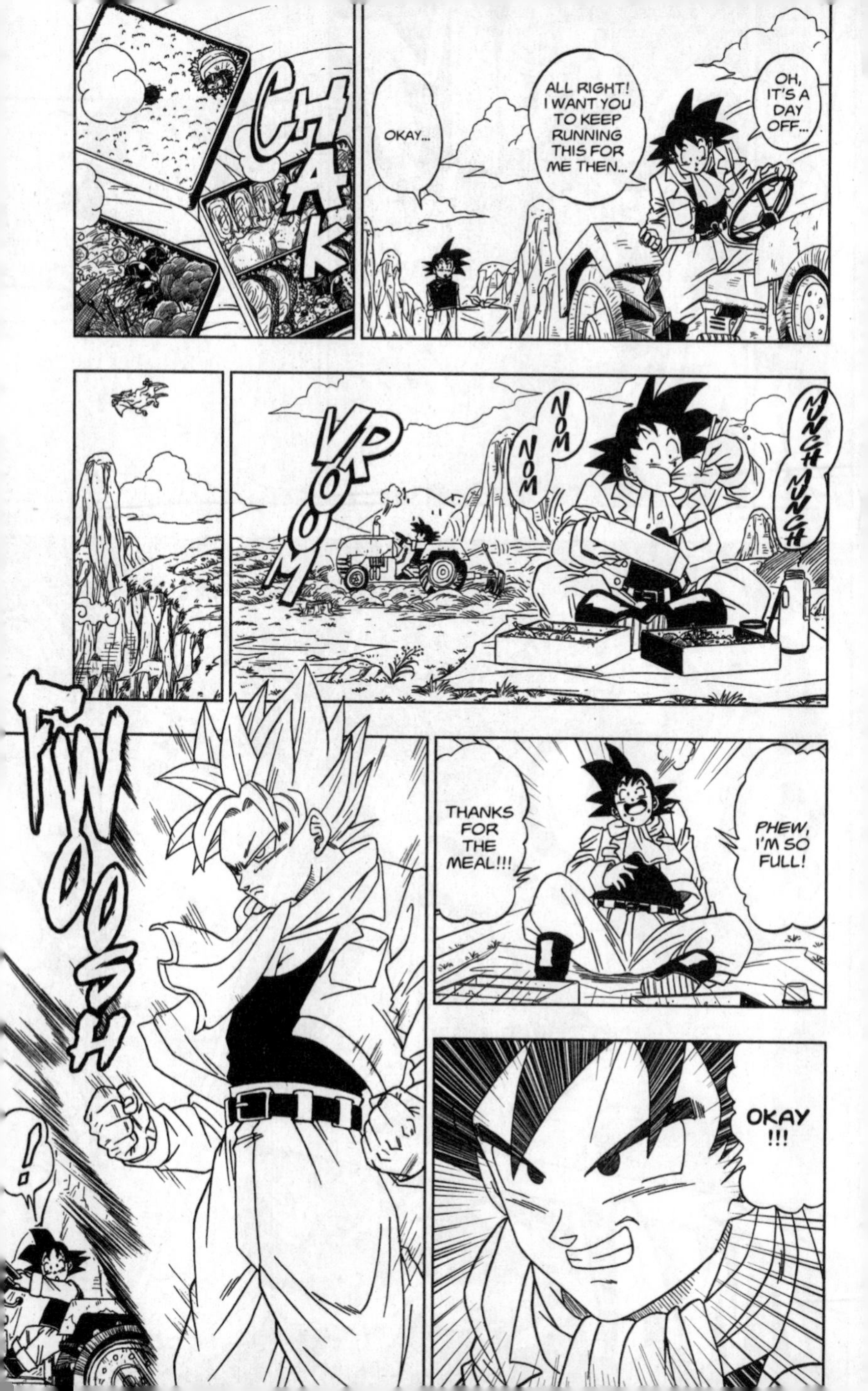
OH, IT'S A DAY OFF...
ALL RIGHT! I WANT YOU TO KEEP RUNNING THIS FOR ME THEN...
OKAY...
CHAK
MUNCH MUNCH
NOM NOM
VROOOM
PHEW, I'M SO FULL!
THANKS FOR THE MEAL!!!
OKAY !!!
FWOOSH
!

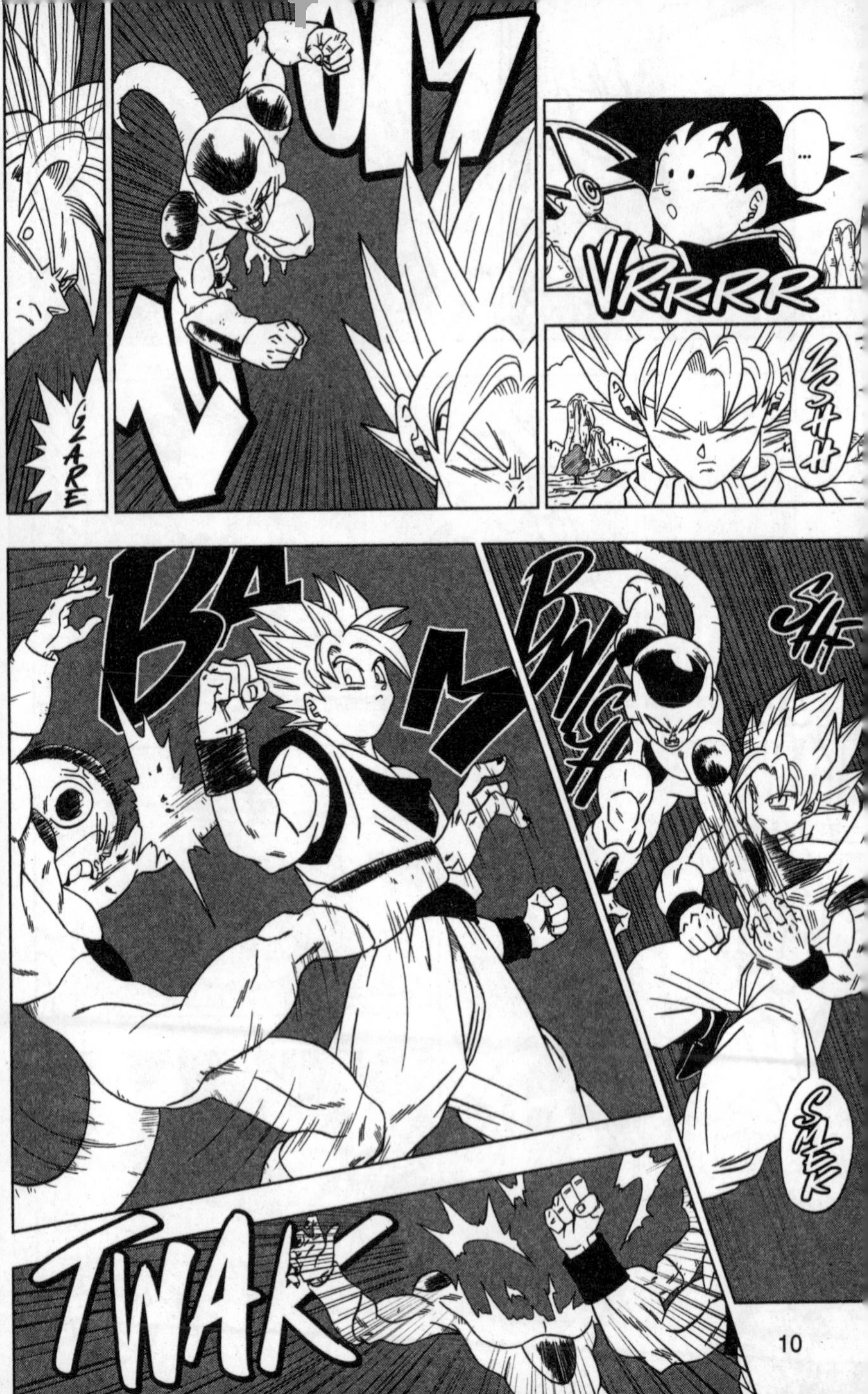
...
VRRRR
ZSHH
OM
GLARE
SHF
BWISH
SMEK
BAM
TWAK

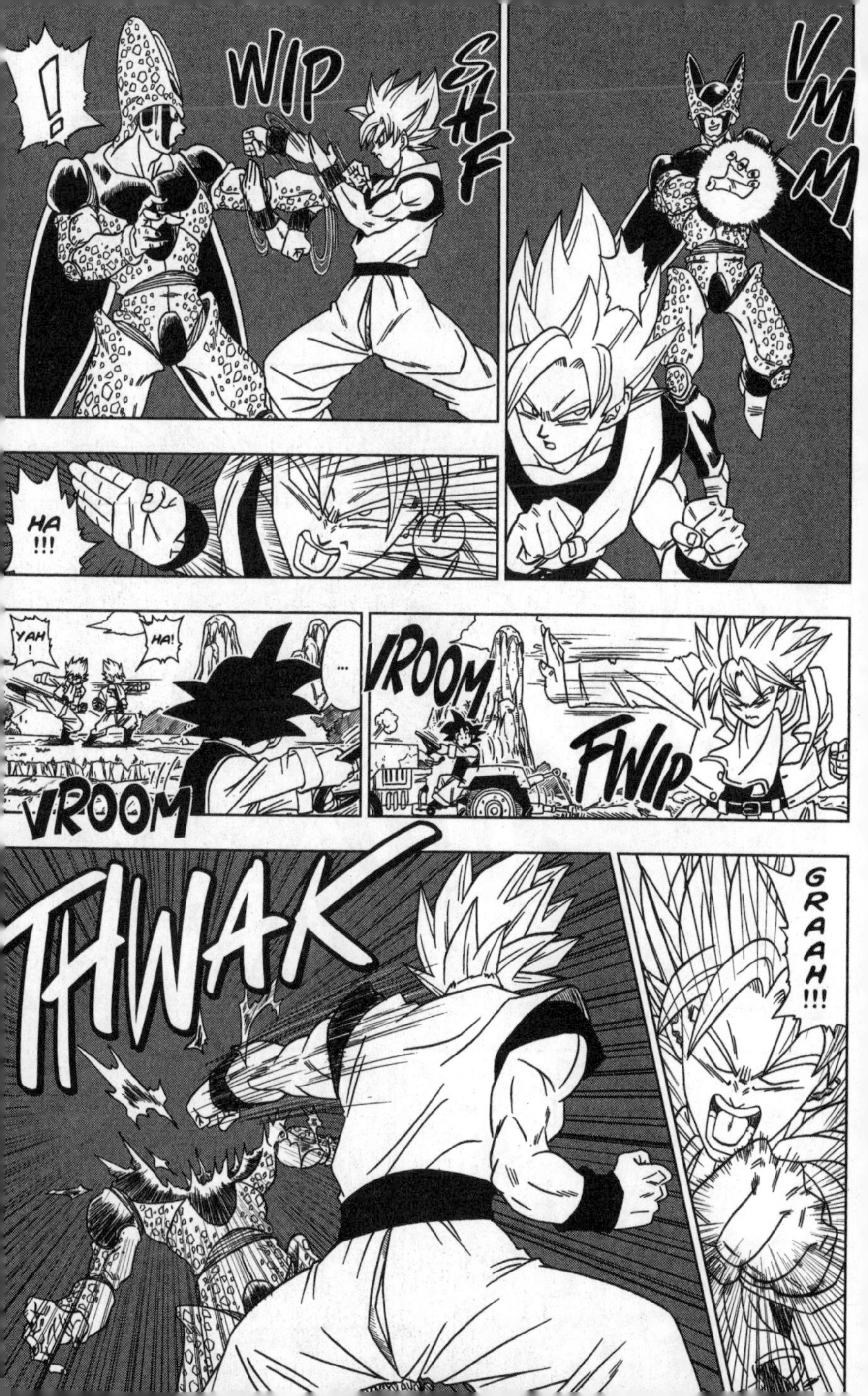
VMM
SHF
WIP
!
HA!!!
FWIP
VROOM
...
HA!
YAH!
VROOM
GRAAH!!!
THWAK

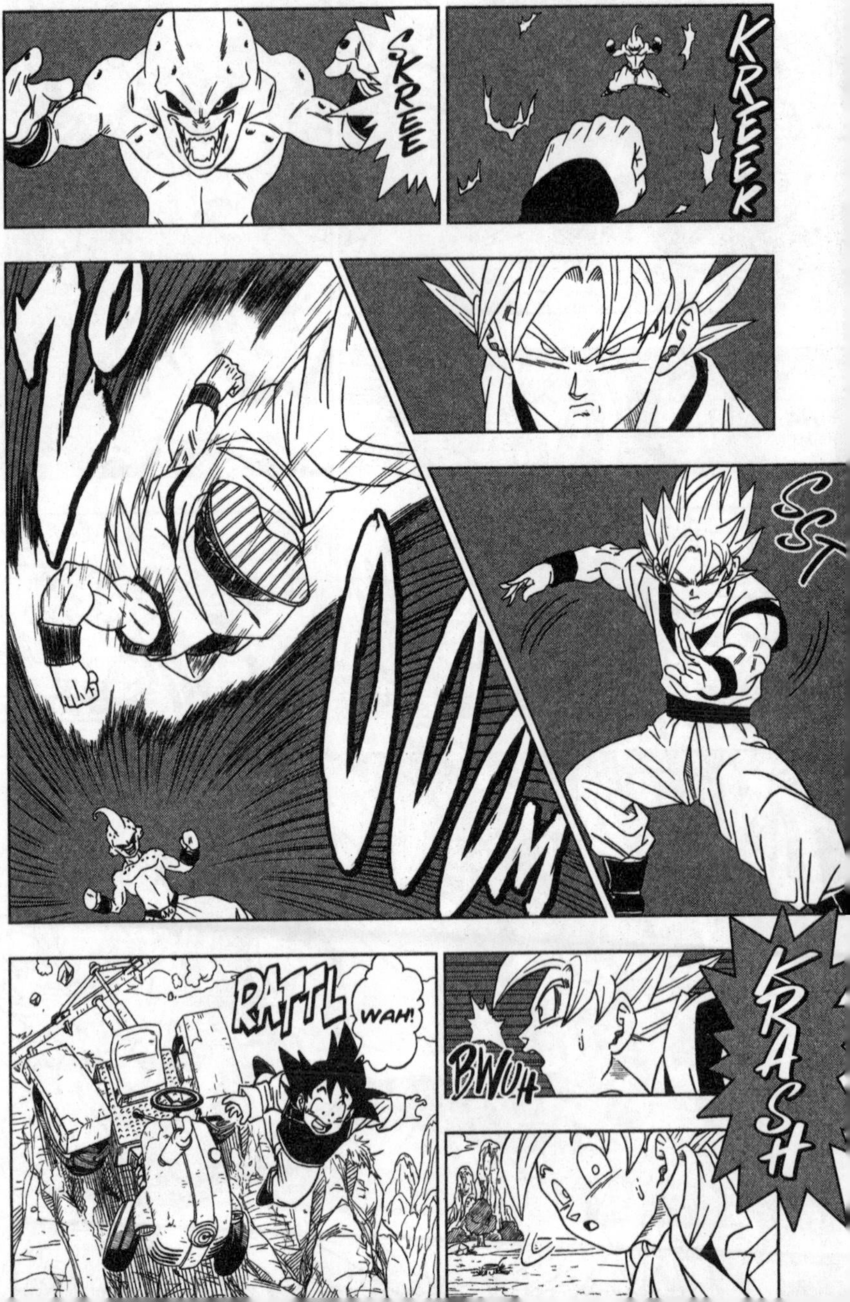
KREEEK
SKREE
SST
VOOOOM
BWUH
KRASH
RATTL
WAH!

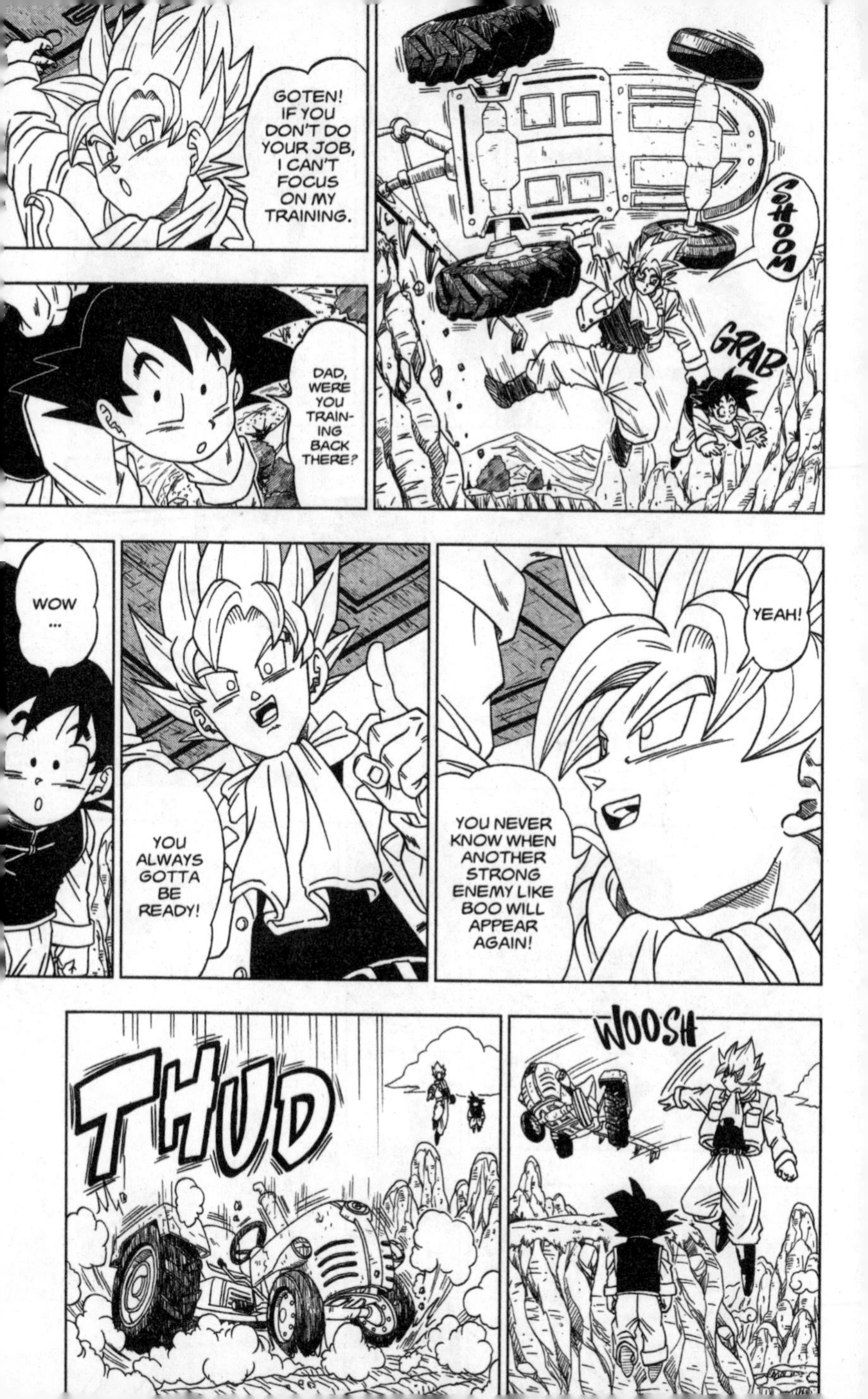
SHOOM
GRAB
GOTEN! IF YOU DON'T DO YOUR JOB, I CAN'T FOCUS ON MY TRAINING.
DAD, WERE YOU TRAINING BACK THERE?
YEAH!
YOU NEVER KNOW WHEN ANOTHER STRONG ENEMY LIKE BOO WILL APPEAR AGAIN!
YOU ALWAYS GOTTA BE READY!
WOW ...
WOOSH
THUD

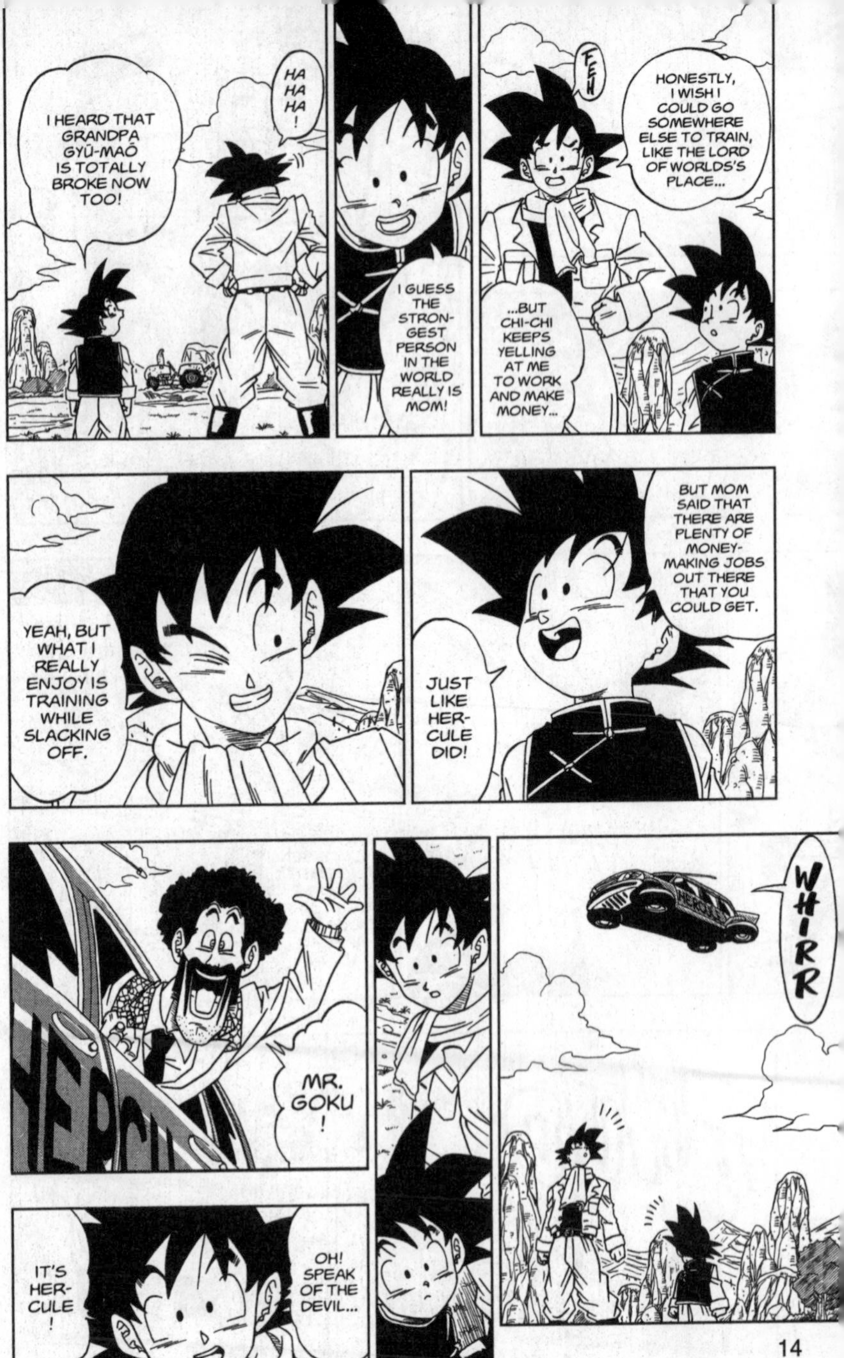
FEH
HONESTLY, I WISH I COULD GO SOMEWHERE ELSE TO TRAIN, LIKE THE LORD OF WORLDS'S PLACE...
...BUT CHI-CHI KEEPS YELLING AT ME TO WORK AND MAKE MONEY...
I GUESS THE STRONGEST PERSON IN THE WORLD REALLY IS MOM!
HA HA HA!
I HEARD THAT GRANDPA GYŪ-MAŌ IS TOTALLY BROKE NOW TOO!
BUT MOM SAID THAT THERE ARE PLENTY OF MONEY-MAKING JOBS OUT THERE THAT YOU COULD GET.
JUST LIKE HERCULE DID!
YEAH, BUT WHAT I REALLY ENJOY IS TRAINING WHILE SLACKING OFF.
WHIRR
MR. GOKU!
OH! SPEAK OF THE DEVIL...
IT'S HERCULE!

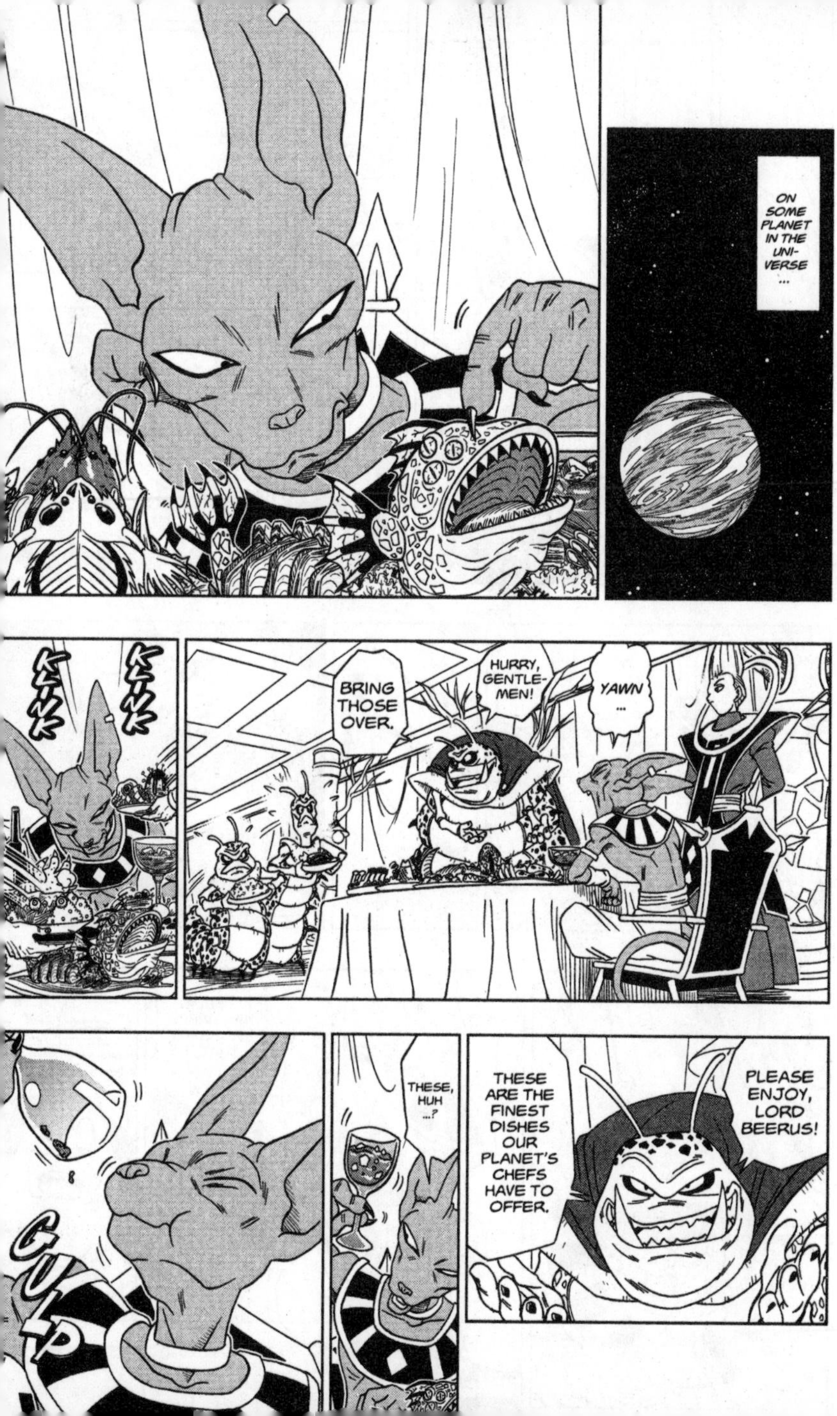
ON SOME PLANET IN THE UNI- VERSE ...
YAWN ...
HURRY, GENTLE- MEN!
BRING THOSE OVER.
KLINK KLINK
PLEASE ENJOY, LORD BEERUS!
THESE ARE THE FINEST DISHES OUR PLANET'S CHEFS HAVE TO OFFER.
THESE, HUH ...?
GULP

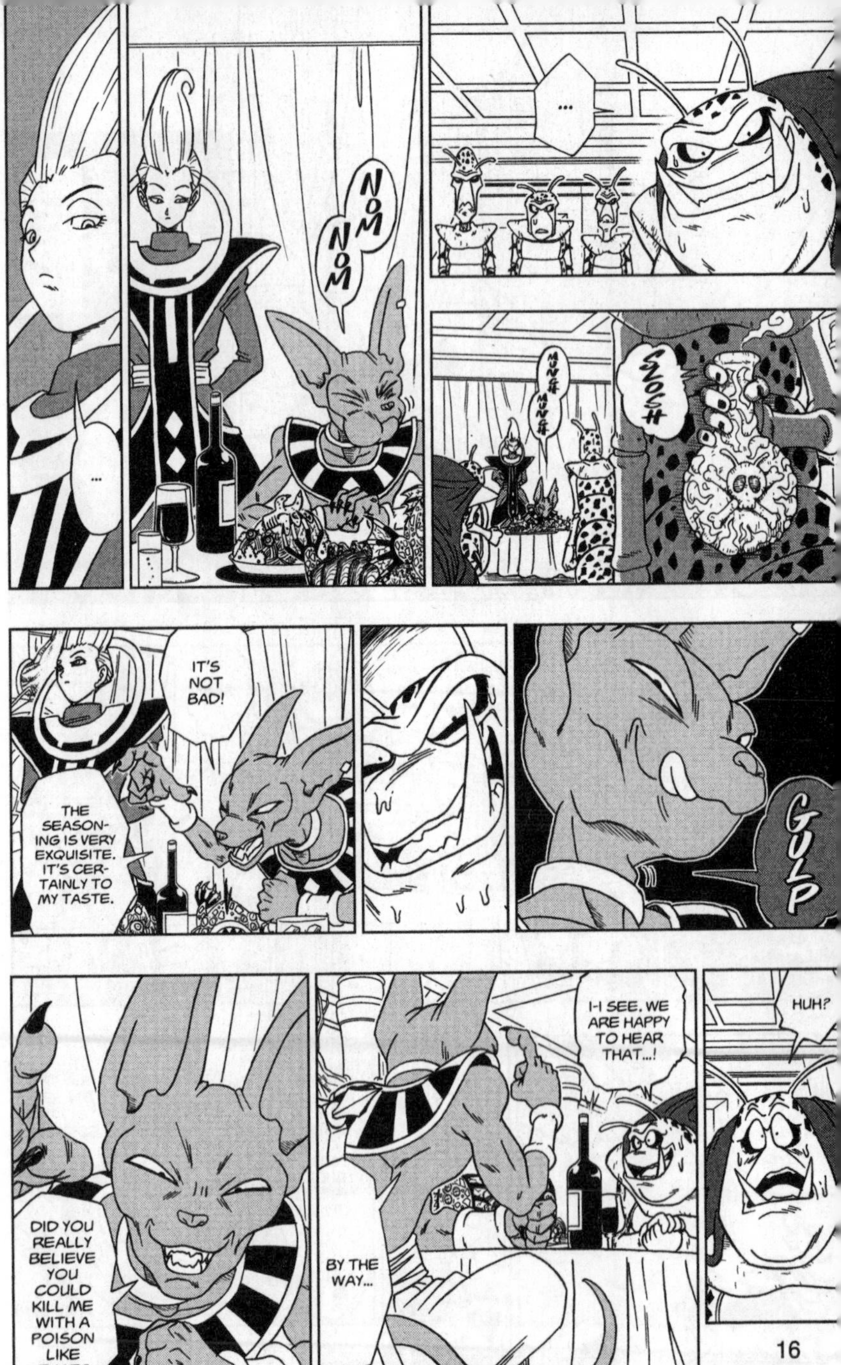
...
SLOSH
MUNCH MUNCH
NOM NOM
...
GULP
IT'S NOT BAD!
THE SEASONING IS VERY EXQUISITE. IT'S CERTAINLY TO MY TASTE.
HUH?
I-I SEE. WE ARE HAPPY TO HEAR THAT...!
BY THE WAY...
DID YOU REALLY BELIEVE YOU COULD KILL ME WITH A POISON LIKE THAT?

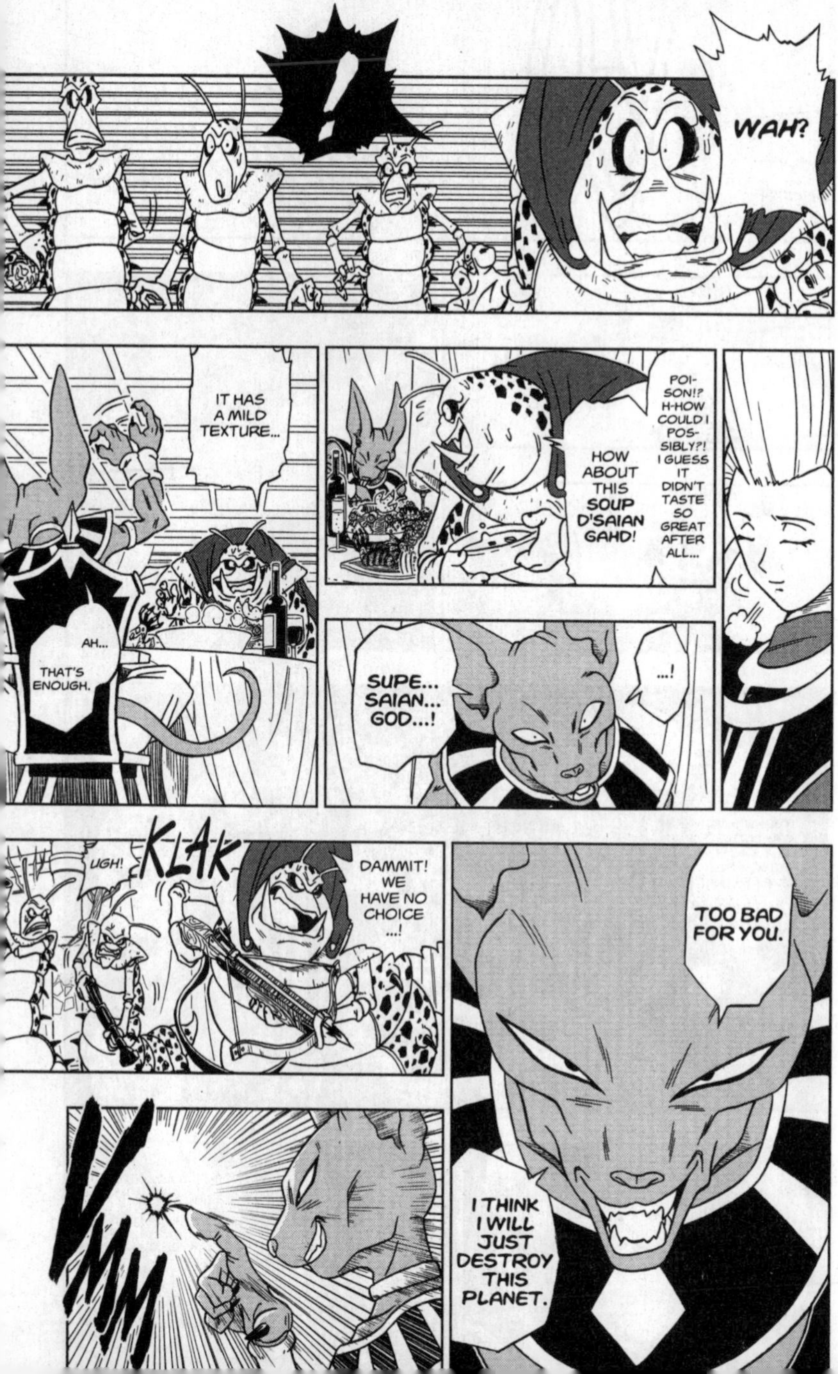
WAH?
!
POI-SON!? H-HOW COULD I POS-SIBLY?! I GUESS IT DIDN'T TASTE SO GREAT AFTER ALL...
HOW ABOUT THIS SOUP D'SAIAN GAHD!
...!
SUPE... SAIAN... GOD...!
IT HAS A MILD TEXTURE...
AH... THAT'S ENOUGH.
TOO BAD FOR YOU.
I THINK I WILL JUST DESTROY THIS PLANET.
DAMMIT! WE HAVE NO CHOICE ...!
KLAK
UGH!
VMM

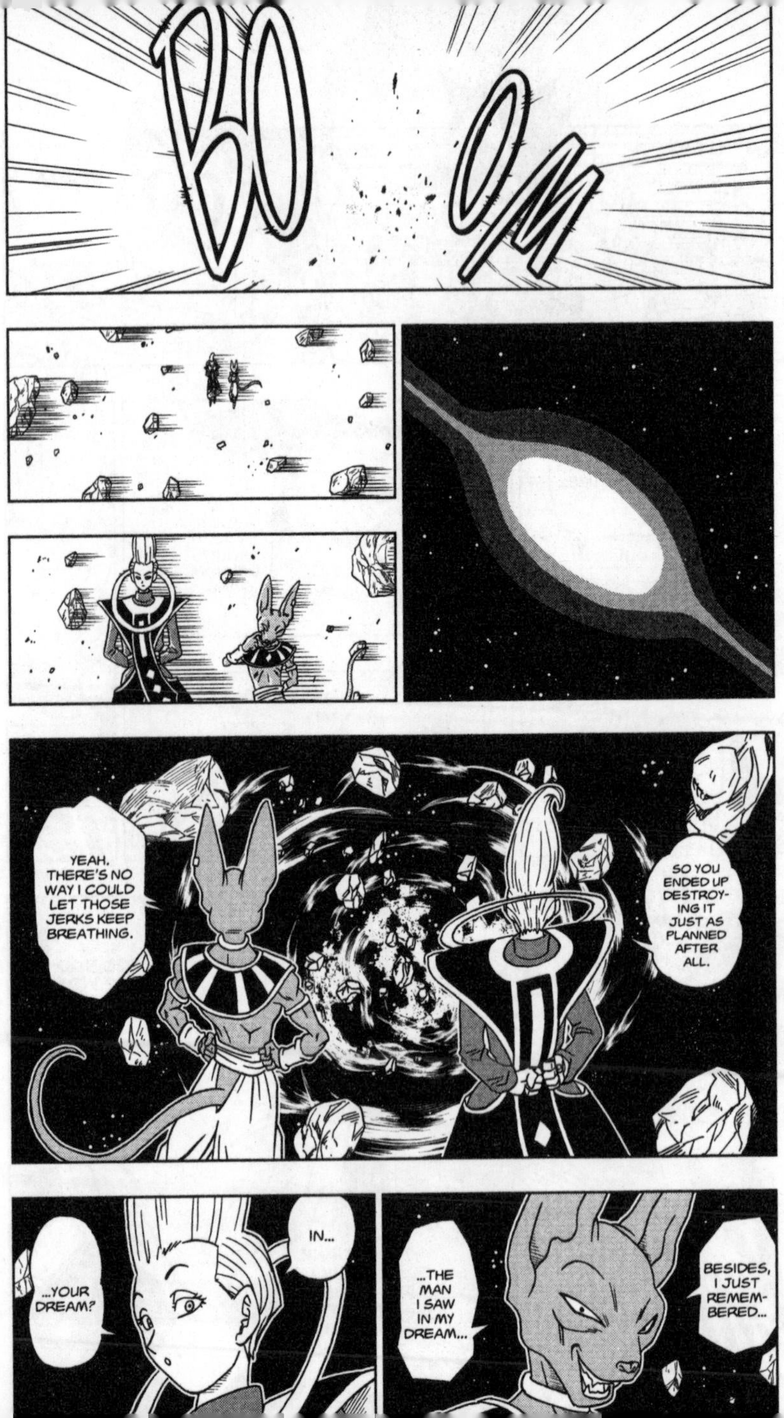
BOOOM
SO YOU ENDED UP DESTROYING IT JUST AS PLANNED AFTER ALL.
YEAH. THERE'S NO WAY I COULD LET THOSE JERKS KEEP BREATHING.
BESIDES, I JUST REMEMBERED...
...THE MAN I SAW IN MY DREAM...
IN...
...YOUR DREAM?

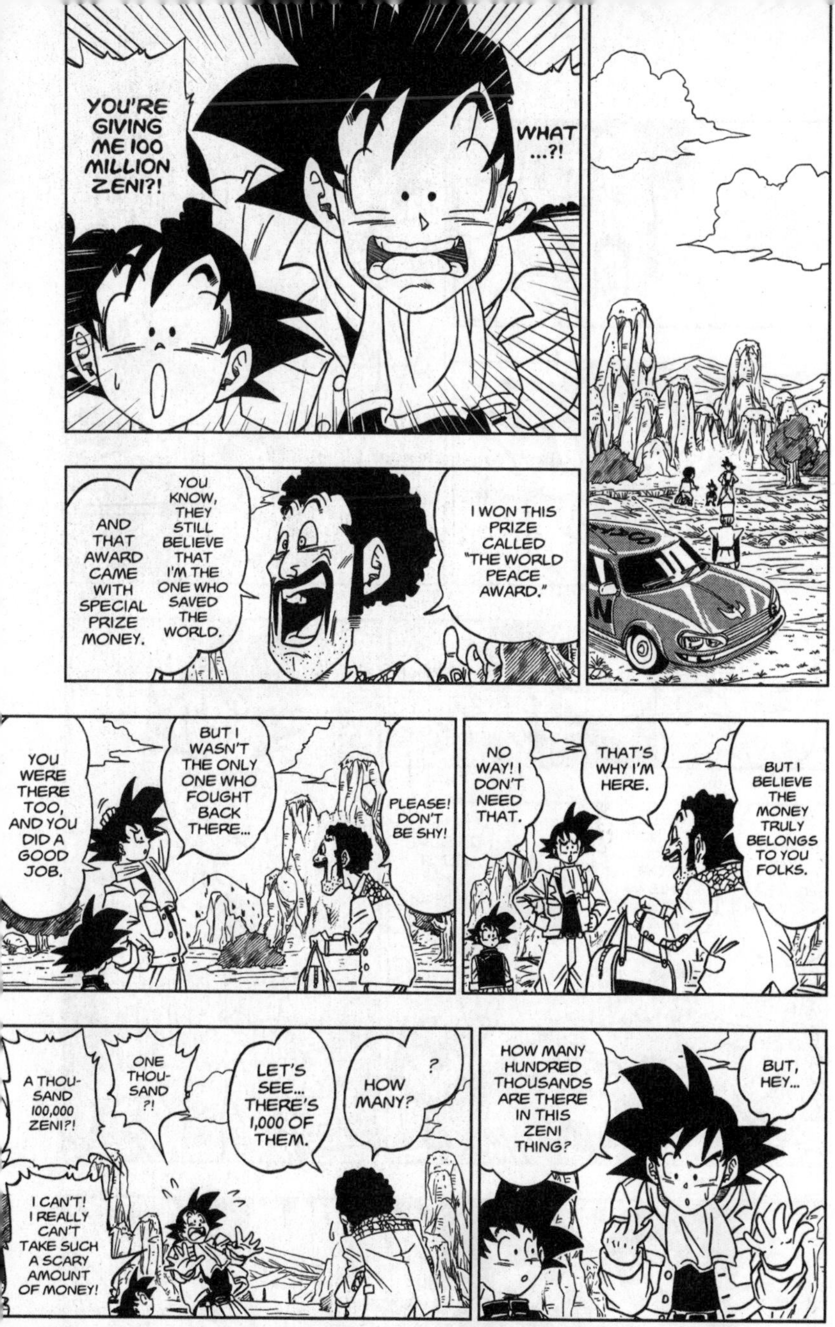
WHAT ...?!
YOU'RE GIVING ME 100 MILLION ZENI?!
I WON THIS PRIZE CALLED "THE WORLD PEACE AWARD."
YOU KNOW, THEY STILL BELIEVE THAT I'M THE ONE WHO SAVED THE WORLD.
AND THAT AWARD CAME WITH SPECIAL PRIZE MONEY.
BUT I BELIEVE THE MONEY TRULY BELONGS TO YOU FOLKS.
THAT'S WHY I'M HERE.
NO WAY! I DON'T NEED THAT.
PLEASE! DON'T BE SHY!
BUT I WASN'T THE ONLY ONE WHO FOUGHT BACK THERE...
YOU WERE THERE TOO, AND YOU DID A GOOD JOB.
BUT, HEY...
HOW MANY HUNDRED THOUSANDS ARE THERE IN THIS ZENI THING?
?
HOW MANY?
LET'S SEE... THERE'S 1,000 OF THEM.
ONE THOUSAND ?!
A THOUSAND 100,000 ZENI?!
I CAN'T! I REALLY CAN'T TAKE SUCH A SCARY AMOUNT OF MONEY!

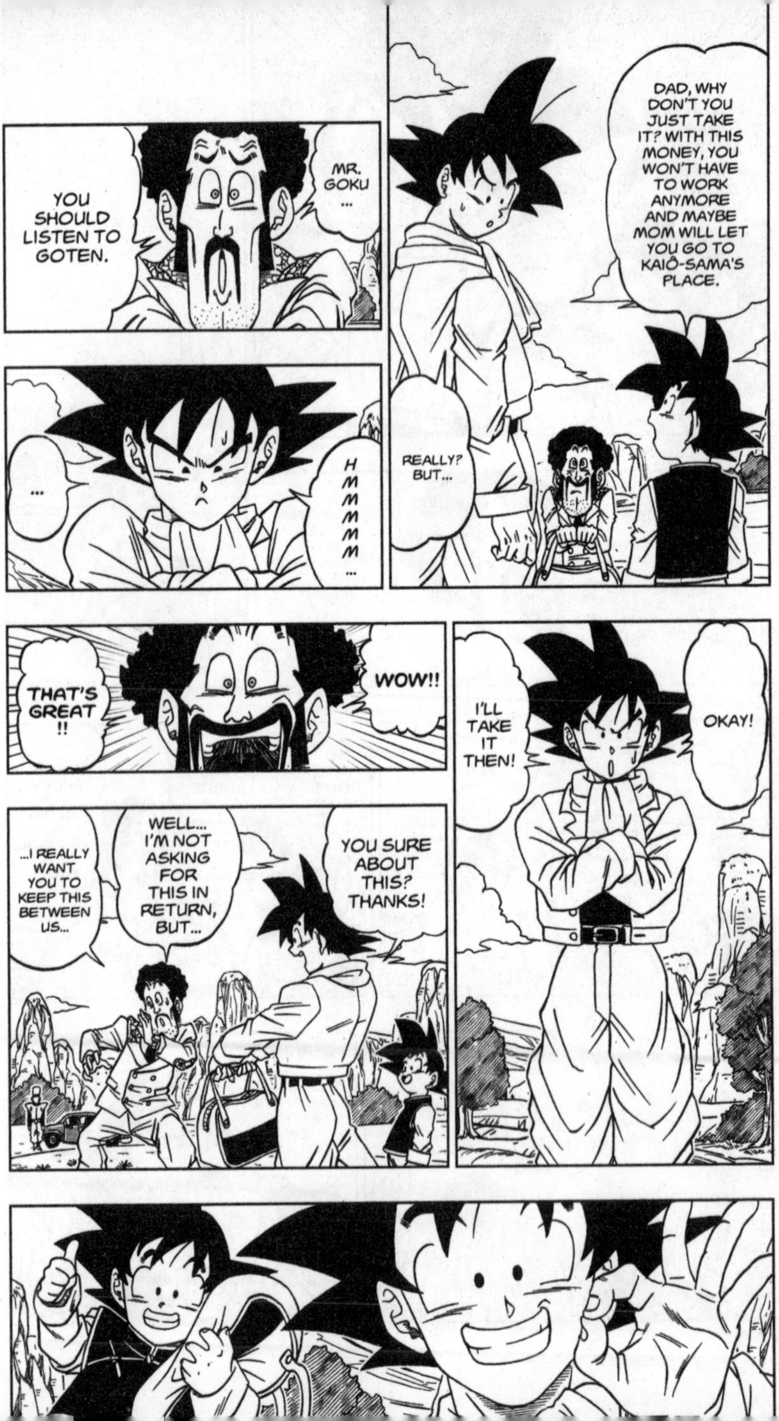
DAD, WHY DON'T YOU JUST TAKE IT? WITH THIS MONEY, YOU WON'T HAVE TO WORK ANYMORE AND MAYBE MOM WILL LET YOU GO TO KAIÔ-SAMA'S PLACE.
REALLY? BUT...
MR. GOKU ...
YOU SHOULD LISTEN TO GOTEN.
HMMMMM...
...
OKAY!
I'LL TAKE IT THEN!
WOW!!
THAT'S GREAT!!
YOU SURE ABOUT THIS? THANKS!
WELL... I'M NOT ASKING FOR THIS IN RETURN, BUT...
...I REALLY WANT YOU TO KEEP THIS BETWEEN US...

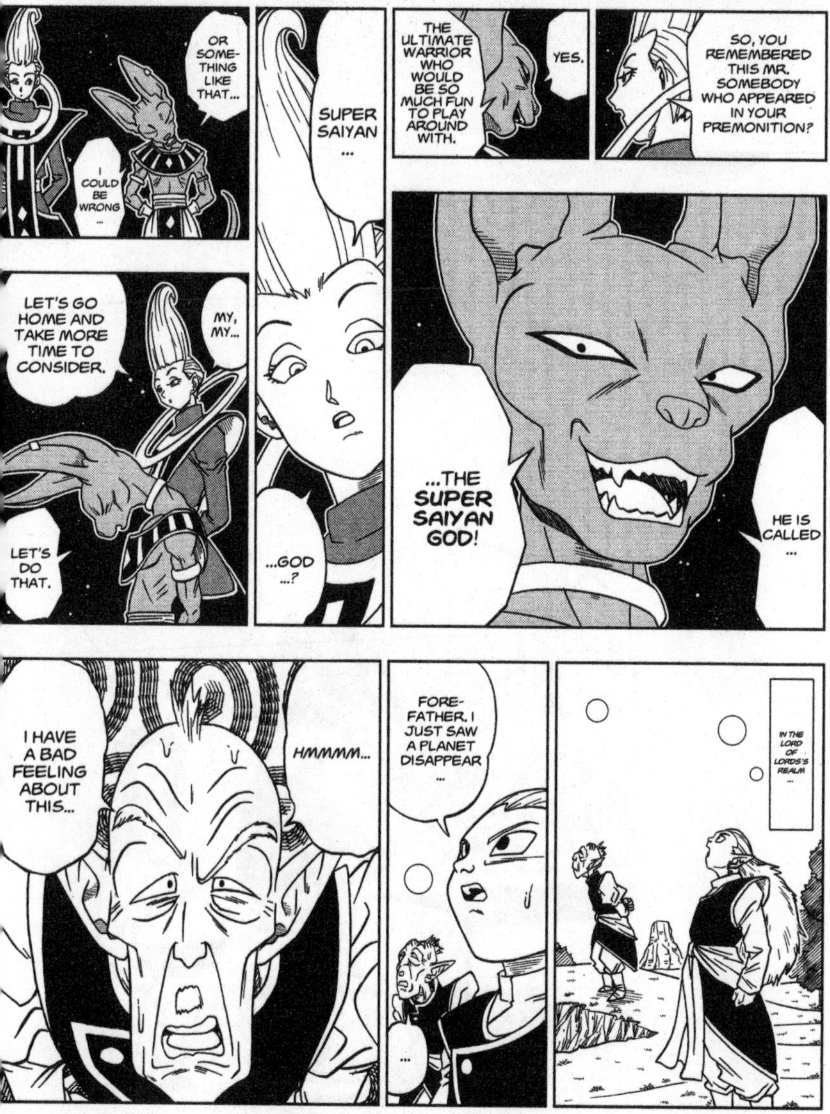
SO, YOU REMEMBERED THIS MR. SOMEBODY WHO APPEARED IN YOUR PREMONITION?
YES.
THE ULTIMATE WARRIOR WHO WOULD BE SO MUCH FUN TO PLAY AROUND WITH.
HE IS CALLED...
...THE **SUPER SAIYAN** GOD!
SUPER SAIYAN...
...GOD...?
OR SOMETHING LIKE THAT...
I COULD BE WRONG...
MY, MY...
LET'S GO HOME AND TAKE MORE TIME TO CONSIDER.
LET'S DO THAT.
IN THE LORD OF LORDS'S REALM...
FOREFATHER, I JUST SAW A PLANET DISAPPEAR...
...
HMMMM...
I HAVE A BAD FEELING ABOUT THIS...

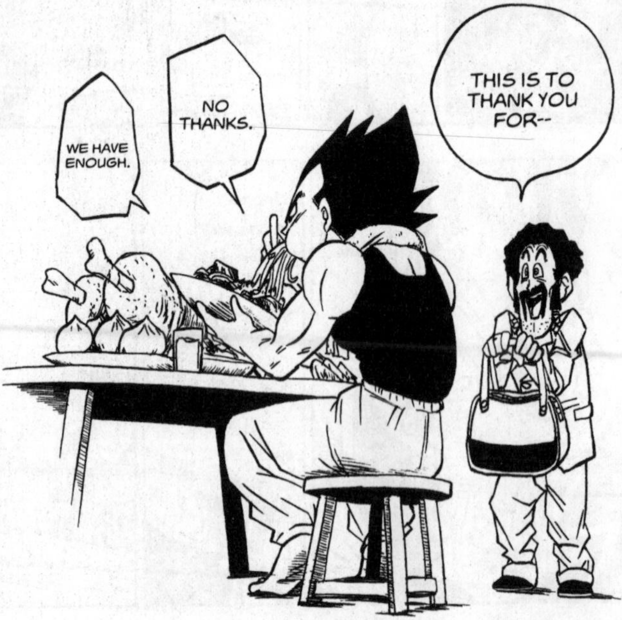
THIS IS TO THANK YOU FOR--
NO THANKS.
WE HAVE ENOUGH.

DRAGON BALL SUPER

CHAPTER 2: GOKU DEFEATED

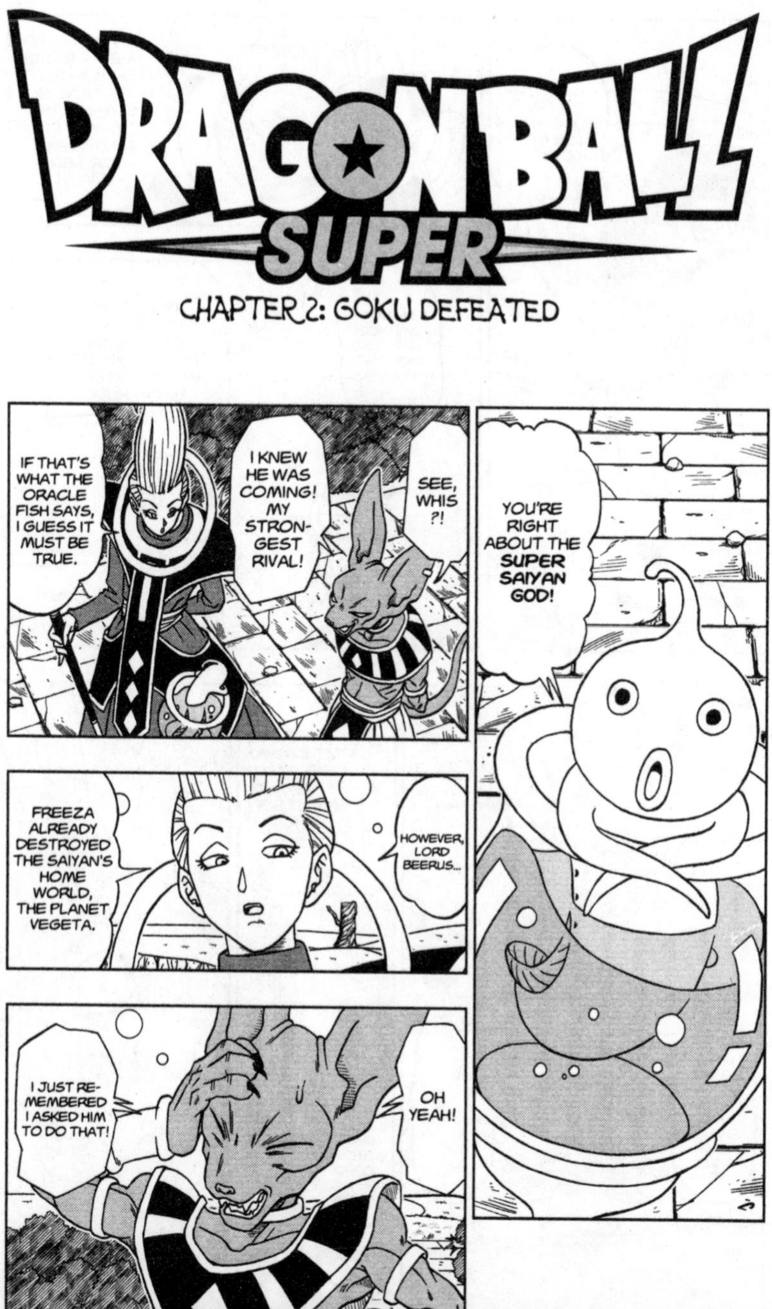
YOU'RE RIGHT ABOUT THE SUPER SAIYAN GOD!
SEE, WHIS?!
I KNEW HE WAS COMING! MY STRONGEST RIVAL!
IF THAT'S WHAT THE ORACLE FISH SAYS, I GUESS IT MUST BE TRUE.
HOWEVER, LORD BEERUS...
FREEZA ALREADY DESTROYED THE SAIYAN'S HOME WORLD, THE PLANET VEGETA.
OH YEAH!
I JUST REMEMBERED I ASKED HIM TO DO THAT!

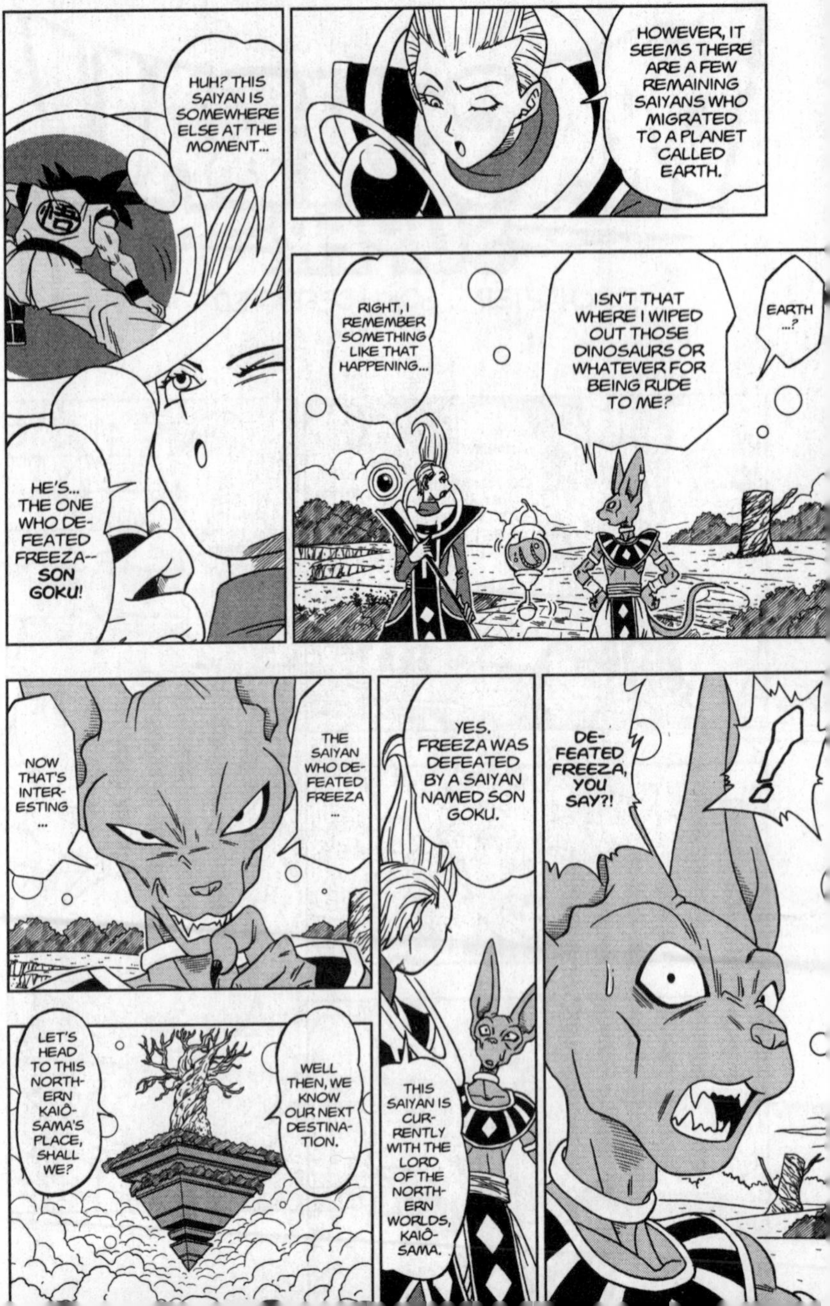
HOWEVER, IT SEEMS THERE ARE A FEW REMAINING SAIYANS WHO MIGRATED TO A PLANET CALLED EARTH.
EARTH ...?
ISN'T THAT WHERE I WIPED OUT THOSE DINOSAURS OR WHATEVER FOR BEING RUDE TO ME?
RIGHT, I REMEMBER SOMETHING LIKE THAT HAPPENING...
HUH? THIS SAIYAN IS SOMEWHERE ELSE AT THE MOMENT...
HE'S... THE ONE WHO DEFEATED FREEZA-- SON GOKU!
!
DEFEATED FREEZA, YOU SAY?!
YES. FREEZA WAS DEFEATED BY A SAIYAN NAMED SON GOKU.
THIS SAIYAN IS CURRENTLY WITH THE LORD OF THE NORTHERN WORLDS, KAIÔ-SAMA.
THE SAIYAN WHO DEFEATED FREEZA ...
NOW THAT'S INTERESTING ...
WELL THEN, WE KNOW OUR NEXT DESTINATION.
LET'S HEAD TO THIS NORTHERN KAIÔ-SAMA'S PLACE, SHALL WE?

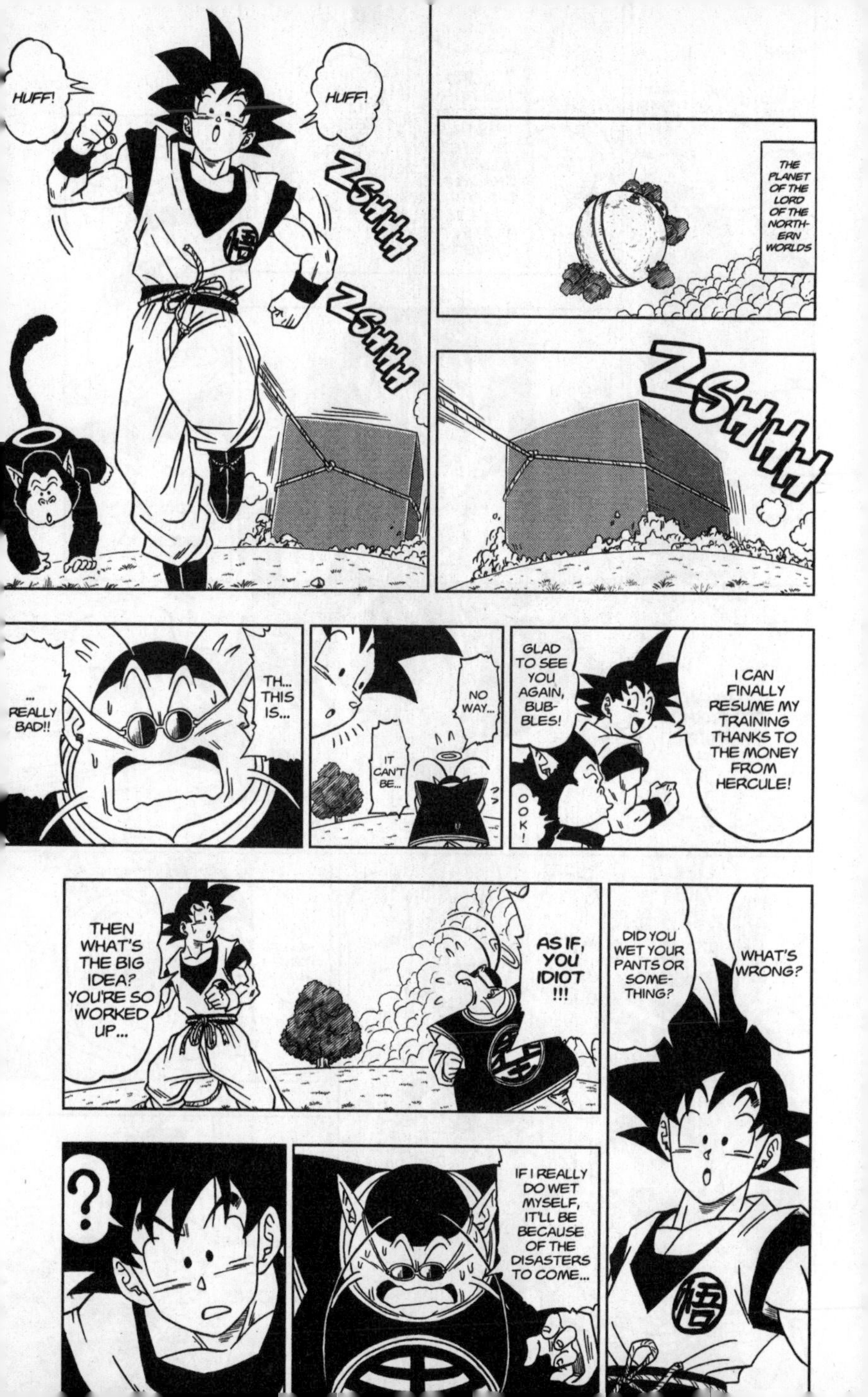
THE PLANET OF THE LORD OF THE NORTHERN WORLDS
ZSHHH
HUFF!
ZSHHH
ZSHHH
HUFF!
I CAN FINALLY RESUME MY TRAINING THANKS TO THE MONEY FROM HERCULE!
GLAD TO SEE YOU AGAIN, BUBBLES!
OOK!
NO WAY...
IT CAN'T BE...
TH... THIS IS...
... REALLY BAD!!
WHAT'S WRONG?
DID YOU WET YOUR PANTS OR SOMETHING?
AS IF, YOU IDIOT!!!
THEN WHAT'S THE BIG IDEA? YOU'RE SO WORKED UP...
IF I REALLY DO WET MYSELF, IT'LL BE BECAUSE OF THE DISASTERS TO COME...
?

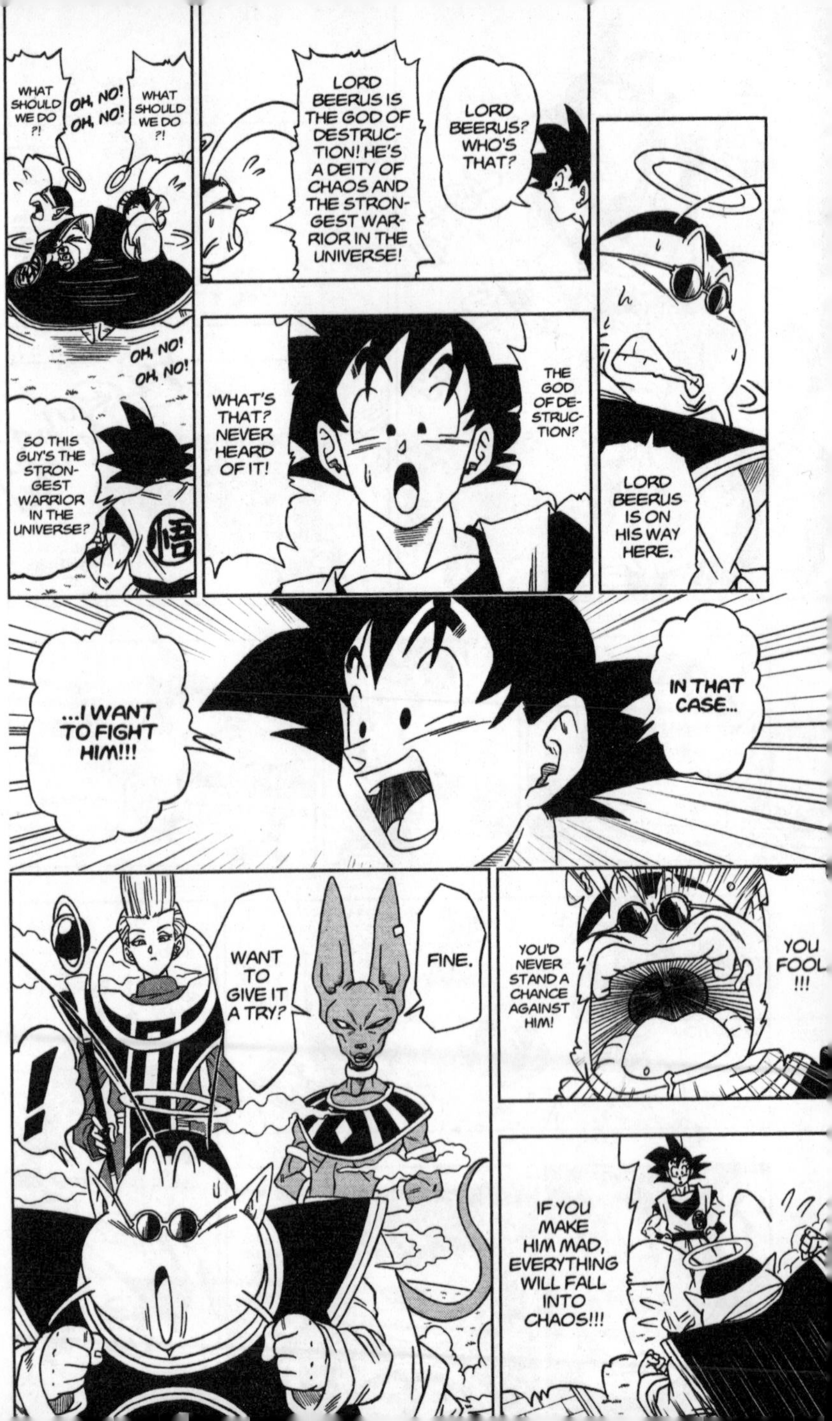
LORD BEERUS IS ON HIS WAY HERE.
LORD BEERUS? WHO'S THAT?
LORD BEERUS IS THE GOD OF DESTRUCTION! HE'S A DEITY OF CHAOS AND THE STRONGEST WARRIOR IN THE UNIVERSE!
THE GOD OF DESTRUCTION?
WHAT'S THAT? NEVER HEARD OF IT!
WHAT SHOULD WE DO ?!
OH, NO! OH, NO!
WHAT SHOULD WE DO ?!
OH, NO! OH, NO!
SO THIS GUY'S THE STRONGEST WARRIOR IN THE UNIVERSE?
IN THAT CASE...
...I WANT TO FIGHT HIM!!!
YOU FOOL!!!
YOU'D NEVER STAND A CHANCE AGAINST HIM!
IF YOU MAKE HIM MAD, EVERYTHING WILL FALL INTO CHAOS!!!
FINE.
WANT TO GIVE IT A TRY?
!

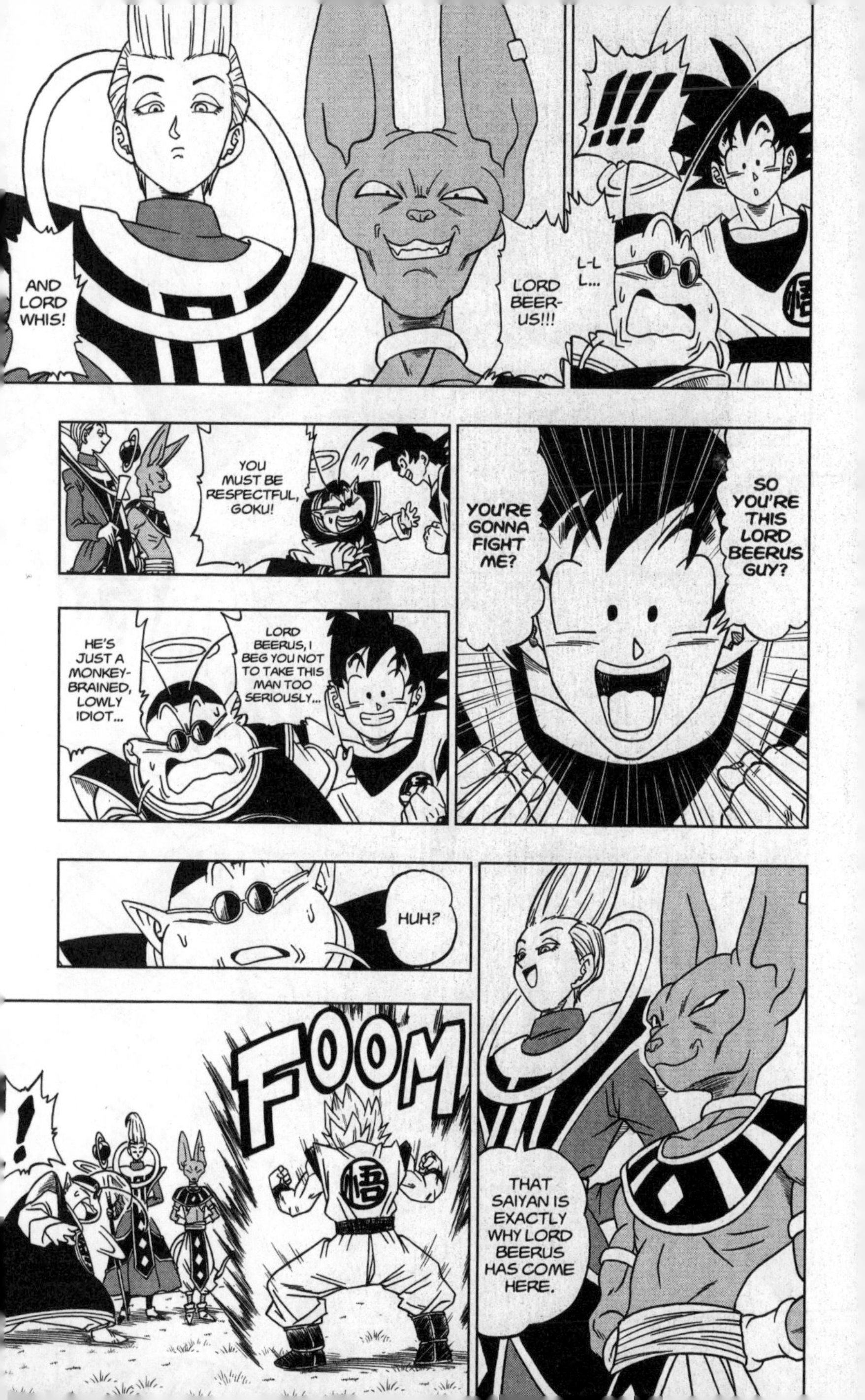
!!!
L-L L...
LORD BEER-US!!!
AND LORD WHIS!
SO YOU'RE THIS LORD BEERUS GUY?
YOU'RE GONNA FIGHT ME?
YOU MUST BE RESPECTFUL, GOKU!
LORD BEERUS, I BEG YOU NOT TO TAKE THIS MAN TOO SERIOUSLY...
HE'S JUST A MONKEY-BRAINED, LOWLY IDIOT...
THAT SAIYAN IS EXACTLY WHY LORD BEERUS HAS COME HERE.
HUH?
FOOM
!

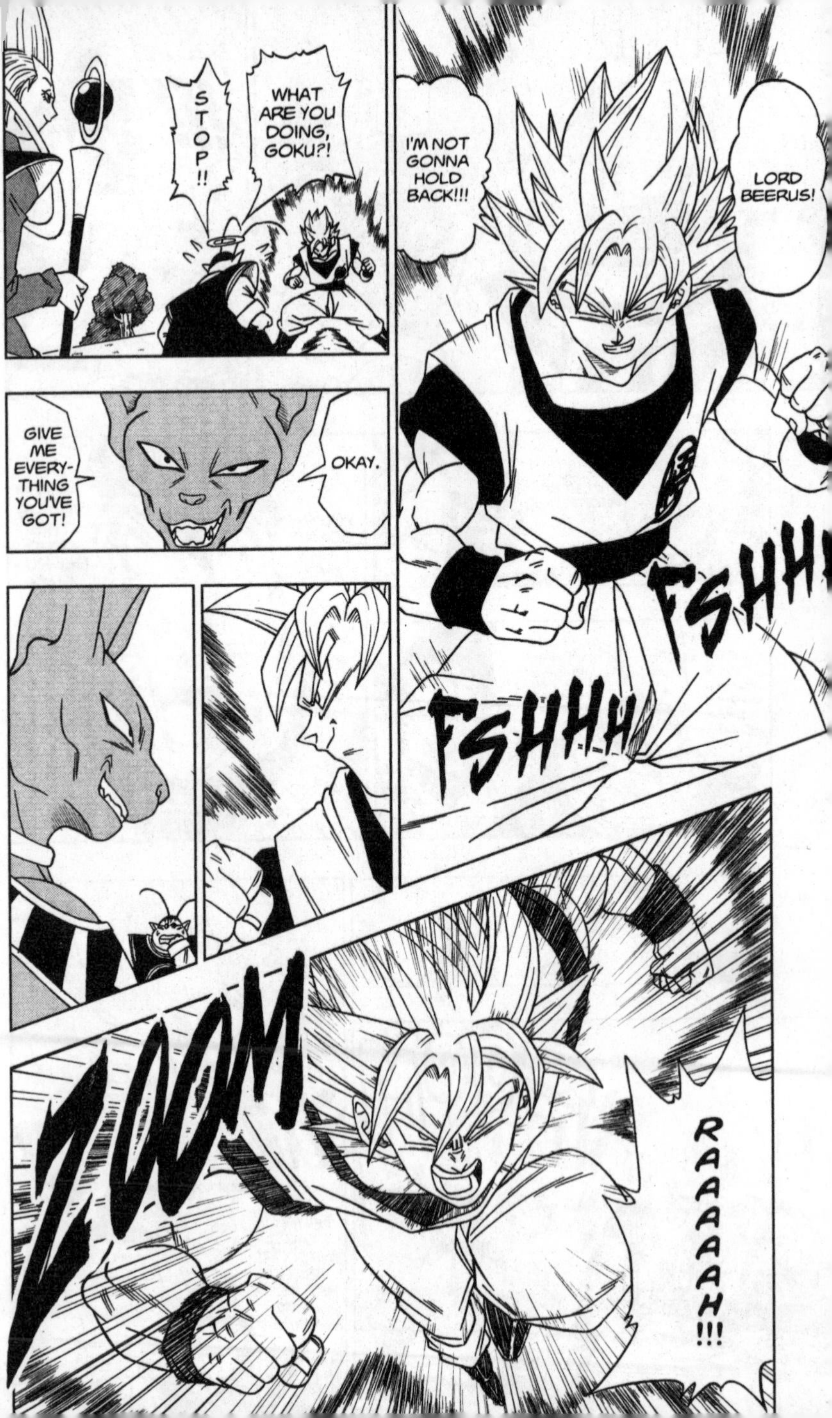
LORD BEERUS!
I'M NOT GONNA HOLD BACK!!!
FSHH
FSHHH
WHAT ARE YOU DOING, GOKU?!
STOP!!
OKAY.
GIVE ME EVERYTHING YOU'VE GOT!
RAAAAAAH!!!
ZOOM

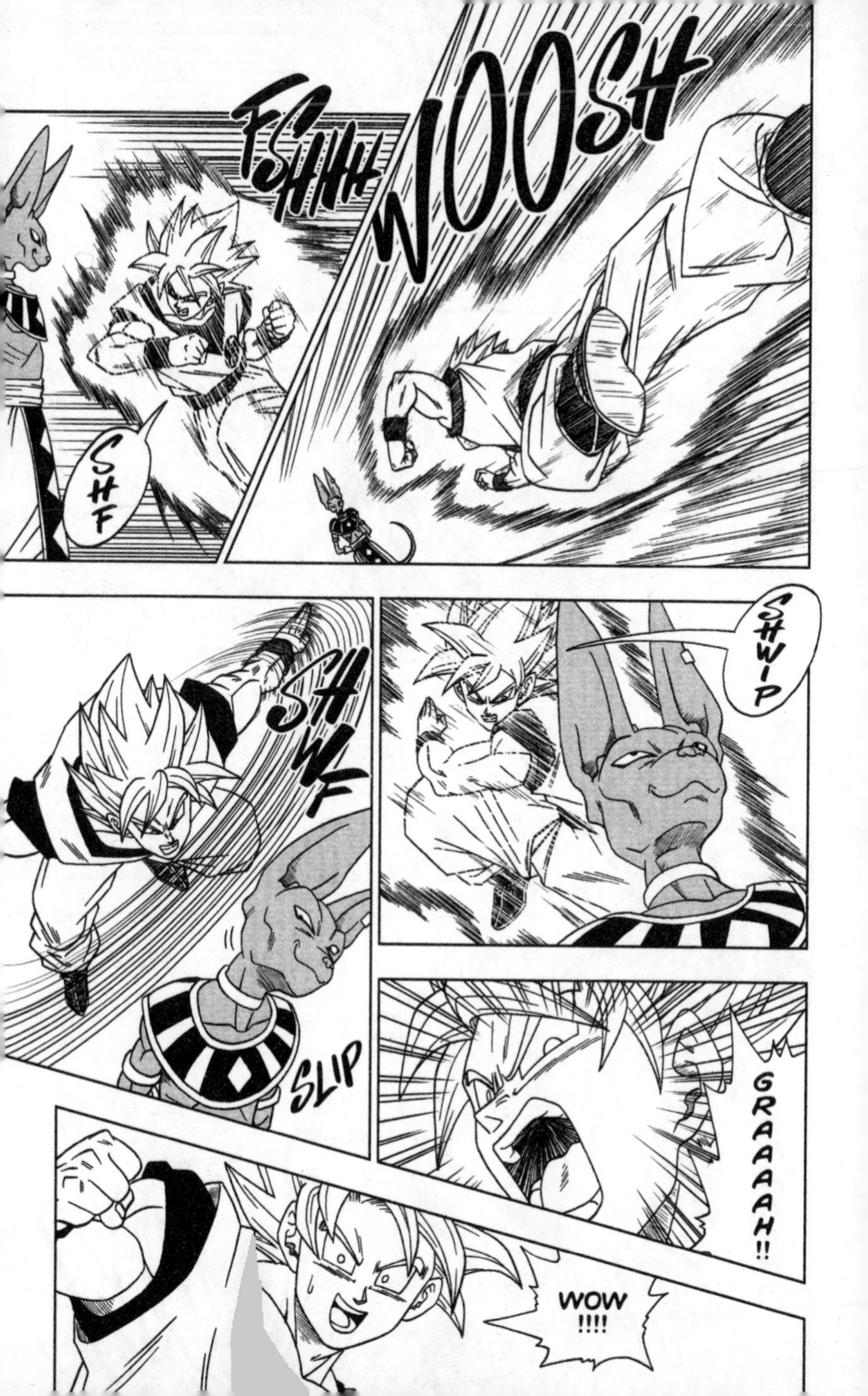
WOOSH
FSHHH
SHF
SHWIP
GRAAAAAH!!
SHWF
SLIP
WOW !!!!

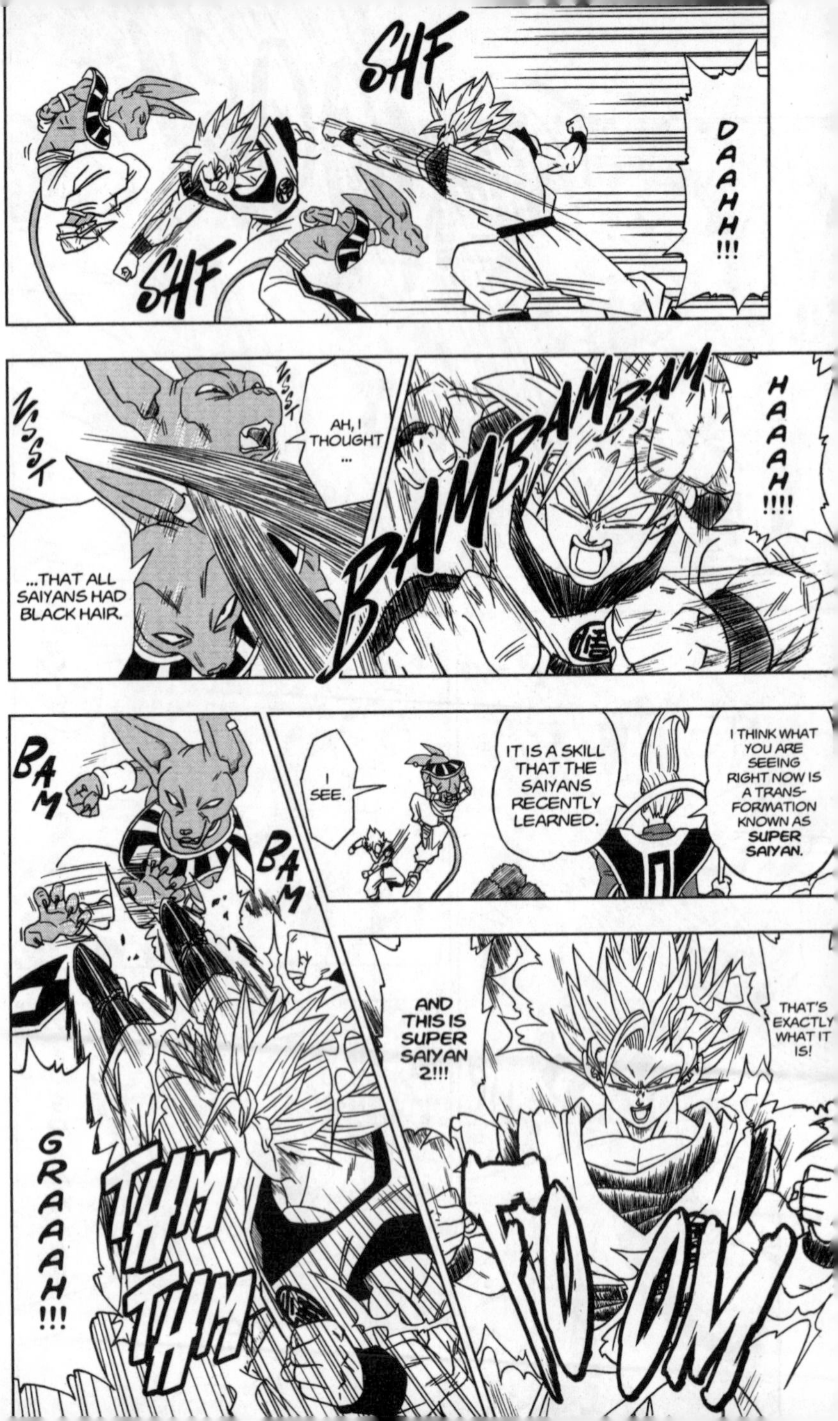
DAAHH!!!
SHF
SHF
HAAAAH!!!!
BAMBAMBAMBAM
AH, I THOUGHT...
NSSK
NSSK
...THAT ALL SAIYANS HAD BLACK HAIR.
I THINK WHAT YOU ARE SEEING RIGHT NOW IS A TRANSFORMATION KNOWN AS SUPER SAIYAN.
IT IS A SKILL THAT THE SAIYANS RECENTLY LEARNED.
I SEE.
THAT'S EXACTLY WHAT IT IS!
AND THIS IS SUPER SAIYAN 2!!!
TOOM
BAM
BAM
GRAAAAH!!!
THM THM

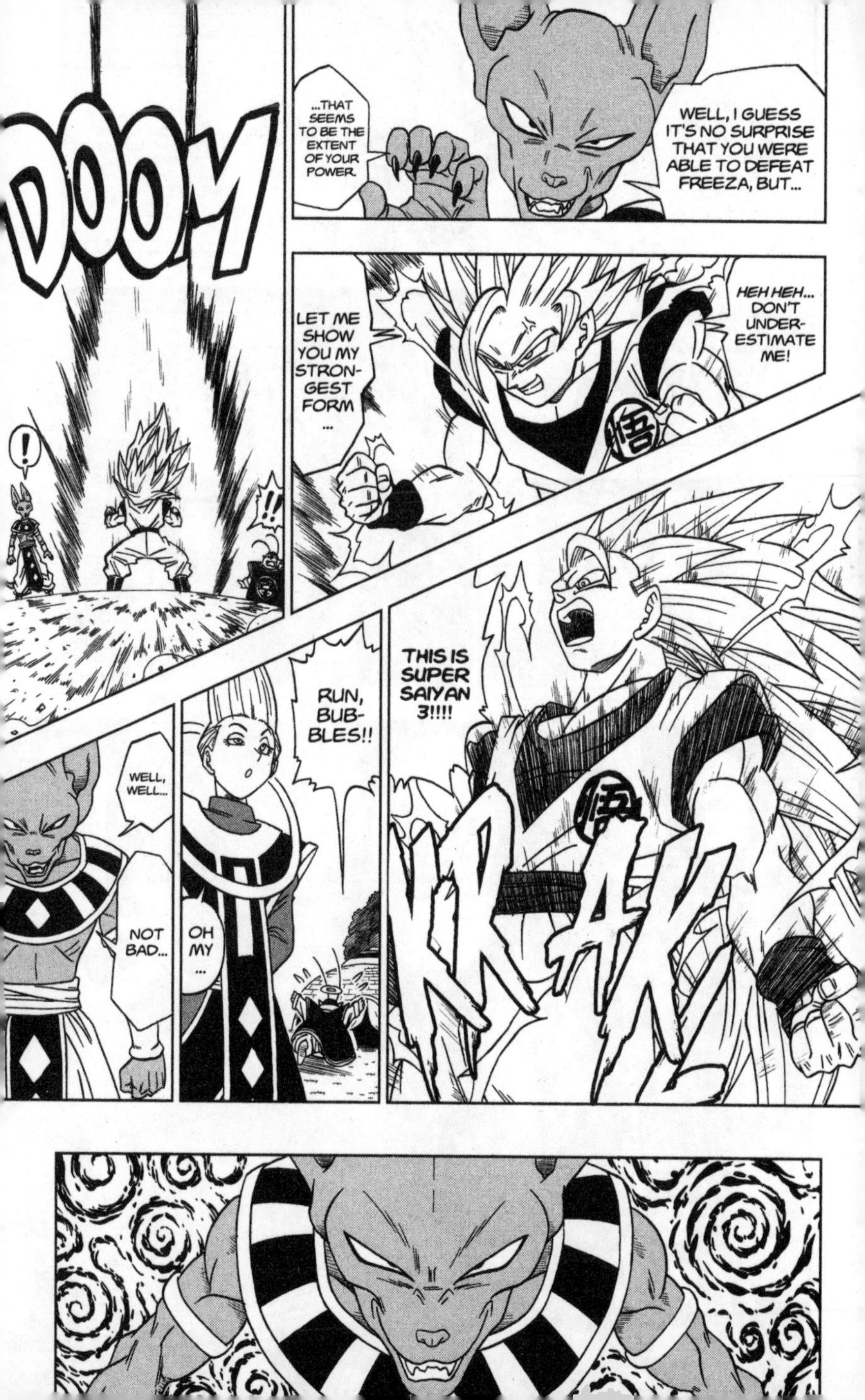
WELL, I GUESS IT'S NO SURPRISE THAT YOU WERE ABLE TO DEFEAT FREEZA, BUT...
...THAT SEEMS TO BE THE EXTENT OF YOUR POWER.
HEH HEH... DON'T UNDER-ESTIMATE ME!
LET ME SHOW YOU MY STRON-GEST FORM ...
DOOM
!
!!
THIS IS SUPER SAIYAN 3!!!!
KRAK
RUN, BUB-BLES!!
OH MY ...
WELL, WELL...
NOT BAD...

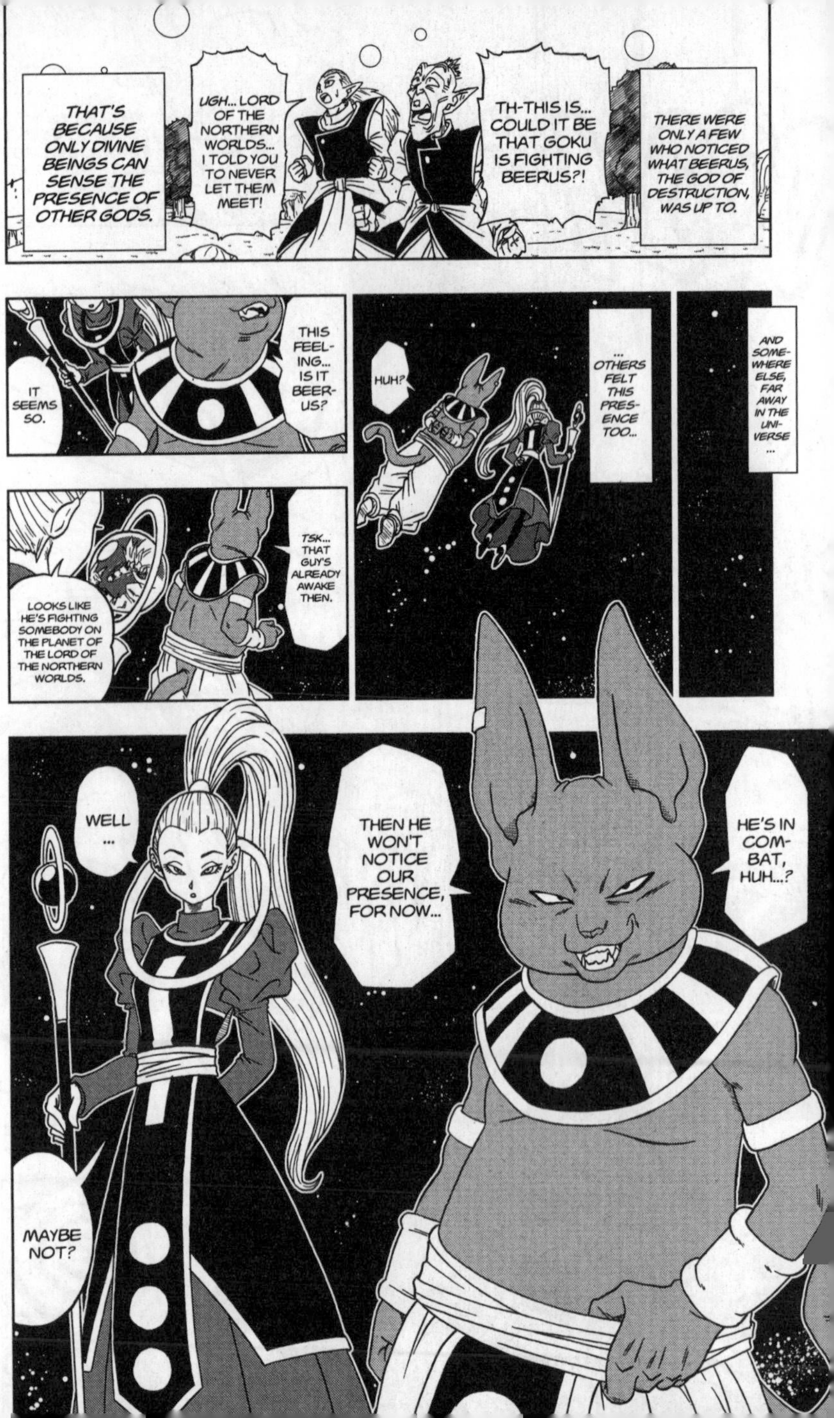
THERE WERE ONLY A FEW WHO NOTICED WHAT BEERUS, THE GOD OF DESTRUCTION, WAS UP TO.
TH-THIS IS... COULD IT BE THAT GOKU IS FIGHTING BEERUS?!
UGH... LORD OF THE NORTHERN WORLDS... I TOLD YOU TO NEVER LET THEM MEET!
THAT'S BECAUSE ONLY DIVINE BEINGS CAN SENSE THE PRESENCE OF OTHER GODS.
AND SOMEWHERE ELSE, FAR AWAY IN THE UNIVERSE...
...OTHERS FELT THIS PRESENCE TOO...
HUH?
THIS FEELING... IS IT BEERUS?
IT SEEMS SO.
TSK... THAT GUY'S ALREADY AWAKE THEN.
LOOKS LIKE HE'S FIGHTING SOMEBODY ON THE PLANET OF THE LORD OF THE NORTHERN WORLDS.
HE'S IN COMBAT, HUH...?
THEN HE WON'T NOTICE OUR PRESENCE, FOR NOW...
WELL...
MAYBE NOT?

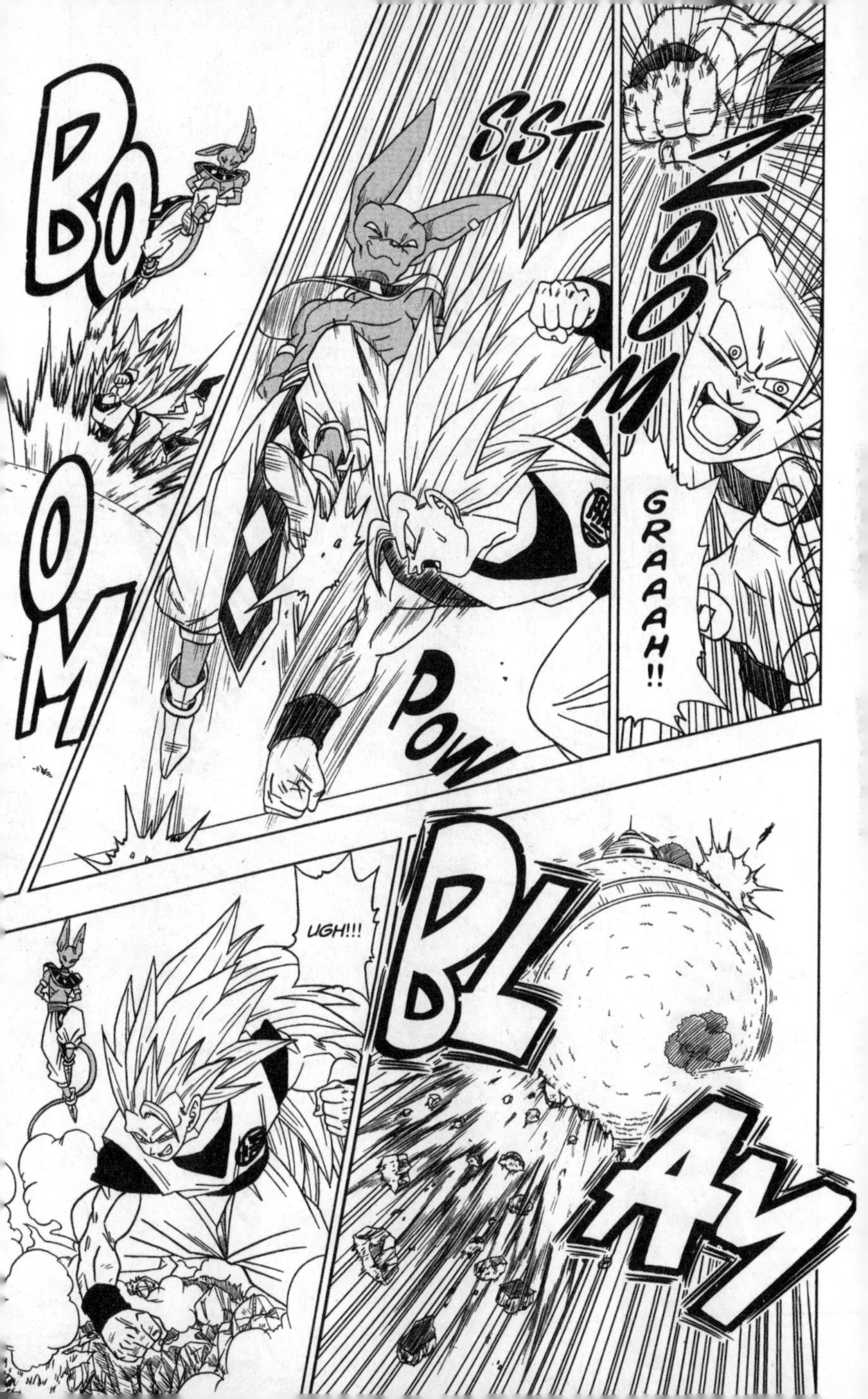
ZOOM
GRAAAAH!!
SST
POW
BOOM
BLAM
UGH!!!

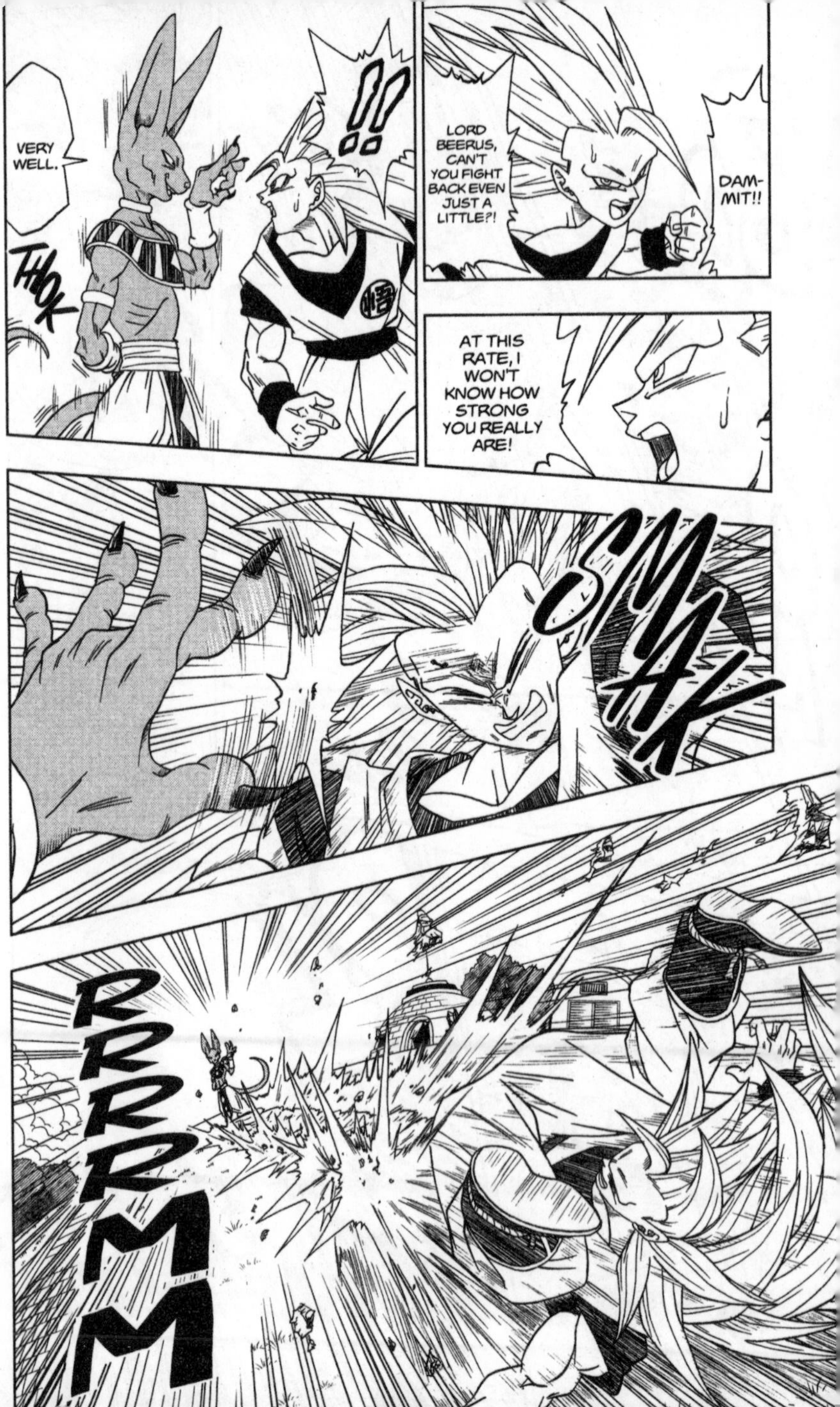

DAM-
MIT!!
LORD BEERUS, CAN'T YOU FIGHT BACK EVEN JUST A LITTLE?!
AT THIS RATE, I WON'T KNOW HOW STRONG YOU REALLY ARE!
!!
VERY WELL.
THOK
SMAK
RRRRMM

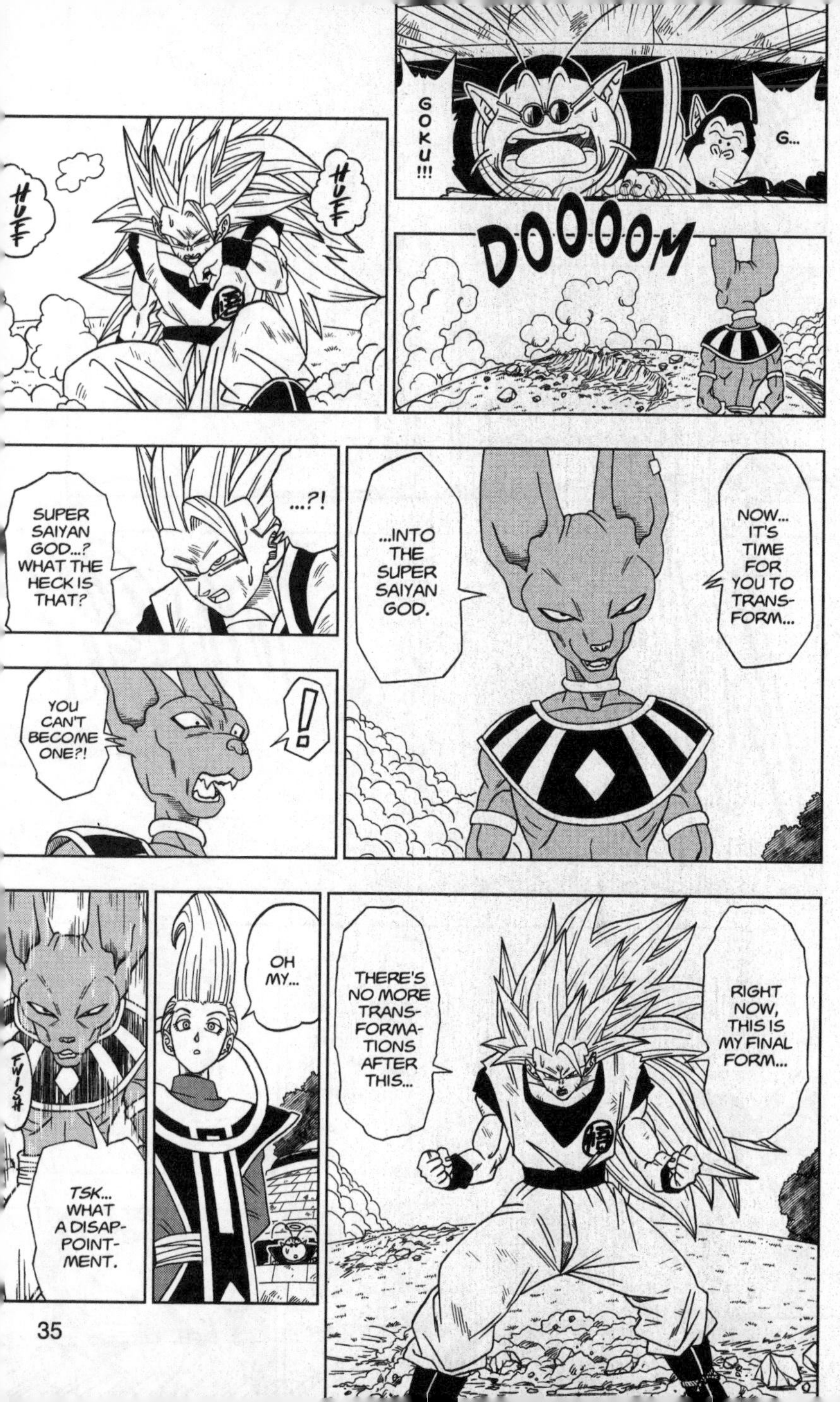
GOKU!!!
G...
DOOOOM
HUFF
HUFF
NOW... IT'S TIME FOR YOU TO TRANS-FORM...
...INTO THE SUPER SAIYAN GOD.
...?!
SUPER SAIYAN GOD...? WHAT THE HECK IS THAT?
!
YOU CAN'T BECOME ONE?!
RIGHT NOW, THIS IS MY FINAL FORM...
THERE'S NO MORE TRANS-FORMA-TIONS AFTER THIS...
OH MY...
FWISH
TSK... WHAT A DISAP-POINT-MENT.

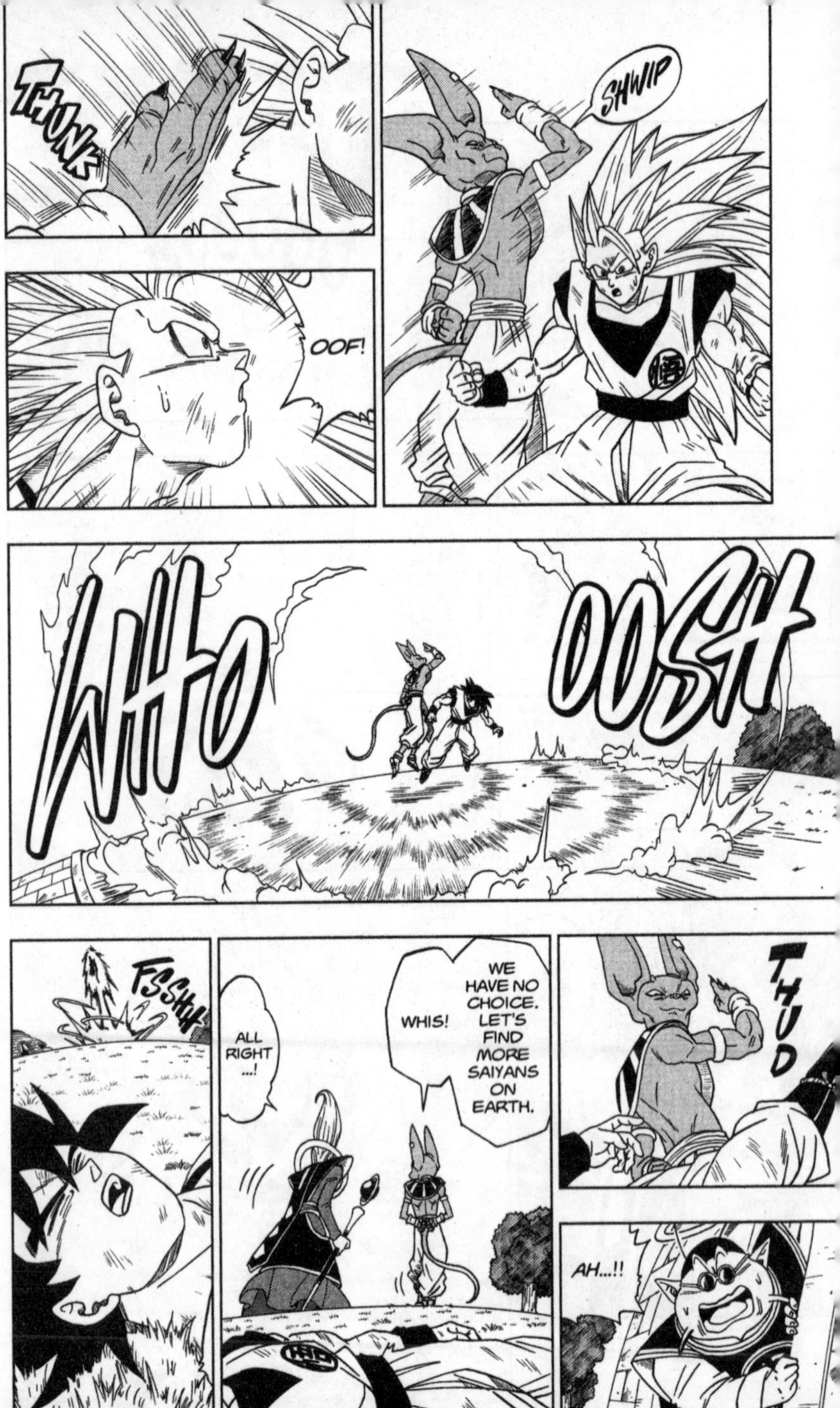
SHWIP
THONK
OOF!
WHOOSH
THUD
AH...!!
WHIS!
WE HAVE NO CHOICE. LET'S FIND MORE SAIYANS ON EARTH.
ALL RIGHT...!
FSSHH

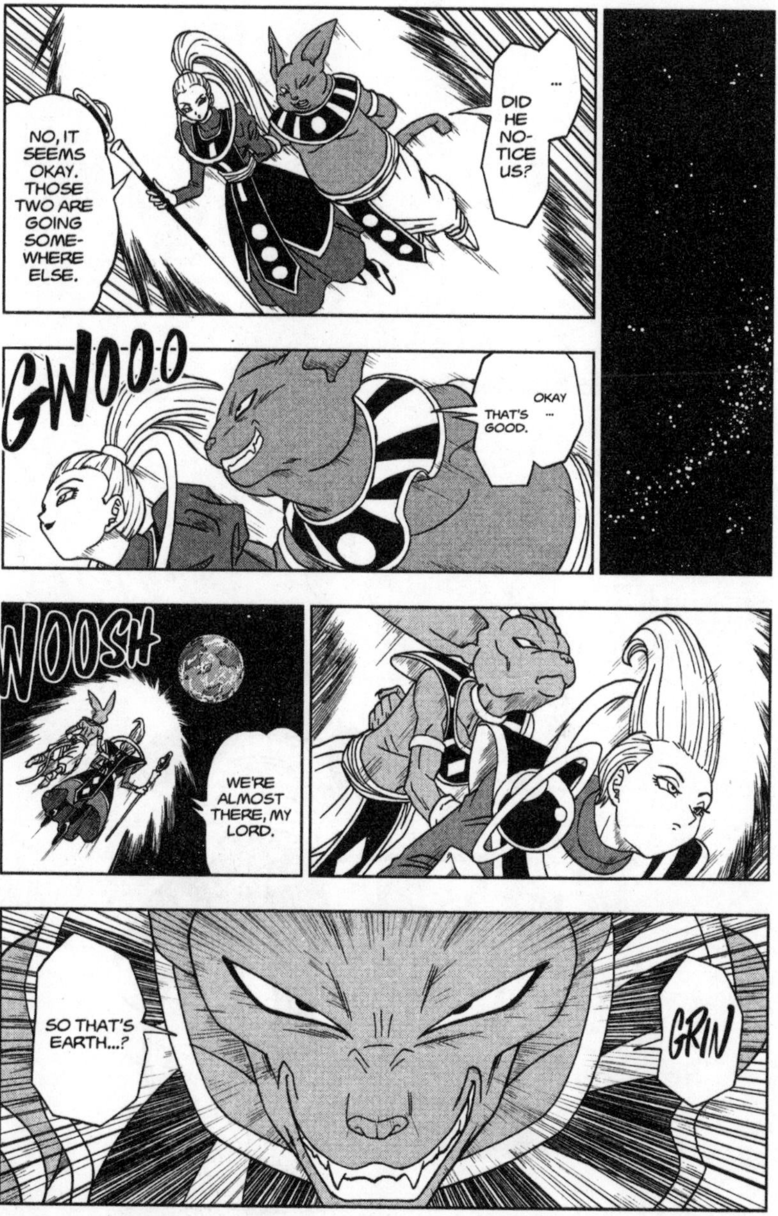
... DID HE NOTICE US?
NO, IT SEEMS OKAY. THOSE TWO ARE GOING SOMEWHERE ELSE.
OKAY... THAT'S GOOD.
GWOOO
WOOSH
WE'RE ALMOST THERE, MY LORD.
GRIN
SO THAT'S EARTH...?

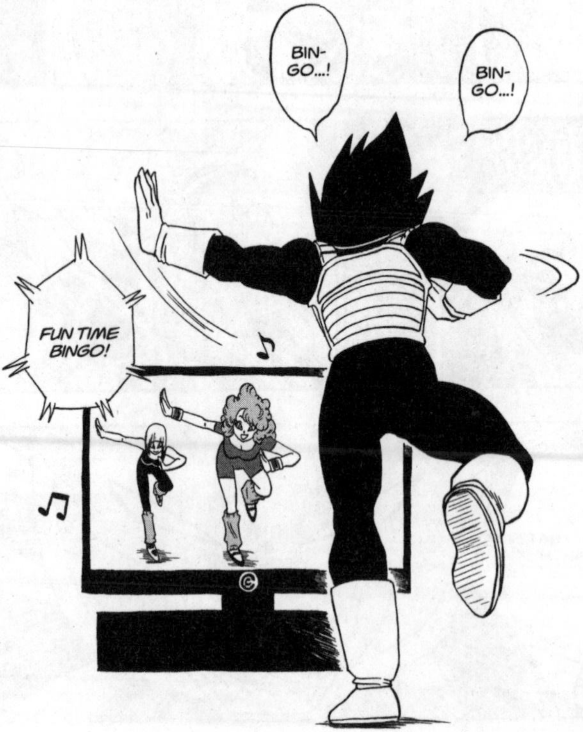
BIN-GO...!
BIN-GO...!
FUN TIME BINGO!

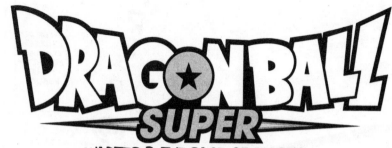

DRAGON BALL SUPER

CHAPTER 3: THE RAGE OF BEERUS

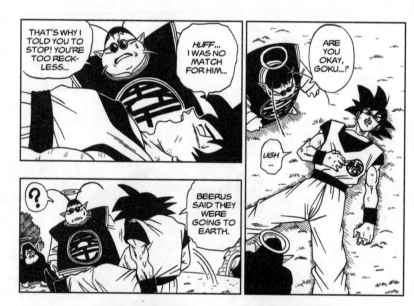

ARE YOU OKAY, GOKU...?
UGH ...
HUFF... I WAS NO MATCH FOR HIM...
THAT'S WHY I TOLD YOU TO STOP! YOU'RE TOO RECK-LESS...
BEERUS SAID THEY WERE GOING TO EARTH.
?
THIS IS BAD...
BULMA'S BIRTHDAY PARTY IS RIGHT NOW...

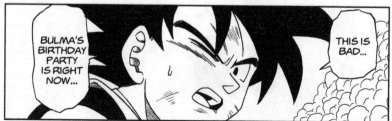

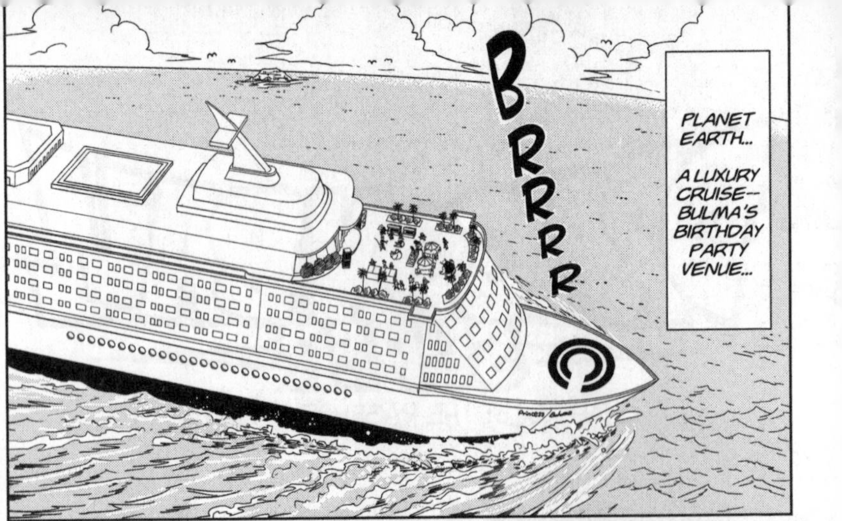
PLANET EARTH...
A LUXURY CRUISE--BULMA'S BIRTHDAY PARTY VENUE...
BRRRR

*EDITOR'S NOTE: IF YOU'D LIKE TO ENJOY THE PARTY IN FULL, CHECK OUT THE *BATTLE OF GODS* MOVIE!

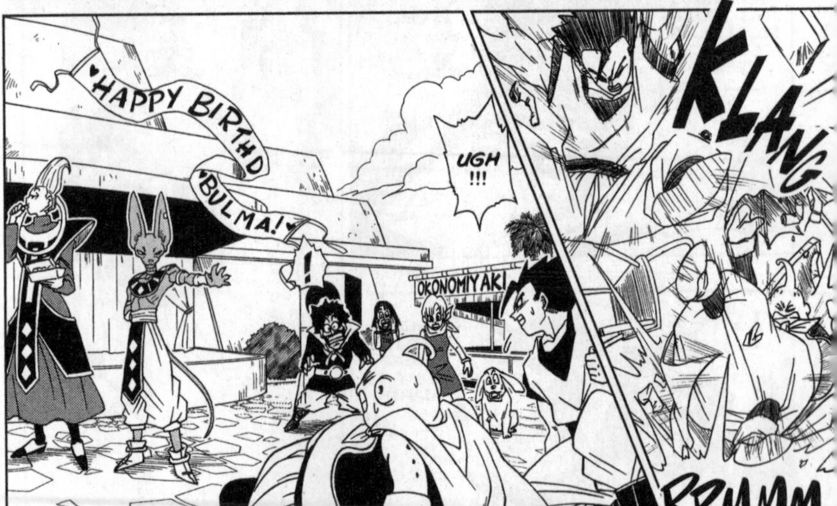
KLANG
UGH !!!
RRMMM
OKONOMIYAKI
HAPPY BIRTHD
BULMA!
!

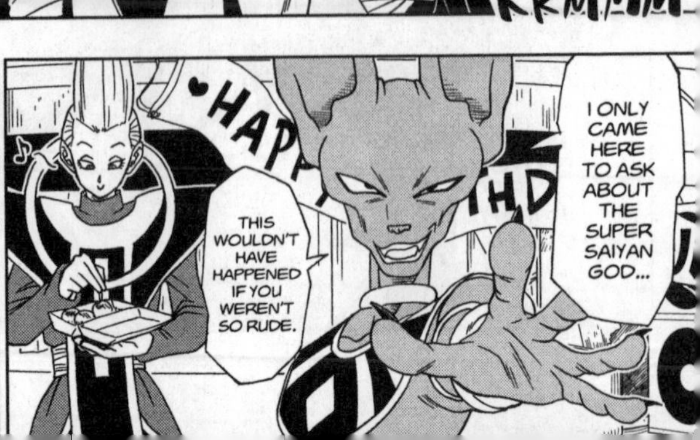
I ONLY CAME HERE TO ASK ABOUT THE SUPER SAIYAN GOD...
THIS WOULDN'T HAVE HAPPENED IF YOU WEREN'T SO RUDE.
HAPP
THD

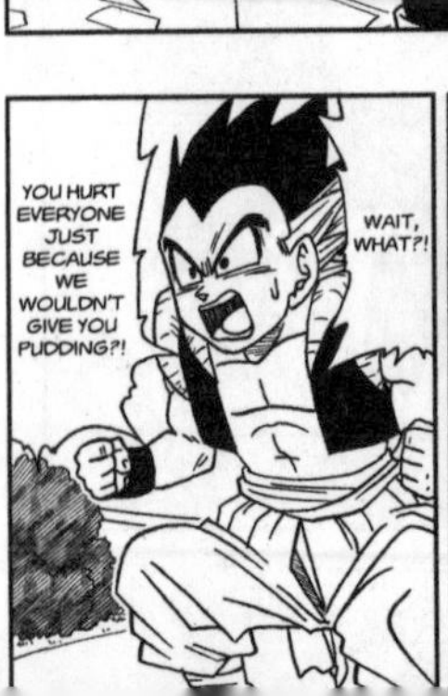
WAIT, WHAT?!
YOU HURT EVERYONE JUST BECAUSE WE WOULDN'T GIVE YOU PUDDING?!

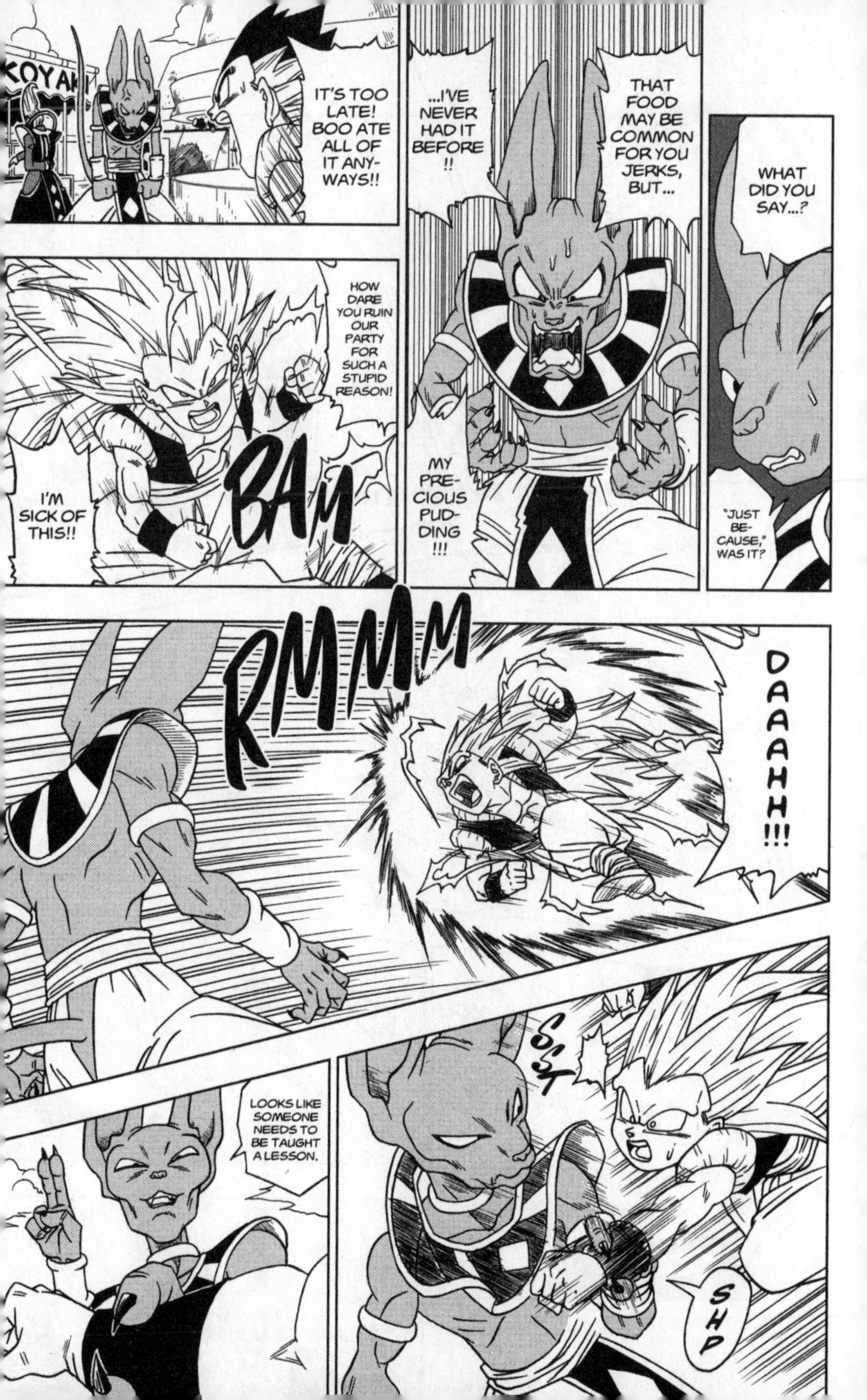
WHAT DID YOU SAY...?
"JUST BE-CAUSE," WAS IT?
THAT FOOD MAY BE COMMON FOR YOU JERKS, BUT...
...I'VE NEVER HAD IT BEFORE!!
MY PRECIOUS PUDDING!!!
KOYAKI
IT'S TOO LATE! BOO ATE ALL OF IT ANY-WAYS!!
HOW DARE YOU RUIN OUR PARTY FOR SUCH A STUPID REASON!
BAM
I'M SICK OF THIS!!
DAAAAHH!!!
RMMMM
SSK
SHP
LOOKS LIKE SOMEONE NEEDS TO BE TAUGHT A LESSON.

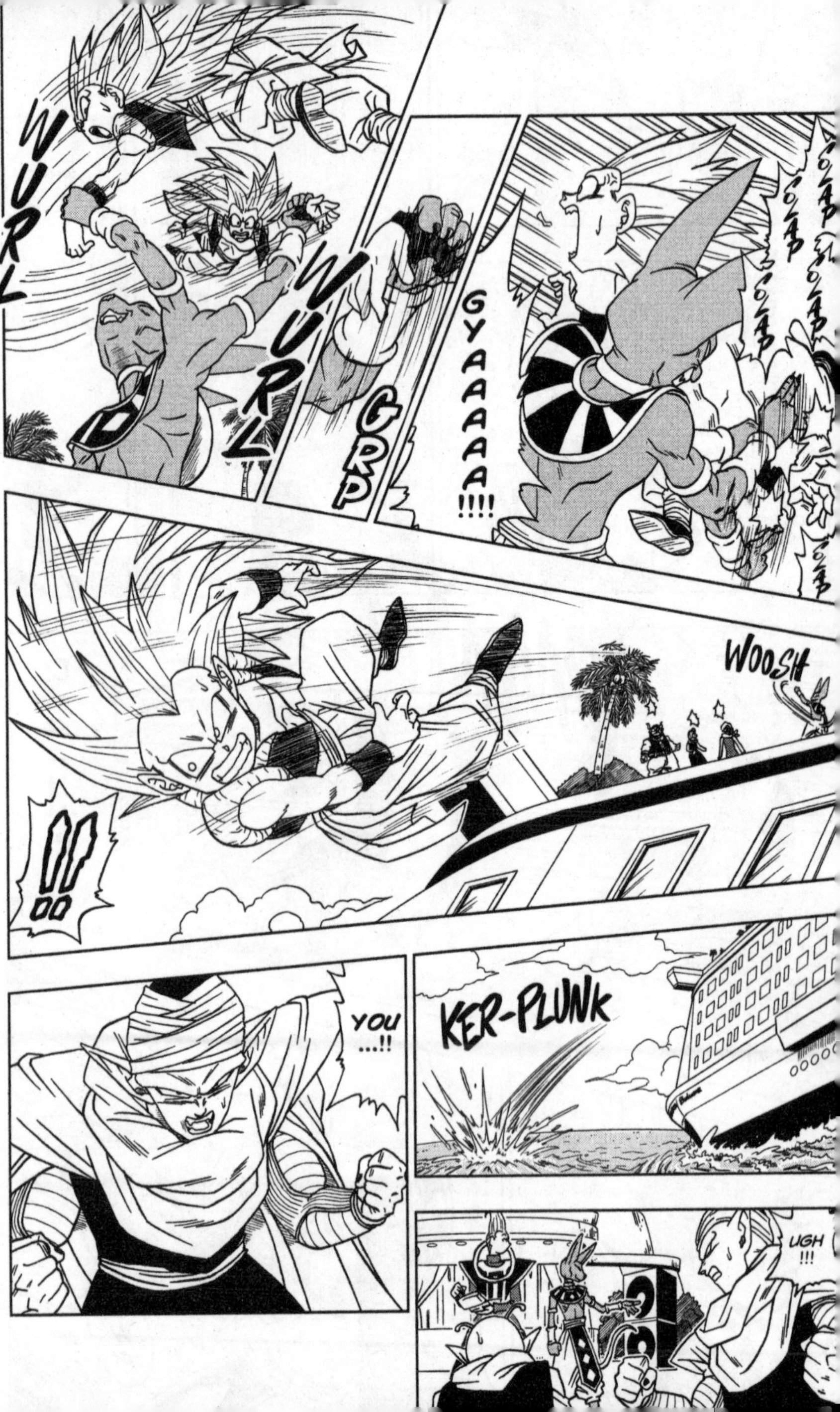

CLAP CLAP
CLAP CLAP
CLAP
GYAAAAAA!!!!
WURL
GRP
WURL
WOOSH
!!
KER-PLUNK
YOU ...!!
UGH !!!

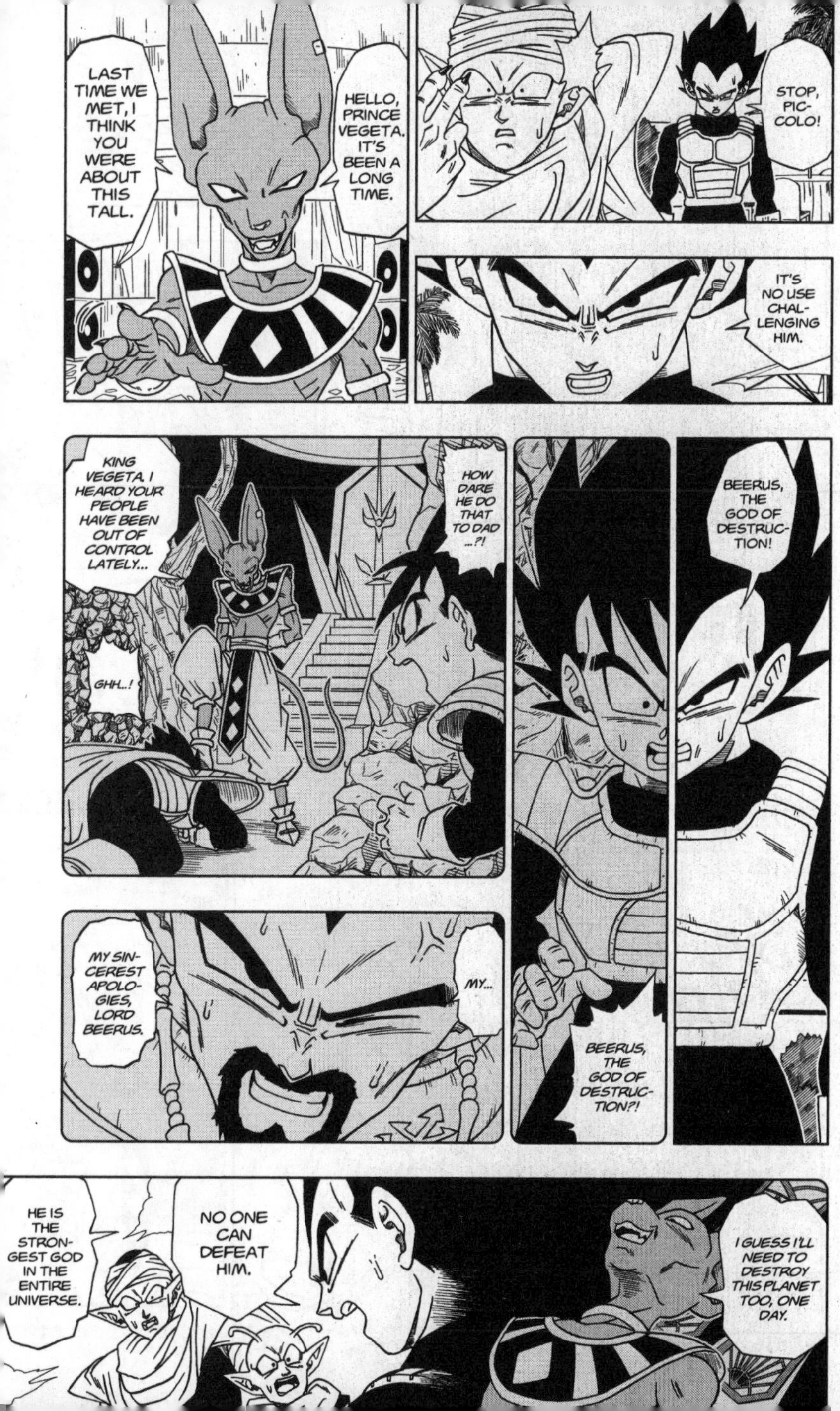
STOP, PIC-COLO!
IT'S NO USE CHAL-LENGING HIM.
HELLO, PRINCE VEGETA. IT'S BEEN A LONG TIME.
LAST TIME WE MET, I THINK YOU WERE ABOUT THIS TALL.
BEERUS, THE GOD OF DESTRUC-TION!
BEERUS, THE GOD OF DESTRUC-TION?!
HOW DARE HE DO THAT TO DAD ...?!
KING VEGETA. I HEARD YOUR PEOPLE HAVE BEEN OUT OF CONTROL LATELY...
GHH...!
MY...
MY SIN-CEREST APOLO-GIES, LORD BEERUS.
I GUESS I'LL NEED TO DESTROY THIS PLANET TOO, ONE DAY.
NO ONE CAN DEFEAT HIM.
HE IS THE STRON-GEST GOD IN THE ENTIRE UNIVERSE.

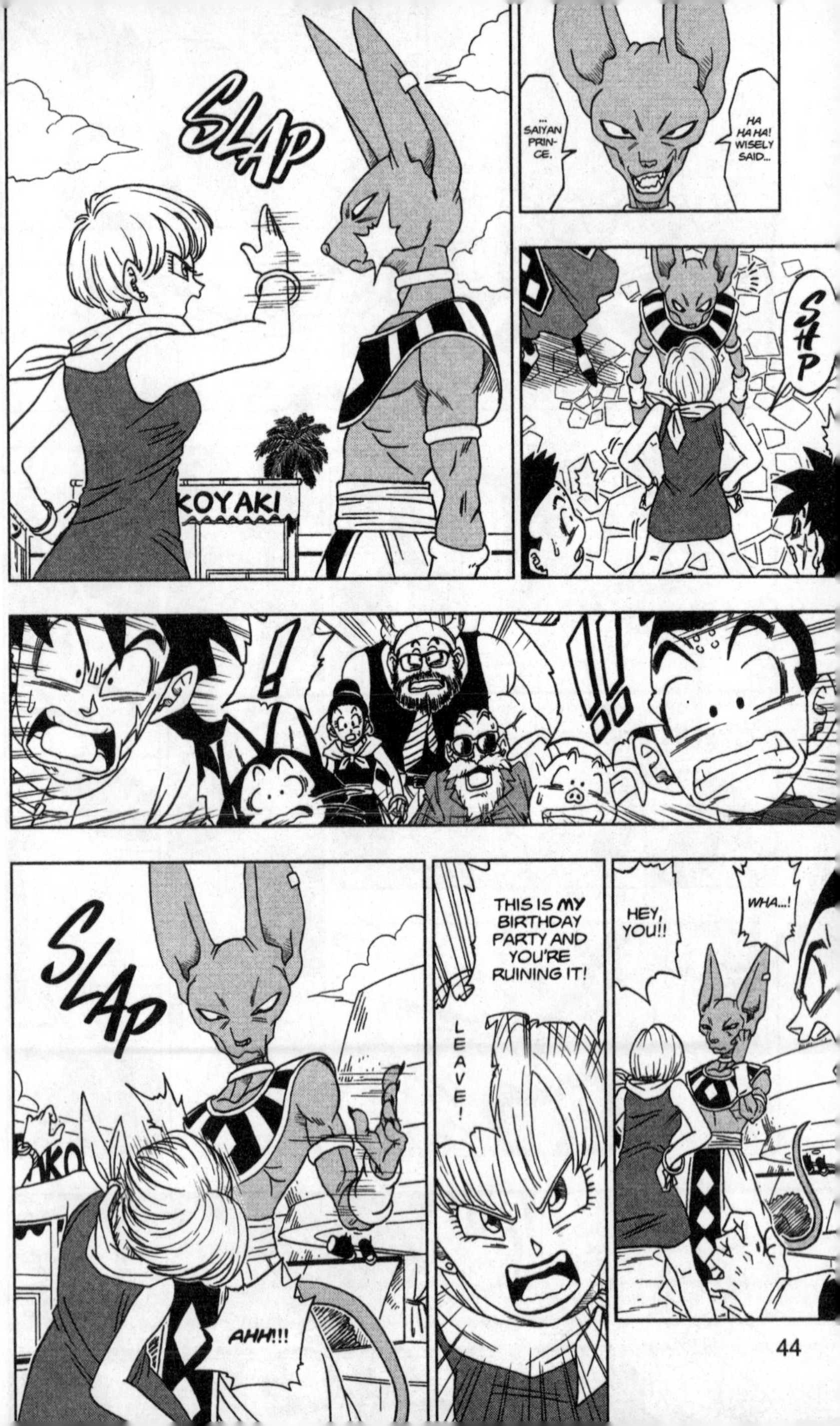
HA HA HA! WISELY SAID...
... SAIYAN PRIN-CE.
SHP
SLAP
KOYAKI
WHA...!
HEY, YOU!!
THIS IS MY BIRTHDAY PARTY AND YOU'RE RUINING IT!
LEAVE!
SLAP
AHH!!!

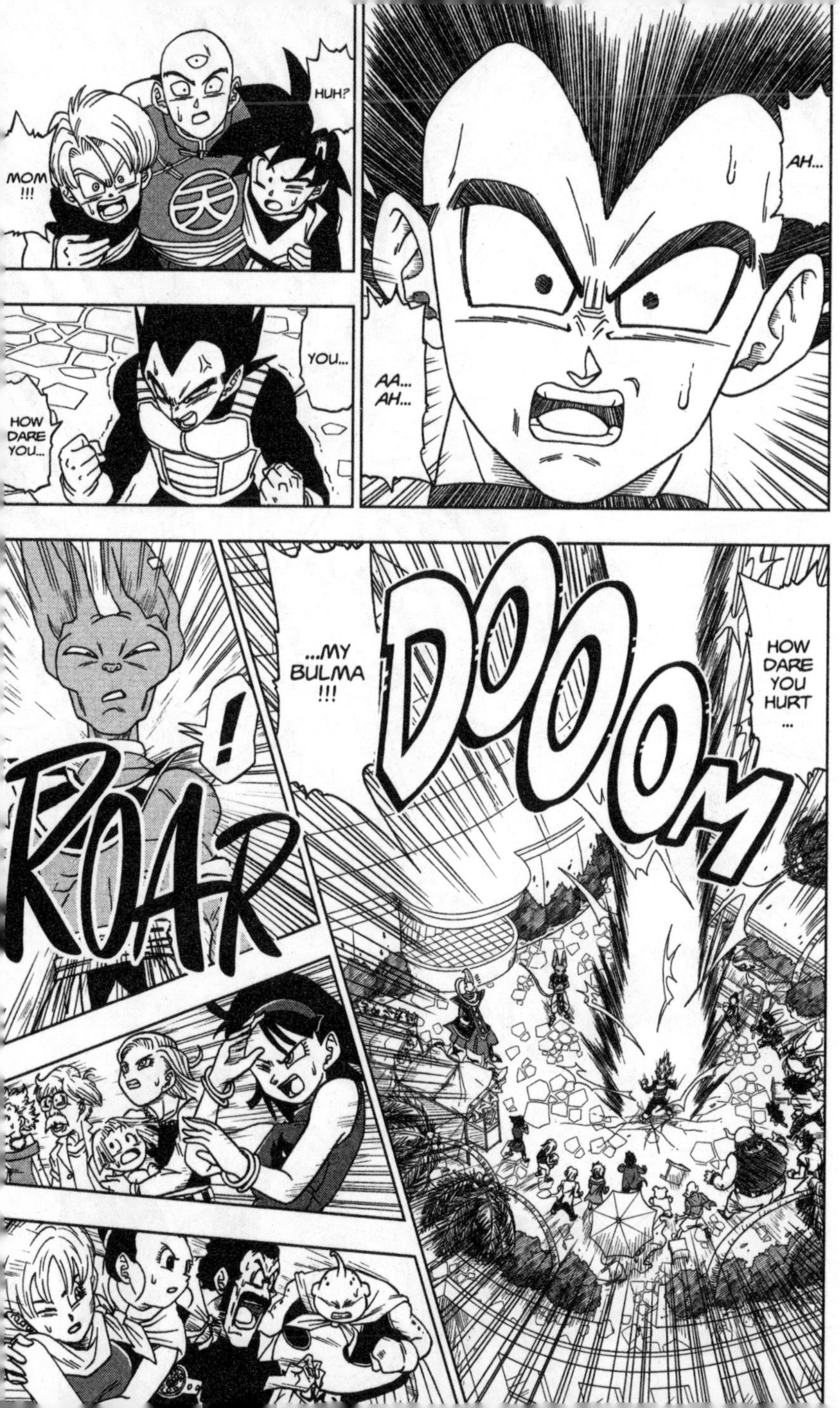
AH...
AA... AH...
HUH?
MOM !!!
YOU...
HOW DARE YOU...
HOW DARE YOU HURT ...
...MY BULMA !!!
DOOOOM
!
ROAR

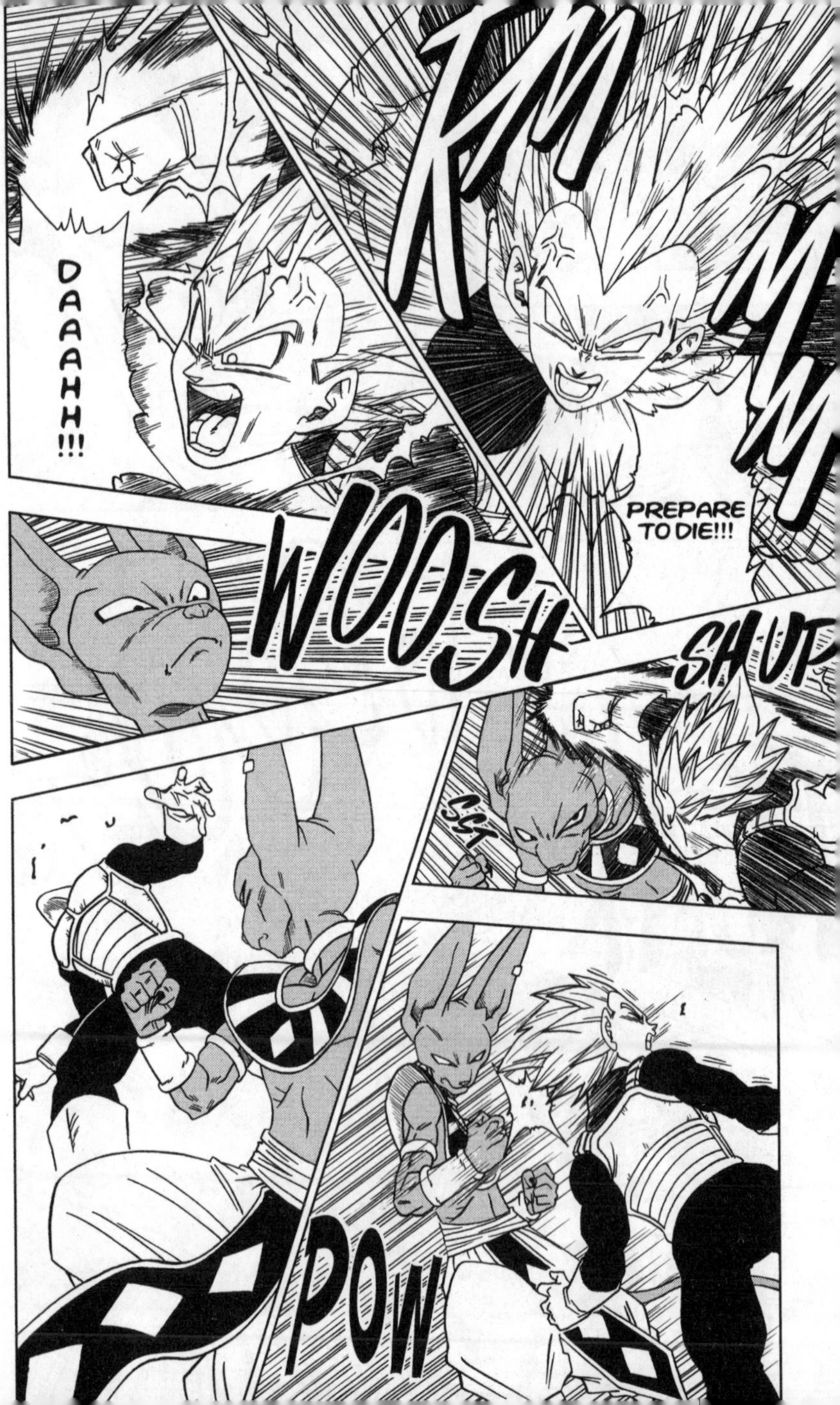
KRMMMM
PREPARE TO DIE!!!
DAAAAHH!!!
SHUP
SST
WOOSH
POW

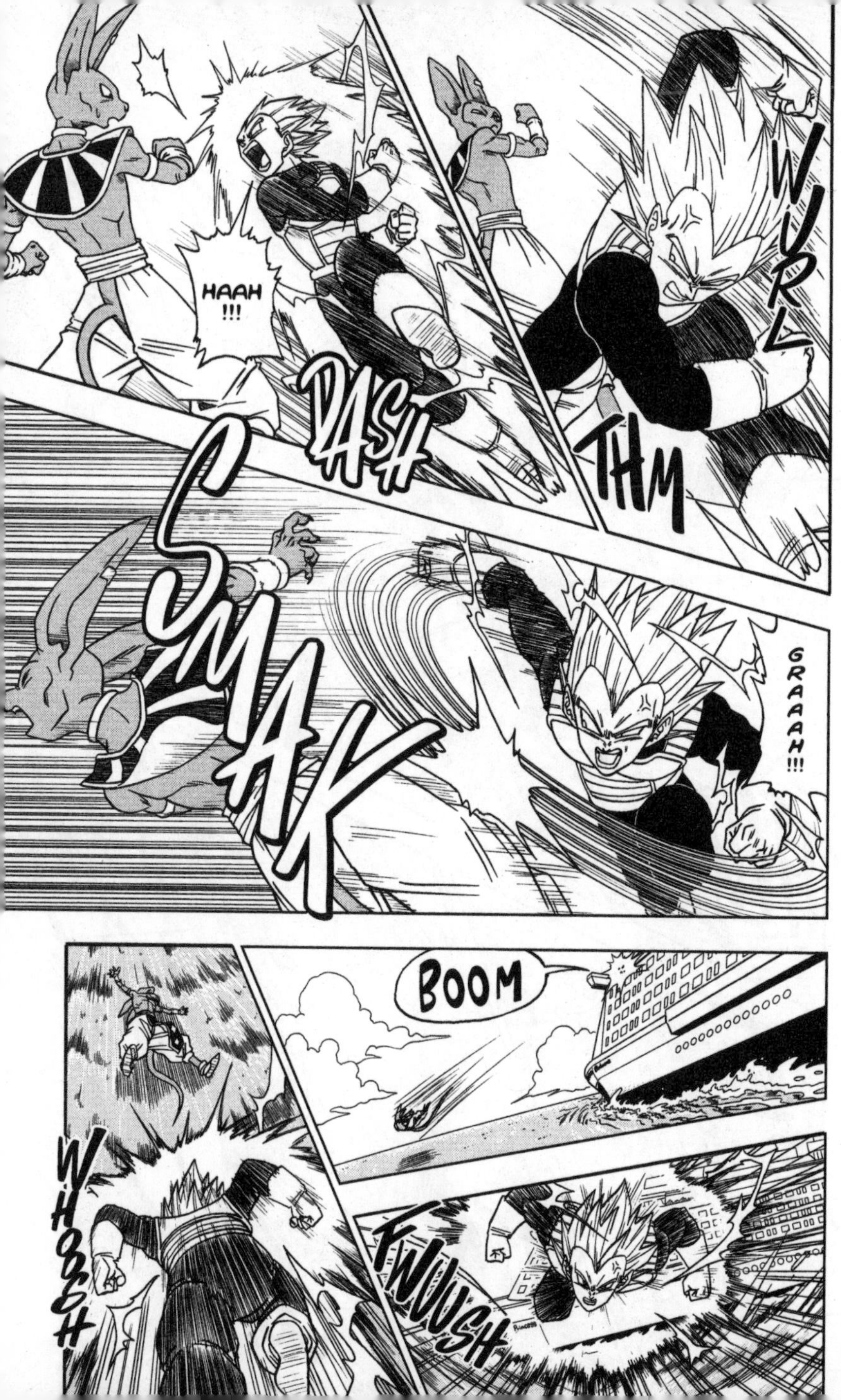
WURL
THM
HAAH !!!
DASH
SMAK
GRAAAH!!!
BOOM
FWUUSH
WHOOSH

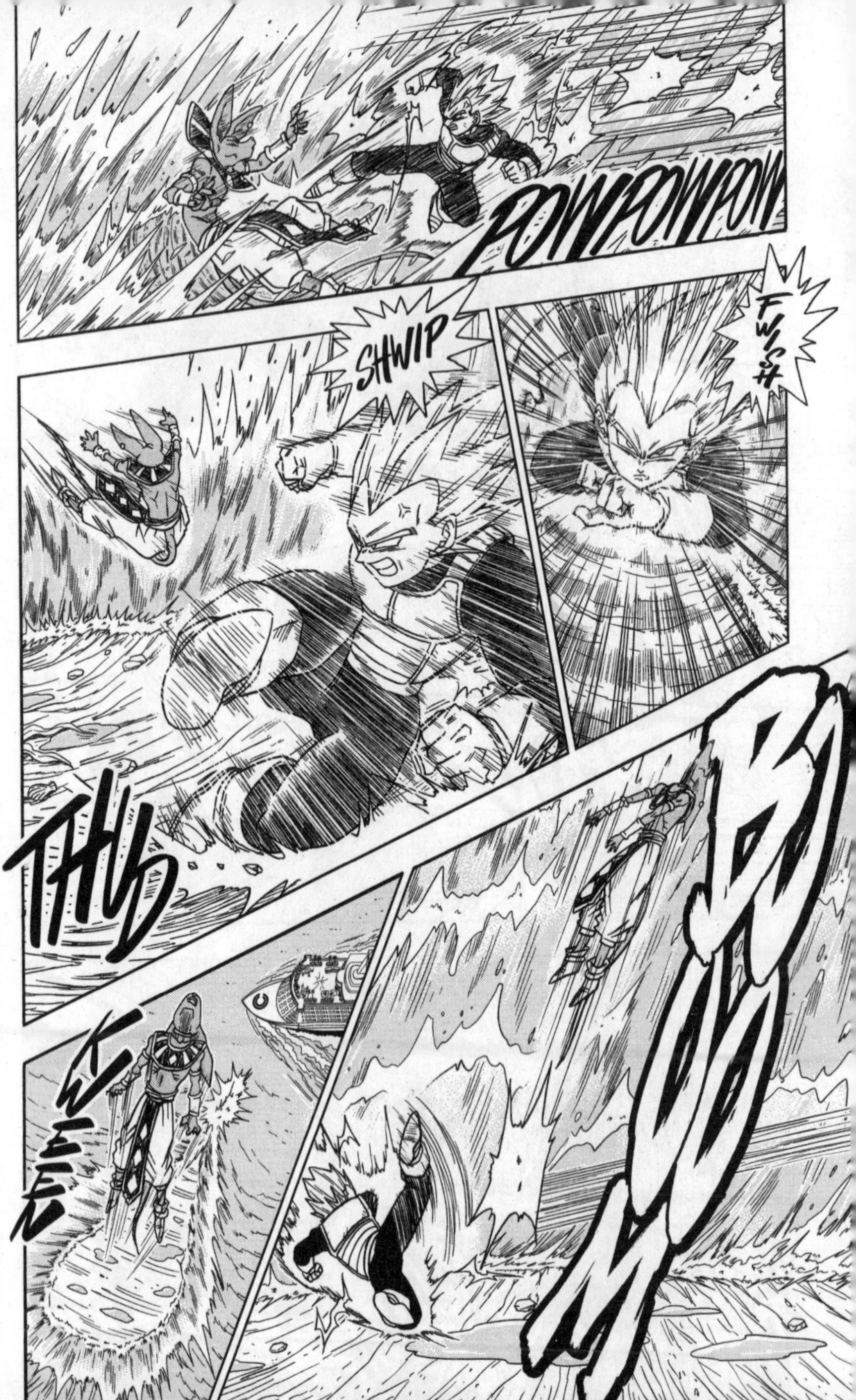
POWPOWPOW
FWISH
SHWIP
THUD
KWEEEN

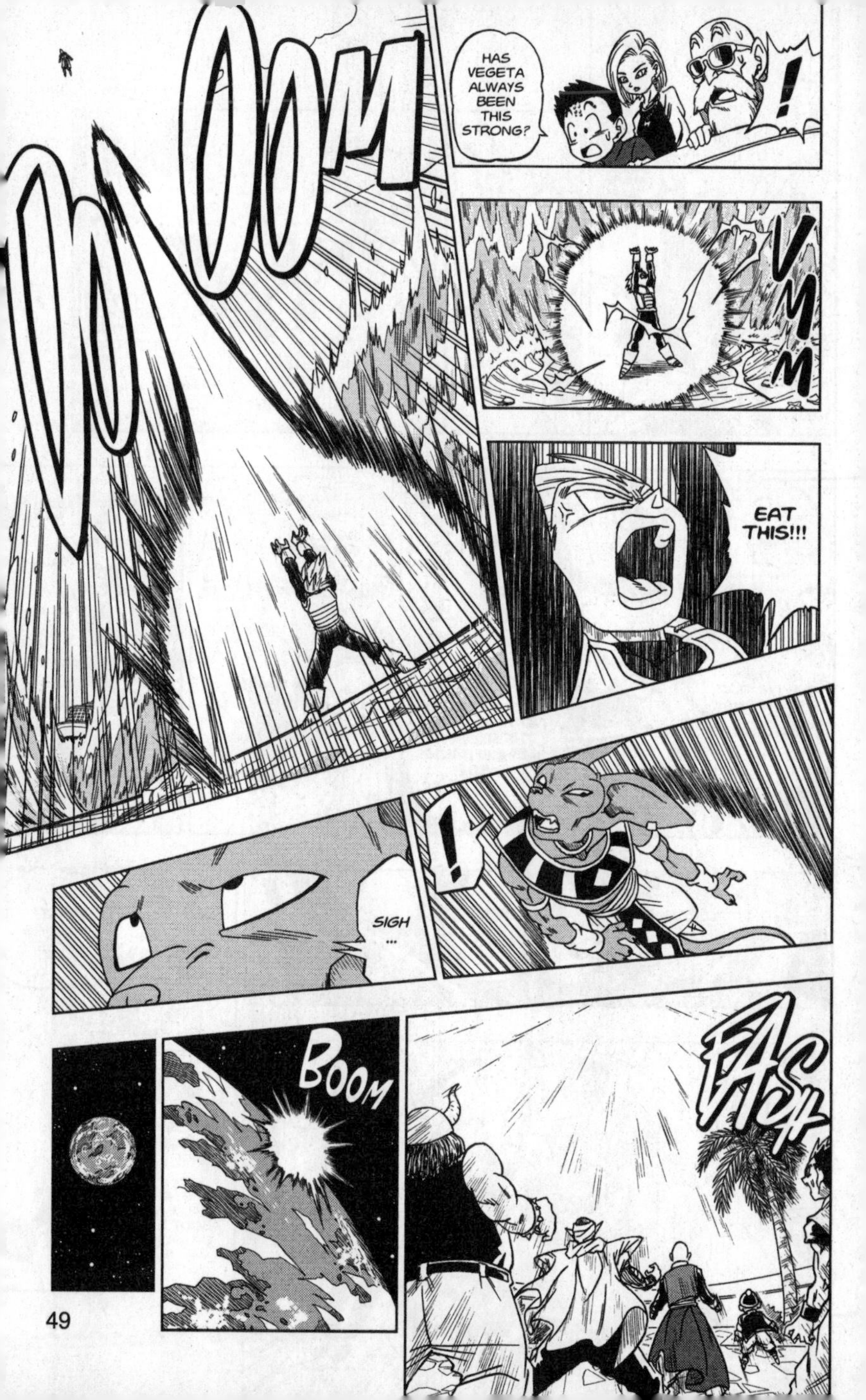
HAS VEGETA ALWAYS BEEN THIS STRONG?
!
VMM
EAT THIS!!!
!
SIGH ...
FASH
BOOM

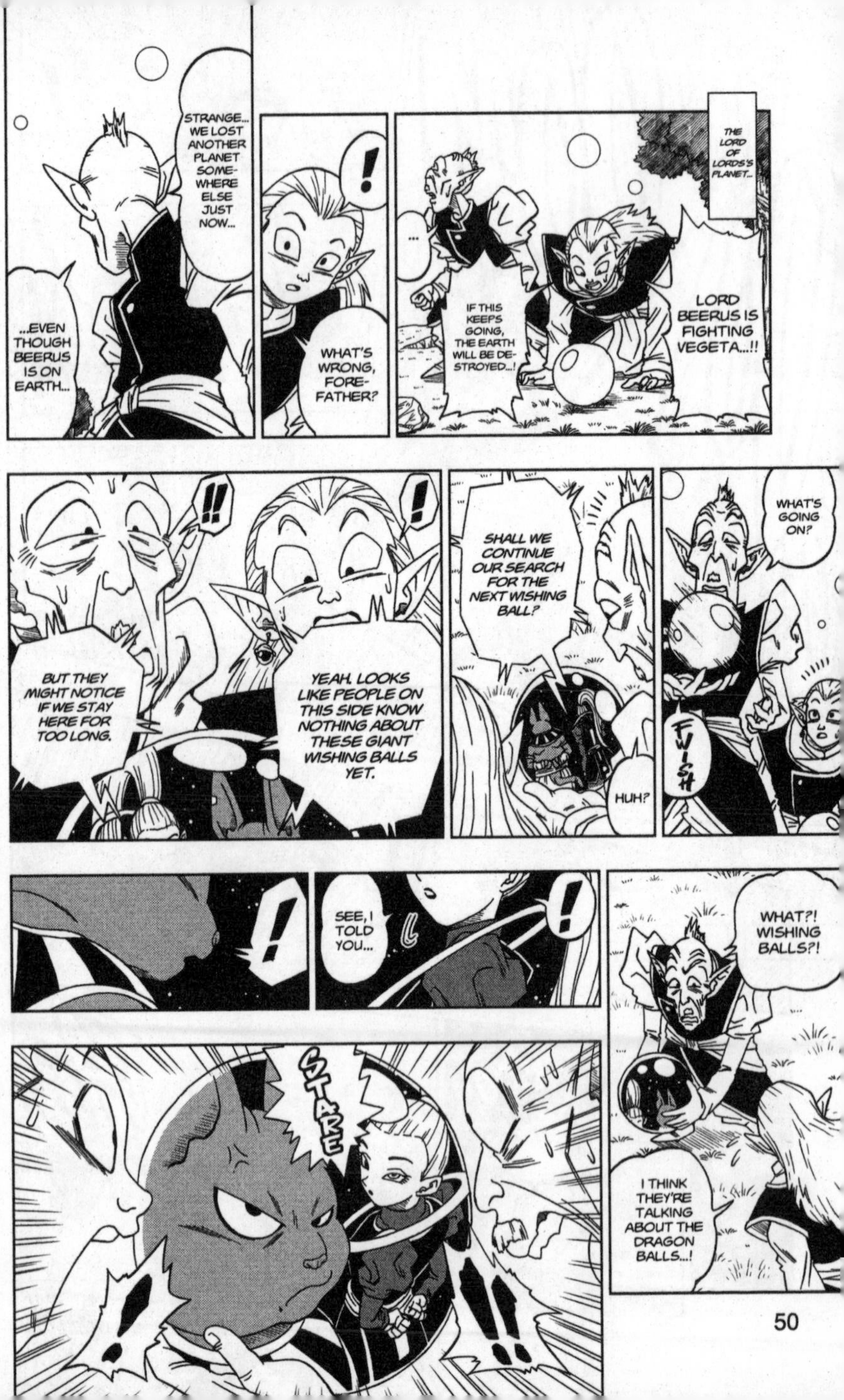
THE LORD OF LORDS'S PLANET...
LORD BEERUS IS FIGHTING VEGETA...!!
IF THIS KEEPS GOING, THE EARTH WILL BE DE-STROYED...!
...
!
WHAT'S WRONG, FORE-FATHER?
STRANGE... WE LOST ANOTHER PLANET SOME-WHERE ELSE JUST NOW...
...EVEN THOUGH BEERUS IS ON EARTH...
WHAT'S GOING ON?
FWISH
HUH?
SHALL WE CONTINUE OUR SEARCH FOR THE NEXT WISHING BALL?
!
YEAH. LOOKS LIKE PEOPLE ON THIS SIDE KNOW NOTHING ABOUT THESE GIANT WISHING BALLS YET.
!!
BUT THEY MIGHT NOTICE IF WE STAY HERE FOR TOO LONG.
WHAT?! WISHING BALLS?!
I THINK THEY'RE TALKING ABOUT THE DRAGON BALLS...!
!
SEE, I TOLD YOU...
!
STARE
!!

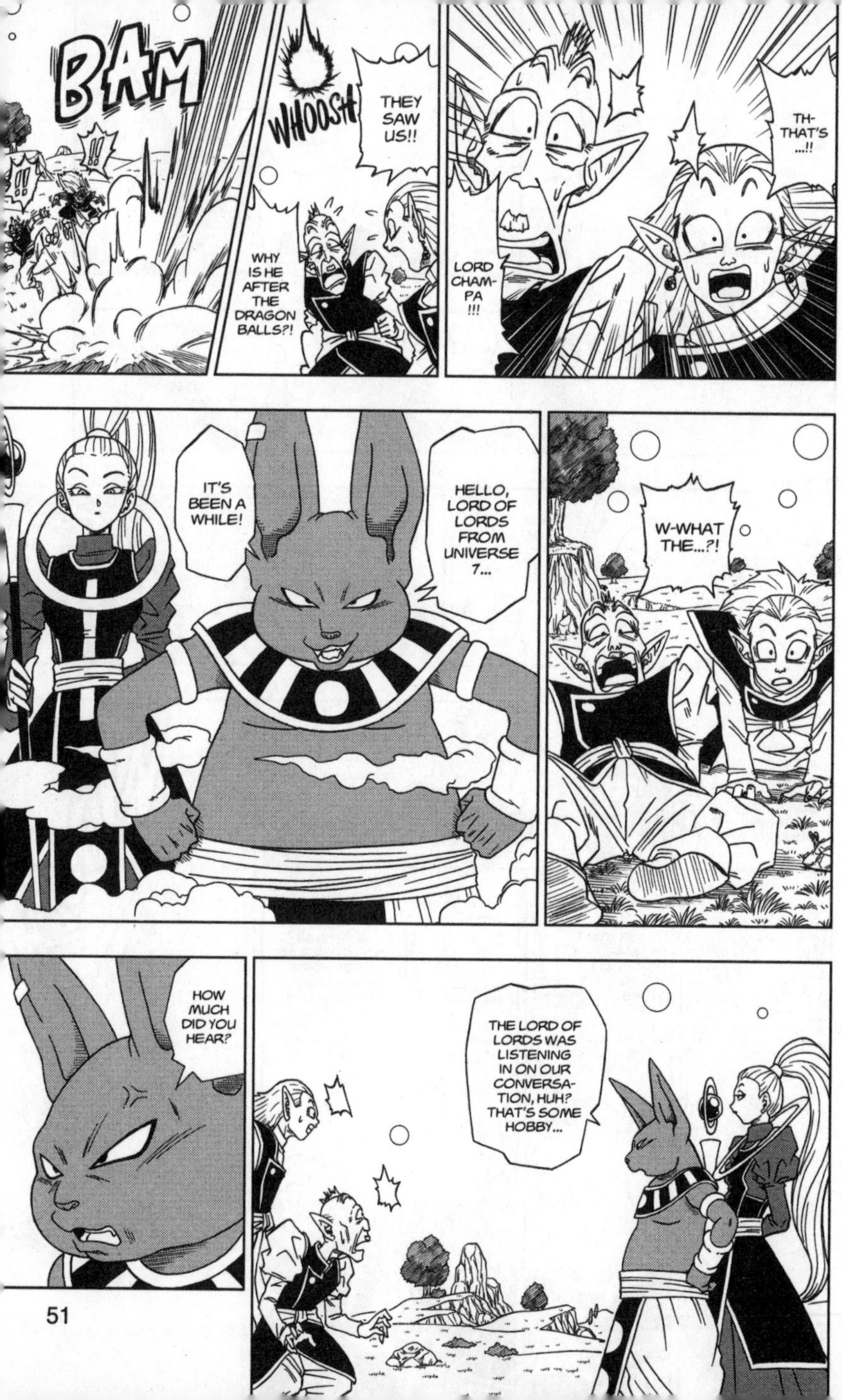
TH-THAT'S ...!!
LORD CHAMPA !!!
THEY SAW US!!
WHOOSH
WHY IS HE AFTER THE DRAGON BALLS?!
BAM
!!
!!
W-WHAT THE...?!
HELLO, LORD OF LORDS FROM UNIVERSE 7...
IT'S BEEN A WHILE!
THE LORD OF LORDS WAS LISTENING IN ON OUR CONVERSATION, HUH? THAT'S SOME HOBBY...
HOW MUCH DID YOU HEAR?

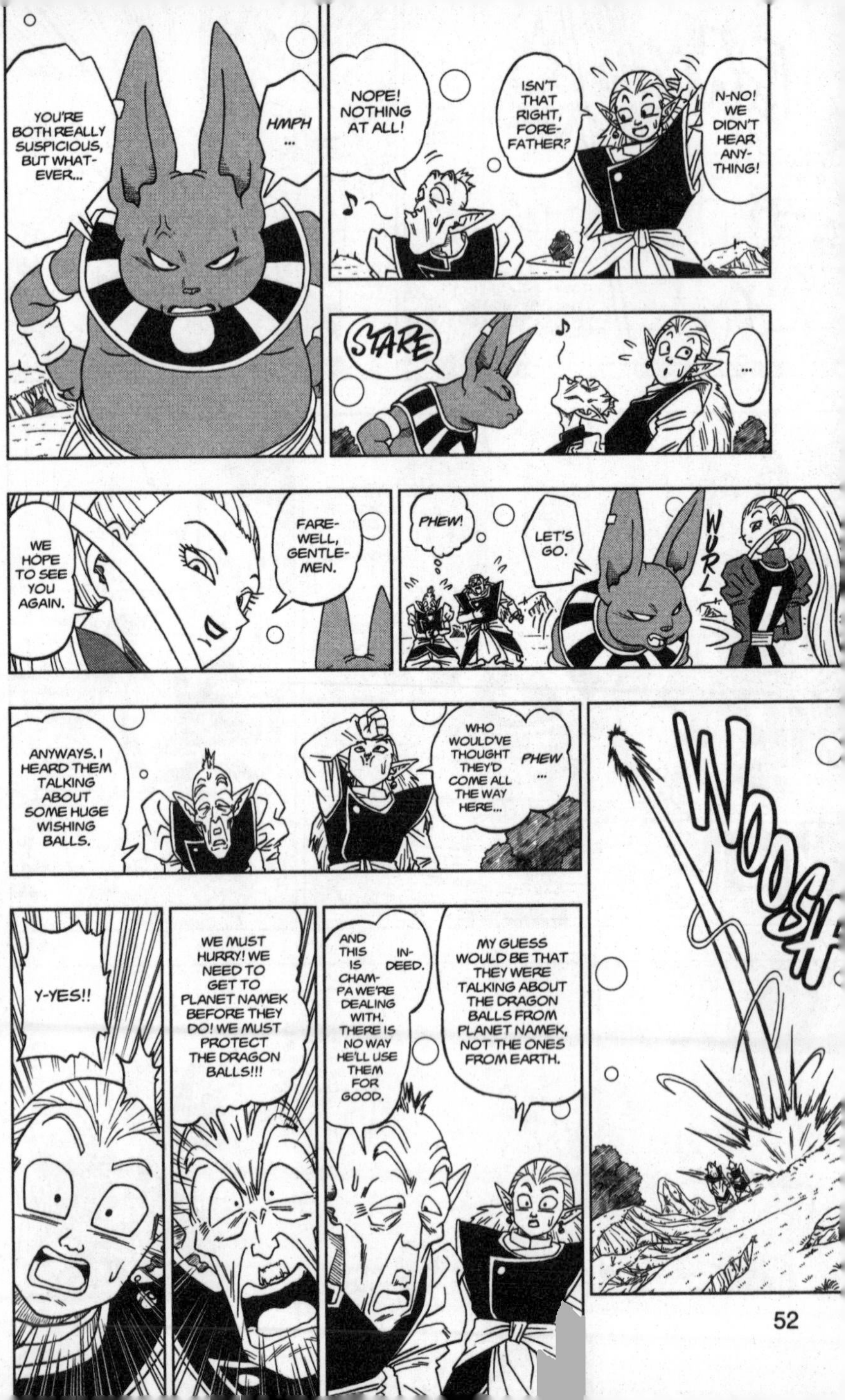
N-NO! WE DIDN'T HEAR ANYTHING!
ISN'T THAT RIGHT, FOREFATHER?
NOPE! NOTHING AT ALL!
...
STARE
HMPH...
YOU'RE BOTH REALLY SUSPICIOUS, BUT WHATEVER...
LET'S GO.
WURL
PHEW!
FAREWELL, GENTLEMEN.
WE HOPE TO SEE YOU AGAIN.
WOOSH
PHEW...
WHO WOULD'VE THOUGHT THEY'D COME ALL THE WAY HERE...
ANYWAYS. I HEARD THEM TALKING ABOUT SOME HUGE WISHING BALLS.
MY GUESS WOULD BE THAT THEY WERE TALKING ABOUT THE DRAGON BALLS FROM PLANET NAMEK, NOT THE ONES FROM EARTH.
INDEED.
AND THIS IS CHAMPA WE'RE DEALING WITH. THERE IS NO WAY HE'LL USE THEM FOR GOOD.
WE MUST HURRY! WE NEED TO GET TO PLANET NAMEK BEFORE THEY DO! WE MUST PROTECT THE DRAGON BALLS!!!
Y-YES!!

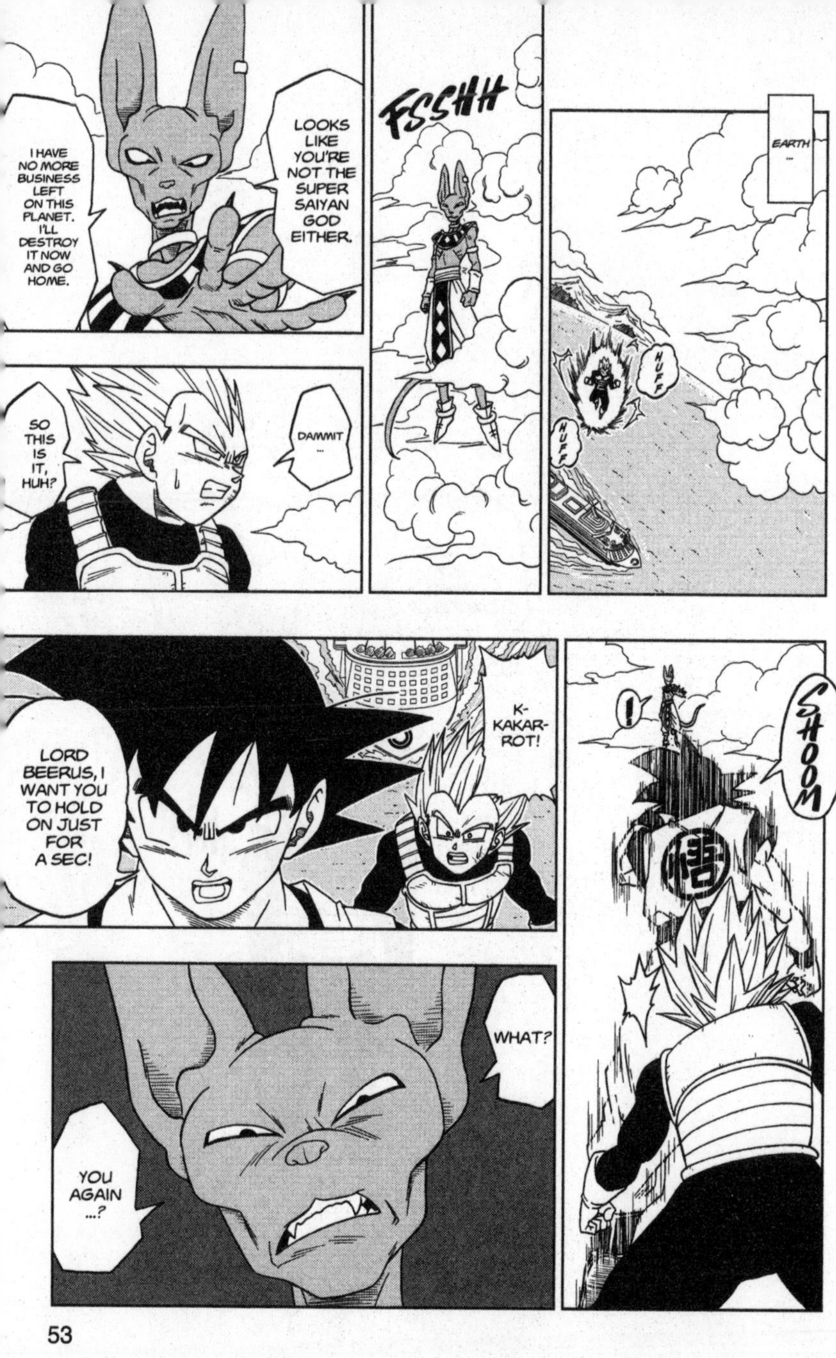
EARTH ...
HUFF
HUFF
FSSHH
LOOKS LIKE YOU'RE NOT THE SUPER SAIYAN GOD EITHER.
I HAVE NO MORE BUSINESS LEFT ON THIS PLANET. I'LL DESTROY IT NOW AND GO HOME.
DAMMIT ...
SO THIS IS IT, HUH?
SHOOM
!
K-KAKARROT!
LORD BEERUS, I WANT YOU TO HOLD ON JUST FOR A SEC!
WHAT?
YOU AGAIN ...?

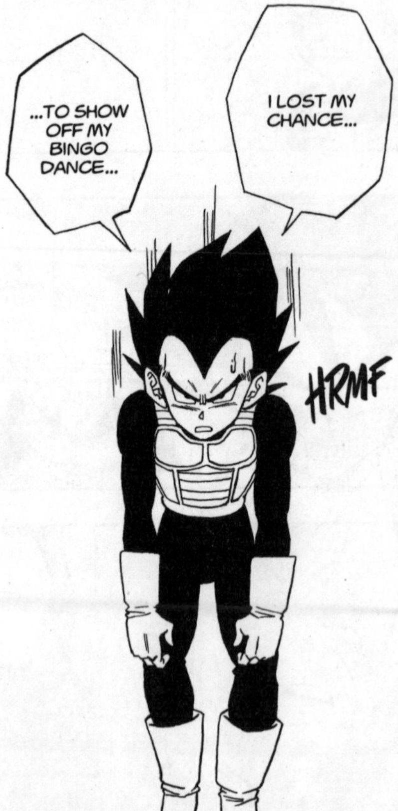
I LOST MY CHANCE...
...TO SHOW OFF MY BINGO DANCE...
HRMF

DRAGON BALL SUPER

CHAPTER 4: BATTLE OF GODS

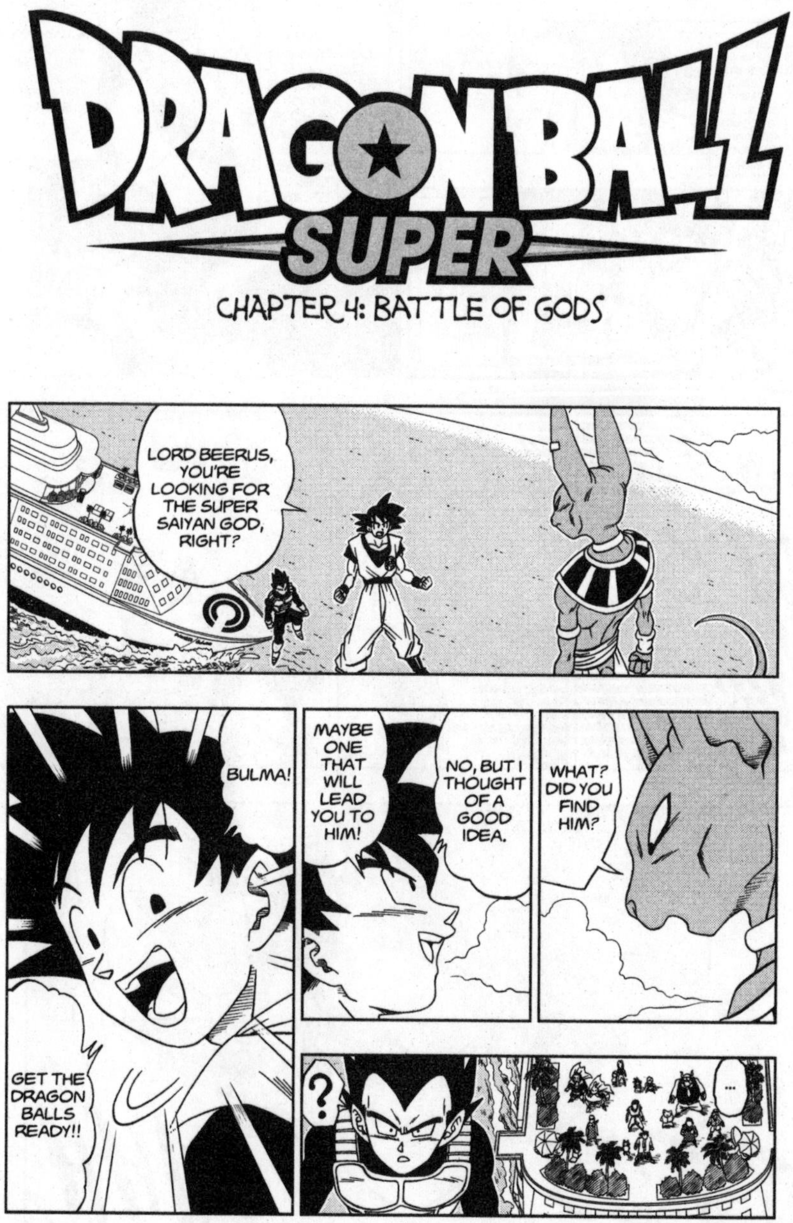
LORD BEERUS, YOU'RE LOOKING FOR THE SUPER SAIYAN GOD, RIGHT?
WHAT? DID YOU FIND HIM?
NO, BUT I THOUGHT OF A GOOD IDEA.
MAYBE ONE THAT WILL LEAD YOU TO HIM!
...
?
BULMA!
GET THE DRAGON BALLS READY!!

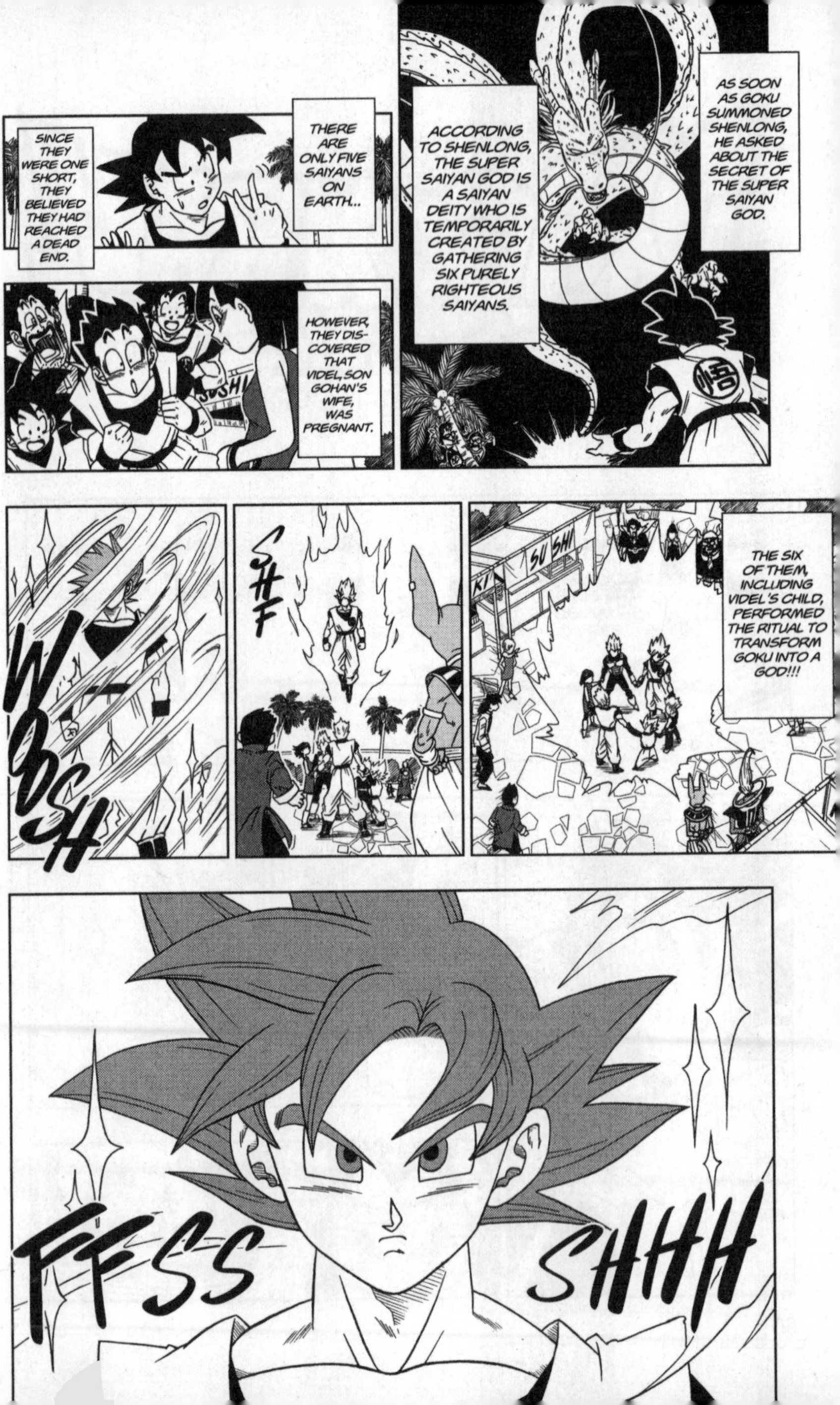
AS SOON AS GOKU SUMMONED SHENLONG, HE ASKED ABOUT THE SECRET OF THE SUPER SAIYAN GOD.
ACCORDING TO SHENLONG, THE SUPER SAIYAN GOD IS A SAIYAN DEITY WHO IS TEMPORARILY CREATED BY GATHERING SIX PURELY RIGHTEOUS SAIYANS.
THERE ARE ONLY FIVE SAIYANS ON EARTH...
SINCE THEY WERE ONE SHORT, THEY BELIEVED THEY HAD REACHED A DEAD END.
HOWEVER, THEY DISCOVERED THAT VIDEL, SON GOHAN'S WIFE, WAS PREGNANT.
SUSHI
THE SIX OF THEM, INCLUDING VIDEL'S CHILD, PERFORMED THE RITUAL TO TRANSFORM GOKU INTO A GOD!!!
KI
SU SHI
SHF
WOOSH
FFSS SHHH

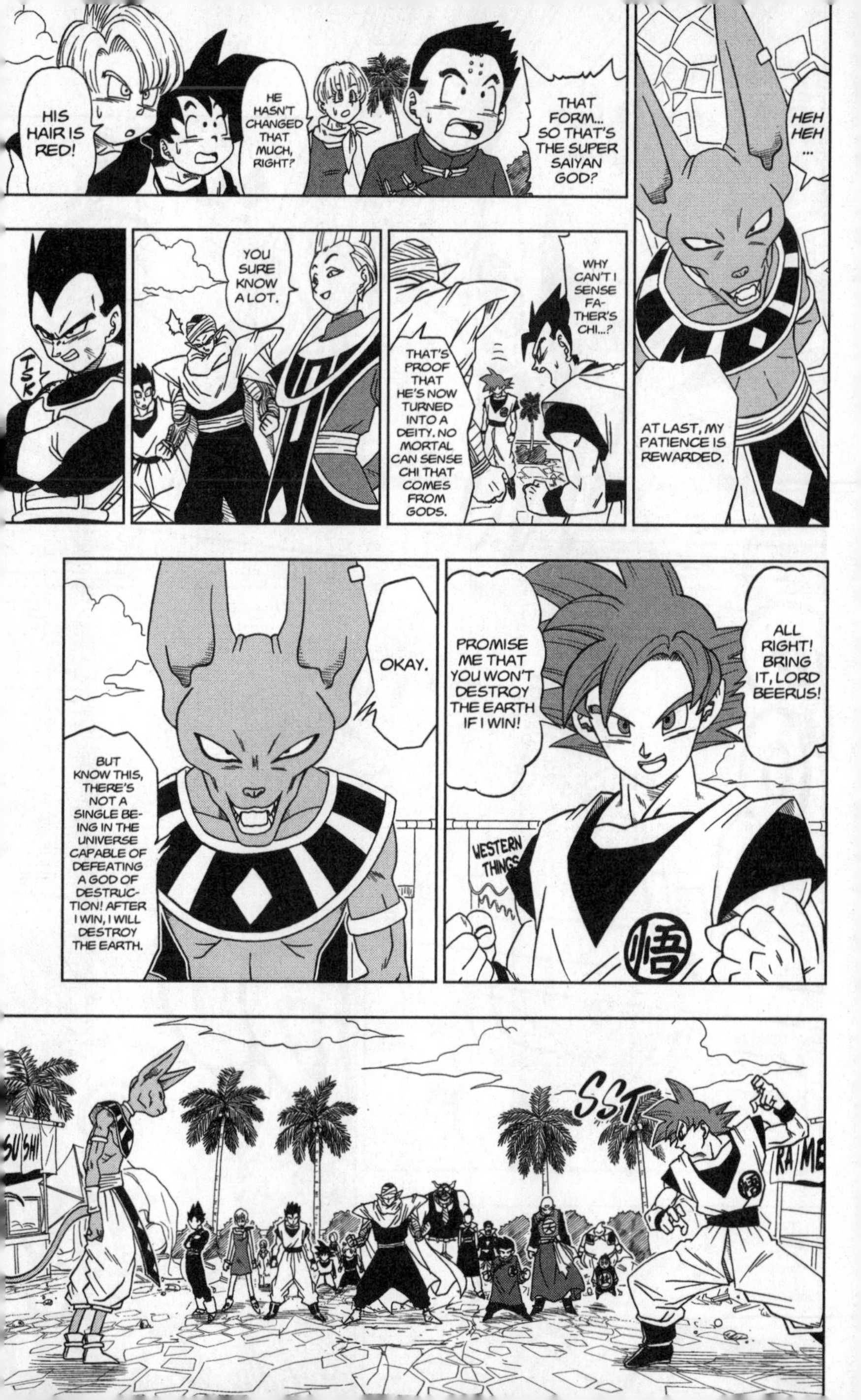
HEH HEH ...
AT LAST, MY PATIENCE IS REWARDED.
THAT FORM... SO THAT'S THE SUPER SAIYAN GOD?
HE HASN'T CHANGED THAT MUCH, RIGHT?
HIS HAIR IS RED!
WHY CAN'T I SENSE FA-THER'S CHI...?
THAT'S PROOF THAT HE'S NOW TURNED INTO A DEITY. NO MORTAL CAN SENSE CHI THAT COMES FROM GODS.
YOU SURE KNOW A LOT.
TSK
ALL RIGHT! BRING IT, LORD BEERUS!
PROMISE ME THAT YOU WON'T DESTROY THE EARTH IF I WIN!
WESTERN THINGS
OKAY.
BUT KNOW THIS, THERE'S NOT A SINGLE BE-ING IN THE UNIVERSE CAPABLE OF DEFEATING A GOD OF DESTRUC-TION! AFTER I WIN, I WILL DESTROY THE EARTH.
SST
SUSHI

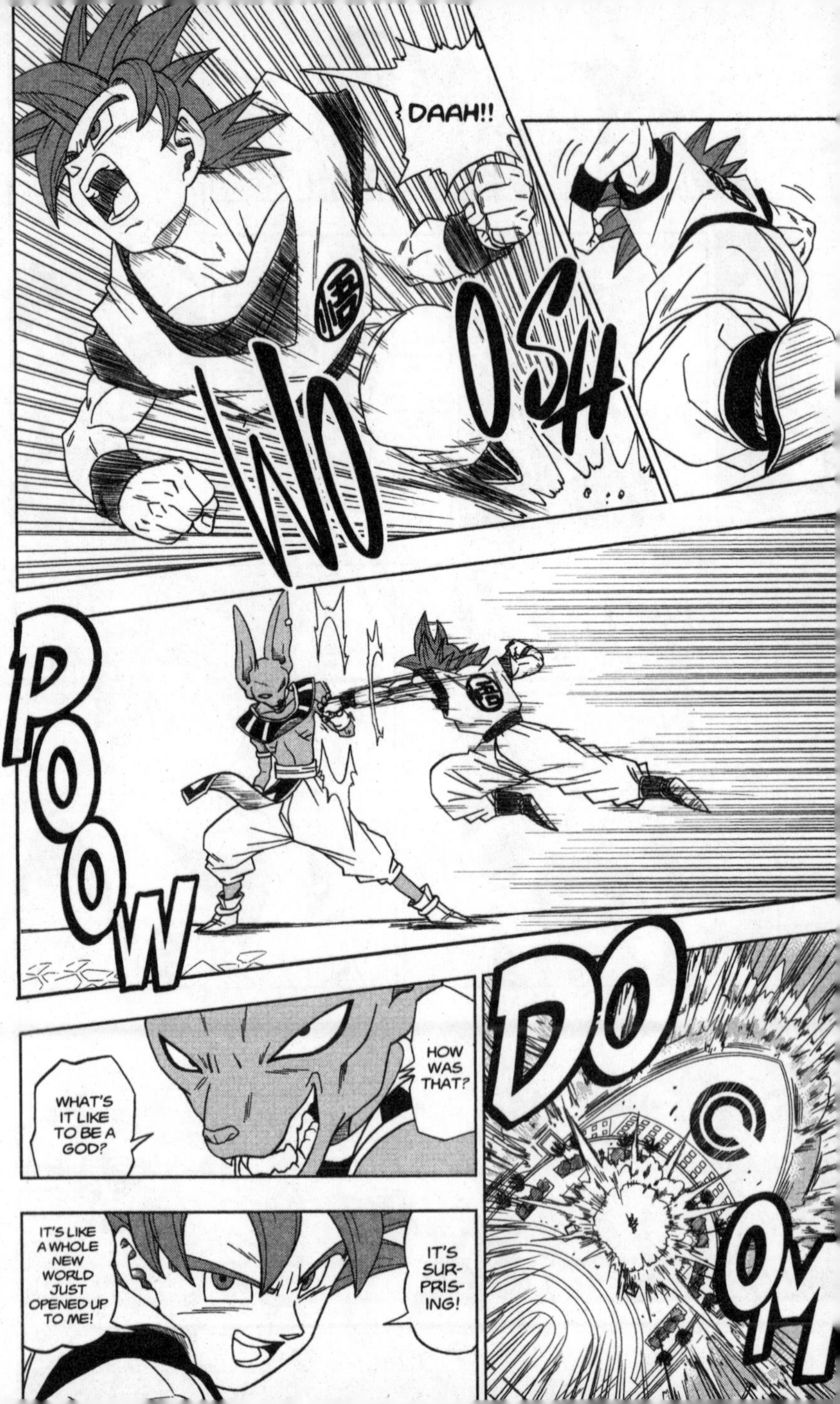
DAAH!!
WOOSH
POOOW
DOOOM
HOW WAS THAT?
WHAT'S IT LIKE TO BE A GOD?
IT'S SURPRISING!
IT'S LIKE A WHOLE NEW WORLD JUST OPENED UP TO ME!

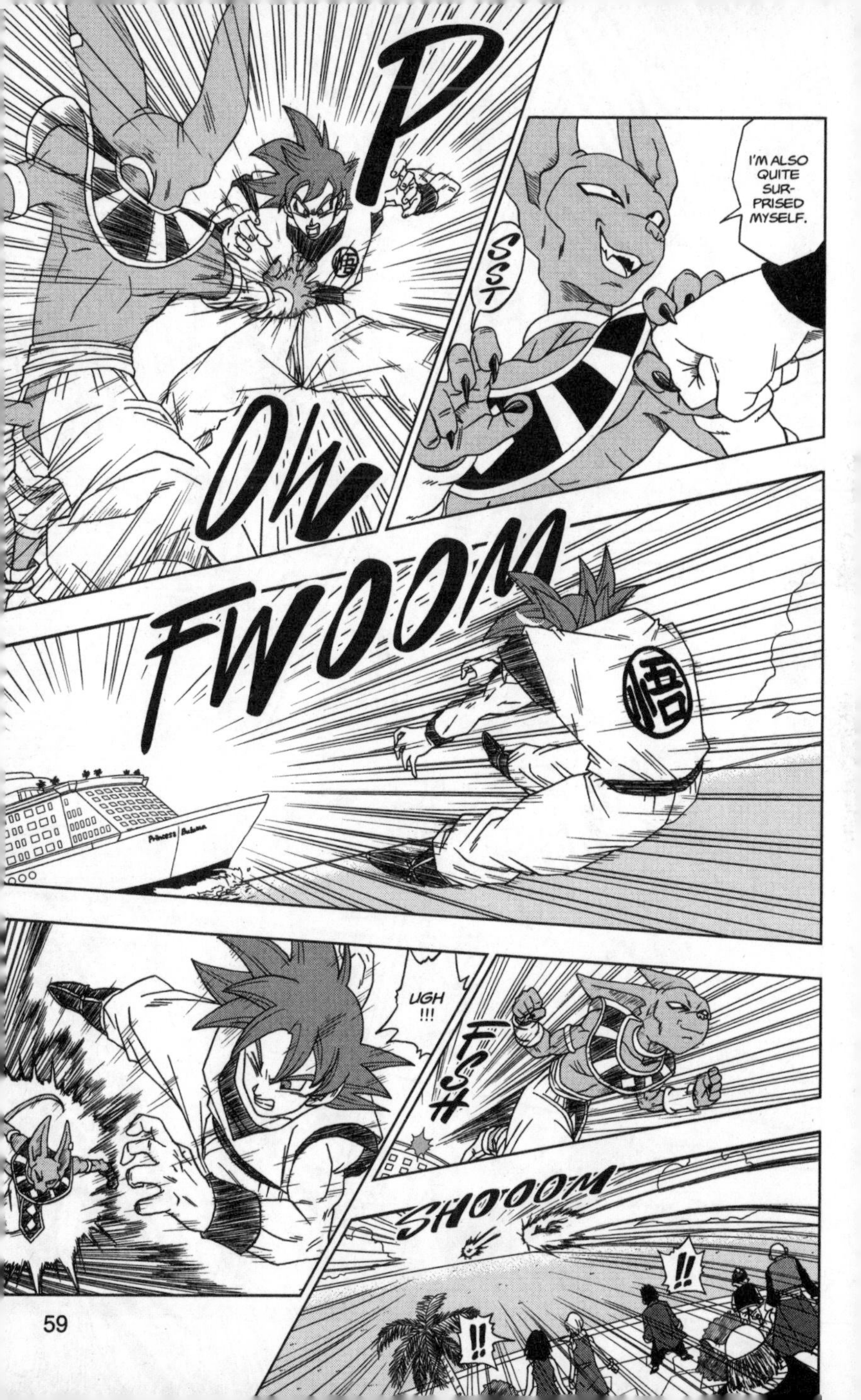

I'M ALSO QUITE SUR-PRISED MYSELF.
SSST
POW
FWOOM
FSH
SHOOOM
!!
!!
UGH !!!

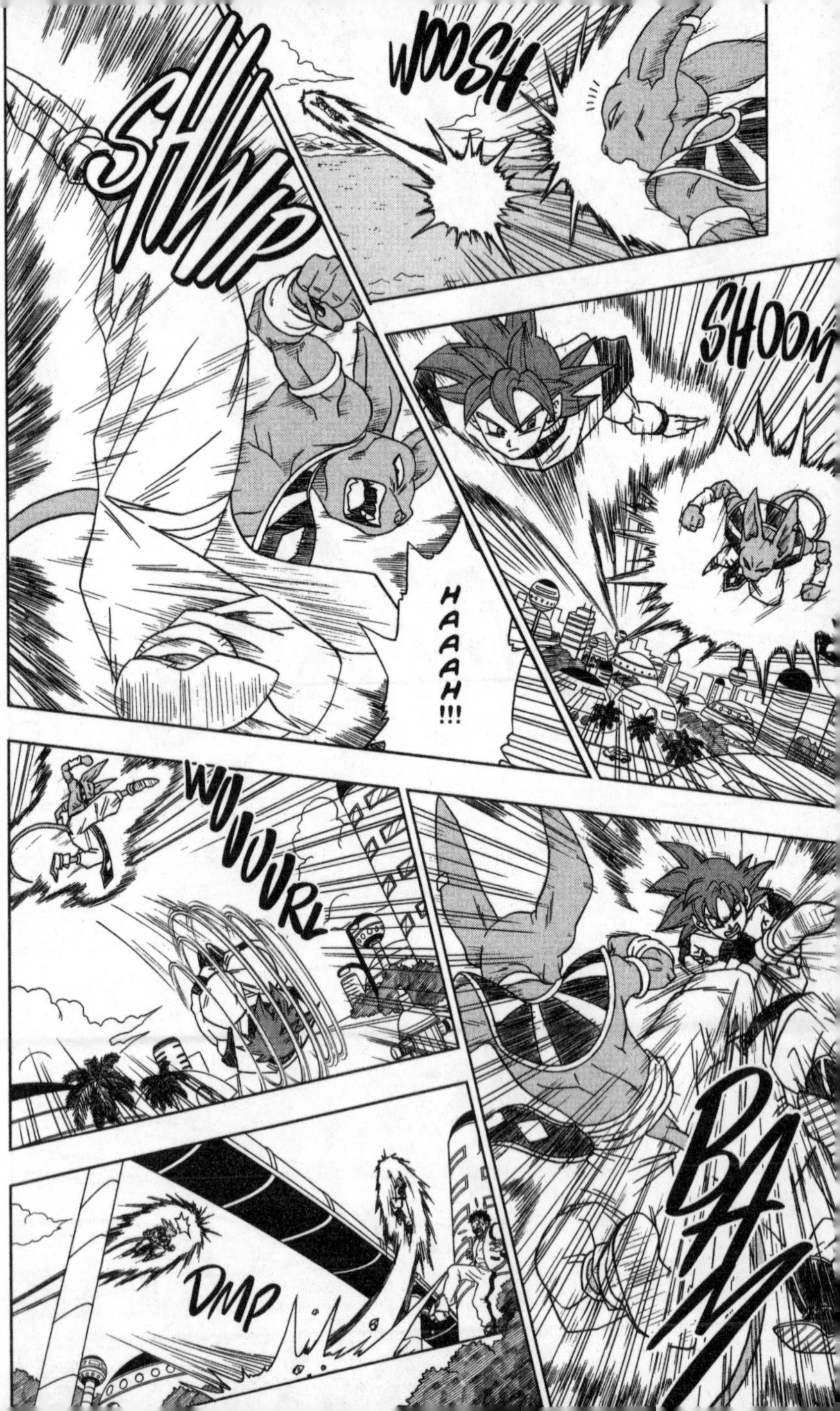
WOOSH
SHWIP
SHOOM
HAAAAH!!!
BAM
WUUUURL
DMP

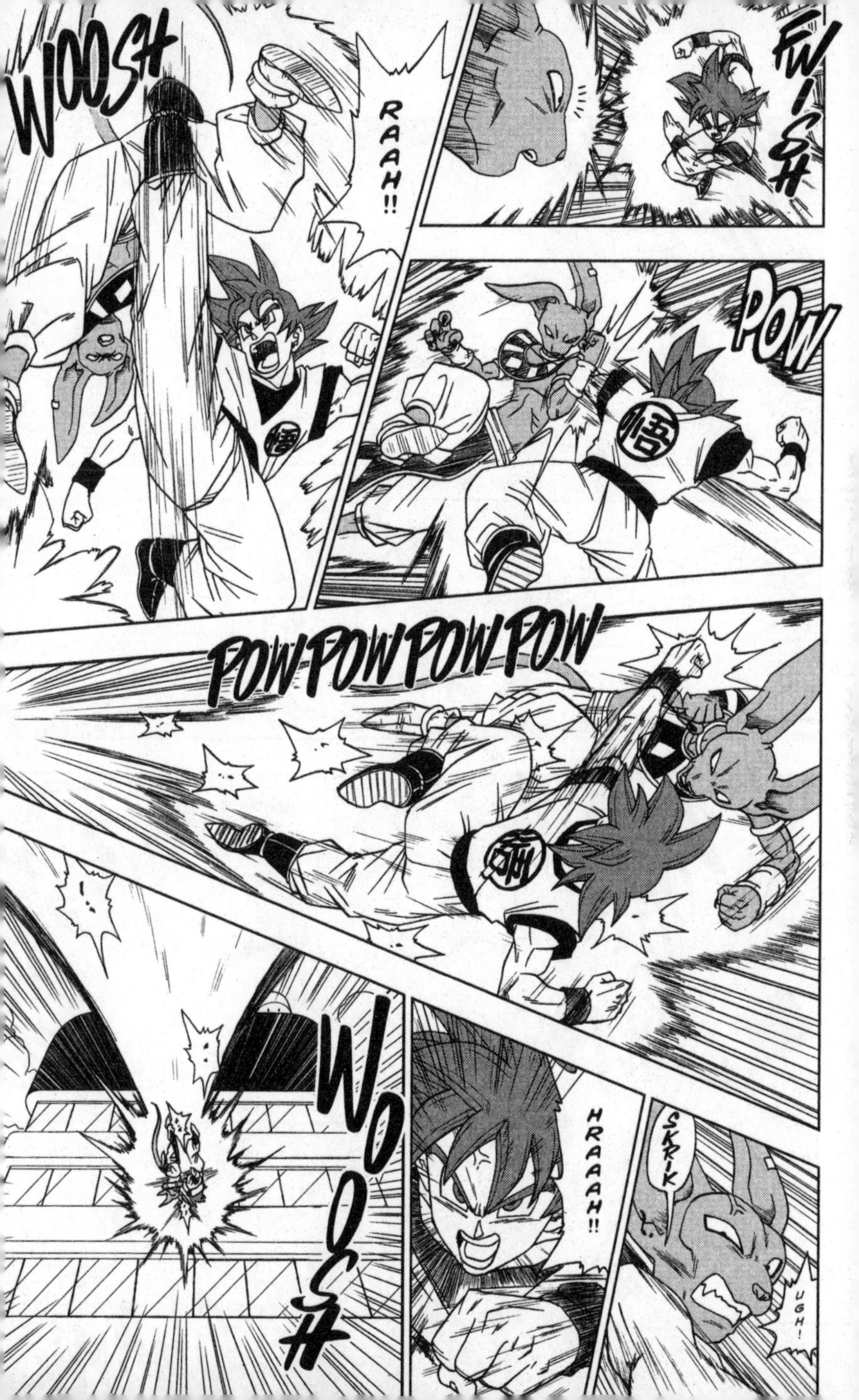
FWISH
POW
WOOSH
RAAAH!!
POW POW POW POW
SKRIK
UGH!
HRAAAAH!!
WOOSH

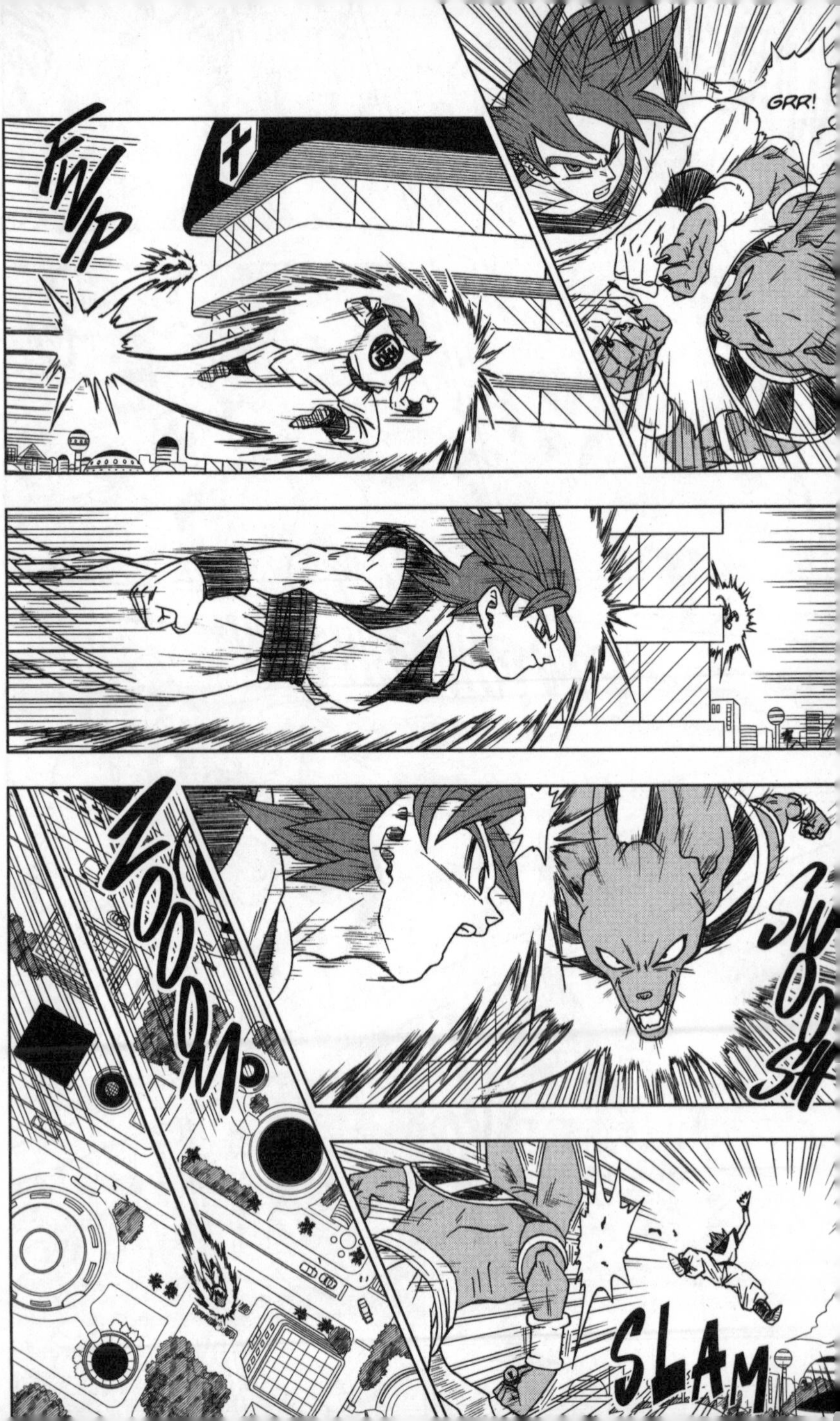
GRR!
FWIP
SWOOSH
ZOOOM
SLAM

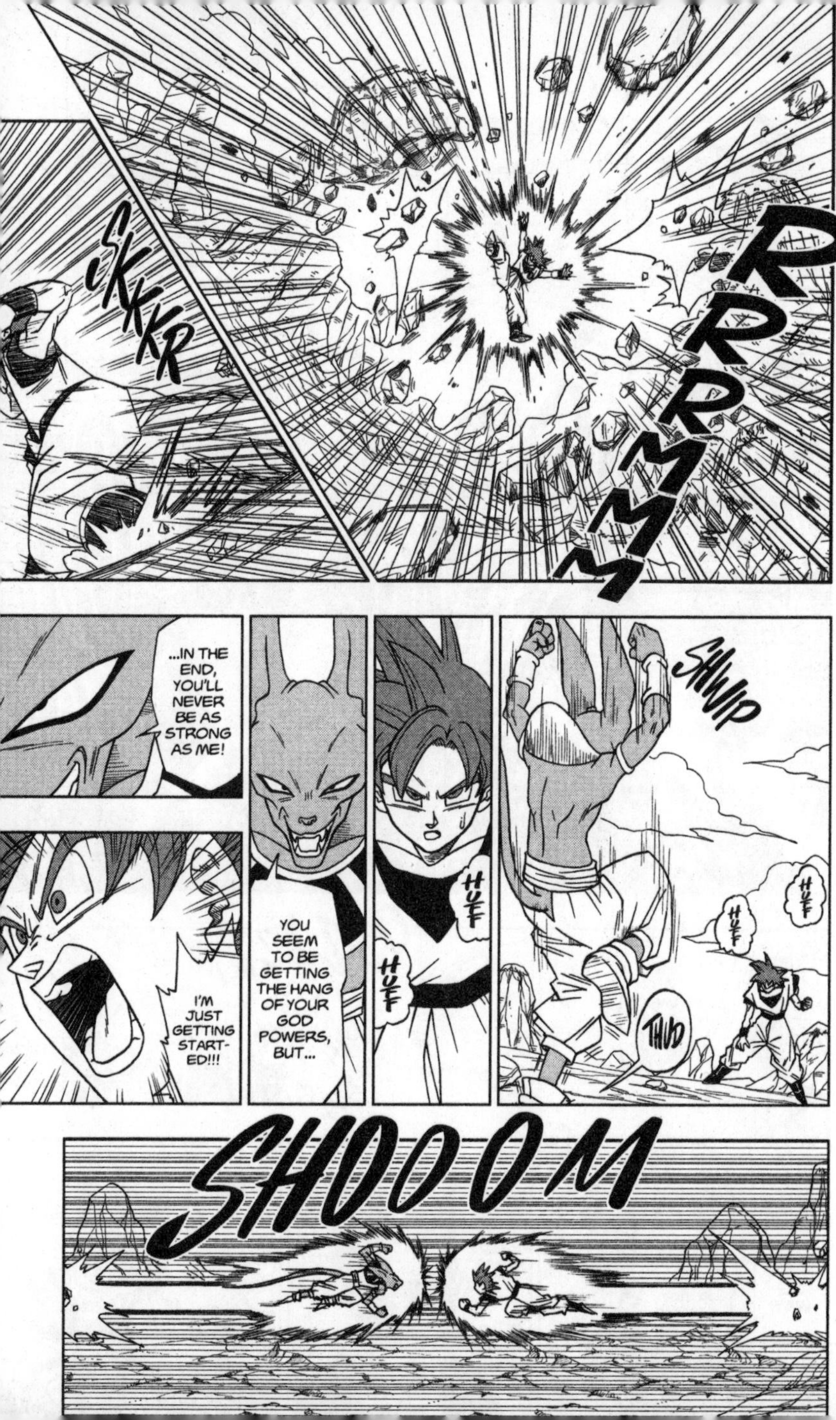
RRRMMM
SKKKR
SHWIP
HUFF
HUFF
THUD
HUFF
HUFF
YOU SEEM TO BE GETTING THE HANG OF YOUR GOD POWERS, BUT...
...IN THE END, YOU'LL NEVER BE AS STRONG AS ME!
I'M JUST GETTING START-ED!!!
SHOOOM

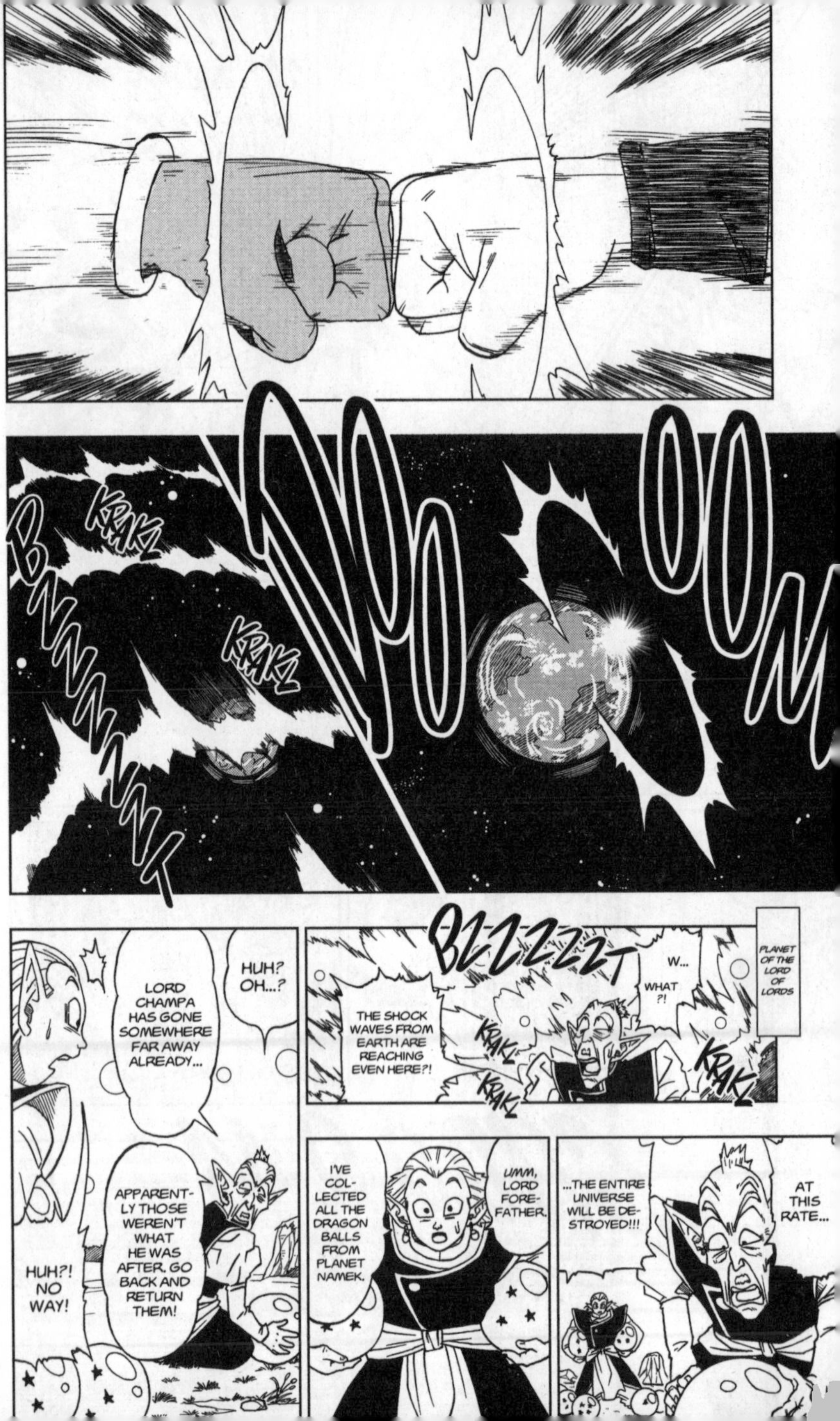
KRAK!
KRAK!
PLANET OF THE LORD OF LORDS
BZZZZZT
W... WHAT ?!
THE SHOCK WAVES FROM EARTH ARE REACHING EVEN HERE?!
KRAK!
KRAK!
KRAK!
AT THIS RATE...
...THE ENTIRE UNIVERSE WILL BE DESTROYED!!!
UMM, LORD FOREFATHER.
I'VE COLLECTED ALL THE DRAGON BALLS FROM PLANET NAMEK.
HUH? OH...?
LORD CHAMPA HAS GONE SOMEWHERE FAR AWAY ALREADY...
APPARENTLY THOSE WEREN'T WHAT HE WAS AFTER. GO BACK AND RETURN THEM!
HUH?! NO WAY!

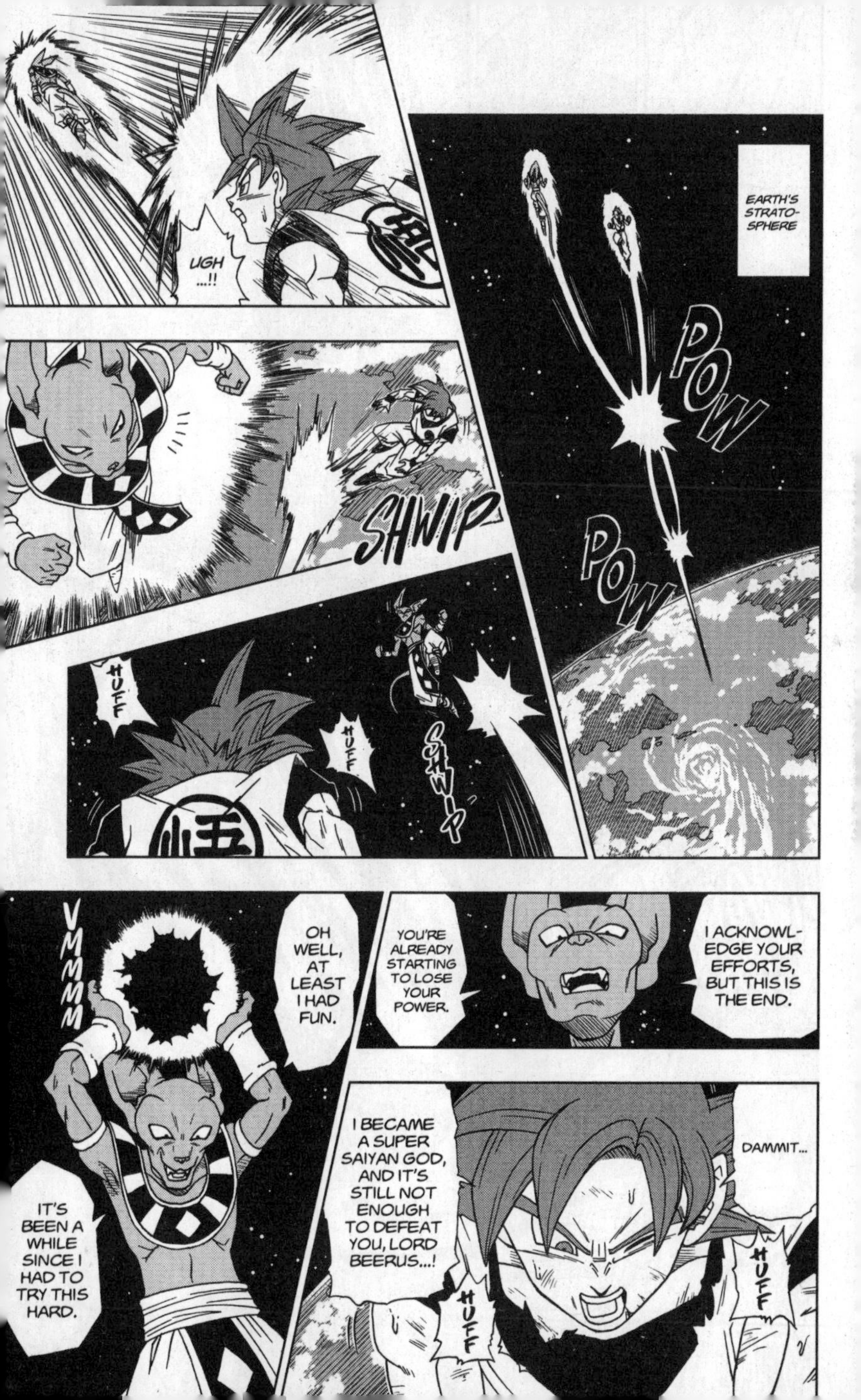
EARTH'S STRATO-SPHERE
POW
POW
UGH ...!!
SHWIP
HUFF
HUFF
SHWIP
I ACKNOWL-EDGE YOUR EFFORTS, BUT THIS IS THE END.
YOU'RE ALREADY STARTING TO LOSE YOUR POWER.
DAMMIT...
HUFF
I BECAME A SUPER SAIYAN GOD, AND IT'S STILL NOT ENOUGH TO DEFEAT YOU, LORD BEERUS...!
HUFF
VMMMM
OH WELL, AT LEAST I HAD FUN.
IT'S BEEN A WHILE SINCE I HAD TO TRY THIS HARD.

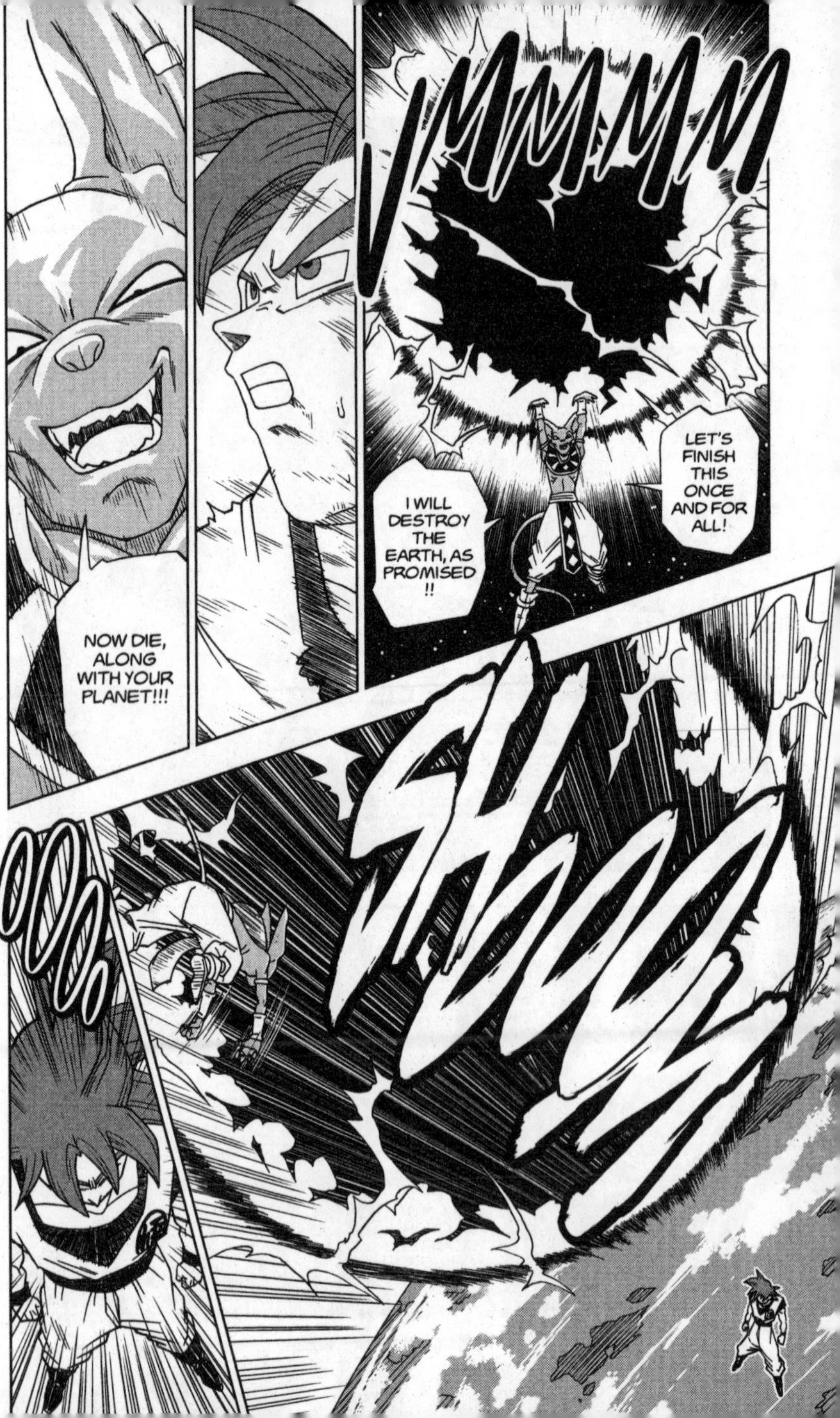
LET'S FINISH THIS ONCE AND FOR ALL!
I WILL DESTROY THE EARTH, AS PROMISED!!
NOW DIE, ALONG WITH YOUR PLANET!!!

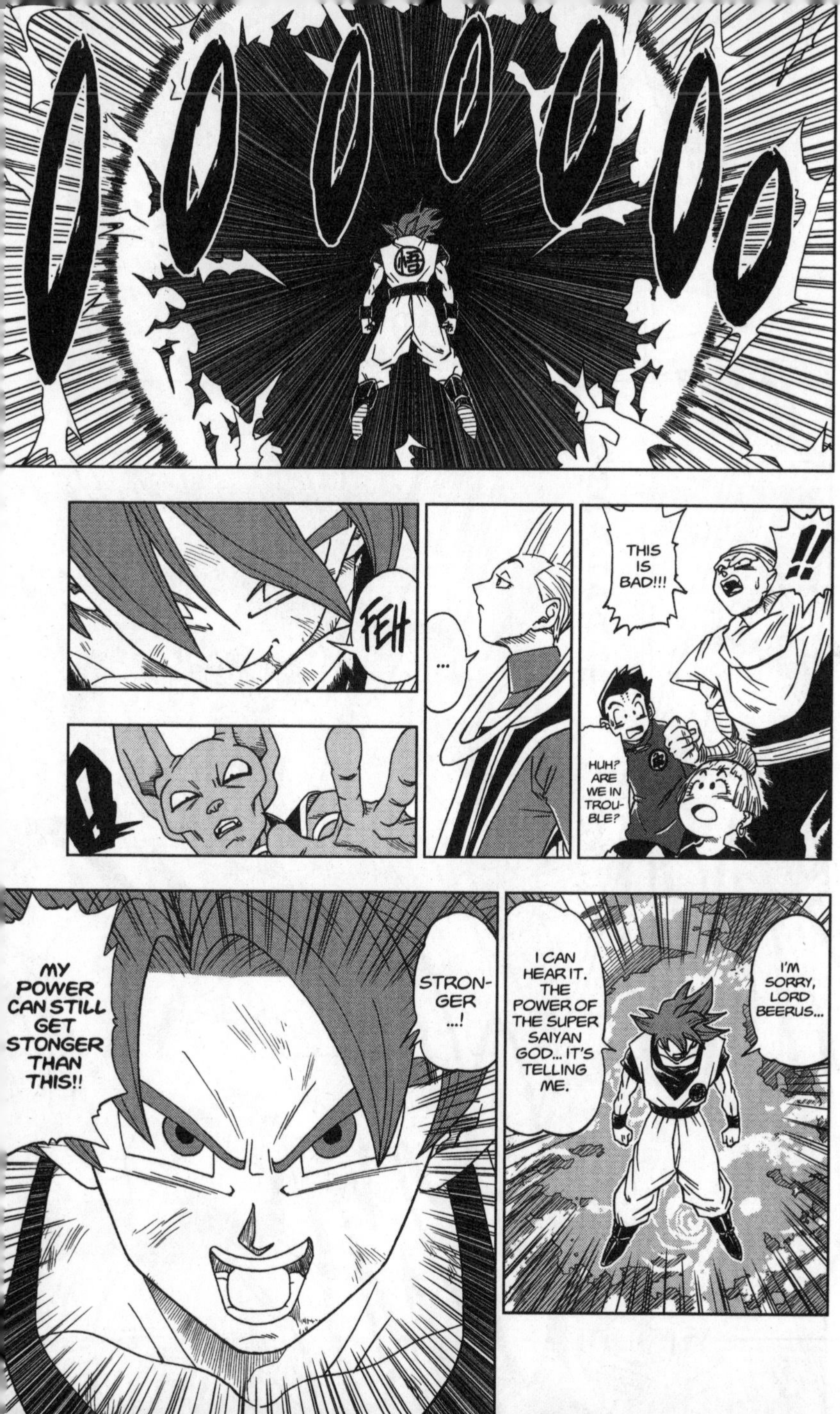
!!
THIS IS BAD!!!
HUH? ARE WE IN TROUBLE?
...
FEH
I'M SORRY, LORD BEERUS...
I CAN HEAR IT. THE POWER OF THE SUPER SAIYAN GOD... IT'S TELLING ME.
STRONGER...!
MY POWER CAN STILL GET STONGER THAN THIS!!

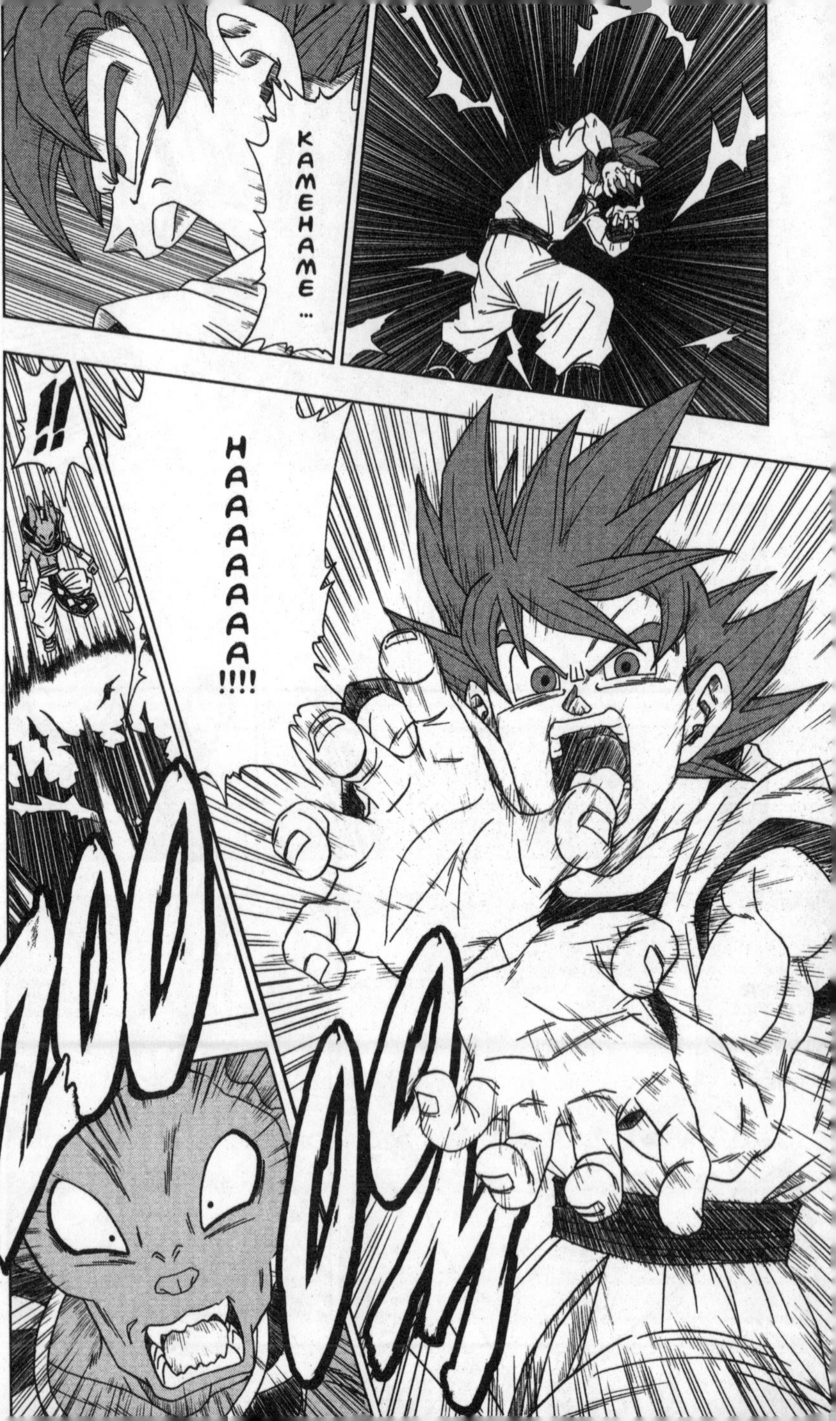
KAMEHAME...
!!
HAAAAAAAAAA!!!!
ZOOOOOM

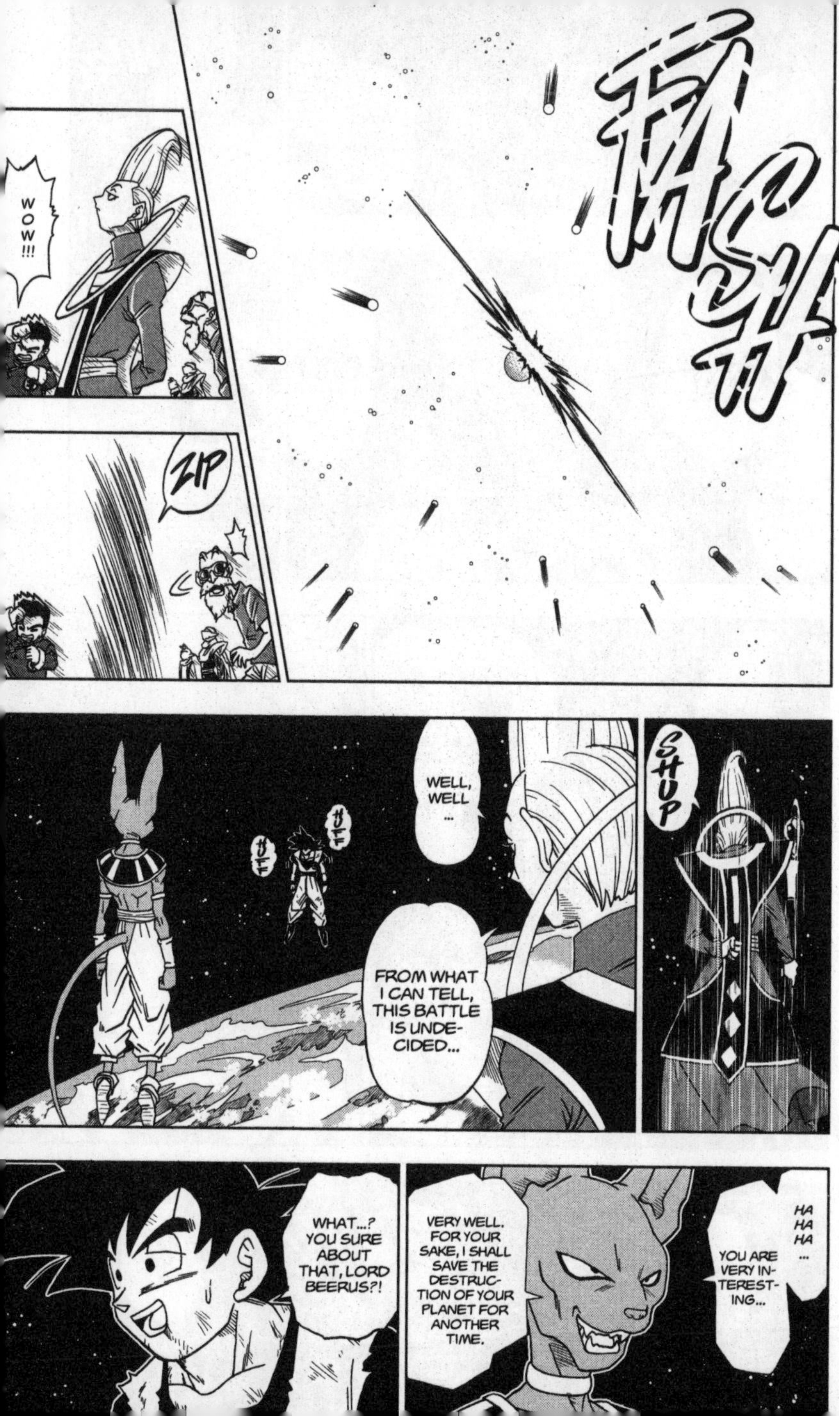
FASH
WOW!!!
ZIP
SHUP
WELL, WELL ...
FROM WHAT I CAN TELL, THIS BATTLE IS UNDECIDED...
HUFF HUFF
HA HA HA ...
YOU ARE VERY INTERESTING...
VERY WELL. FOR YOUR SAKE, I SHALL SAVE THE DESTRUCTION OF YOUR PLANET FOR ANOTHER TIME.
WHAT...? YOU SURE ABOUT THAT, LORD BEERUS?!

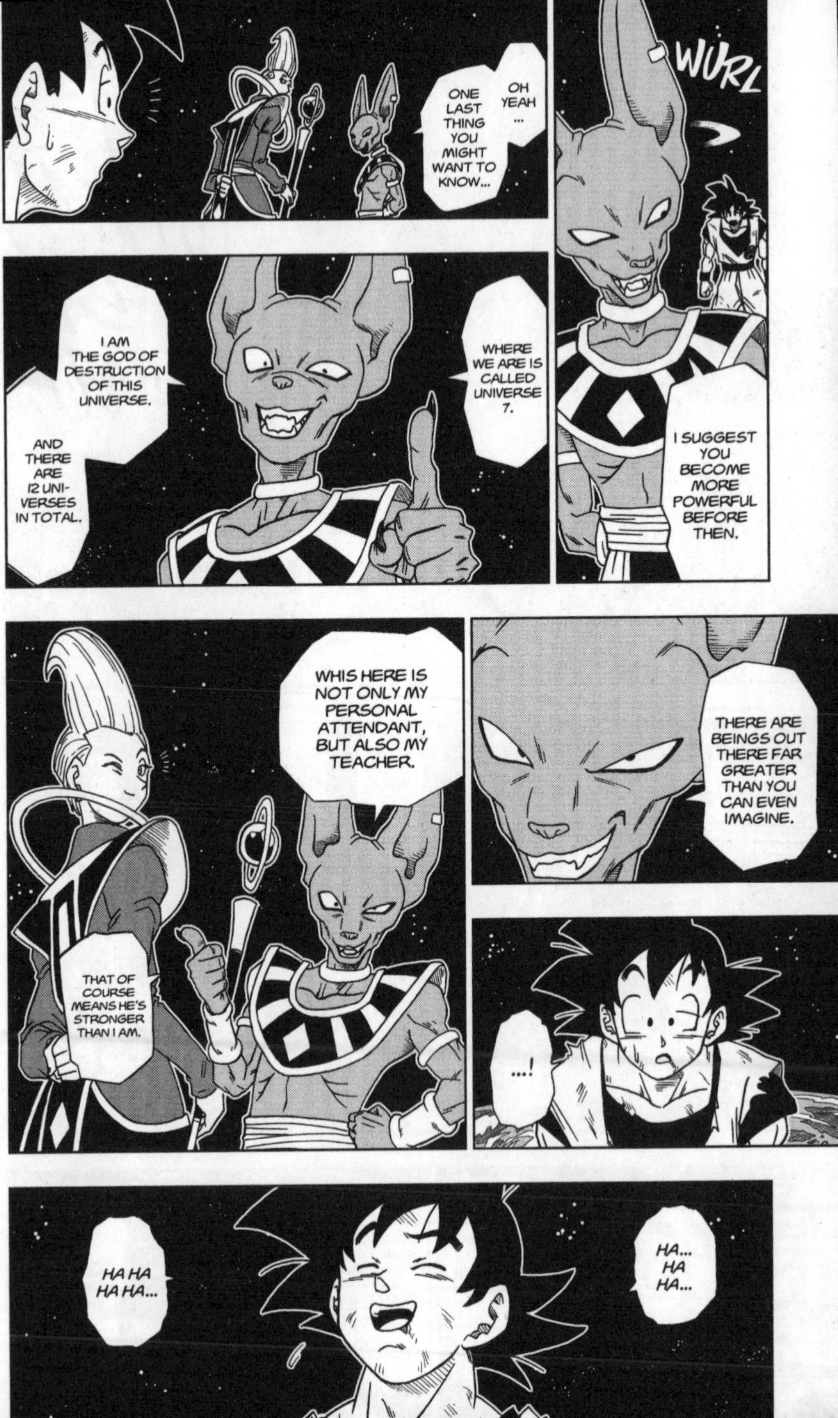
WURL
I SUGGEST YOU BECOME MORE POWERFUL BEFORE THEN.
OH YEAH ...
ONE LAST THING YOU MIGHT WANT TO KNOW...
WHERE WE ARE IS CALLED UNIVERSE 7.
I AM THE GOD OF DESTRUCTION OF THIS UNIVERSE.
AND THERE ARE 12 UNIVERSES IN TOTAL.
THERE ARE BEINGS OUT THERE FAR GREATER THAN YOU CAN EVEN IMAGINE.
...!
WHIS HERE IS NOT ONLY MY PERSONAL ATTENDANT, BUT ALSO MY TEACHER.
THAT OF COURSE MEANS HE'S STRONGER THAN I AM.
HA... HA HA...
HA HA HA HA...

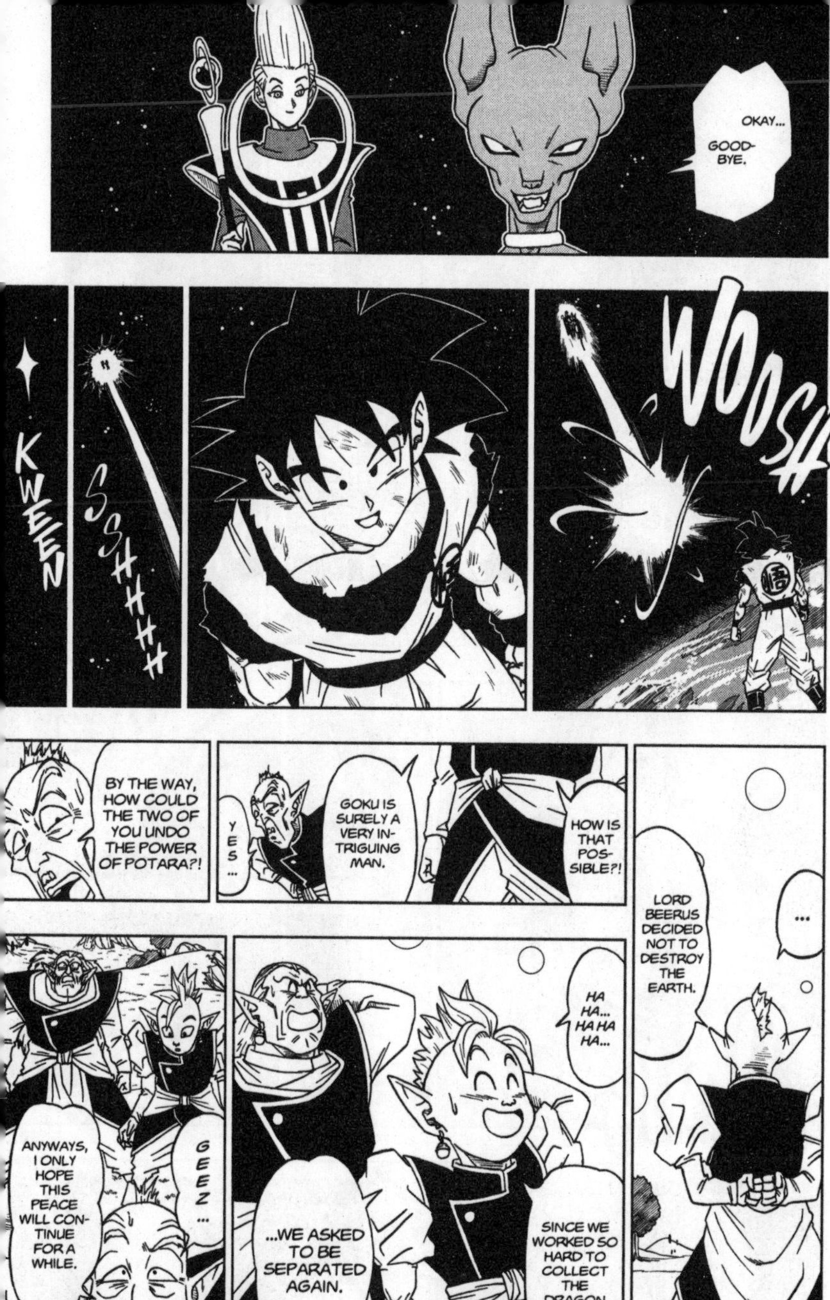
OKAY...
GOOD-BYE.
WOOSH
SSHHHHHH
KWEEN
...
LORD BEERUS DECIDED NOT TO DESTROY THE EARTH.
HOW IS THAT POSSIBLE?!
GOKU IS SURELY A VERY INTRIGUING MAN.
YES...
BY THE WAY, HOW COULD THE TWO OF YOU UNDO THE POWER OF POTARA?!
HA HA... HA HA HA...
SINCE WE WORKED SO HARD TO COLLECT THE DRAGON BALLS...
...WE ASKED TO BE SEPARATED AGAIN.
GEEZ...
ANYWAYS, I ONLY HOPE THIS PEACE WILL CONTINUE FOR A WHILE.

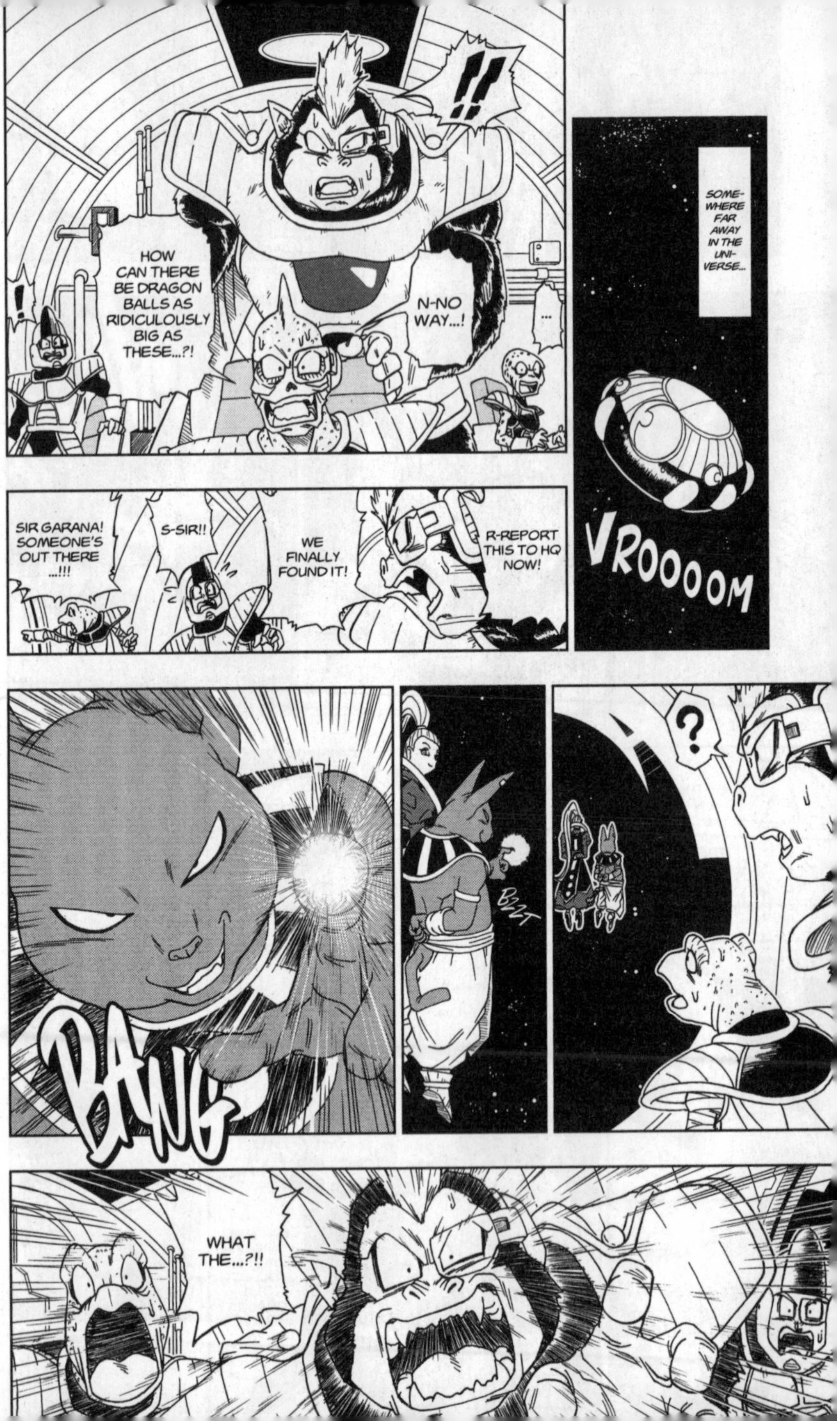
SOMEWHERE FAR AWAY IN THE UNIVERSE...
VROOOOM
!!
...
N-NO WAY...!
HOW CAN THERE BE DRAGON BALLS AS RIDICULOUSLY BIG AS THESE...?!
!
R-REPORT THIS TO HQ NOW!
WE FINALLY FOUND IT!
S-SIR!!
SIR GARANA! SOMEONE'S OUT THERE ...!!!
?
BZZT
BANG
WHAT THE...?!!

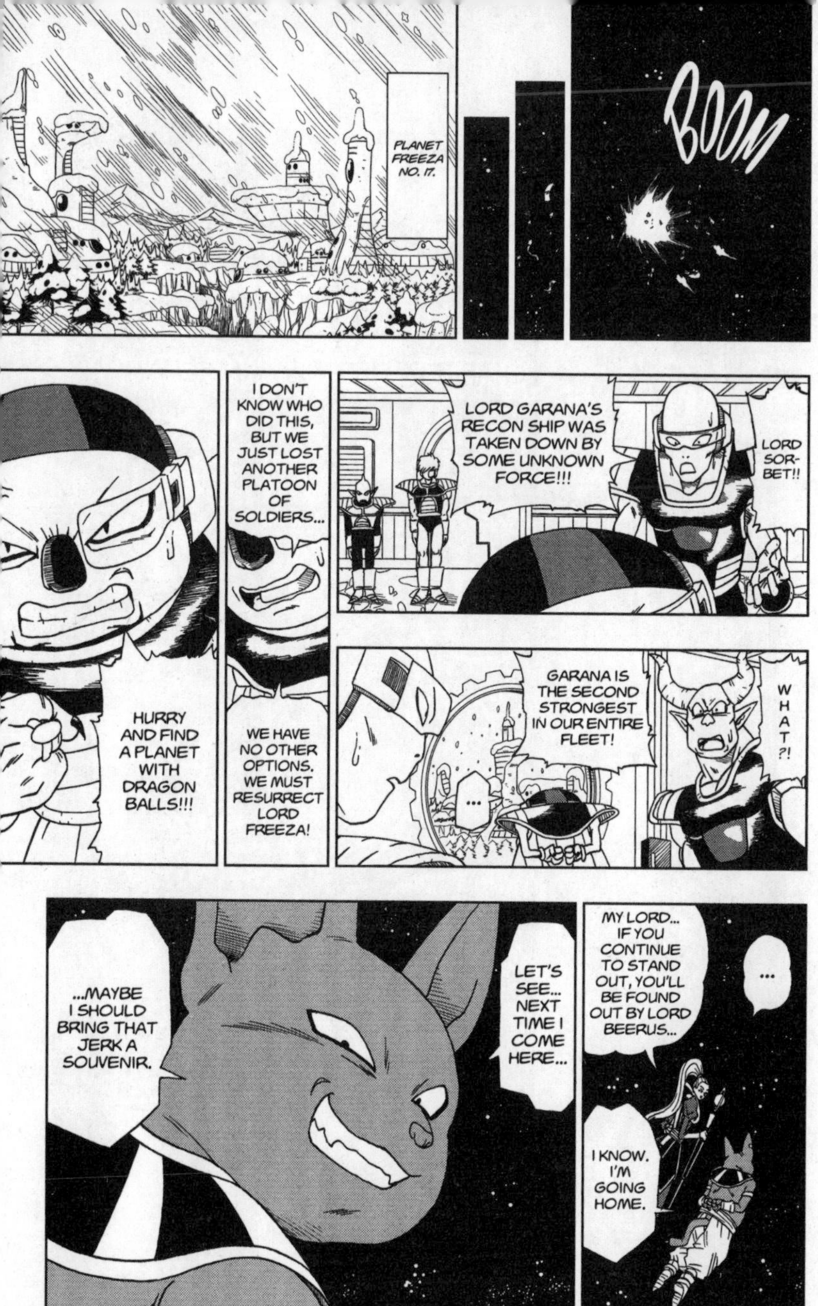
BOOM
PLANET FREEZA NO. 17.
LORD SORBET!!
LORD GARANA'S RECON SHIP WAS TAKEN DOWN BY SOME UNKNOWN FORCE!!!
WHAT?!
GARANA IS THE SECOND STRONGEST IN OUR ENTIRE FLEET!
...
I DON'T KNOW WHO DID THIS, BUT WE JUST LOST ANOTHER PLATOON OF SOLDIERS...
WE HAVE NO OTHER OPTIONS. WE MUST RESURRECT LORD FREEZA!
HURRY AND FIND A PLANET WITH DRAGON BALLS!!!
...
MY LORD... IF YOU CONTINUE TO STAND OUT, YOU'LL BE FOUND OUT BY LORD BEERUS...
I KNOW. I'M GOING HOME.
LET'S SEE... NEXT TIME I COME HERE...
...MAYBE I SHOULD BRING THAT JERK A SOUVENIR.

DRAGON BALL SUPER

CHAPTER 5: BEERUS AND CHAMPA

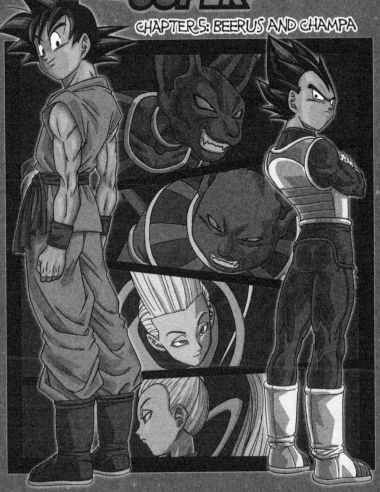

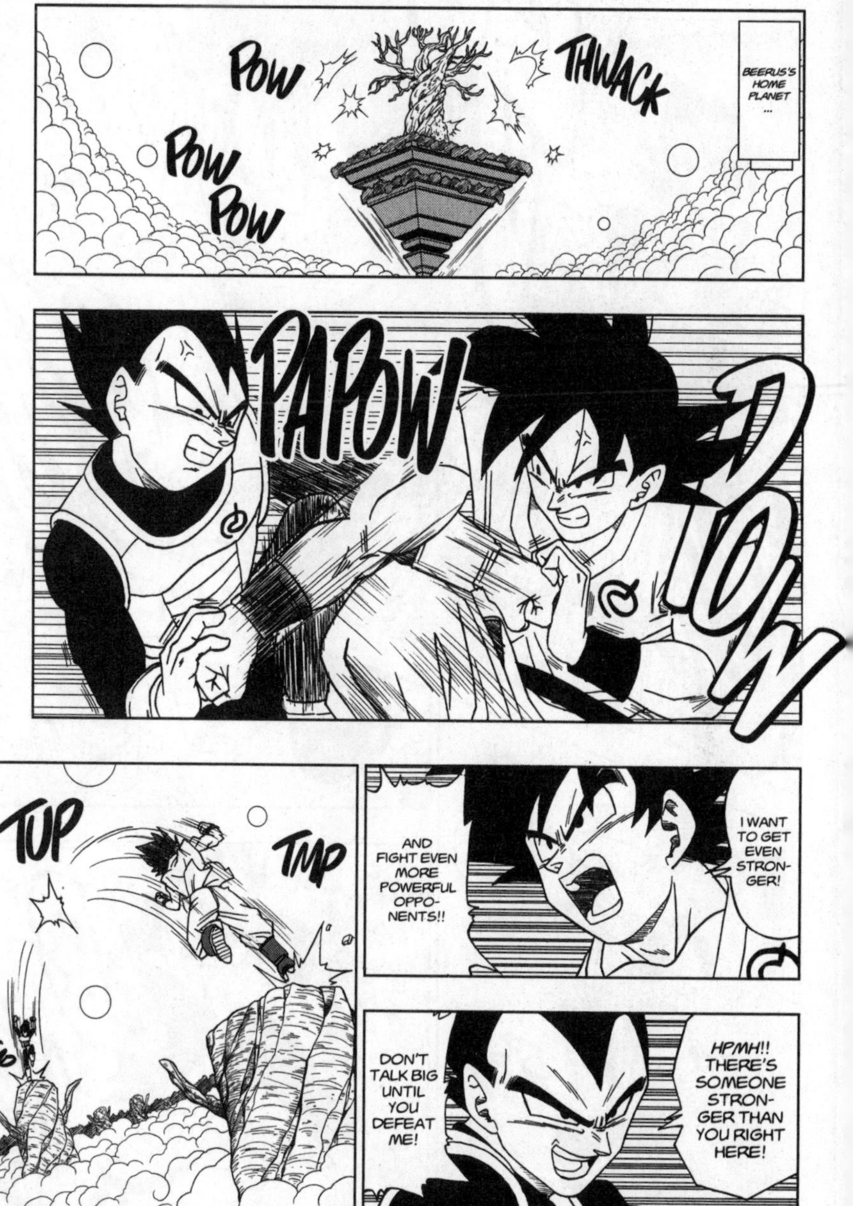
BEERUS'S HOME PLANET ...
THWACK
POW
POW POW
PAPOW
I WANT TO GET EVEN STRONGER!
AND FIGHT EVEN MORE POWERFUL OPPONENTS!!
HPMH!! THERE'S SOMEONE STRONGER THAN YOU RIGHT HERE!
DON'T TALK BIG UNTIL YOU DEFEAT ME!
TMP
TUP
TMP

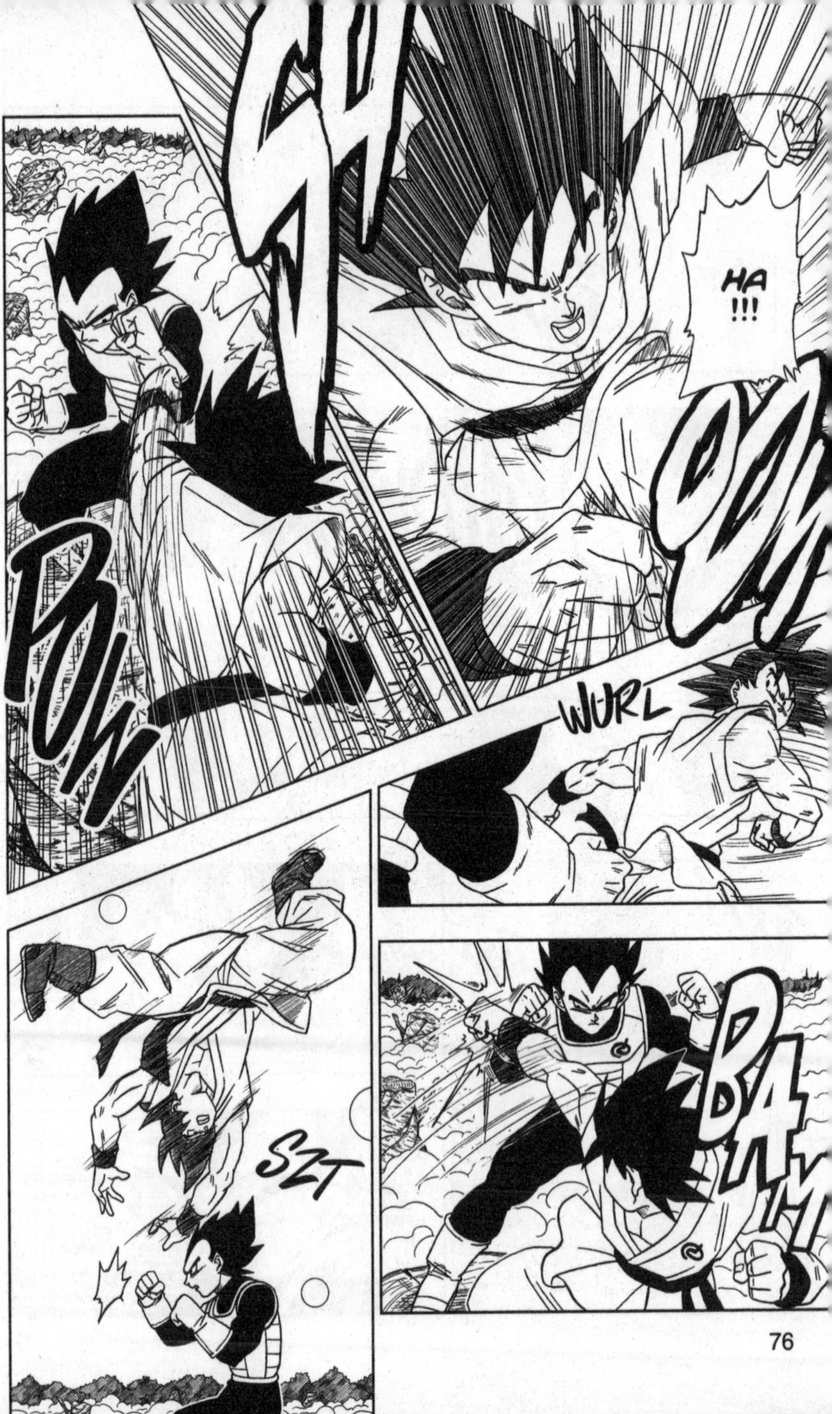
HA!!!
WURL
BAM
SZT

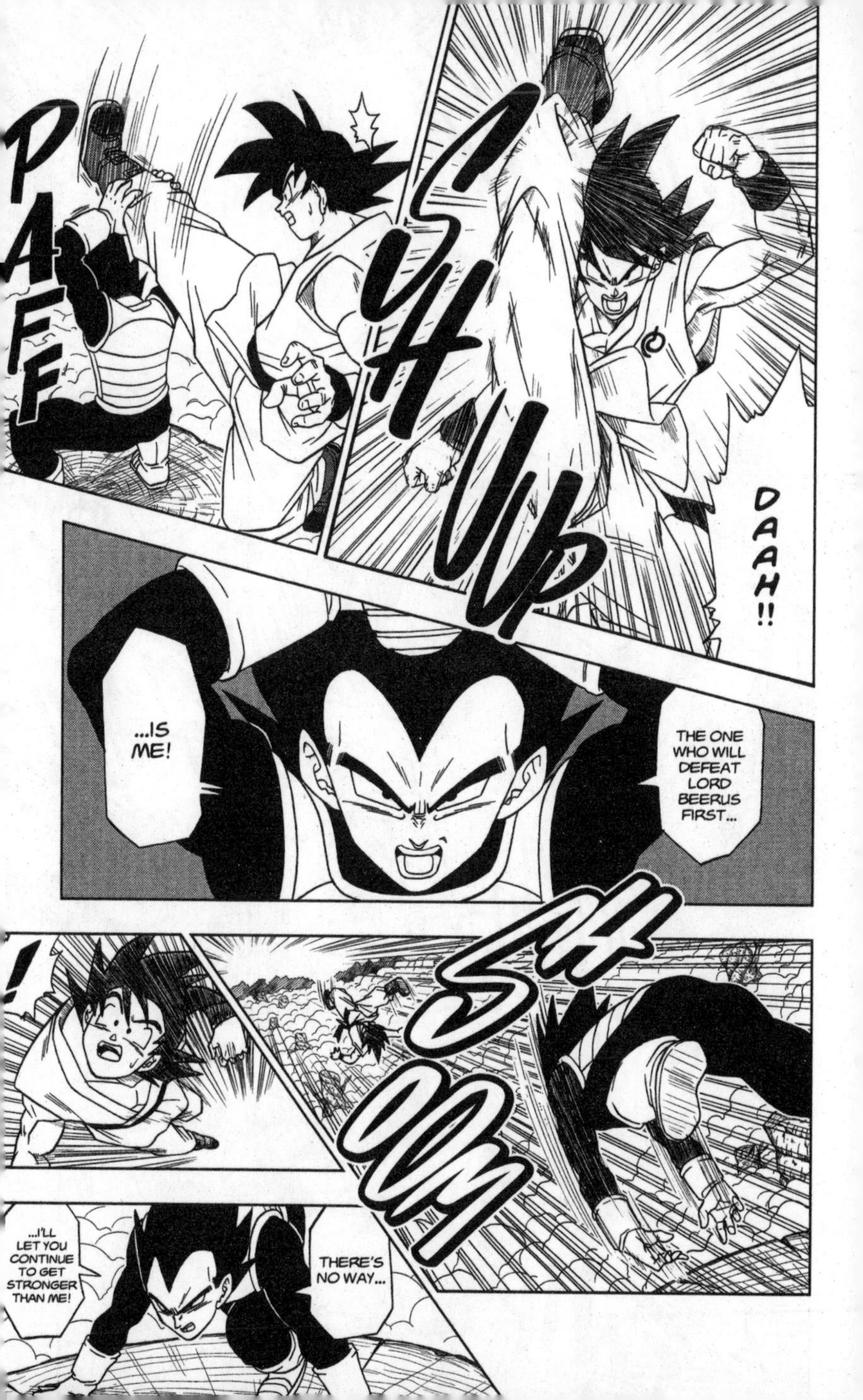
DAAAH!!
SHUP
PAFF
THE ONE WHO WILL DEFEAT LORD BEERUS FIRST...
...IS ME!
SHOOM
!
THERE'S NO WAY...
...I'LL LET YOU CONTINUE TO GET STRONGER THAN ME!

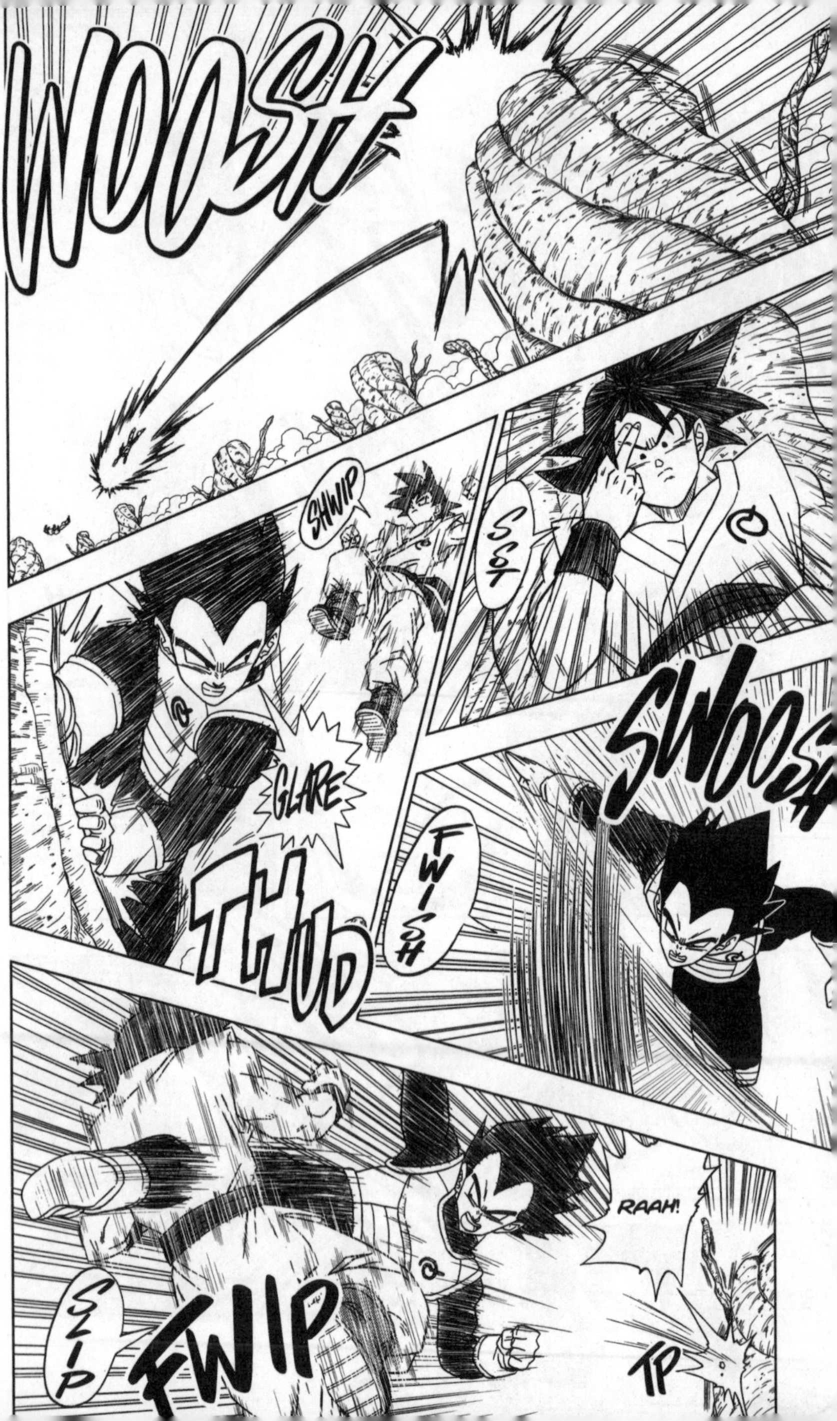
WOOSH
SST
SHWIP
GLARE
THUD
SWOOSH
FWISH
RAAH!
TP
FWIP
SLIP

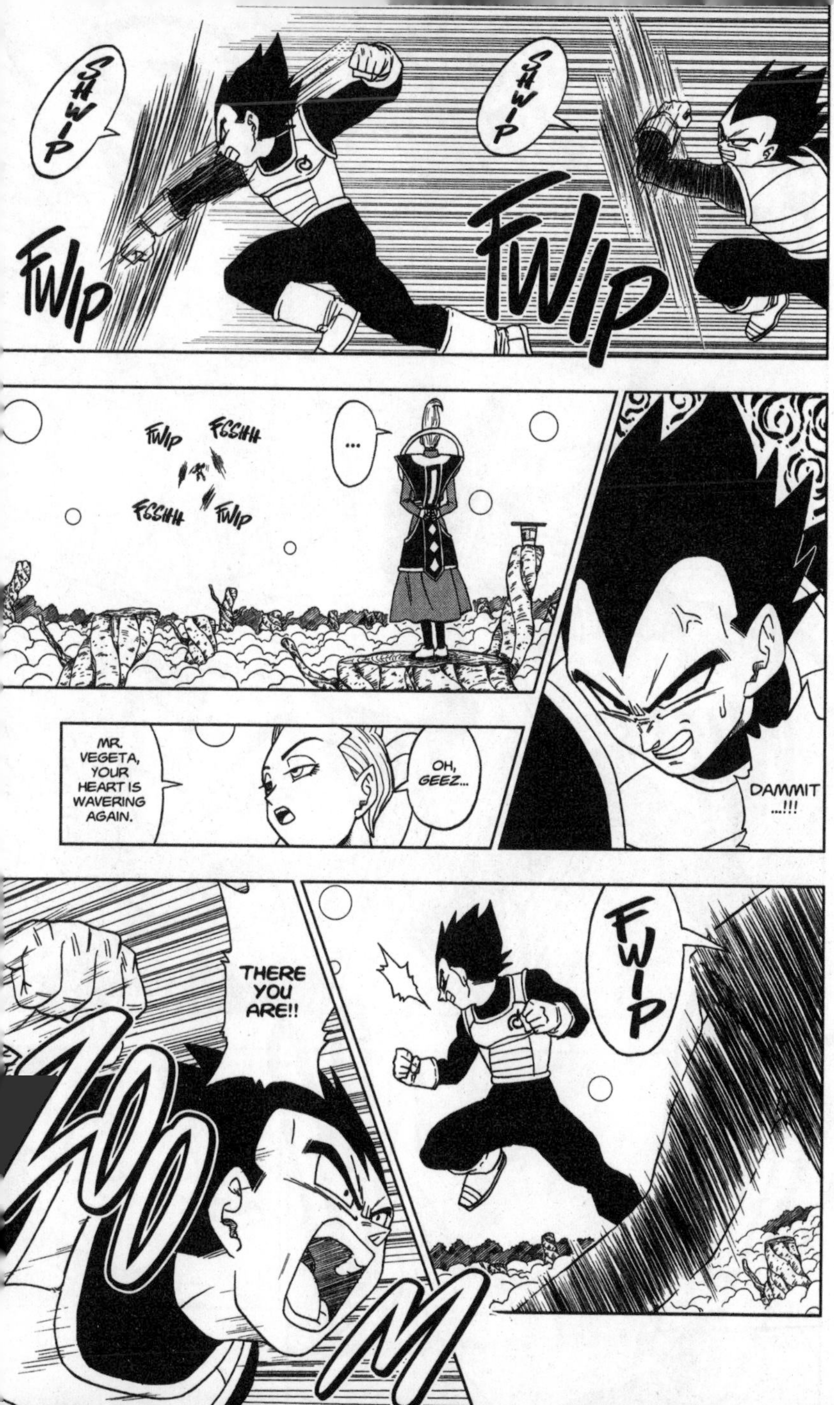
SHWIP
FWIP
SHWIP
FWIP
DAMMIT ...!!!
...
FSSHH
FWIP
FWIP
FSSHH
OH, GEEZ...
MR. VEGETA, YOUR HEART IS WAVERING AGAIN.
FWIP
THERE YOU ARE!!
ZOOM

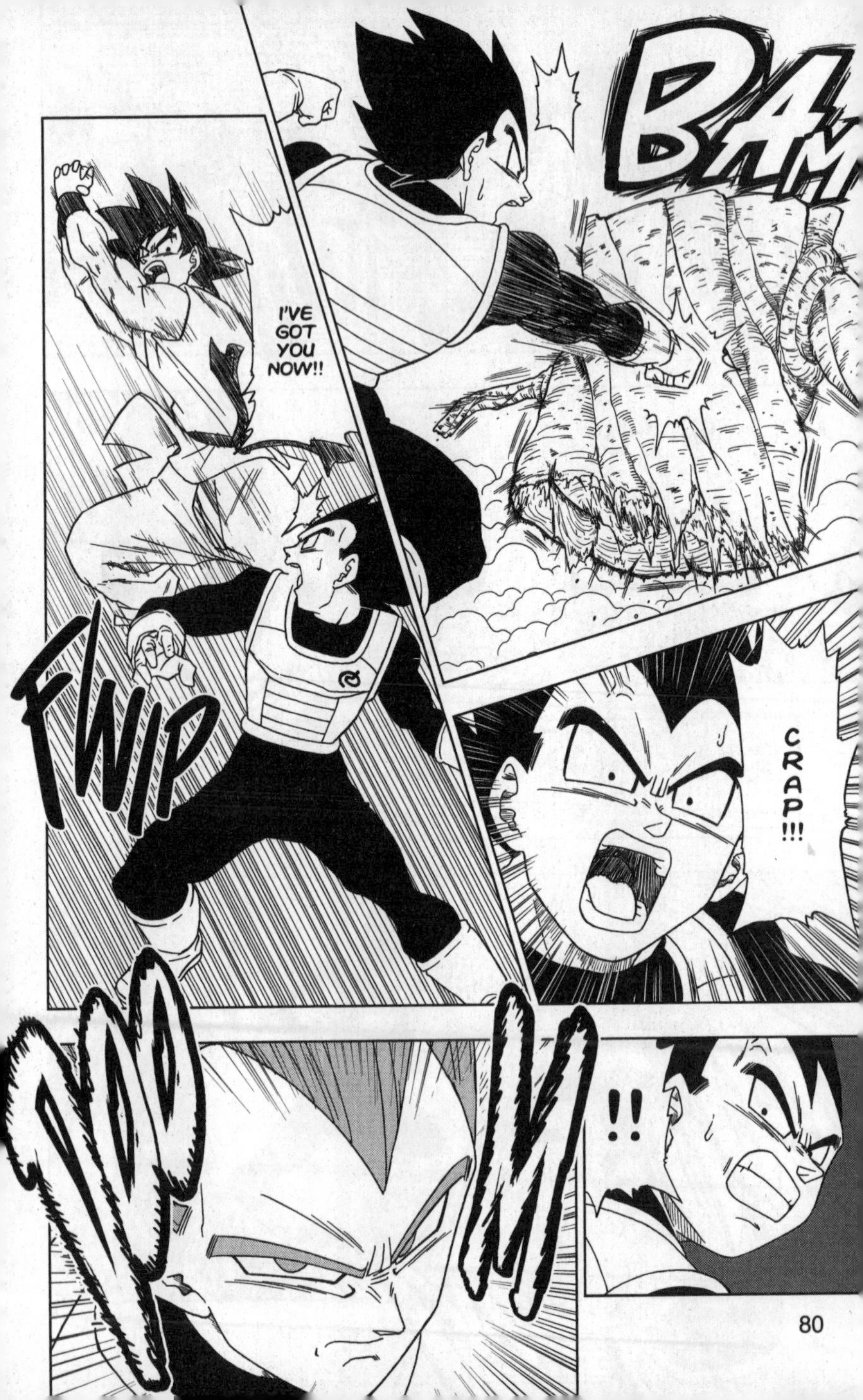
BAM
I'VE GOT YOU NOW!!
FWIP
CRAP!!!
!!

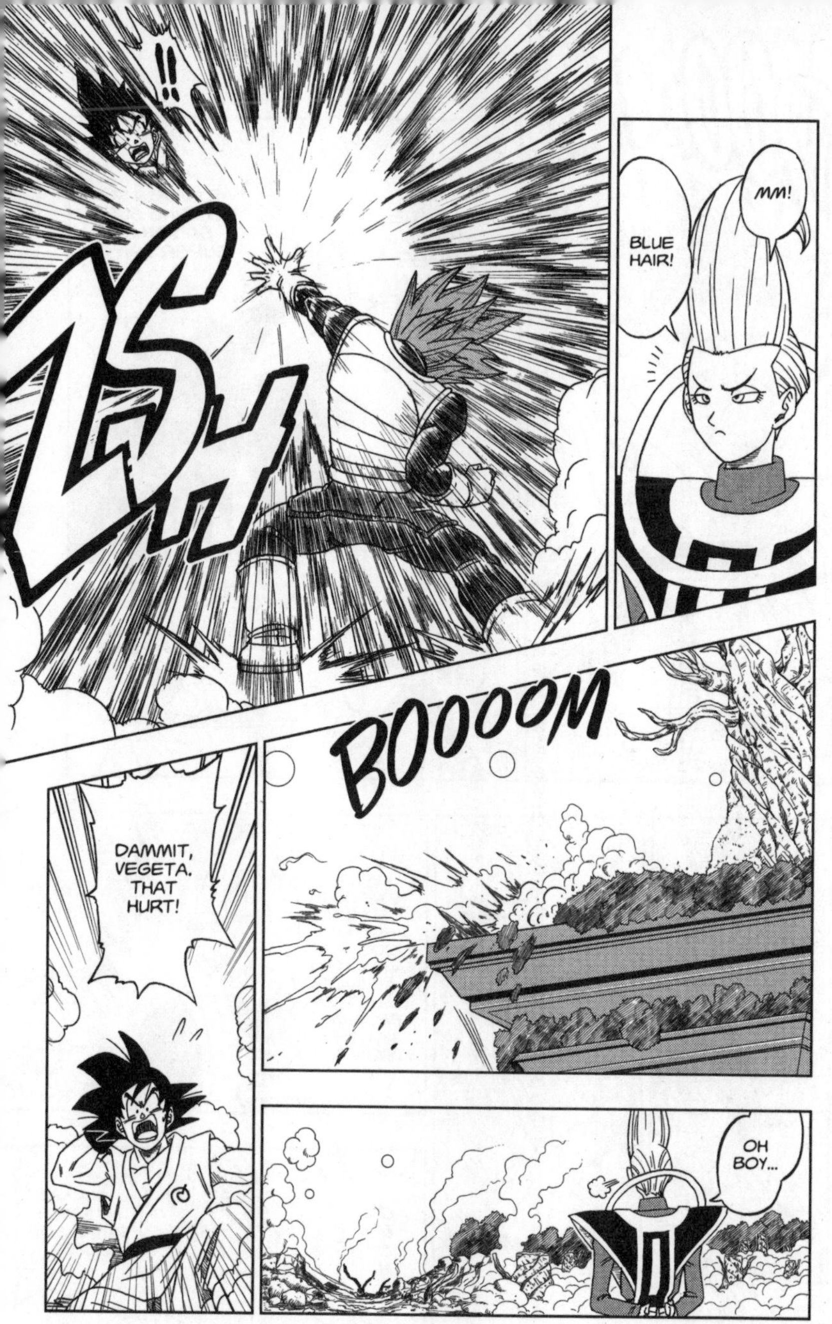
MM!
BLUE HAIR!
!!
ZSH
BOOOOM
OH BOY...
DAMMIT, VEGETA. THAT HURT!

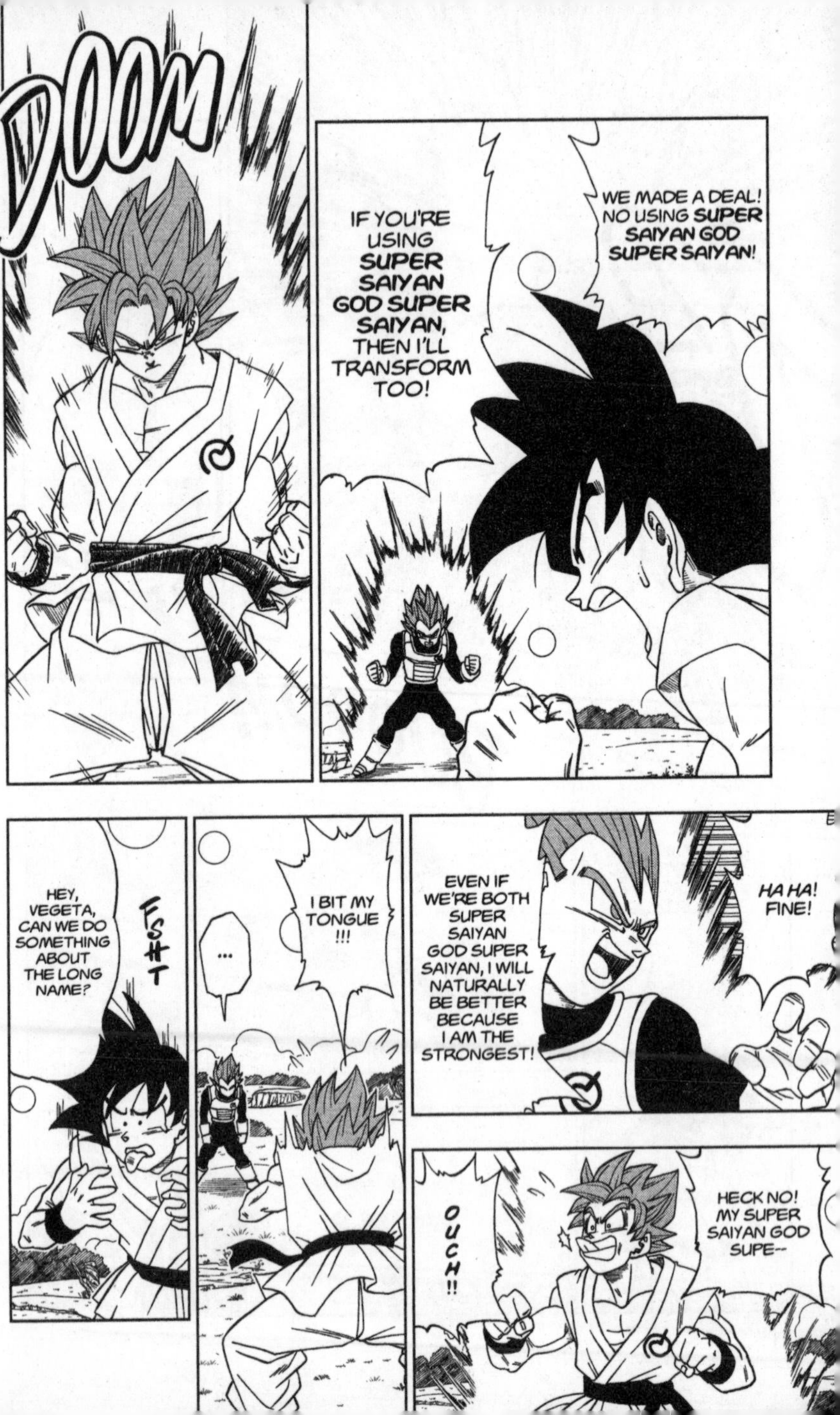
WE MADE A DEAL! NO USING SUPER SAIYAN GOD SUPER SAIYAN!
IF YOU'RE USING SUPER SAIYAN GOD SUPER SAIYAN, THEN I'LL TRANSFORM TOO!
DOOM
HA HA! FINE!
EVEN IF WE'RE BOTH SUPER SAIYAN GOD SUPER SAIYAN, I WILL NATURALLY BE BETTER BECAUSE I AM THE STRONGEST!
HECK NO! MY SUPER SAIYAN GOD SUPE--
OUCH!!
I BIT MY TONGUE!!!
...
FSHT
HEY, VEGETA, CAN WE DO SOMETHING ABOUT THE LONG NAME?

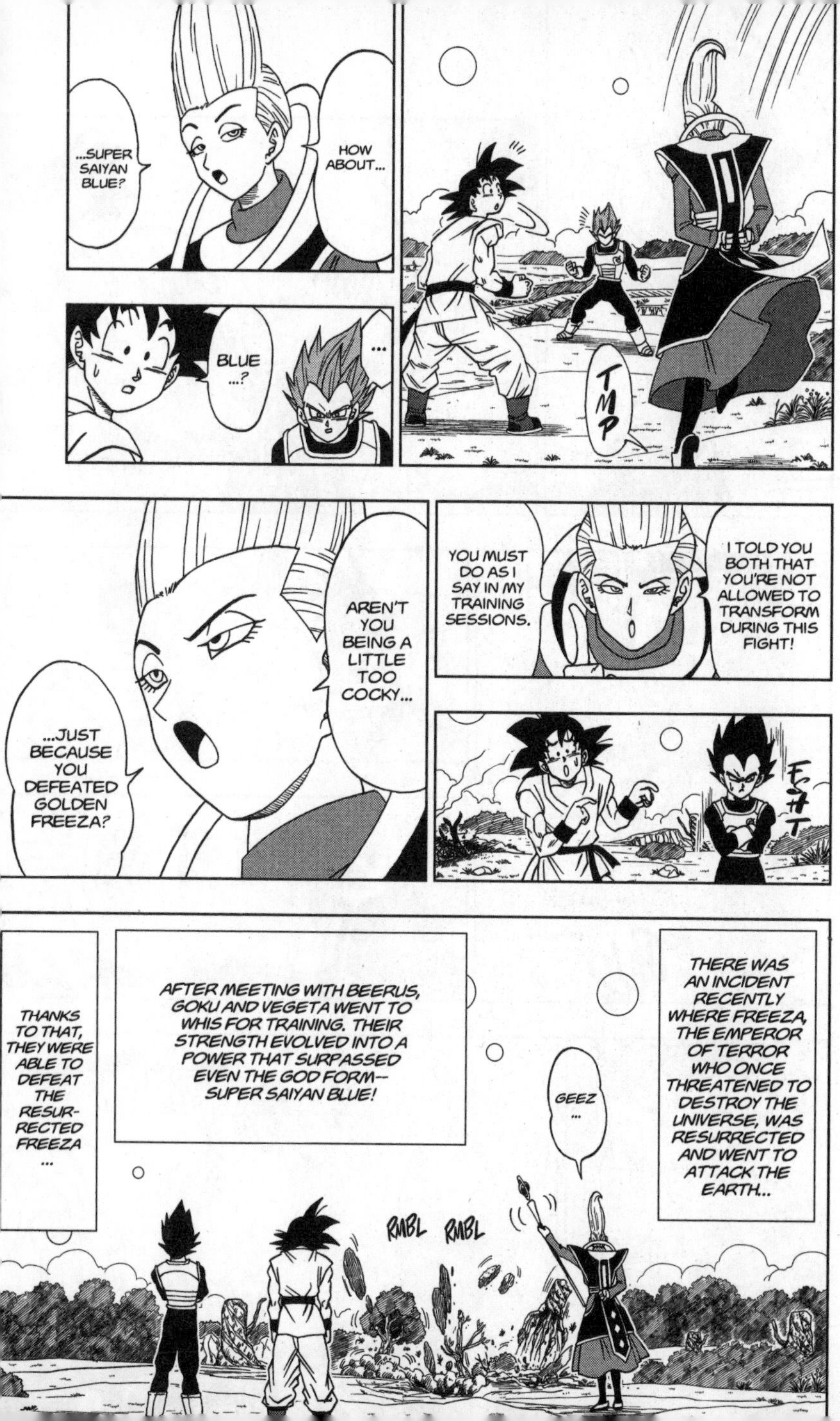
TMP
HOW ABOUT...
...SUPER SAIYAN BLUE?
...
BLUE ...?
I TOLD YOU BOTH THAT YOU'RE NOT ALLOWED TO TRANSFORM DURING THIS FIGHT!
YOU MUST DO AS I SAY IN MY TRAINING SESSIONS.
FSHT
AREN'T YOU BEING A LITTLE TOO COCKY...
...JUST BECAUSE YOU DEFEATED GOLDEN FREEZA?
THERE WAS AN INCIDENT RECENTLY WHERE FREEZA, THE EMPEROR OF TERROR WHO ONCE THREATENED TO DESTROY THE UNIVERSE, WAS RESURRECTED AND WENT TO ATTACK THE EARTH...
GEEZ ...
AFTER MEETING WITH BEERUS, GOKU AND VEGETA WENT TO WHIS FOR TRAINING. THEIR STRENGTH EVOLVED INTO A POWER THAT SURPASSED EVEN THE GOD FORM-- SUPER SAIYAN BLUE!
THANKS TO THAT, THEY WERE ABLE TO DEFEAT THE RESUR-RECTED FREEZA ...
RMBL RMBL

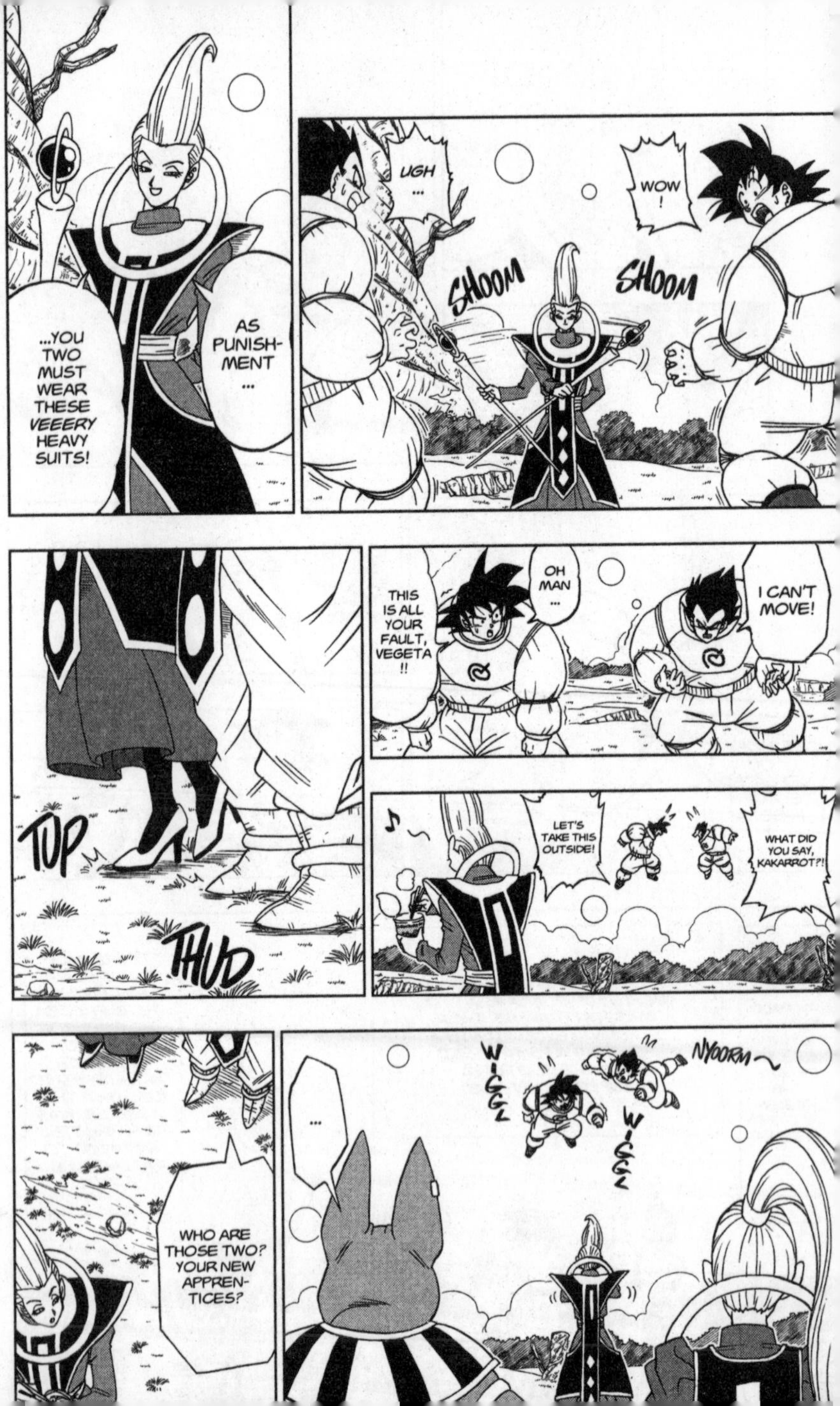
WOW!
UGH...
SHOOM
SHOOM
AS PUNISHMENT...
...YOU TWO MUST WEAR THESE VEEERY HEAVY SUITS!
I CAN'T MOVE!
OH MAN...
THIS IS ALL YOUR FAULT, VEGETA!!
WHAT DID YOU SAY, KAKARROT?!
LET'S TAKE THIS OUTSIDE!
♪~
TUP
THUD
NYOORM~
WIGGL
WIGGL
...
WHO ARE THOSE TWO? YOUR NEW APPRENTICES?

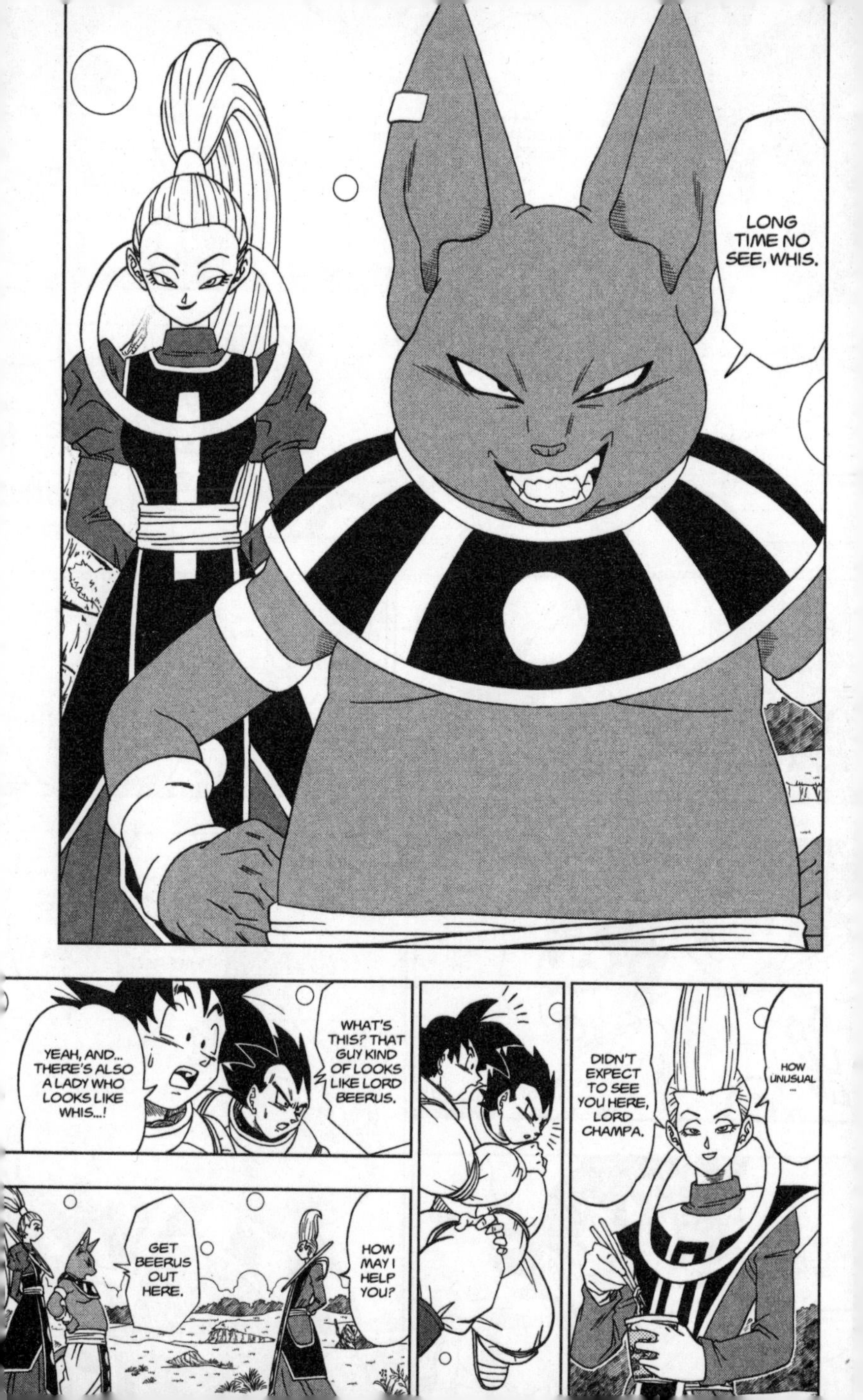
LONG TIME NO SEE, WHIS.
HOW UNUSUAL...
DIDN'T EXPECT TO SEE YOU HERE, LORD CHAMPA.
WHAT'S THIS? THAT GUY KIND OF LOOKS LIKE LORD BEERUS.
YEAH, AND... THERE'S ALSO A LADY WHO LOOKS LIKE WHIS...!
HOW MAY I HELP YOU?
GET BEERUS OUT HERE.

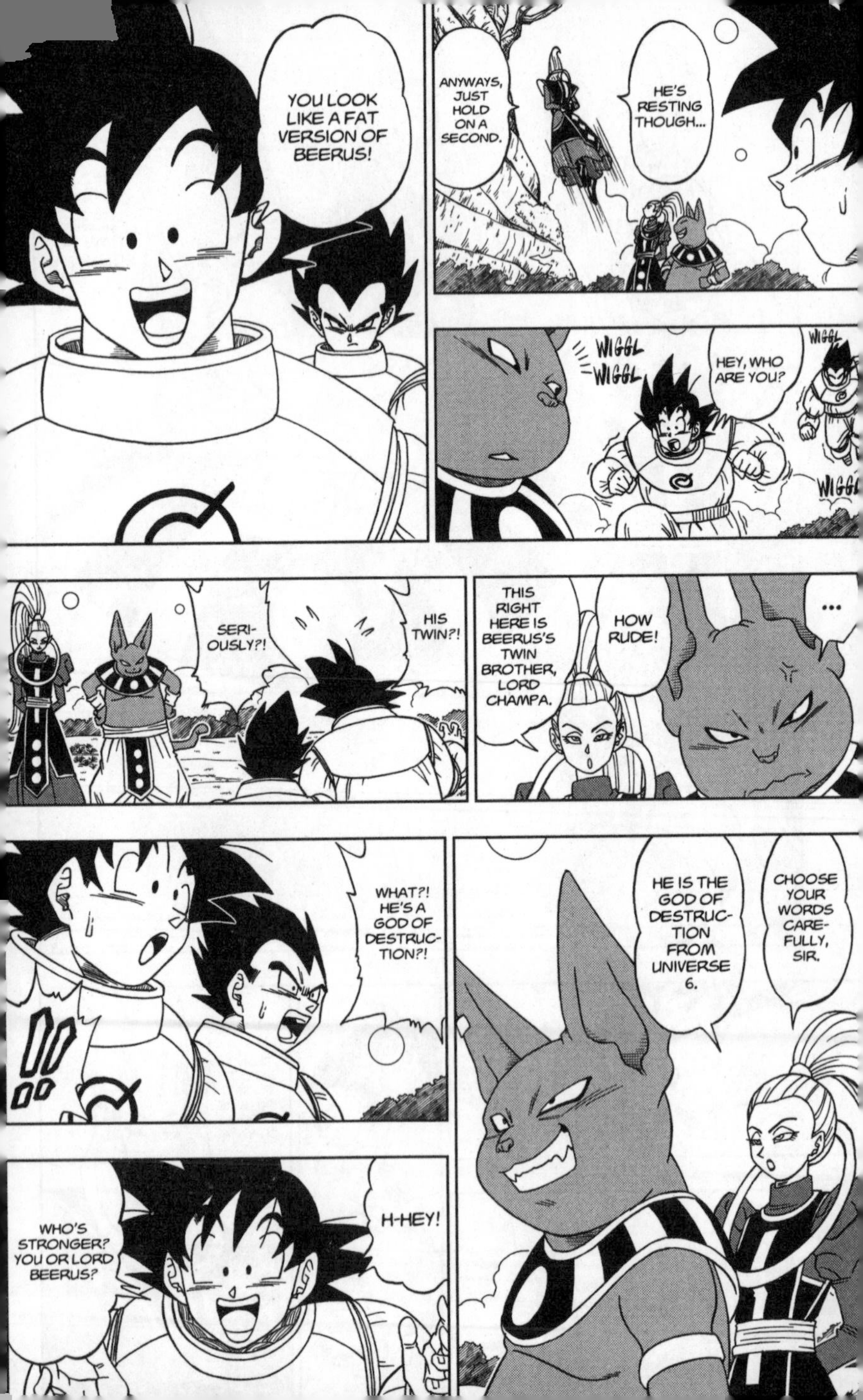
HE'S RESTING THOUGH...
ANYWAYS, JUST HOLD ON A SECOND.
WIGGL
HEY, WHO ARE YOU?
WIGGL
WIGGL
WIGGL
YOU LOOK LIKE A FAT VERSION OF BEERUS!
...
HOW RUDE!
THIS RIGHT HERE IS BEERUS'S TWIN BROTHER, LORD CHAMPA.
HIS TWIN?!
SERI-OUSLY?!
CHOOSE YOUR WORDS CARE-FULLY, SIR.
HE IS THE GOD OF DESTRUC-TION FROM UNIVERSE 6.
WHAT?! HE'S A GOD OF DESTRUC-TION?!
H-HEY!
WHO'S STRONGER? YOU OR LORD BEERUS?

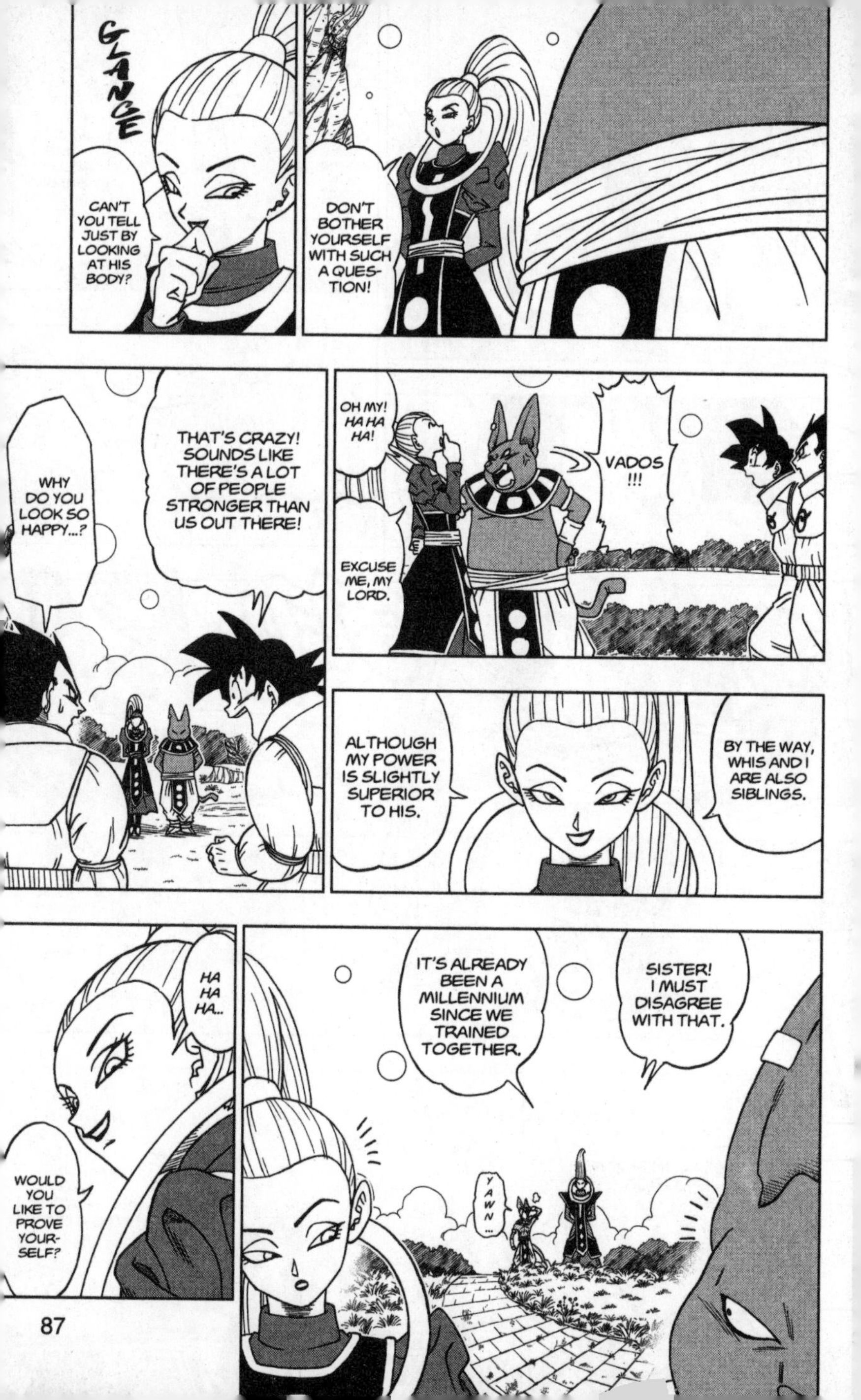
DON'T BOTHER YOURSELF WITH SUCH A QUESTION!
GLANCE
CAN'T YOU TELL JUST BY LOOKING AT HIS BODY?
VADOS!!!
OH MY! HA HA HA!
EXCUSE ME, MY LORD.
BY THE WAY, WHIS AND I ARE ALSO SIBLINGS.
ALTHOUGH MY POWER IS SLIGHTLY SUPERIOR TO HIS.
THAT'S CRAZY! SOUNDS LIKE THERE'S A LOT OF PEOPLE STRONGER THAN US OUT THERE!
WHY DO YOU LOOK SO HAPPY...?
SISTER! I MUST DISAGREE WITH THAT.
IT'S ALREADY BEEN A MILLENNIUM SINCE WE TRAINED TOGETHER.
YAWN...
HA HA HA...
WOULD YOU LIKE TO PROVE YOURSELF?

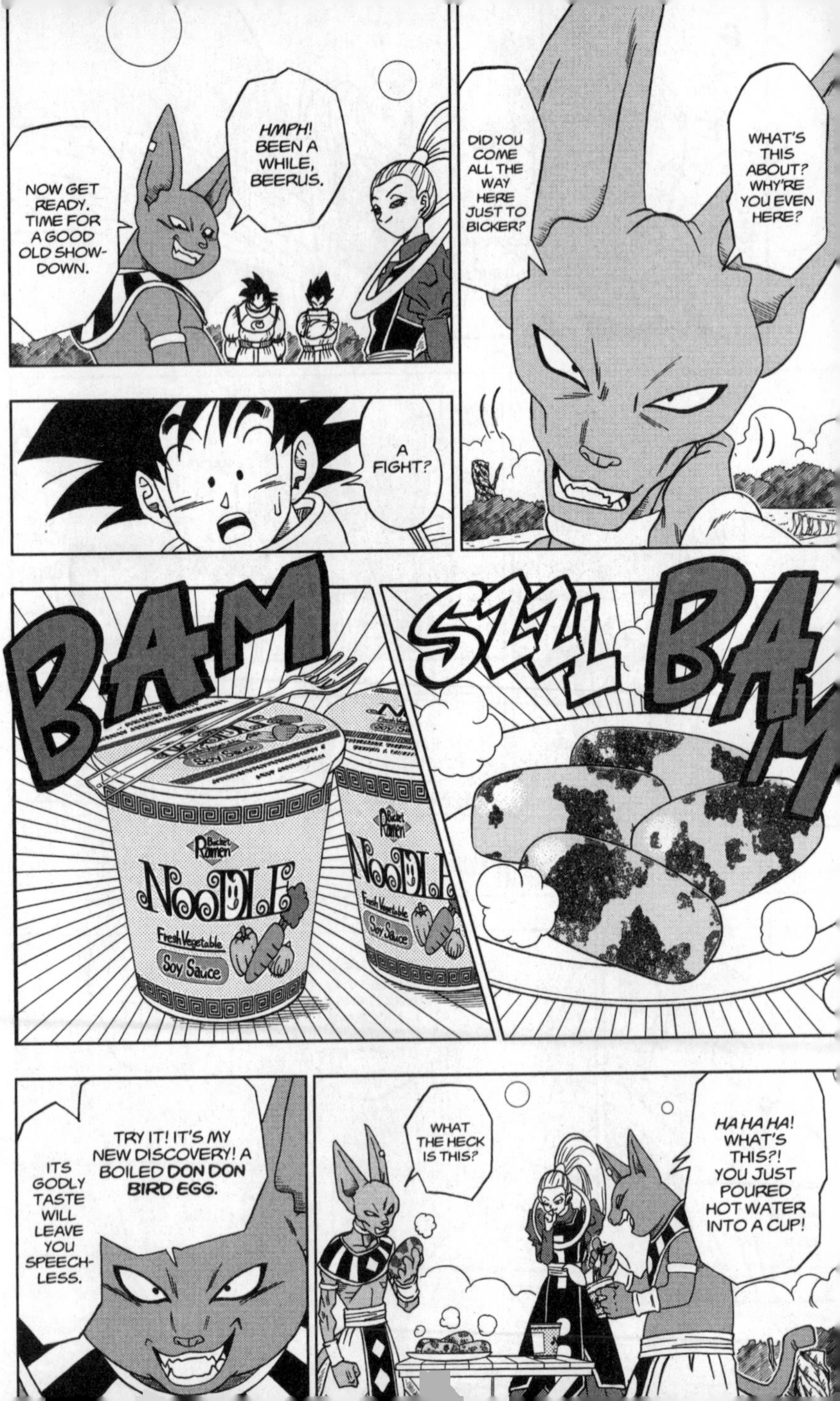

WHAT'S THIS ABOUT? WHY'RE YOU EVEN HERE?
DID YOU COME ALL THE WAY HERE JUST TO BICKER?
HMPH! BEEN A WHILE, BEERUS.
NOW GET READY. TIME FOR A GOOD OLD SHOW-DOWN.
A FIGHT?
SIZZL
BAM
Bucket Ramen
NOODLE
Fresh Vegetable
Soy Sauce
BAM
HA HA HA! WHAT'S THIS?! YOU JUST POURED HOT WATER INTO A CUP!
WHAT THE HECK IS THIS?
TRY IT! IT'S MY NEW DISCOVERY! A BOILED DON DON BIRD EGG.
ITS GODLY TASTE WILL LEAVE YOU SPEECHLESS.

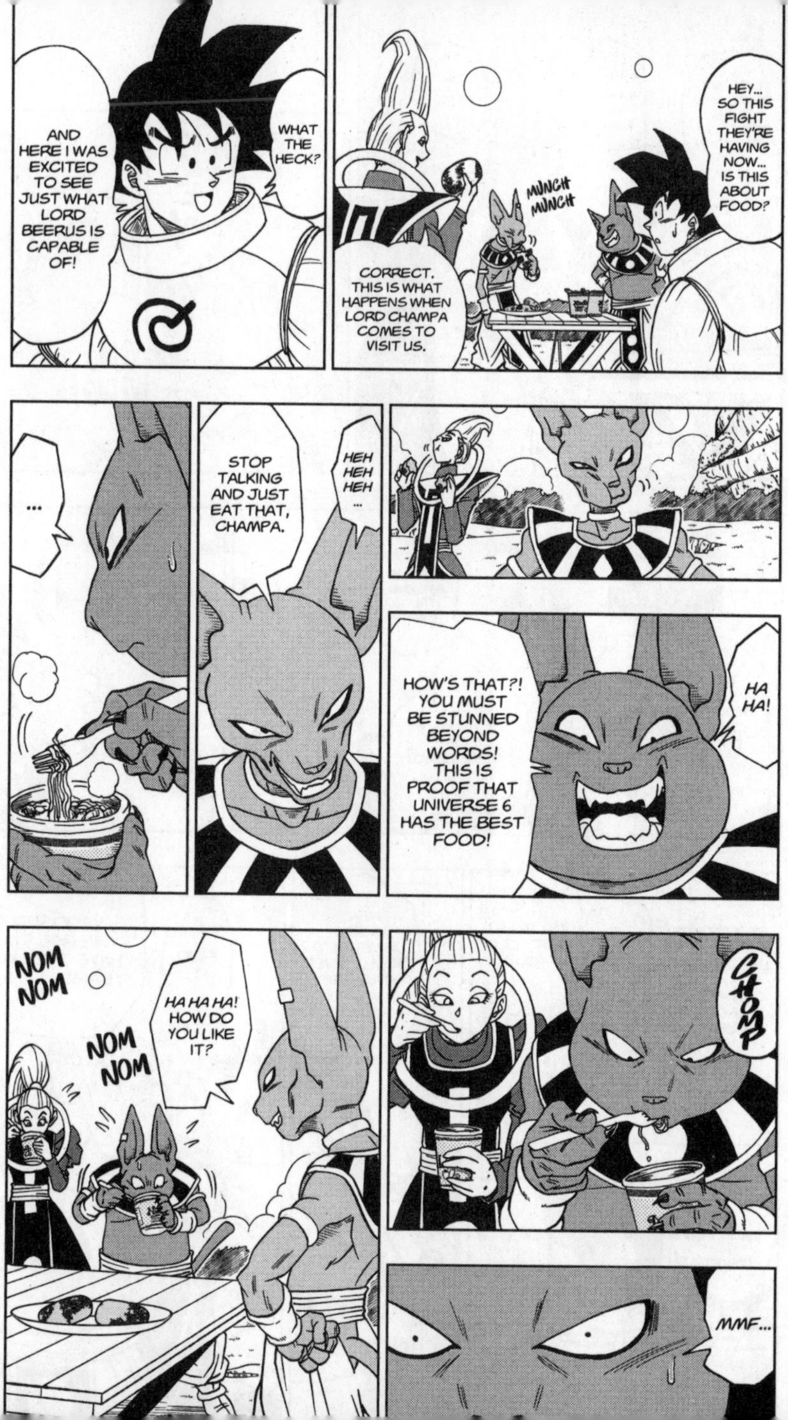
HEY... SO THIS FIGHT THEY'RE HAVING NOW... IS THIS ABOUT FOOD?
MUNCH MUNCH
CORRECT. THIS IS WHAT HAPPENS WHEN LORD CHAMPA COMES TO VISIT US.
WHAT THE HECK?
AND HERE I WAS EXCITED TO SEE JUST WHAT LORD BEERUS IS CAPABLE OF!
HA HA!
HOW'S THAT?! YOU MUST BE STUNNED BEYOND WORDS! THIS IS PROOF THAT UNIVERSE 6 HAS THE BEST FOOD!
HEH HEH HEH...
STOP TALKING AND JUST EAT THAT, CHAMPA.
...
CHOMP
MMF...
HA HA HA! HOW DO YOU LIKE IT?
NOM NOM
NOM NOM

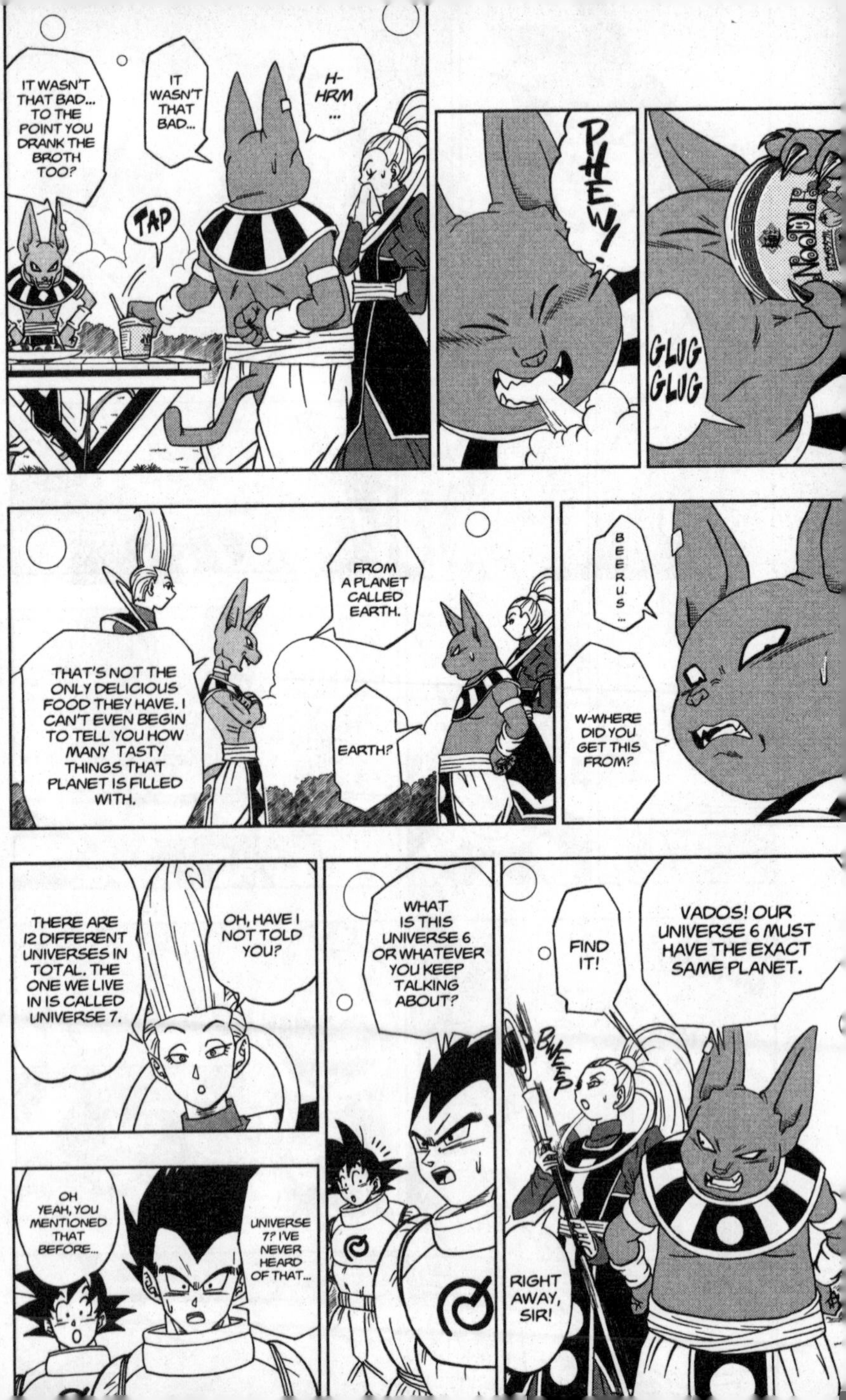
GLUG GLUG
PHEW!
H-HRM...
IT WASN'T THAT BAD...
IT WASN'T THAT BAD... TO THE POINT YOU DRANK THE BROTH TOO?
TAP
BEERUS...
W-WHERE DID YOU GET THIS FROM?
FROM A PLANET CALLED EARTH.
EARTH?
THAT'S NOT THE ONLY DELICIOUS FOOD THEY HAVE. I CAN'T EVEN BEGIN TO TELL YOU HOW MANY TASTY THINGS THAT PLANET IS FILLED WITH.
VADOS! OUR UNIVERSE 6 MUST HAVE THE EXACT SAME PLANET.
FIND IT!
RIGHT AWAY, SIR!
WHAT IS THIS UNIVERSE 6 OR WHATEVER YOU KEEP TALKING ABOUT?
OH, HAVE I NOT TOLD YOU?
THERE ARE 12 DIFFERENT UNIVERSES IN TOTAL. THE ONE WE LIVE IN IS CALLED UNIVERSE 7.
UNIVERSE 7? I'VE NEVER HEARD OF THAT...
OH YEAH, YOU MENTIONED THAT BEFORE...

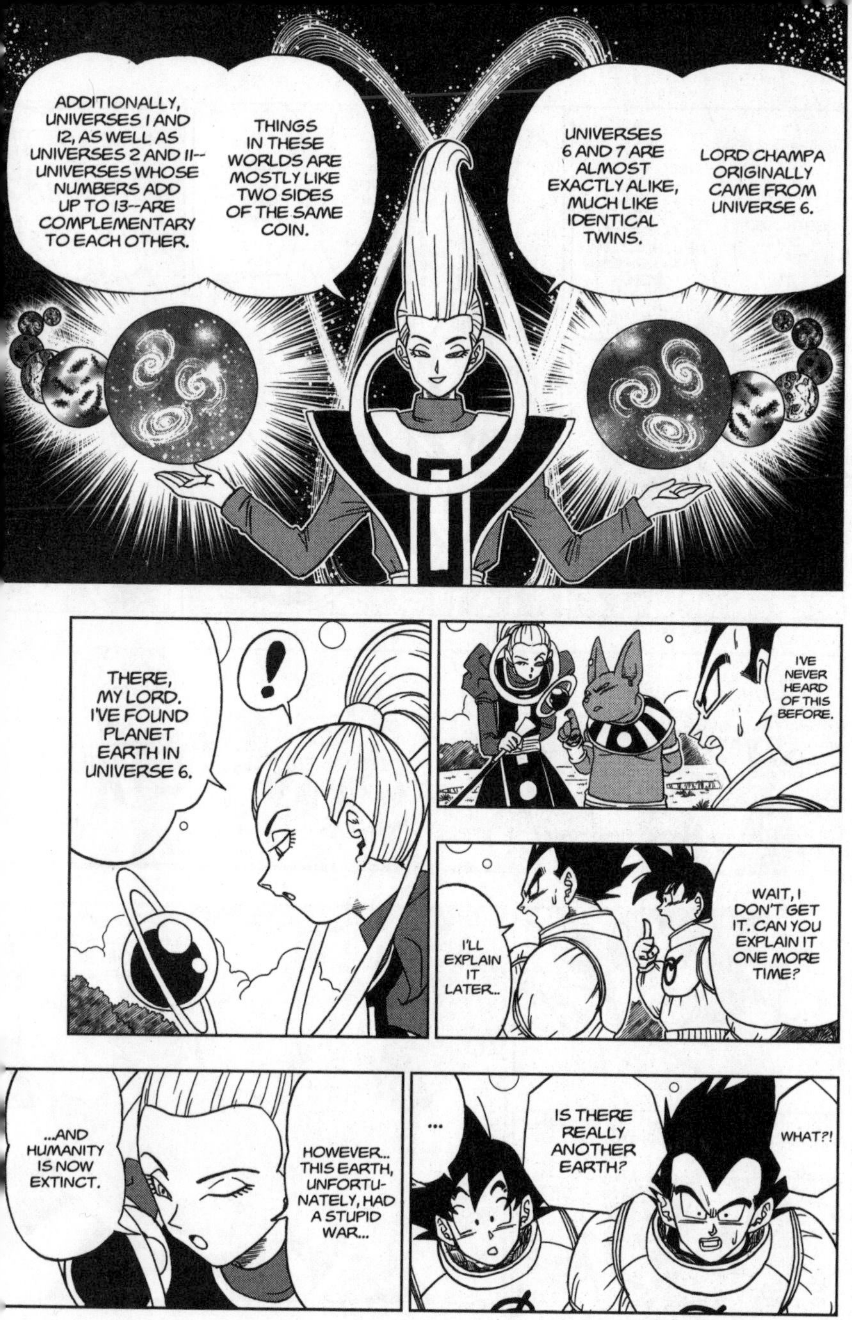
LORD CHAMPA ORIGINALLY CAME FROM UNIVERSE 6.
UNIVERSES 6 AND 7 ARE ALMOST EXACTLY ALIKE, MUCH LIKE IDENTICAL TWINS.
THINGS IN THESE WORLDS ARE MOSTLY LIKE TWO SIDES OF THE SAME COIN.
ADDITIONALLY, UNIVERSES 1 AND 12, AS WELL AS UNIVERSES 2 AND 11--UNIVERSES WHOSE NUMBERS ADD UP TO 13--ARE COMPLEMENTARY TO EACH OTHER.
I'VE NEVER HEARD OF THIS BEFORE.
WAIT, I DON'T GET IT. CAN YOU EXPLAIN IT ONE MORE TIME?
I'LL EXPLAIN IT LATER..
!
THERE, MY LORD. I'VE FOUND PLANET EARTH IN UNIVERSE 6.
WHAT?!
IS THERE REALLY ANOTHER EARTH?
...
HOWEVER.. THIS EARTH, UNFORTU-NATELY, HAD A STUPID WAR...
...AND HUMANITY IS NOW EXTINCT.

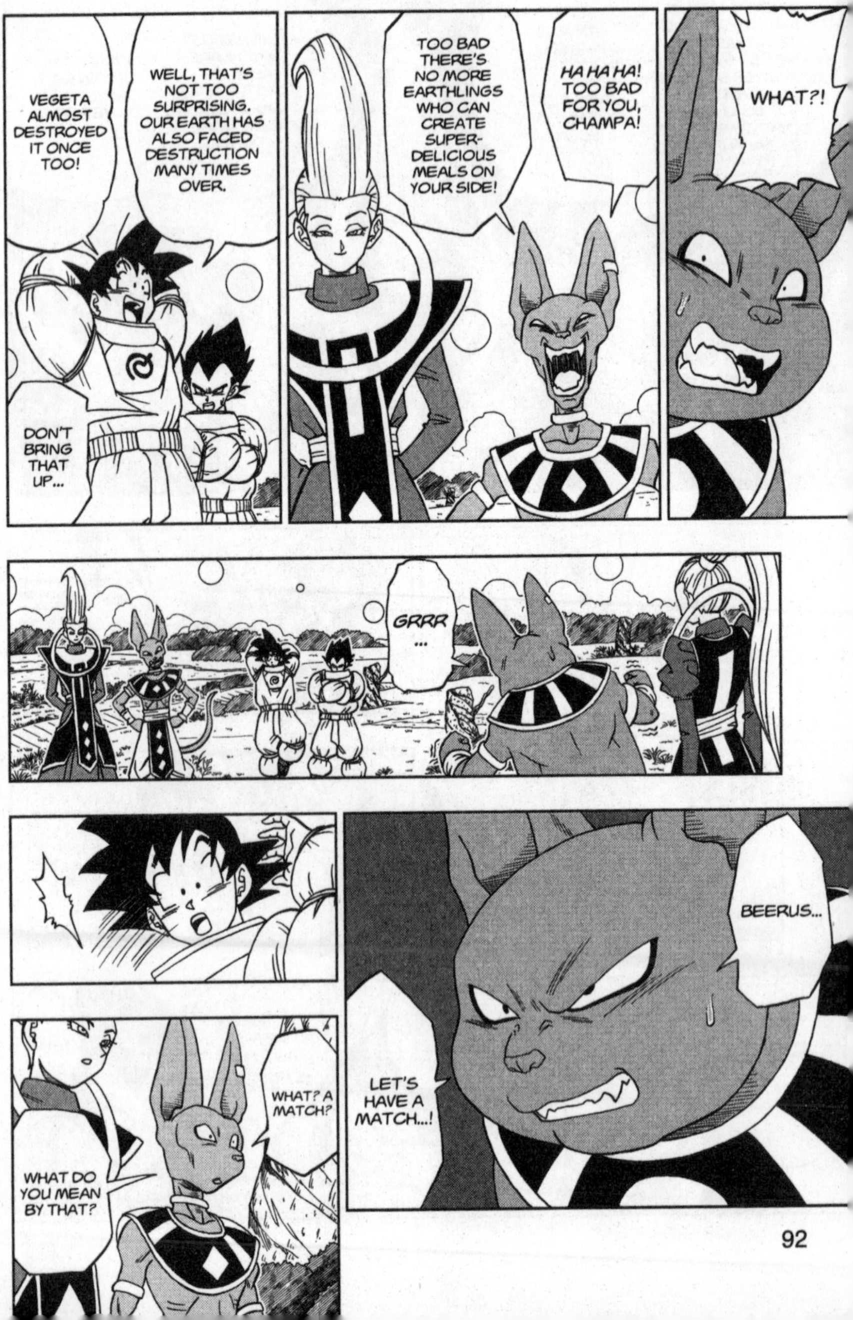
WHAT?!
HA HA HA! TOO BAD FOR YOU, CHAMPA!
TOO BAD THERE'S NO MORE EARTHLINGS WHO CAN CREATE SUPER-DELICIOUS MEALS ON YOUR SIDE!
WELL, THAT'S NOT TOO SURPRISING. OUR EARTH HAS ALSO FACED DESTRUCTION MANY TIMES OVER.
VEGETA ALMOST DESTROYED IT ONCE TOO!
DON'T BRING THAT UP...
GRRR ...
BEERUS...
LET'S HAVE A MATCH...!
WHAT? A MATCH?
WHAT DO YOU MEAN BY THAT?

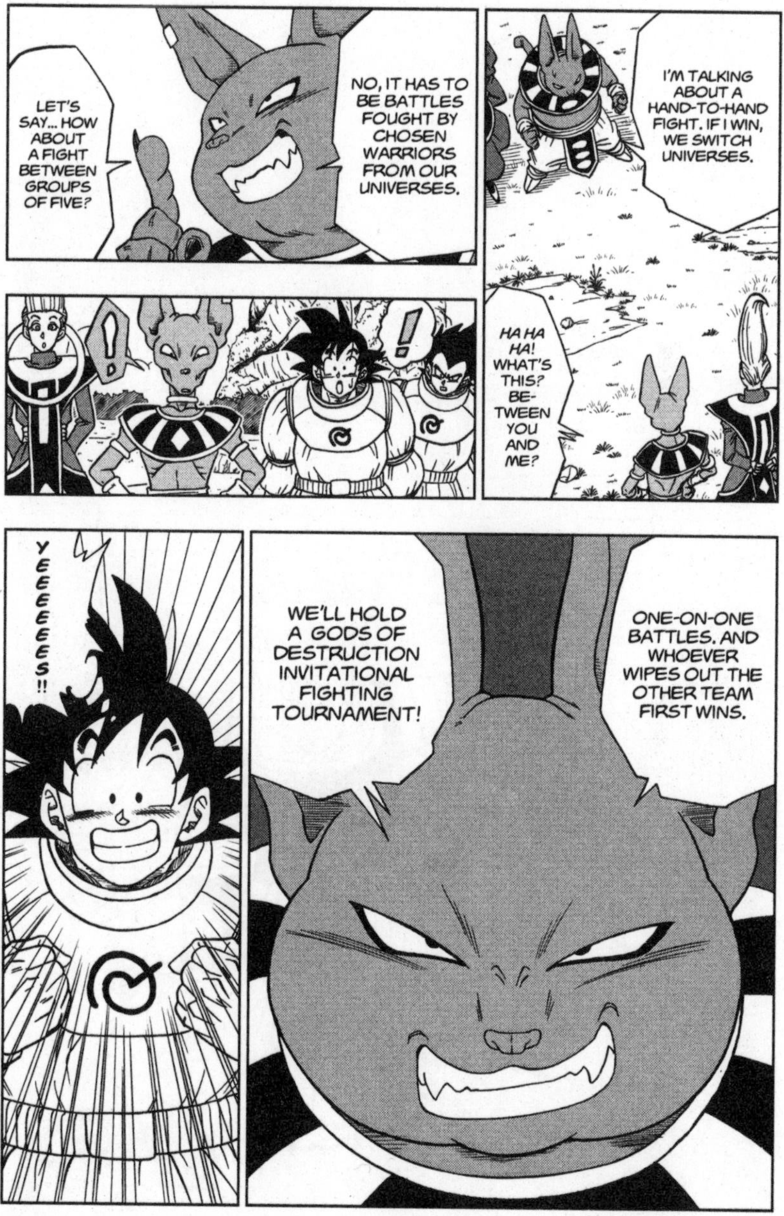
I'M TALKING ABOUT A HAND-TO-HAND FIGHT. IF I WIN, WE SWITCH UNIVERSES.
HA HA HA! WHAT'S THIS? BE-TWEEN YOU AND ME?
NO, IT HAS TO BE BATTLES FOUGHT BY CHOSEN WARRIORS FROM OUR UNIVERSES.
LET'S SAY... HOW ABOUT A FIGHT BETWEEN GROUPS OF FIVE?
!
!
ONE-ON-ONE BATTLES. AND WHOEVER WIPES OUT THE OTHER TEAM FIRST WINS.
WE'LL HOLD A GODS OF DESTRUCTION INVITATIONAL FIGHTING TOURNAMENT!
YEEEEEEES!!

I... WAS FLOWN DOWN HERE...

DRAGON BALL SUPER

CHAPTER 6: TOURNAMENT PREPARATION

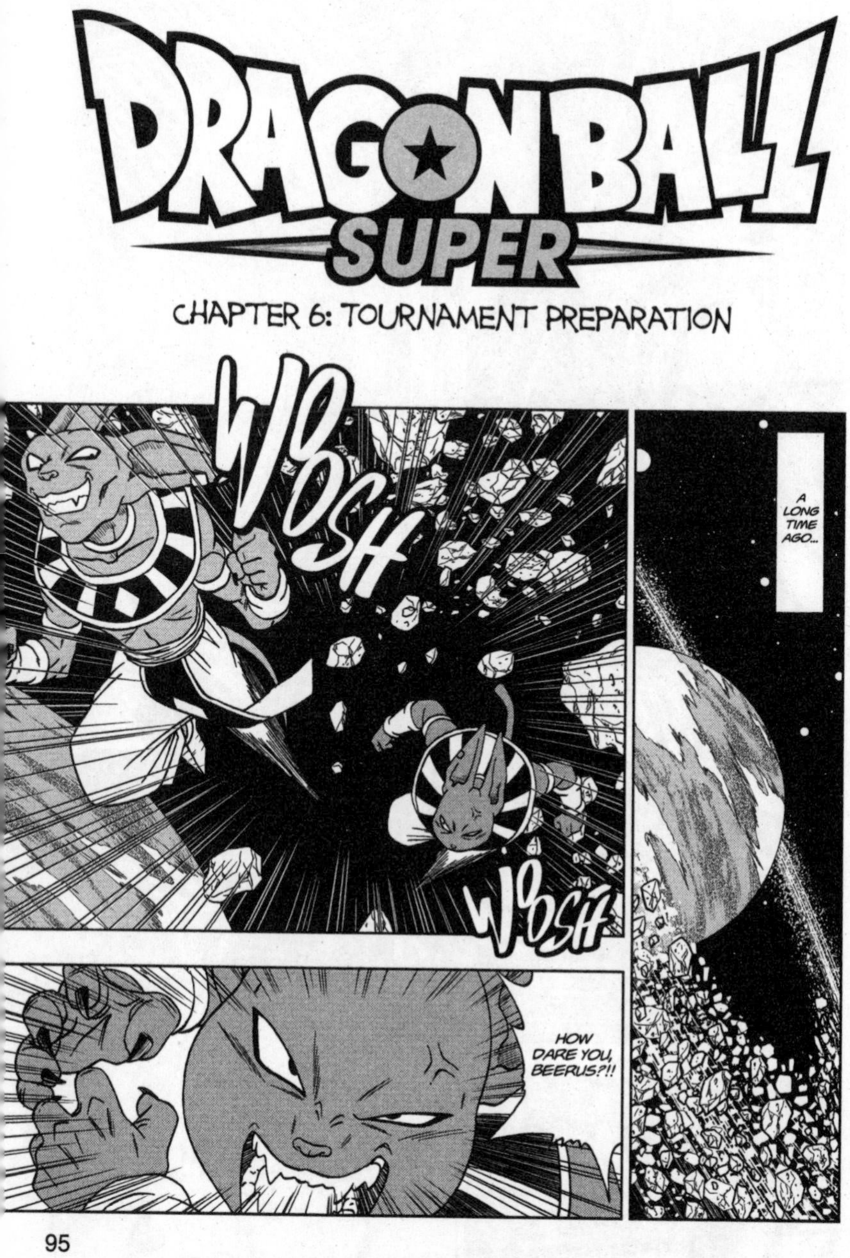

A LONG TIME AGO...
WOOSH
WOOSH
HOW DARE YOU, BEERUS?!!

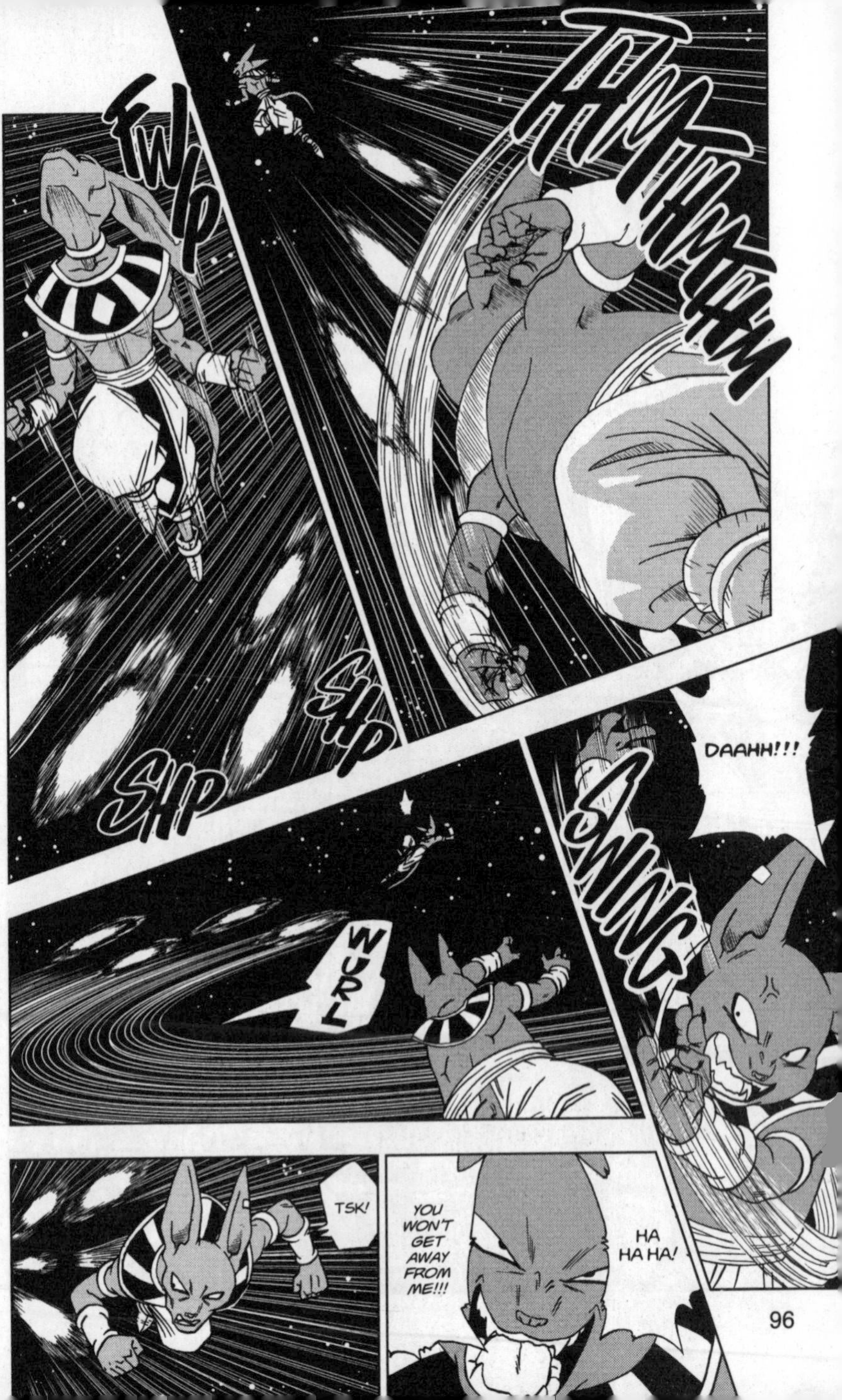
FWIP
SHP
SHP
DAAHH!!!
SWING
WURL
HA HA HA!
YOU WON'T GET AWAY FROM ME!!!
TSK!

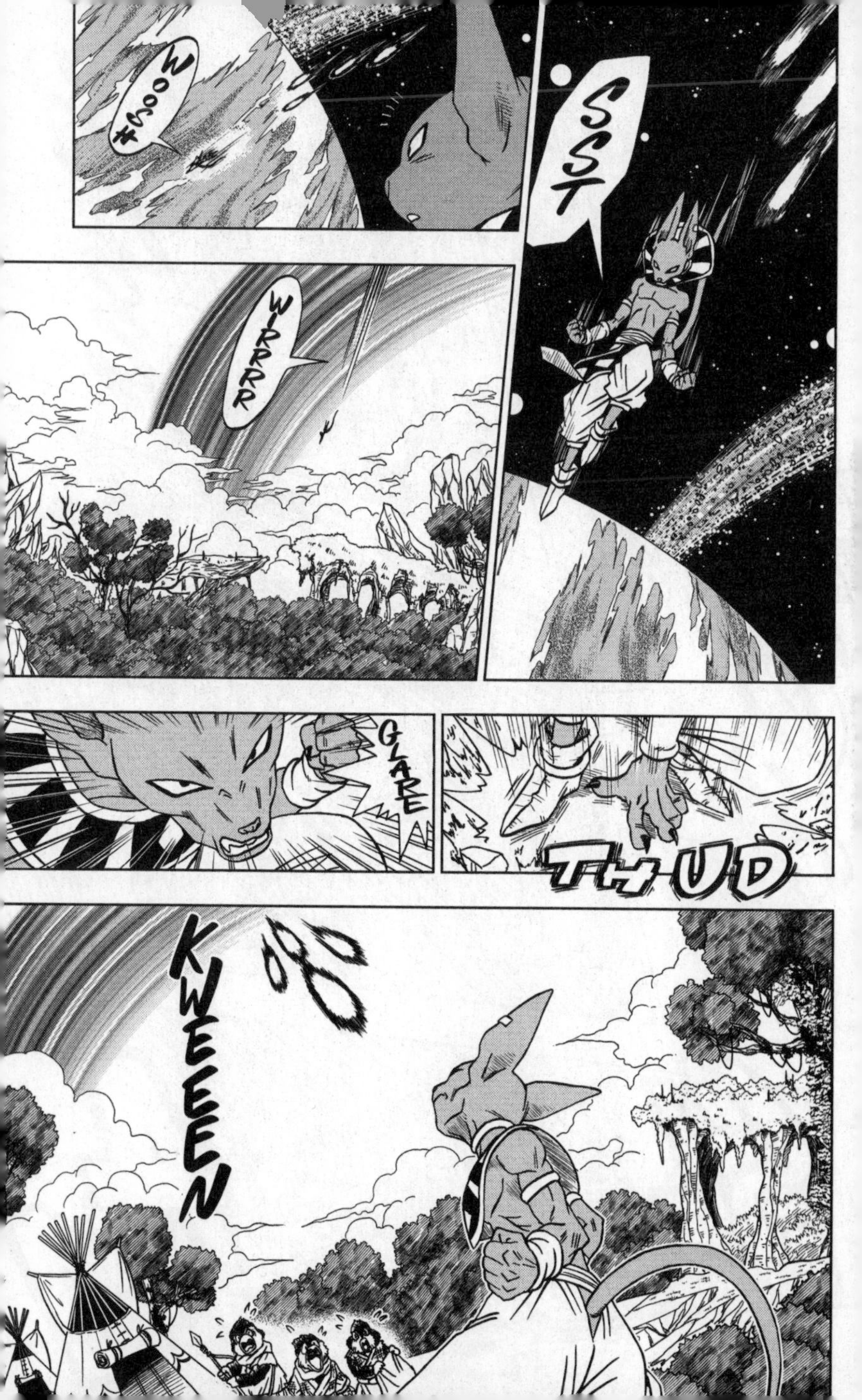
SSST
WOOOSH
WIRRRR
THUD
GLARE
KWEEEEN

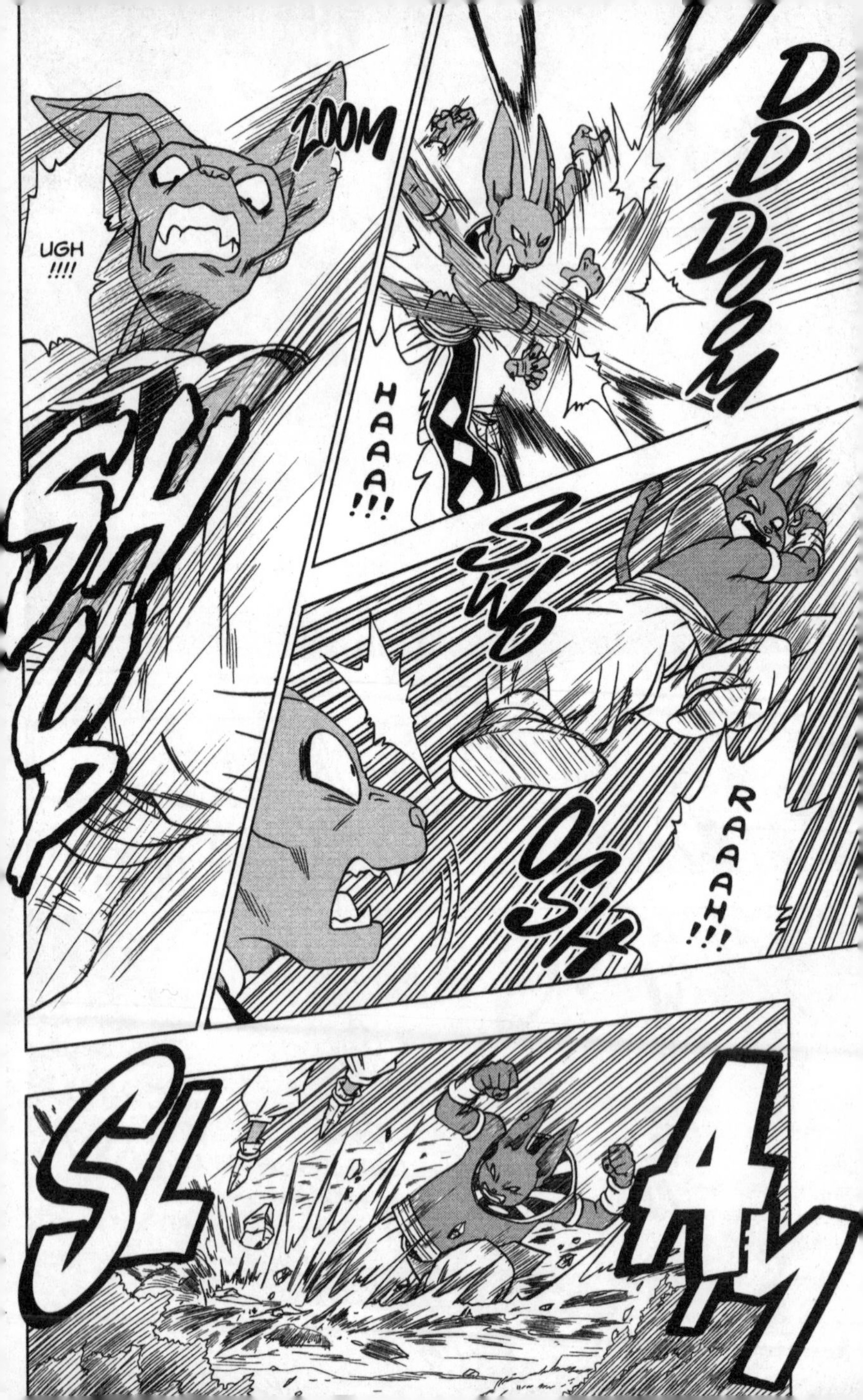
DDDOOM
HAAAA!!!
SWOOSH
RAAAAH!!!
ZOOM
UGH!!!!
SLAM

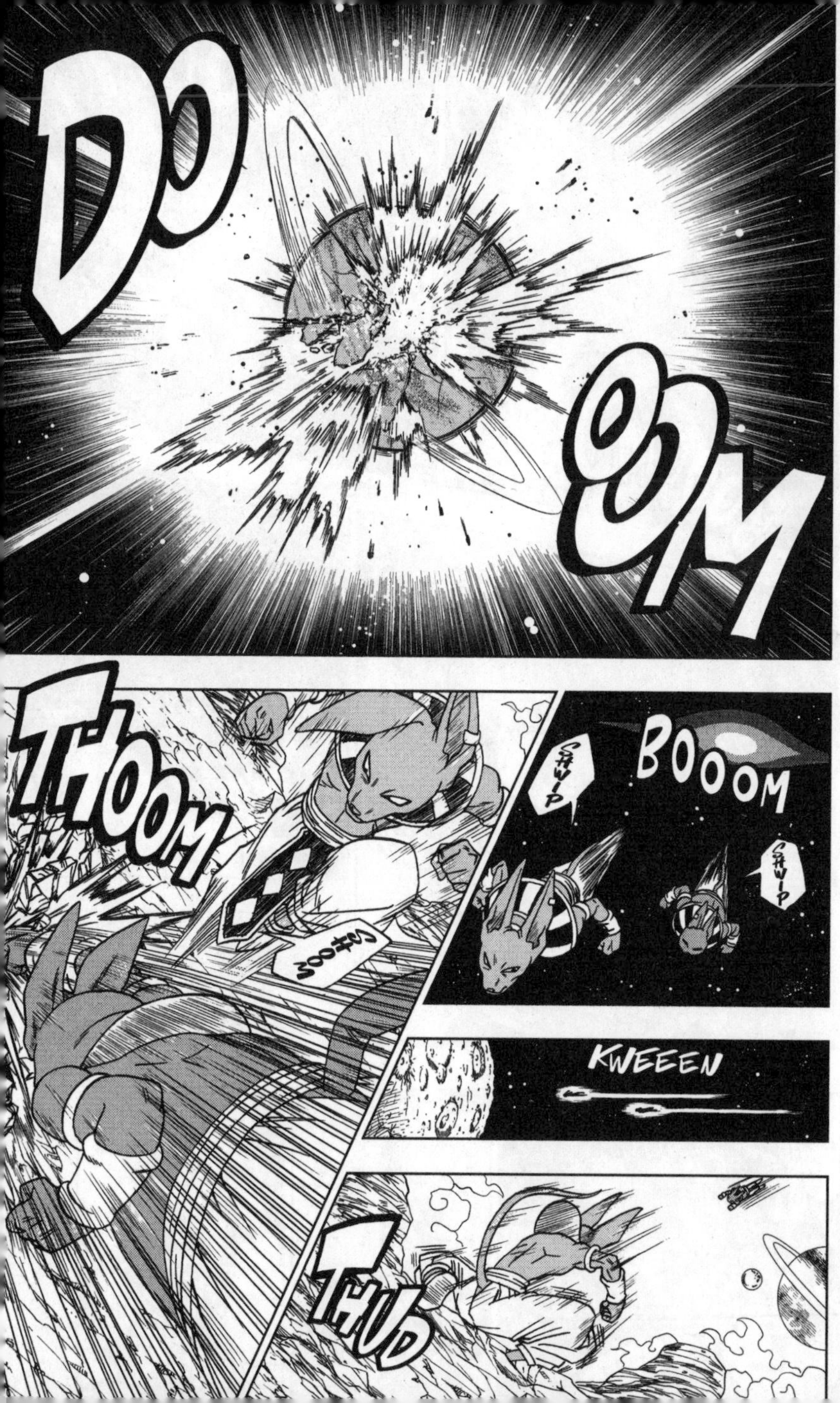
DOOOM
BOOOM
SHWIP
SHWIP
KWEEEN
THUD
THOOM
SHOOSH

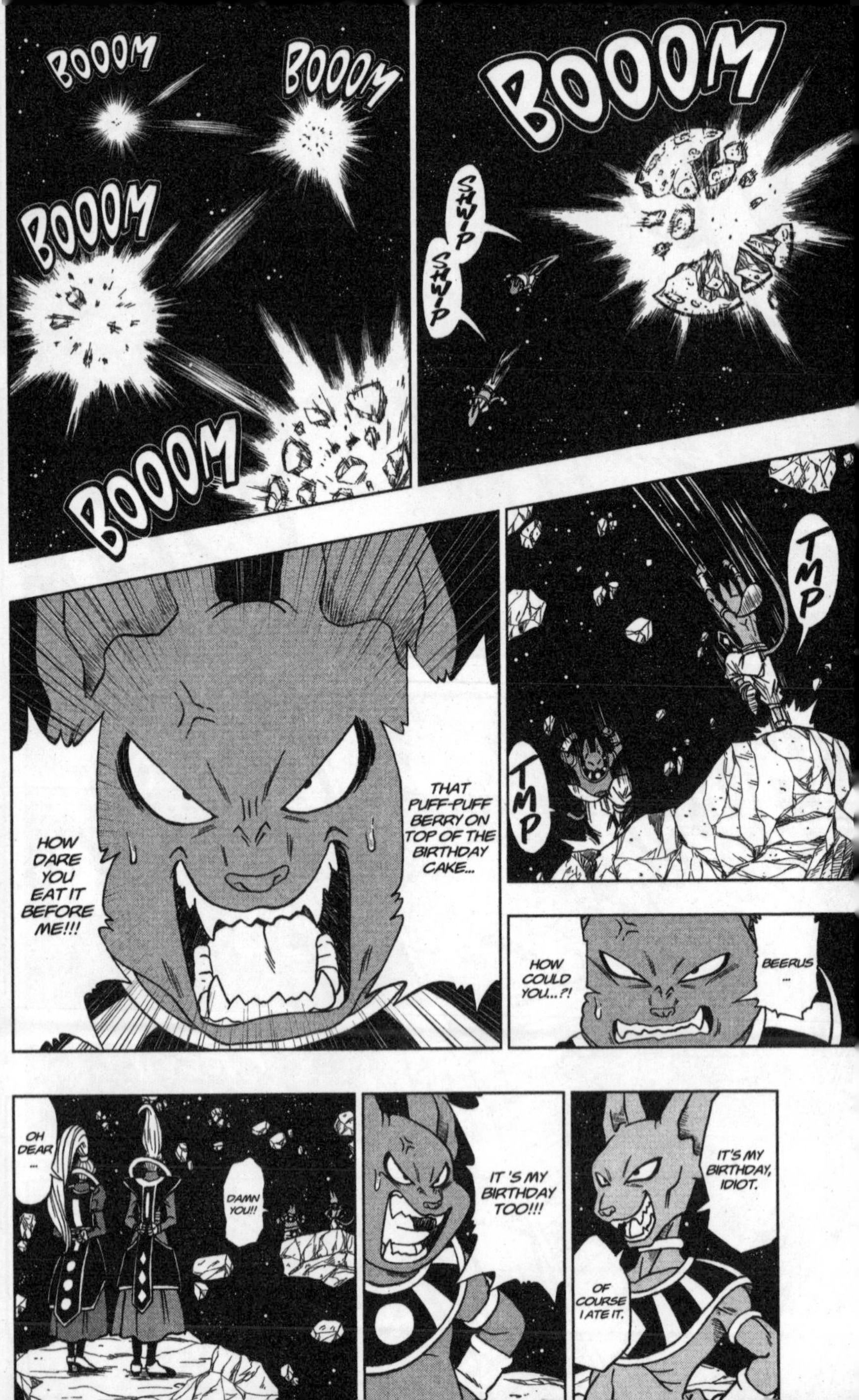
BOOOM
SHWIP
SHWIP
BOOOM
BOOOM
BOOOM
BOOOM
TMP
TMP
BEERUS ...
HOW COULD YOU...?!
THAT PUFF-PUFF BERRY ON TOP OF THE BIRTHDAY CAKE...
HOW DARE YOU EAT IT BEFORE ME!!!
IT'S MY BIRTHDAY, IDIOT.
OF COURSE I ATE IT.
IT'S MY BIRTHDAY TOO!!!
OH DEAR ...
DAMN YOU!!

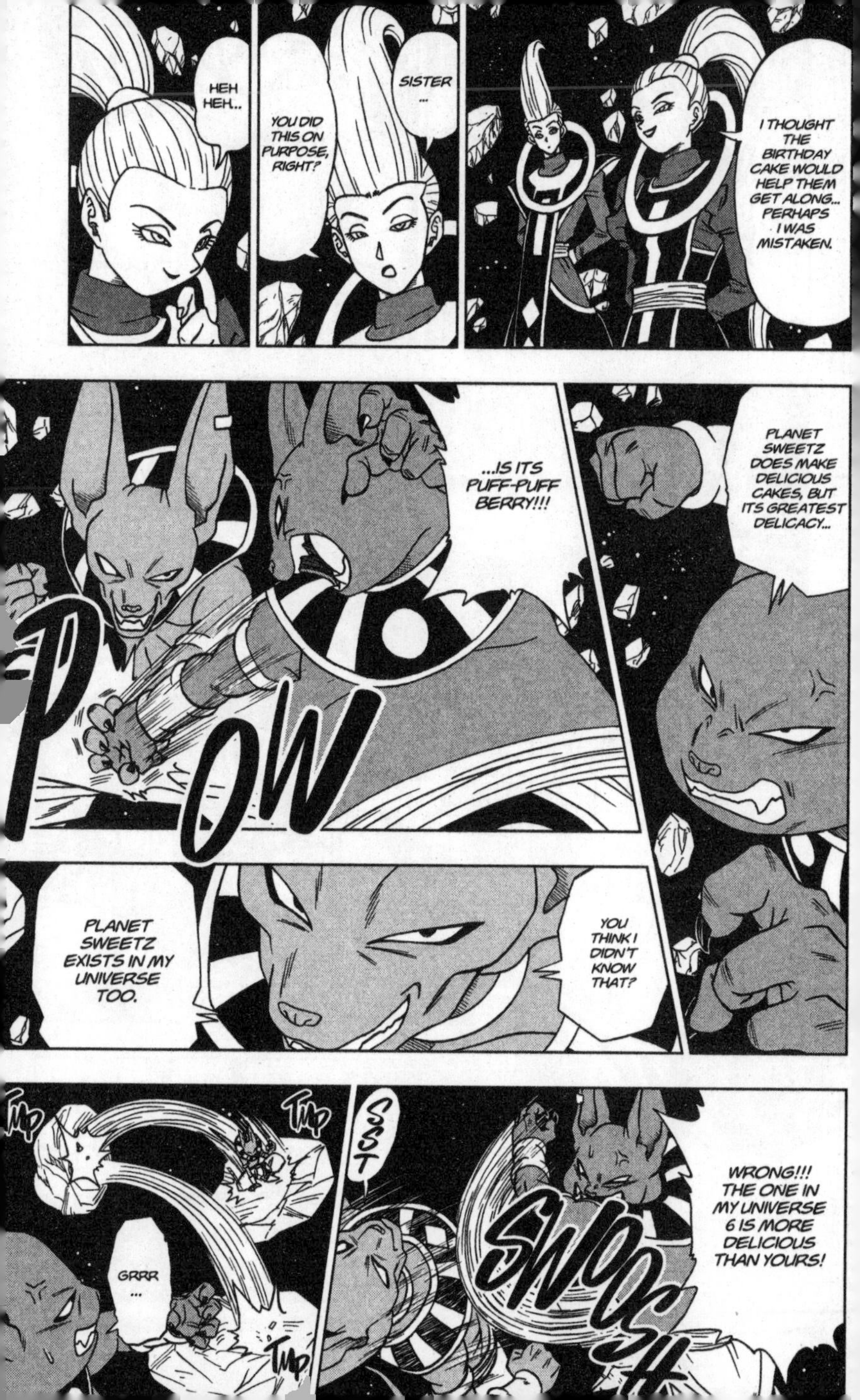
I THOUGHT THE BIRTHDAY CAKE WOULD HELP THEM GET ALONG... PERHAPS I WAS MISTAKEN.
SISTER ...
YOU DID THIS ON PURPOSE, RIGHT?
HEH HEH...
PLANET SWEETZ DOES MAKE DELICIOUS CAKES, BUT ITS GREATEST DELICACY...
...IS ITS PUFF-PUFF BERRY!!!
POW
YOU THINK I DIDN'T KNOW THAT?
PLANET SWEETZ EXISTS IN MY UNIVERSE TOO.
WRONG!!! THE ONE IN MY UNIVERSE 6 IS MORE DELICIOUS THAN YOURS!
SSST
SWOOSH
TMP
TMP
GRRR ...
TMP

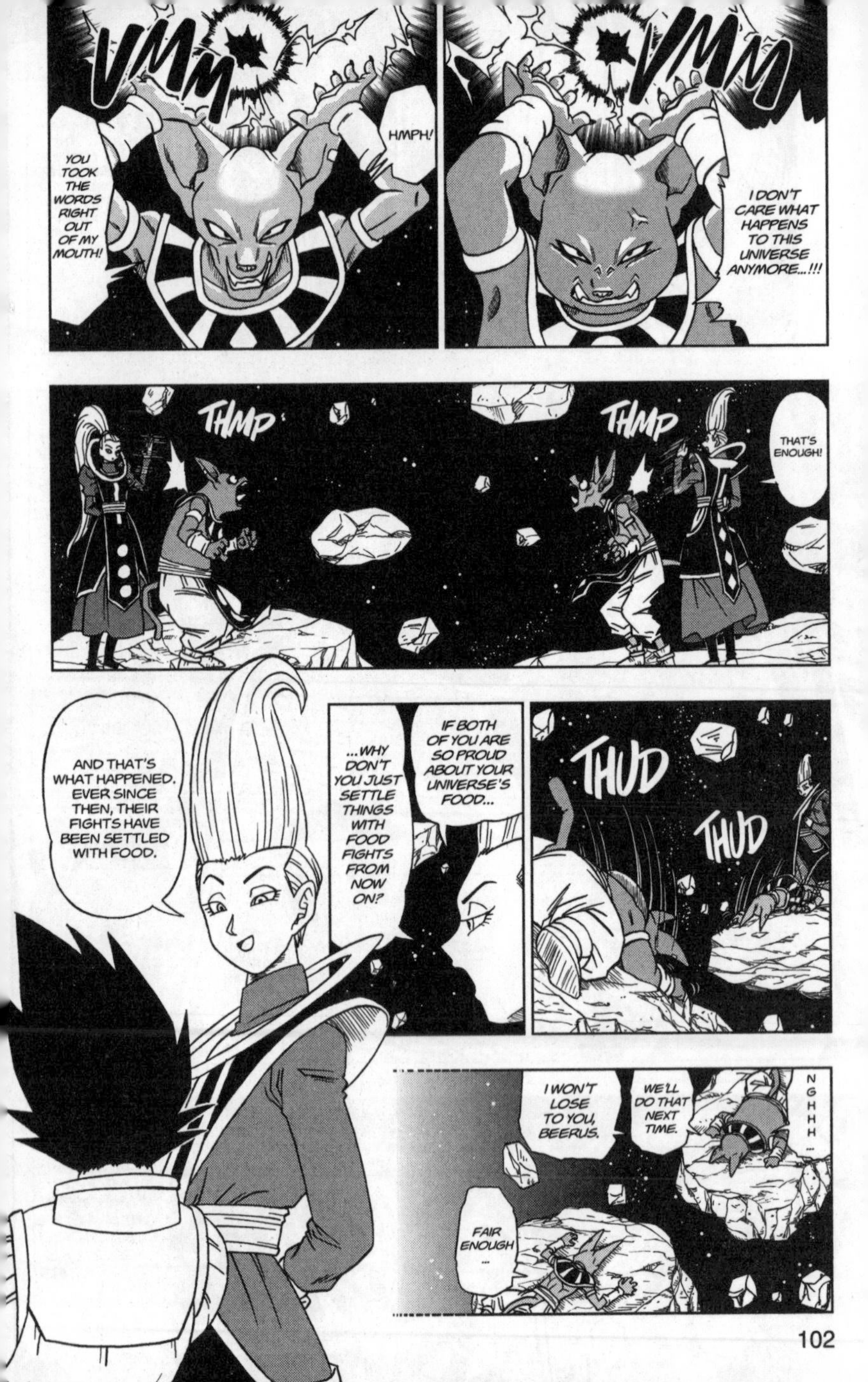
VMM
I DON'T CARE WHAT HAPPENS TO THIS UNIVERSE ANYMORE...!!!
VMM
HMPH!
YOU TOOK THE WORDS RIGHT OUT OF MY MOUTH!
THAT'S ENOUGH!
THMP
THMP
THUD
THUD
IF BOTH OF YOU ARE SO PROUD ABOUT YOUR UNIVERSE'S FOOD...
...WHY DON'T YOU JUST SETTLE THINGS WITH FOOD FIGHTS FROM NOW ON?
NGHHH...
WE'LL DO THAT NEXT TIME.
I WON'T LOSE TO YOU, BEERUS.
FAIR ENOUGH...
AND THAT'S WHAT HAPPENED. EVER SINCE THEN, THEIR FIGHTS HAVE BEEN SETTLED WITH FOOD.

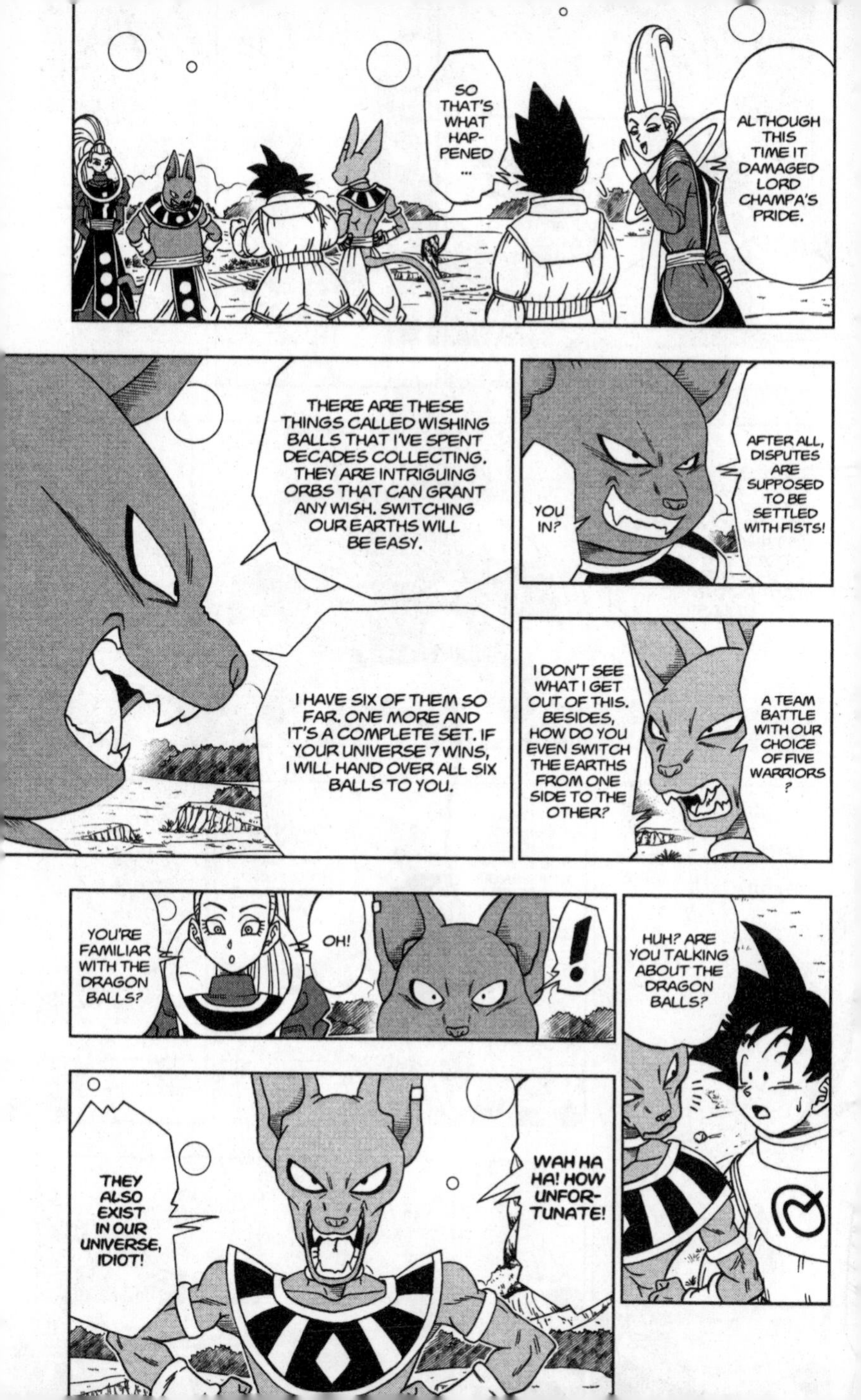
ALTHOUGH THIS TIME IT DAMAGED LORD CHAMPA'S PRIDE.
SO THAT'S WHAT HAP-PENED ...
AFTER ALL, DISPUTES ARE SUPPOSED TO BE SETTLED WITH FISTS!
YOU IN?
A TEAM BATTLE WITH OUR CHOICE OF FIVE WARRIORS?
I DON'T SEE WHAT I GET OUT OF THIS. BESIDES, HOW DO YOU EVEN SWITCH THE EARTHS FROM ONE SIDE TO THE OTHER?
THERE ARE THESE THINGS CALLED WISHING BALLS THAT I'VE SPENT DECADES COLLECTING. THEY ARE INTRIGUING ORBS THAT CAN GRANT ANY WISH. SWITCHING OUR EARTHS WILL BE EASY.
I HAVE SIX OF THEM SO FAR. ONE MORE AND IT'S A COMPLETE SET. IF YOUR UNIVERSE 7 WINS, I WILL HAND OVER ALL SIX BALLS TO YOU.
HUH? ARE YOU TALKING ABOUT THE DRAGON BALLS?
!
OH!
YOU'RE FAMILIAR WITH THE DRAGON BALLS?
WAH HA HA! HOW UNFOR-TUNATE!
THEY ALSO EXIST IN OUR UNIVERSE, IDIOT!

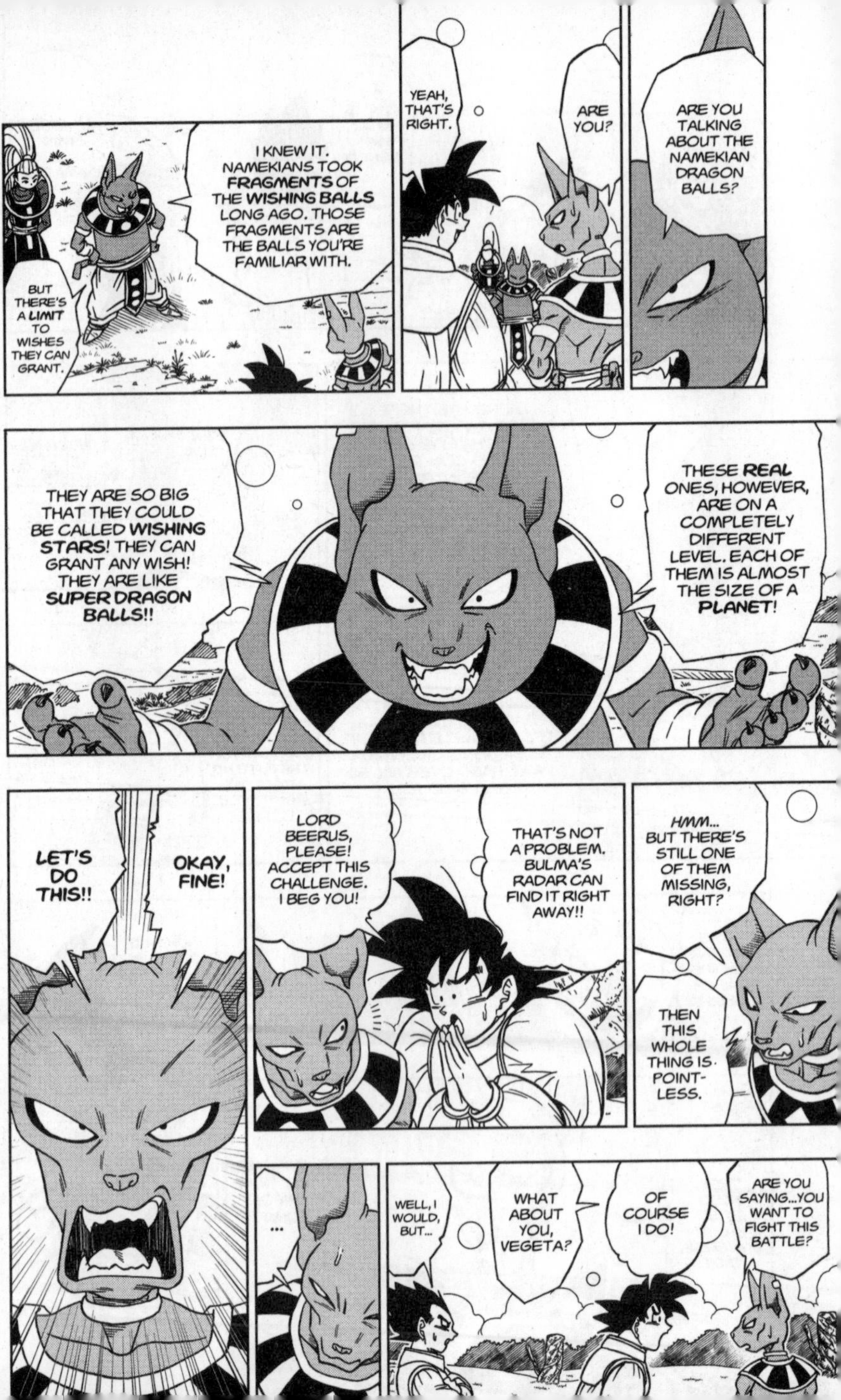
ARE YOU TALKING ABOUT THE NAMEKIAN DRAGON BALLS?
ARE YOU?
YEAH, THAT'S RIGHT.
I KNEW IT. NAMEKIANS TOOK FRAGMENTS OF THE WISHING BALLS LONG AGO. THOSE FRAGMENTS ARE THE BALLS YOU'RE FAMILIAR WITH.
BUT THERE'S A LIMIT TO WISHES THEY CAN GRANT.
THESE REAL ONES, HOWEVER, ARE ON A COMPLETELY DIFFERENT LEVEL. EACH OF THEM IS ALMOST THE SIZE OF A PLANET!
THEY ARE SO BIG THAT THEY COULD BE CALLED WISHING STARS! THEY CAN GRANT ANY WISH! THEY ARE LIKE SUPER DRAGON BALLS!!
HMM... BUT THERE'S STILL ONE OF THEM MISSING, RIGHT?
THEN THIS WHOLE THING IS POINTLESS.
THAT'S NOT A PROBLEM. BULMA'S RADAR CAN FIND IT RIGHT AWAY!!
LORD BEERUS, PLEASE! ACCEPT THIS CHALLENGE. I BEG YOU!
ARE YOU SAYING...YOU WANT TO FIGHT THIS BATTLE?
OF COURSE I DO!
WHAT ABOUT YOU, VEGETA?
WELL, I WOULD, BUT...
...
OKAY, FINE!
LET'S DO THIS!!

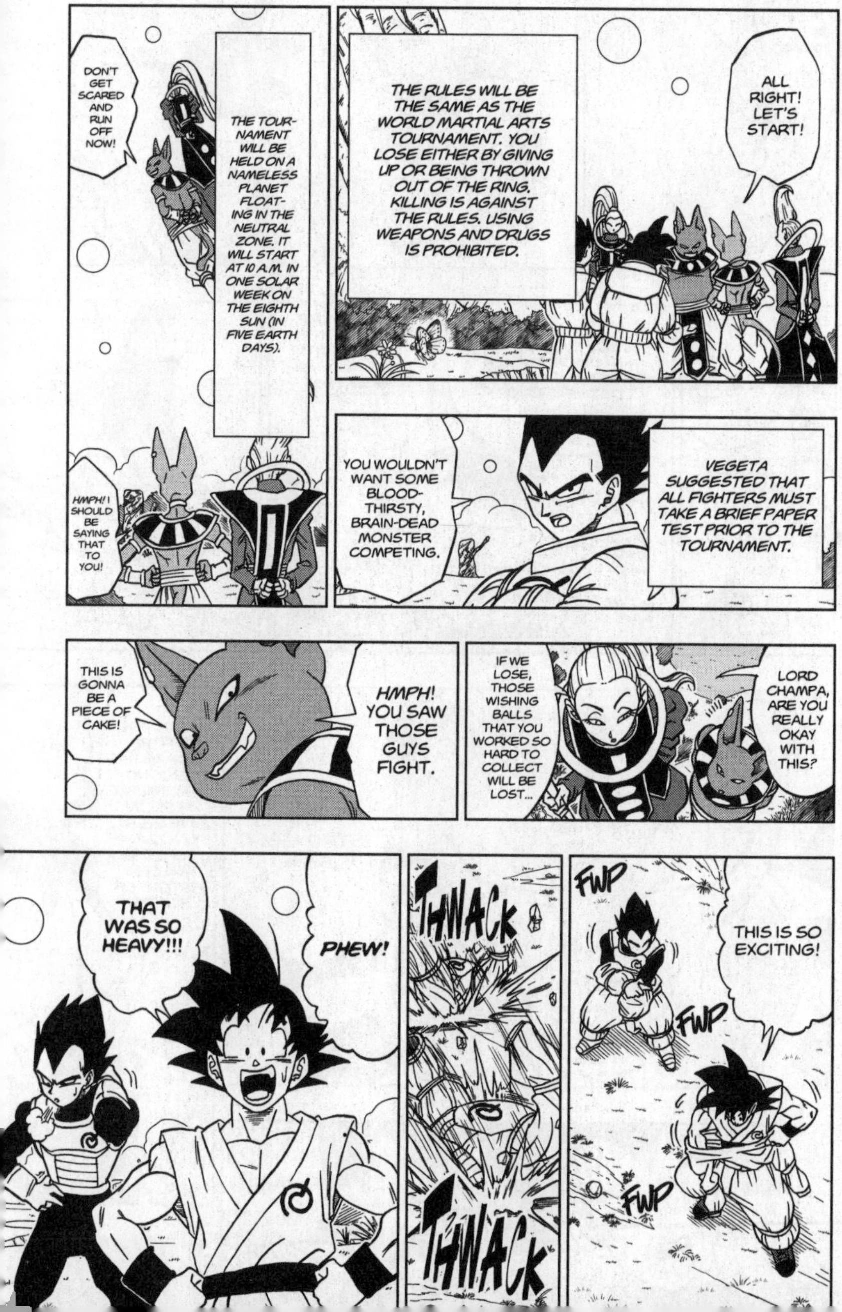
ALL RIGHT! LET'S START!
THE RULES WILL BE THE SAME AS THE WORLD MARTIAL ARTS TOURNAMENT. YOU LOSE EITHER BY GIVING UP OR BEING THROWN OUT OF THE RING. KILLING IS AGAINST THE RULES. USING WEAPONS AND DRUGS IS PROHIBITED.
VEGETA SUGGESTED THAT ALL FIGHTERS MUST TAKE A BRIEF PAPER TEST PRIOR TO THE TOURNAMENT.
YOU WOULDN'T WANT SOME BLOOD-THIRSTY, BRAIN-DEAD MONSTER COMPETING.
THE TOURNAMENT WILL BE HELD ON A NAMELESS PLANET FLOATING IN THE NEUTRAL ZONE. IT WILL START AT 10 A.M. IN ONE SOLAR WEEK ON THE EIGHTH SUN (IN FIVE EARTH DAYS).
DON'T GET SCARED AND RUN OFF NOW!
HMPH! I SHOULD BE SAYING THAT TO YOU!
LORD CHAMPA, ARE YOU REALLY OKAY WITH THIS?
IF WE LOSE, THOSE WISHING BALLS THAT YOU WORKED SO HARD TO COLLECT WILL BE LOST...
HMPH! YOU SAW THOSE GUYS FIGHT.
THIS IS GONNA BE A PIECE OF CAKE!
FWP
THIS IS SO EXCITING!
FWP
FWP
THWACK
THWACK
PHEW!
THAT WAS SO HEAVY!!!

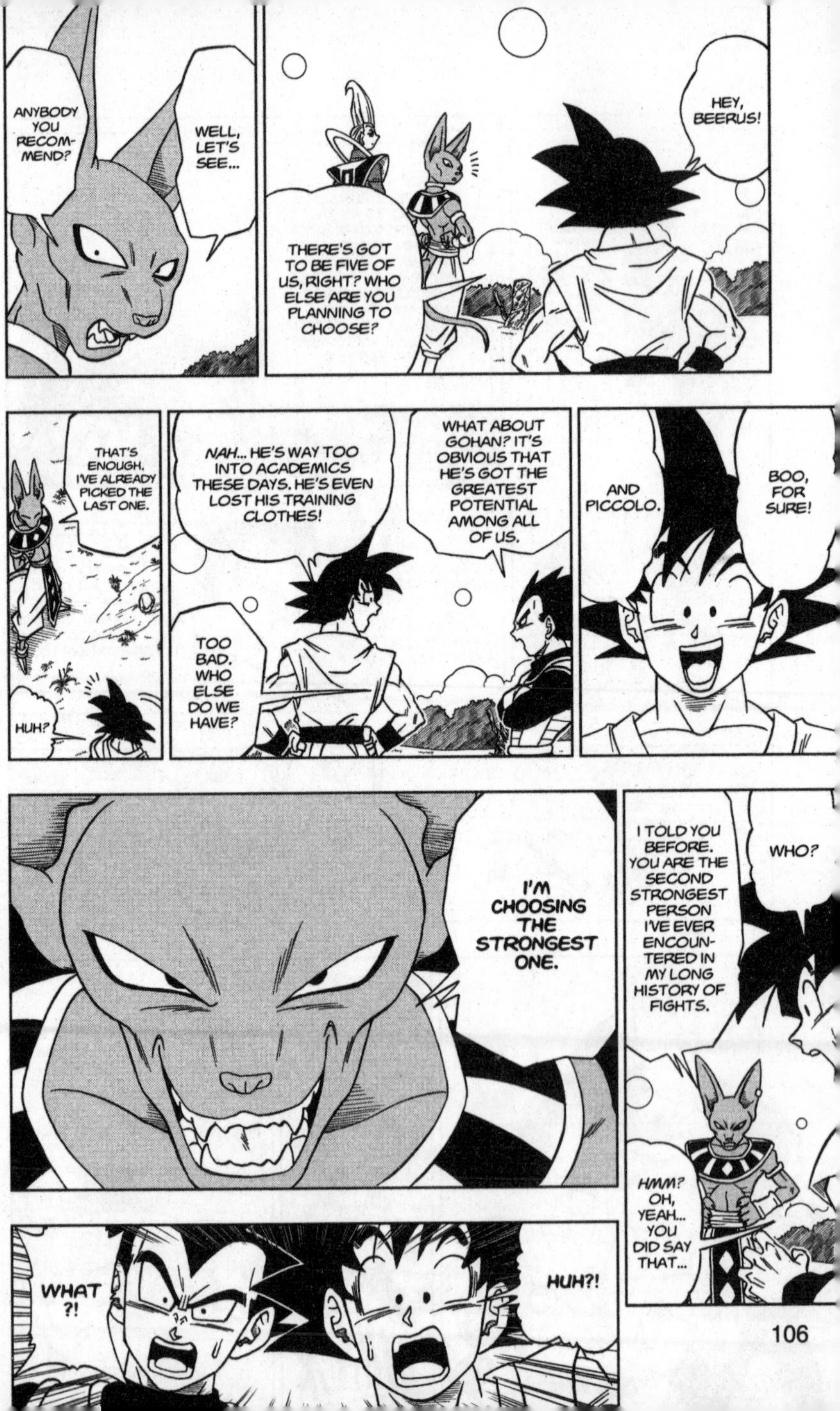
HEY, BEERUS!
THERE'S GOT TO BE FIVE OF US, RIGHT? WHO ELSE ARE YOU PLANNING TO CHOOSE?
WELL, LET'S SEE...
ANYBODY YOU RECOM-MEND?
BOO, FOR SURE!
AND PICCOLO.
WHAT ABOUT GOHAN? IT'S OBVIOUS THAT HE'S GOT THE GREATEST POTENTIAL AMONG ALL OF US.
NAH... HE'S WAY TOO INTO ACADEMICS THESE DAYS. HE'S EVEN LOST HIS TRAINING CLOTHES!
TOO BAD. WHO ELSE DO WE HAVE?
THAT'S ENOUGH. I'VE ALREADY PICKED THE LAST ONE.
HUH?
WHO?
I TOLD YOU BEFORE. YOU ARE THE SECOND STRONGEST PERSON I'VE EVER ENCOUN-TERED IN MY LONG HISTORY OF FIGHTS.
HMM? OH, YEAH... YOU DID SAY THAT...
I'M CHOOSING THE STRONGEST ONE.
HUH?!
WHAT ?!

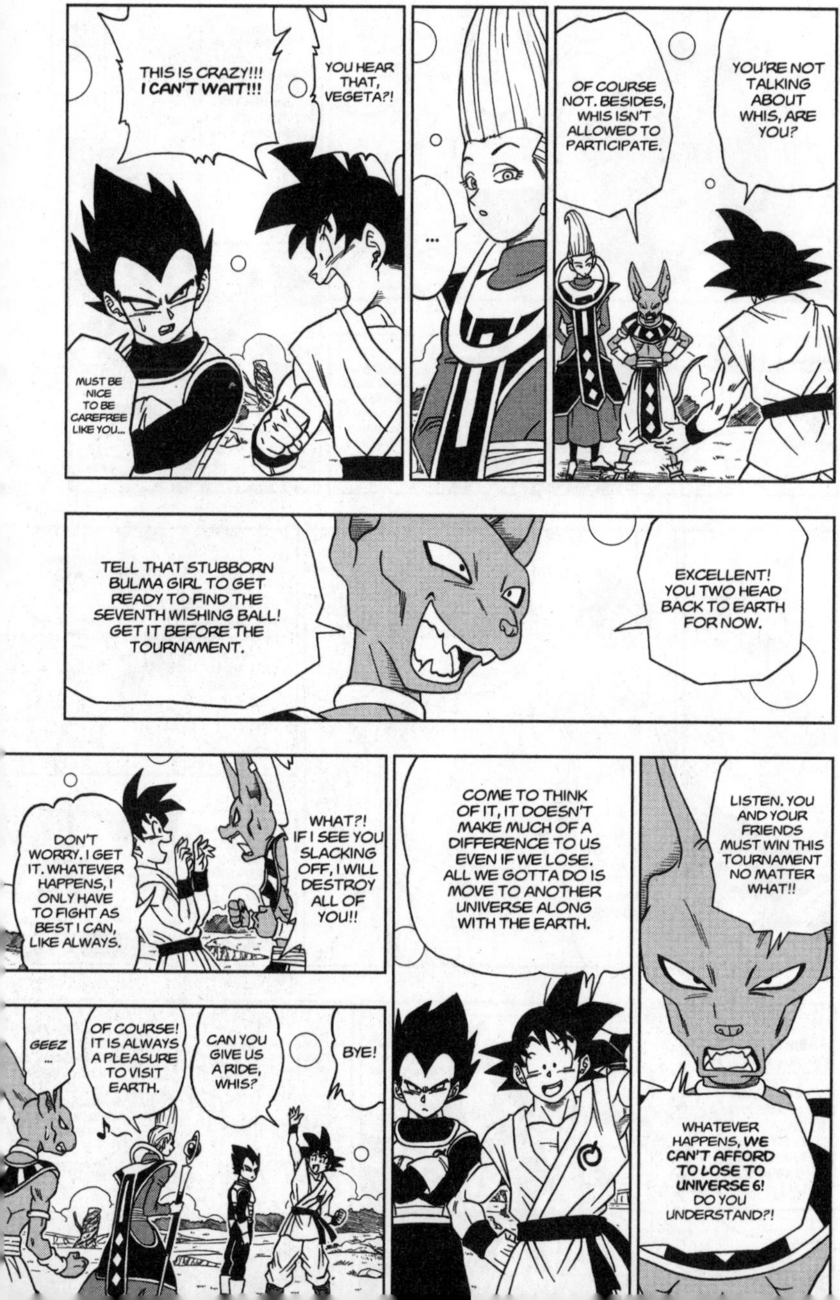
YOU'RE NOT TALKING ABOUT WHIS, ARE YOU?
OF COURSE NOT. BESIDES, WHIS ISN'T ALLOWED TO PARTICIPATE.
...
YOU HEAR THAT, VEGETA?!
THIS IS CRAZY!!! I CAN'T WAIT!!!
MUST BE NICE TO BE CAREFREE LIKE YOU...
EXCELLENT! YOU TWO HEAD BACK TO EARTH FOR NOW.
TELL THAT STUBBORN BULMA GIRL TO GET READY TO FIND THE SEVENTH WISHING BALL! GET IT BEFORE THE TOURNAMENT.
LISTEN. YOU AND YOUR FRIENDS MUST WIN THIS TOURNAMENT NO MATTER WHAT!!
WHATEVER HAPPENS, WE CAN'T AFFORD TO LOSE TO UNIVERSE 6! DO YOU UNDERSTAND?!
COME TO THINK OF IT, IT DOESN'T MAKE MUCH OF A DIFFERENCE TO US EVEN IF WE LOSE. ALL WE GOTTA DO IS MOVE TO ANOTHER UNIVERSE ALONG WITH THE EARTH.
WHAT?! IF I SEE YOU SLACKING OFF, I WILL DESTROY ALL OF YOU!!
DON'T WORRY. I GET IT. WHATEVER HAPPENS, I ONLY HAVE TO FIGHT AS BEST I CAN, LIKE ALWAYS.
BYE!
CAN YOU GIVE US A RIDE, WHIS?
OF COURSE! IT IS ALWAYS A PLEASURE TO VISIT EARTH.
GEEZ ...

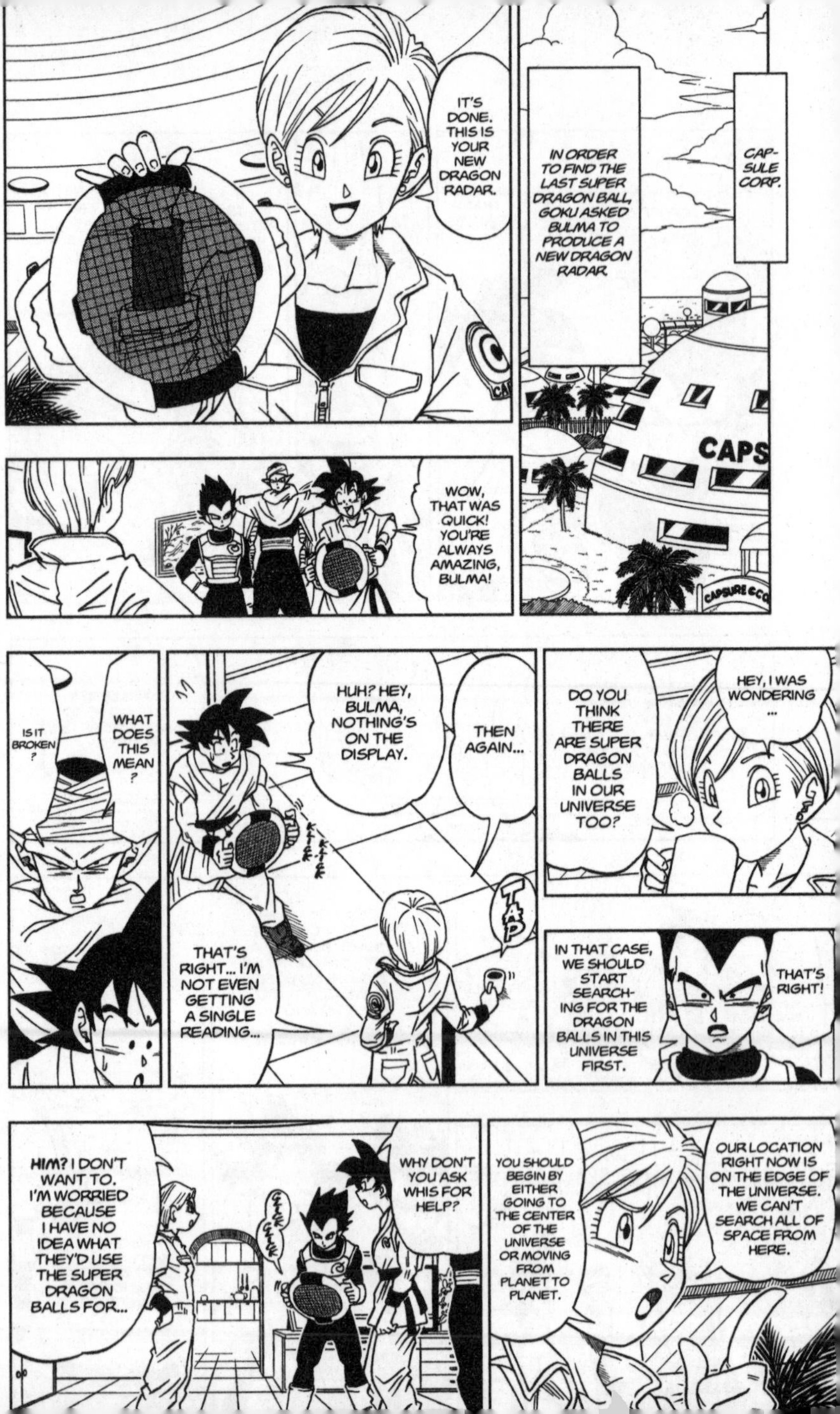

CAPSULE CORP.
IN ORDER TO FIND THE LAST SUPER DRAGON BALL, GOKU ASKED BULMA TO PRODUCE A NEW DRAGON RADAR.
CAPS
IT'S DONE. THIS IS YOUR NEW DRAGON RADAR.
WOW, THAT WAS QUICK! YOU'RE ALWAYS AMAZING, BULMA!
HEY, I WAS WONDERING ...
DO YOU THINK THERE ARE SUPER DRAGON BALLS IN OUR UNIVERSE TOO?
THAT'S RIGHT!
IN THAT CASE, WE SHOULD START SEARCHING FOR THE DRAGON BALLS IN THIS UNIVERSE FIRST.
HUH? HEY, BULMA, NOTHING'S ON THE DISPLAY.
THEN AGAIN...
TAP
THAT'S RIGHT... I'M NOT EVEN GETTING A SINGLE READING...
WHAT DOES THIS MEAN?
IS IT BROKEN?
OUR LOCATION RIGHT NOW IS ON THE EDGE OF THE UNIVERSE. WE CAN'T SEARCH ALL OF SPACE FROM HERE.
YOU SHOULD BEGIN BY EITHER GOING TO THE CENTER OF THE UNIVERSE OR MOVING FROM PLANET TO PLANET.
WHY DON'T YOU ASK WHIS FOR HELP?
HIM? I DON'T WANT TO. I'M WORRIED BECAUSE I HAVE NO IDEA WHAT THEY'D USE THE SUPER DRAGON BALLS FOR...

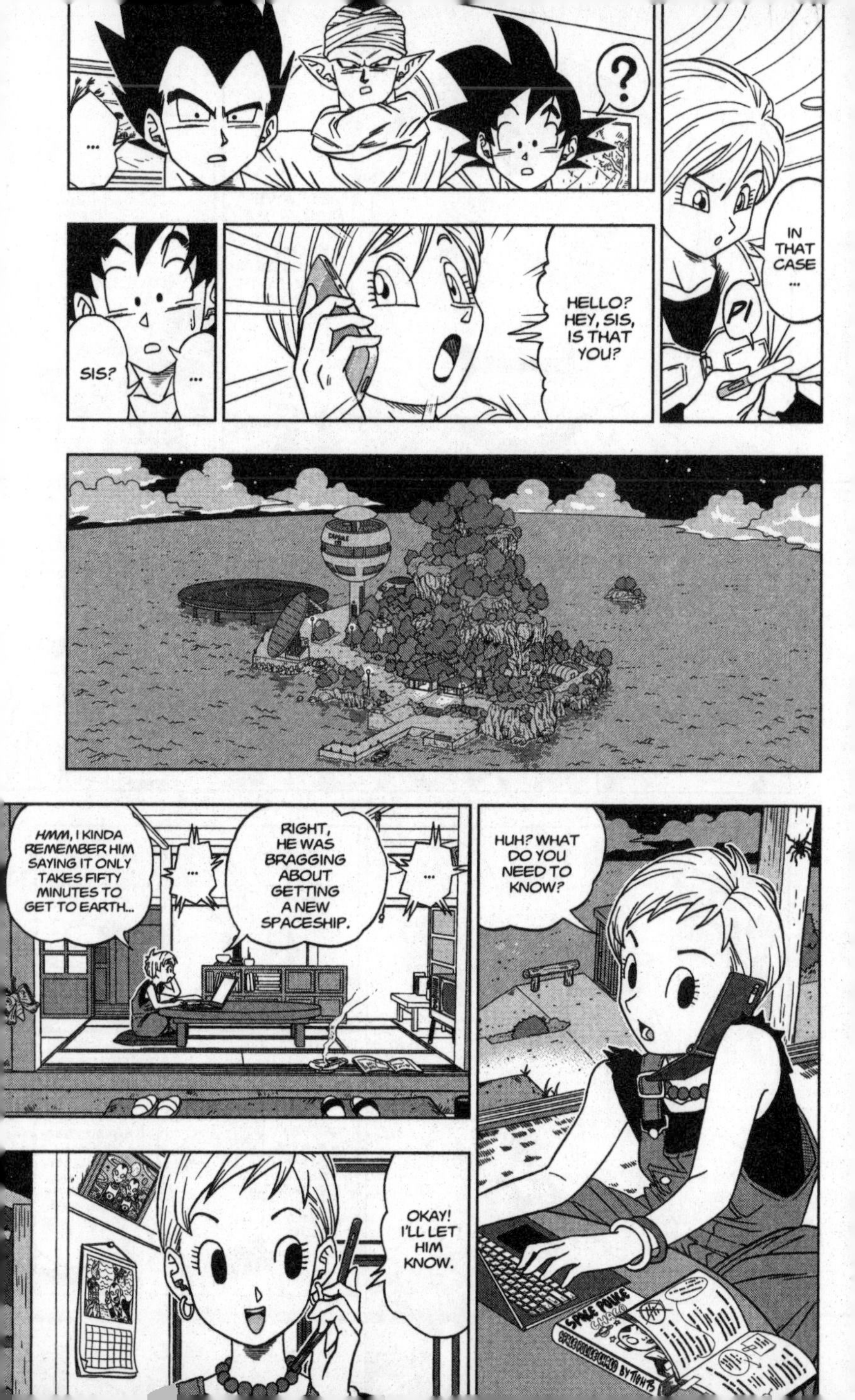
IN THAT CASE ...
PI
?
...
HELLO? HEY, SIS, IS THAT YOU?
...
SIS?
HUH? WHAT DO YOU NEED TO KNOW?
SPACE POLICE
...
RIGHT, HE WAS BRAGGING ABOUT GETTING A NEW SPACESHIP.
...
HMM, I KINDA REMEMBER HIM SAYING IT ONLY TAKES FIFTY MINUTES TO GET TO EARTH...
OKAY! I'LL LET HIM KNOW.

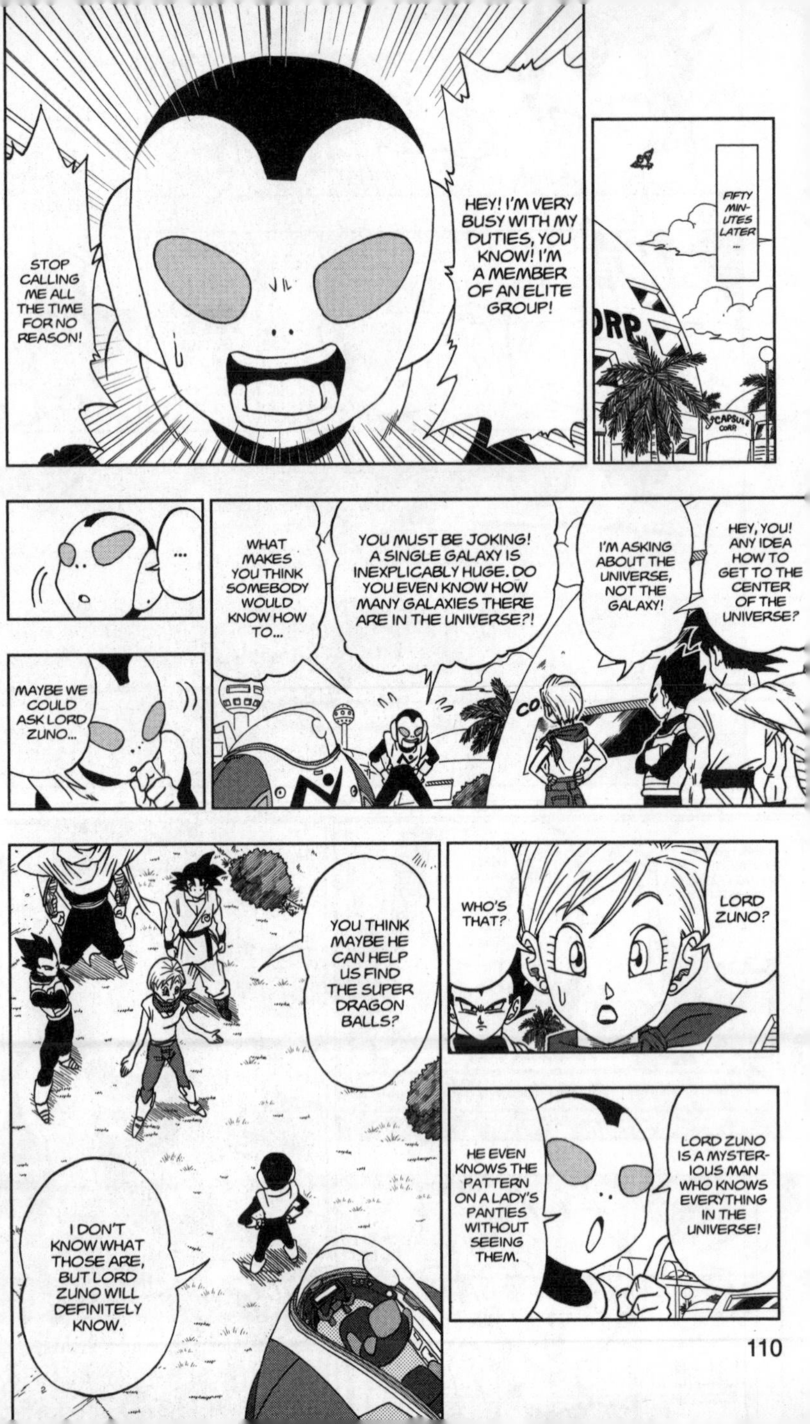
FIFTY MIN-UTES LATER ...
CAPSULE CORP
HEY! I'M VERY BUSY WITH MY DUTIES, YOU KNOW! I'M A MEMBER OF AN ELITE GROUP!
STOP CALLING ME ALL THE TIME FOR NO REASON!
HEY, YOU! ANY IDEA HOW TO GET TO THE CENTER OF THE UNIVERSE?
YOU MUST BE JOKING! A SINGLE GALAXY IS INEXPLICABLY HUGE. DO YOU EVEN KNOW HOW MANY GALAXIES THERE ARE IN THE UNIVERSE?!
I'M ASKING ABOUT THE UNIVERSE, NOT THE GALAXY!
WHAT MAKES YOU THINK SOMEBODY WOULD KNOW HOW TO...
...
MAYBE WE COULD ASK LORD ZUNO...
LORD ZUNO?
WHO'S THAT?
LORD ZUNO IS A MYSTER-IOUS MAN WHO KNOWS EVERYTHING IN THE UNIVERSE!
HE EVEN KNOWS THE PATTERN ON A LADY'S PANTIES WITHOUT SEEING THEM.
YOU THINK MAYBE HE CAN HELP US FIND THE SUPER DRAGON BALLS?
I DON'T KNOW WHAT THOSE ARE, BUT LORD ZUNO WILL DEFINITELY KNOW.

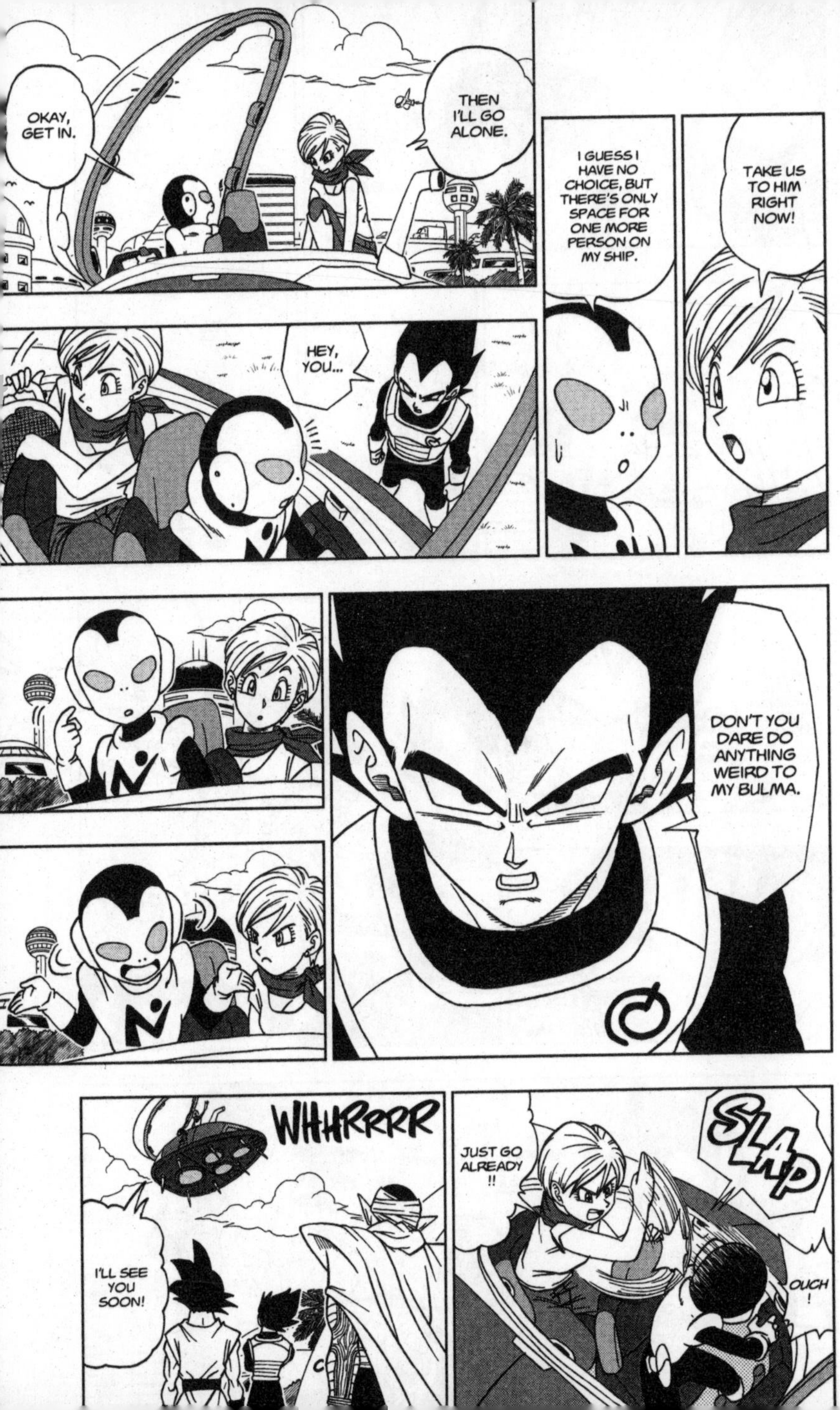
TAKE US TO HIM RIGHT NOW!
I GUESS I HAVE NO CHOICE, BUT THERE'S ONLY SPACE FOR ONE MORE PERSON ON MY SHIP.
THEN I'LL GO ALONE.
OKAY, GET IN.
HEY, YOU...
DON'T YOU DARE DO ANYTHING WEIRD TO MY BULMA.
SLAP
JUST GO ALREADY !!
OUCH !
WHHRRRR
I'LL SEE YOU SOON!

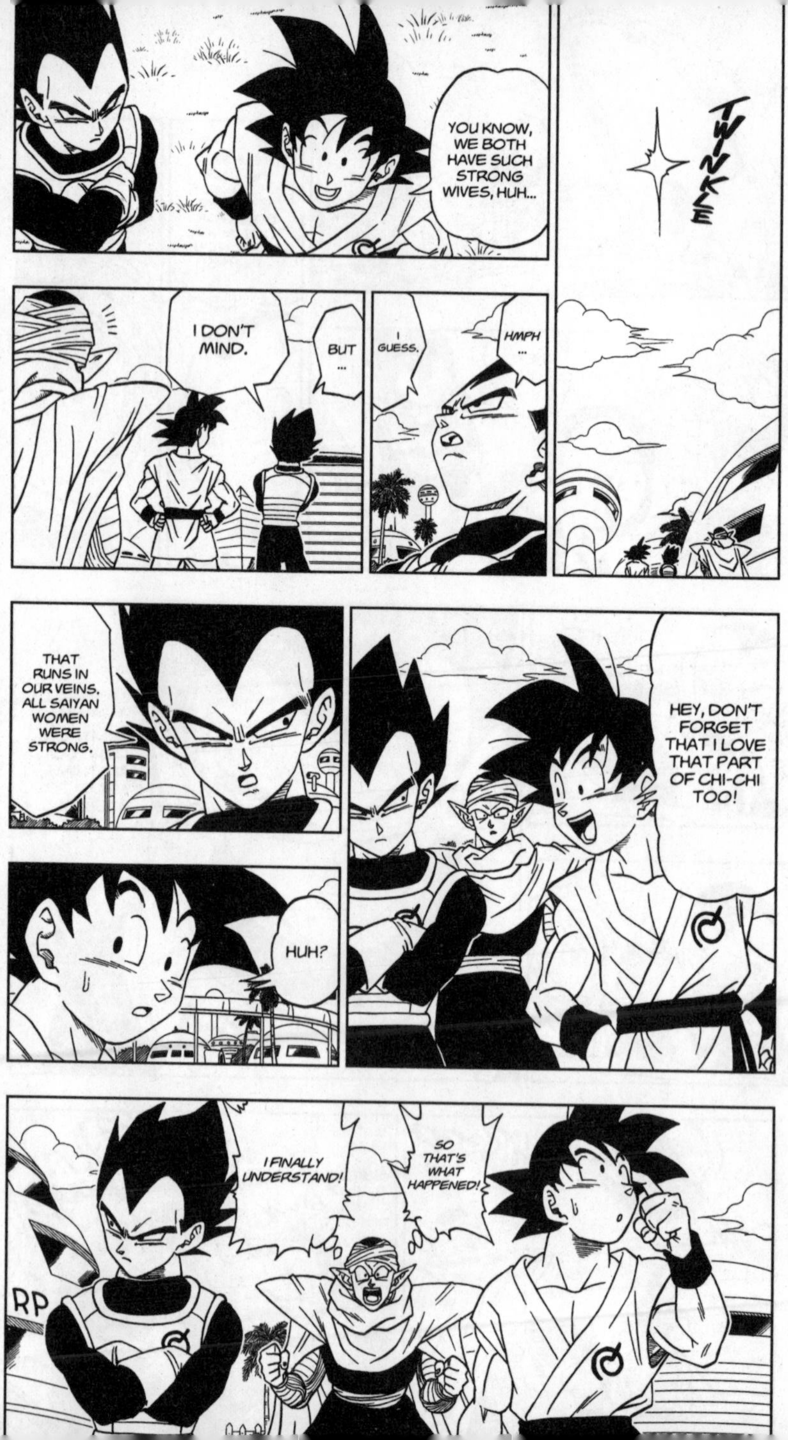
TWINKLE
YOU KNOW, WE BOTH HAVE SUCH STRONG WIVES, HUH...
HMPH ...
I GUESS.
BUT ...
I DON'T MIND.
HEY, DON'T FORGET THAT I LOVE THAT PART OF CHI-CHI TOO!
THAT RUNS IN OUR VEINS. ALL SAIYAN WOMEN WERE STRONG.
HUH?
SO THAT'S WHAT HAPPENED!
I FINALLY UNDERSTAND!
RP

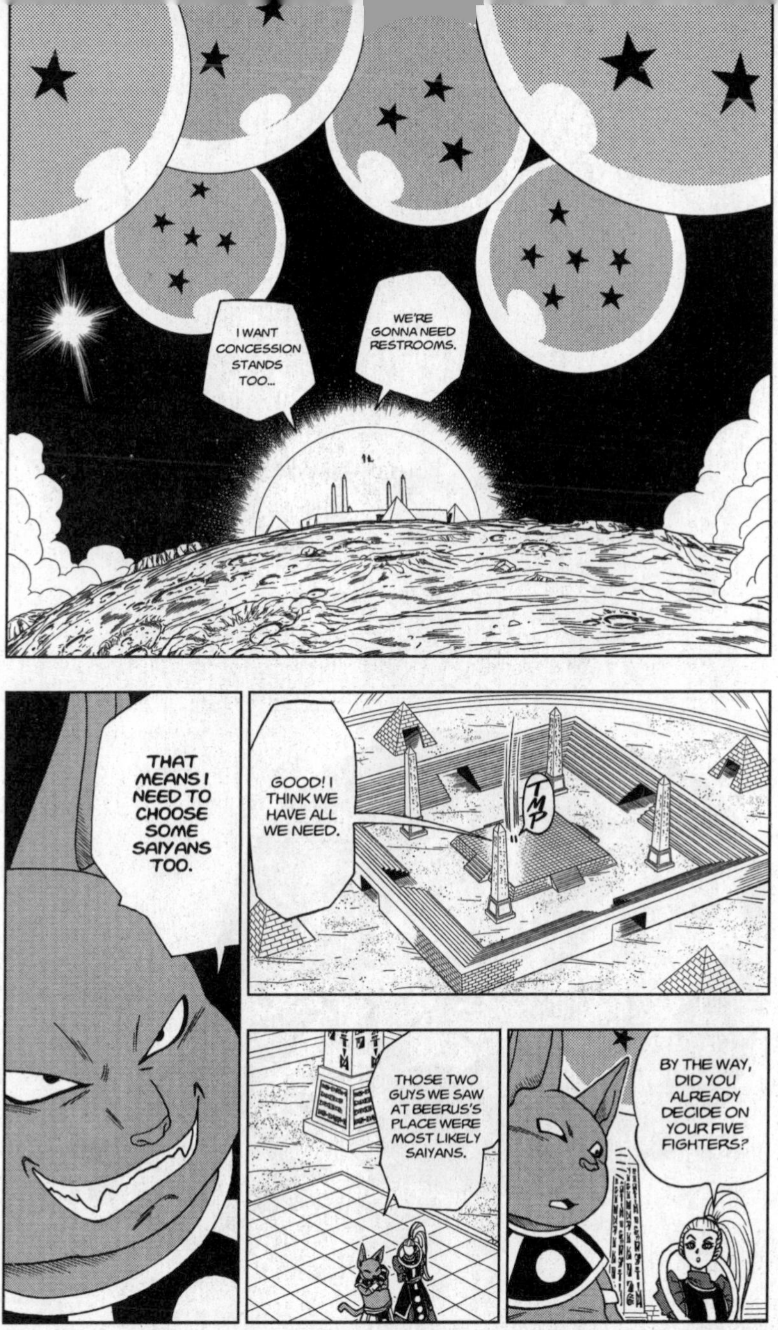
WE'RE GONNA NEED RESTROOMS.
I WANT CONCESSION STANDS TOO...
GOOD! I THINK WE HAVE ALL WE NEED.
TMP
BY THE WAY, DID YOU ALREADY DECIDE ON YOUR FIVE FIGHTERS?
THOSE TWO GUYS WE SAW AT BEERUS'S PLACE WERE MOST LIKELY SAIYANS.
THAT MEANS I NEED TO CHOOSE SOME SAIYANS TOO.

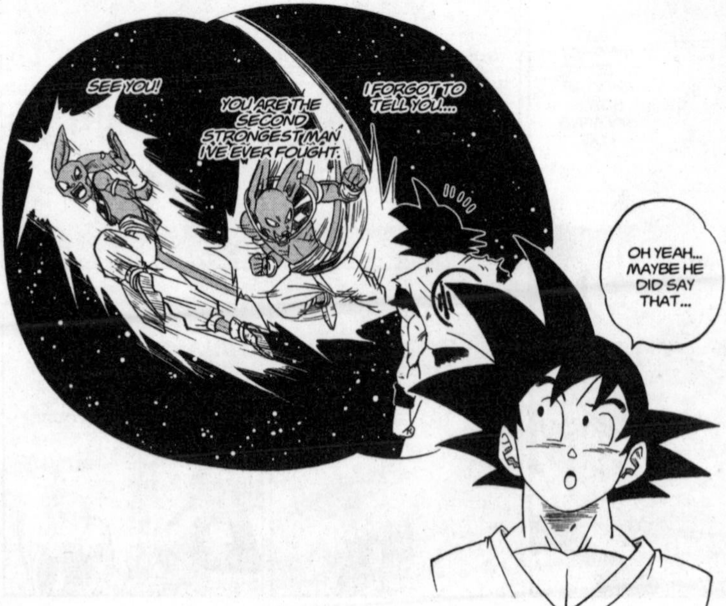
OH YEAH... MAYBE HE DID SAY THAT...
I FORGOT TO TELL YOU...
YOU ARE THE SECOND STRONGEST MAN I'VE EVER FOUGHT.
SEE YOU!

DRAGON BALL SUPER

CHAPTER 7: WARRIORS FROM UNIVERSE 6

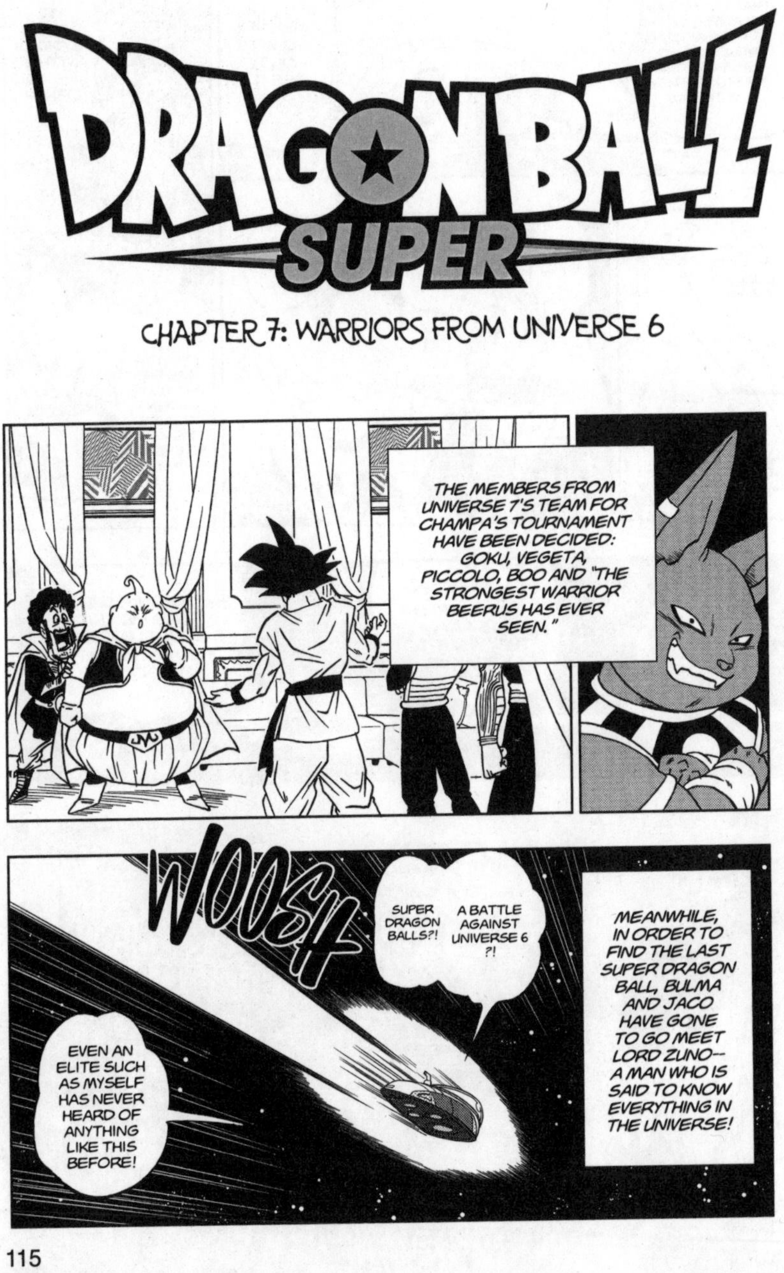
THE MEMBERS FROM UNIVERSE 7'S TEAM FOR CHAMPA'S TOURNAMENT HAVE BEEN DECIDED: GOKU, VEGETA, PICCOLO, BOO AND "THE STRONGEST WARRIOR BEERUS HAS EVER SEEN."
MEANWHILE, IN ORDER TO FIND THE LAST SUPER DRAGON BALL, BULMA AND JACO HAVE GONE TO GO MEET LORD ZUNO-- A MAN WHO IS SAID TO KNOW EVERYTHING IN THE UNIVERSE!
A BATTLE AGAINST UNIVERSE 6 ?!
SUPER DRAGON BALLS?!
WOOSH
EVEN AN ELITE SUCH AS MYSELF HAS NEVER HEARD OF ANYTHING LIKE THIS BEFORE!

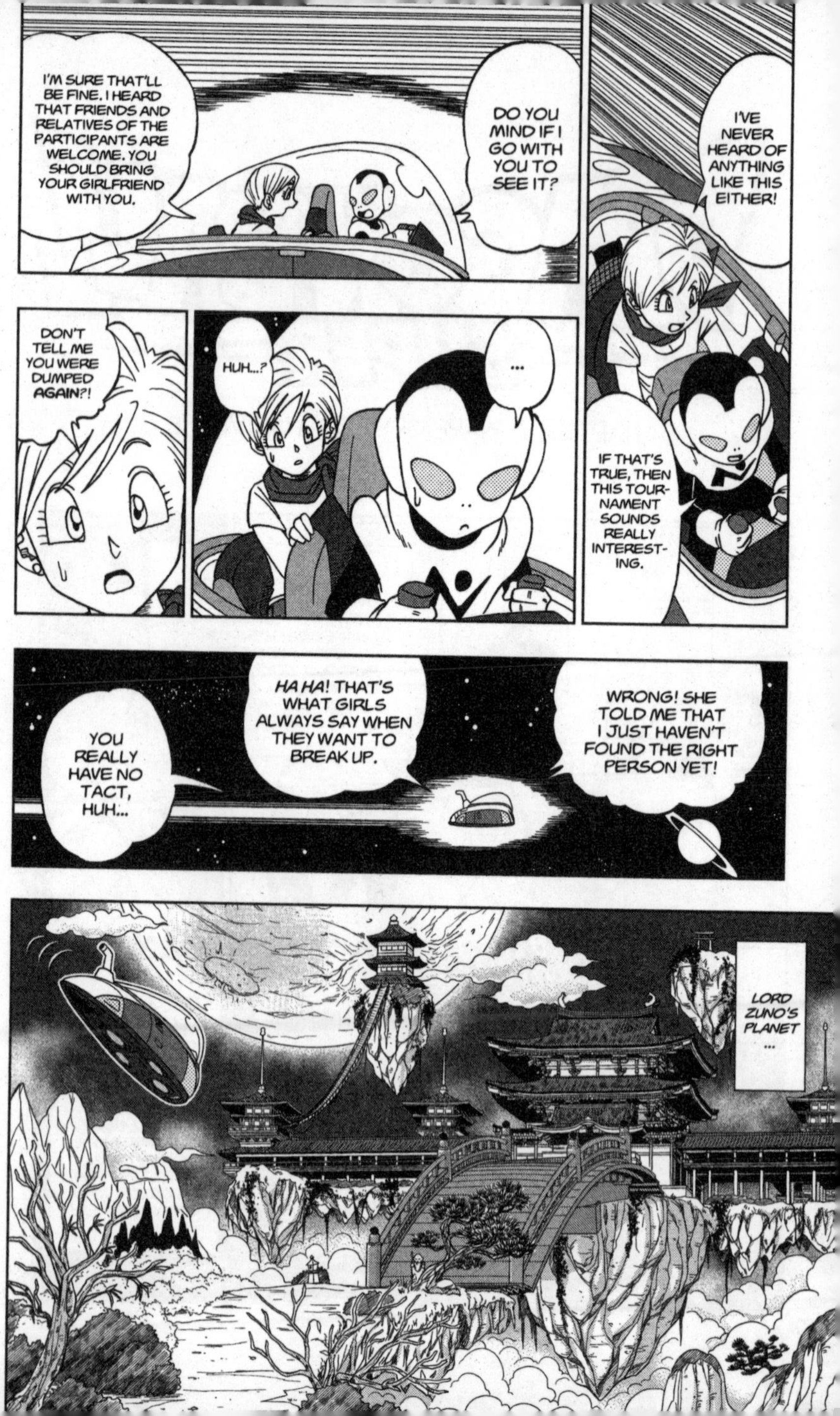
I'VE NEVER HEARD OF ANYTHING LIKE THIS EITHER!
IF THAT'S TRUE, THEN THIS TOURNAMENT SOUNDS REALLY INTERESTING.
DO YOU MIND IF I GO WITH YOU TO SEE IT?
I'M SURE THAT'LL BE FINE. I HEARD THAT FRIENDS AND RELATIVES OF THE PARTICIPANTS ARE WELCOME. YOU SHOULD BRING YOUR GIRLFRIEND WITH YOU.
...
HUH...?
DON'T TELL ME YOU WERE DUMPED **AGAIN**?!
WRONG! SHE TOLD ME THAT I JUST HAVEN'T FOUND THE RIGHT PERSON YET!
HA HA! THAT'S WHAT GIRLS ALWAYS SAY WHEN THEY WANT TO BREAK UP.
YOU REALLY HAVE NO TACT, HUH...
LORD ZUNO'S PLANET ...

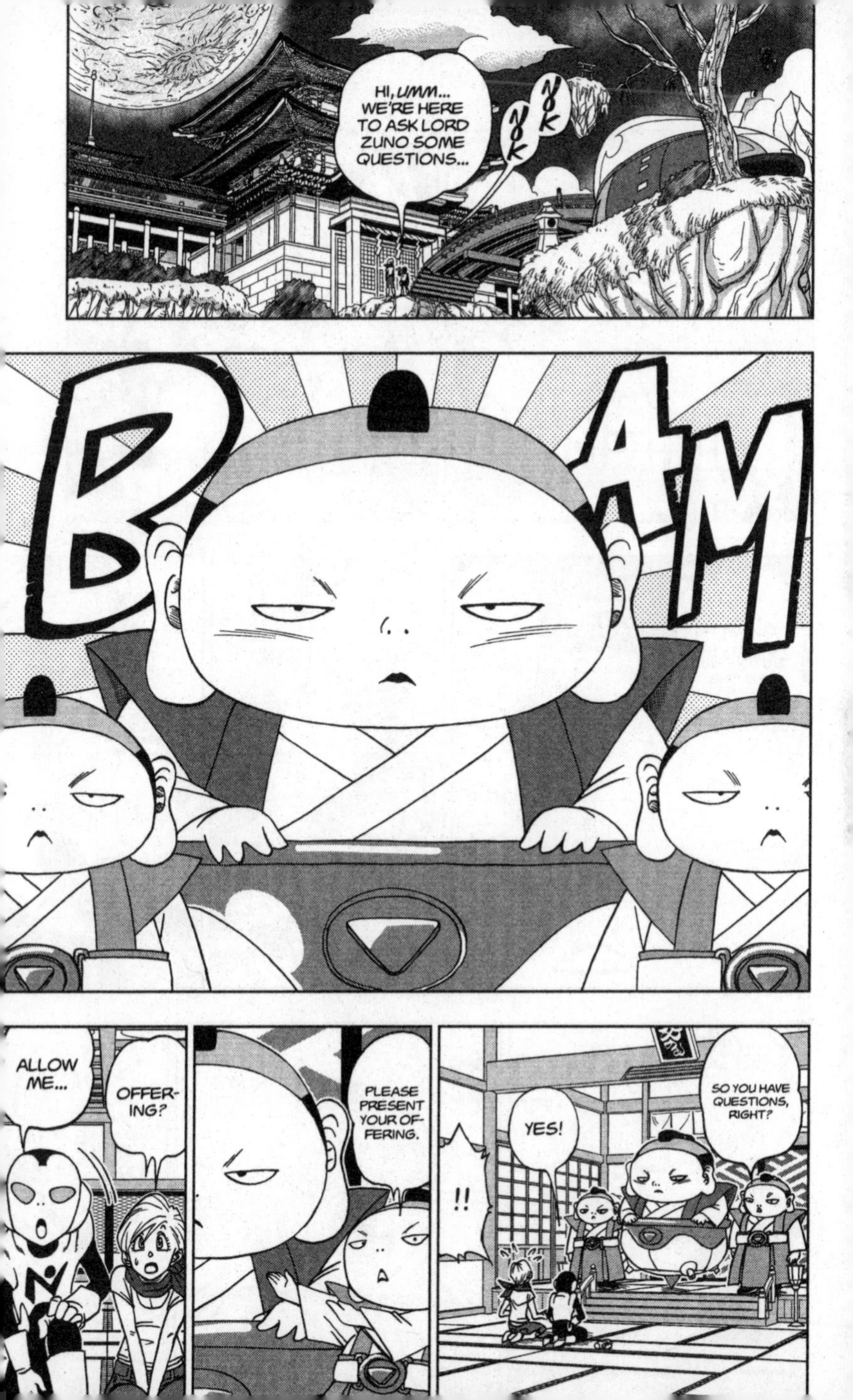
NOK
NOK
HI, UMM... WE'RE HERE TO ASK LORD ZUNO SOME QUESTIONS...
BAM
SO YOU HAVE QUESTIONS, RIGHT?
YES!
!!
PLEASE PRESENT YOUR OF-FERING.
OFFER-ING?
ALLOW ME...

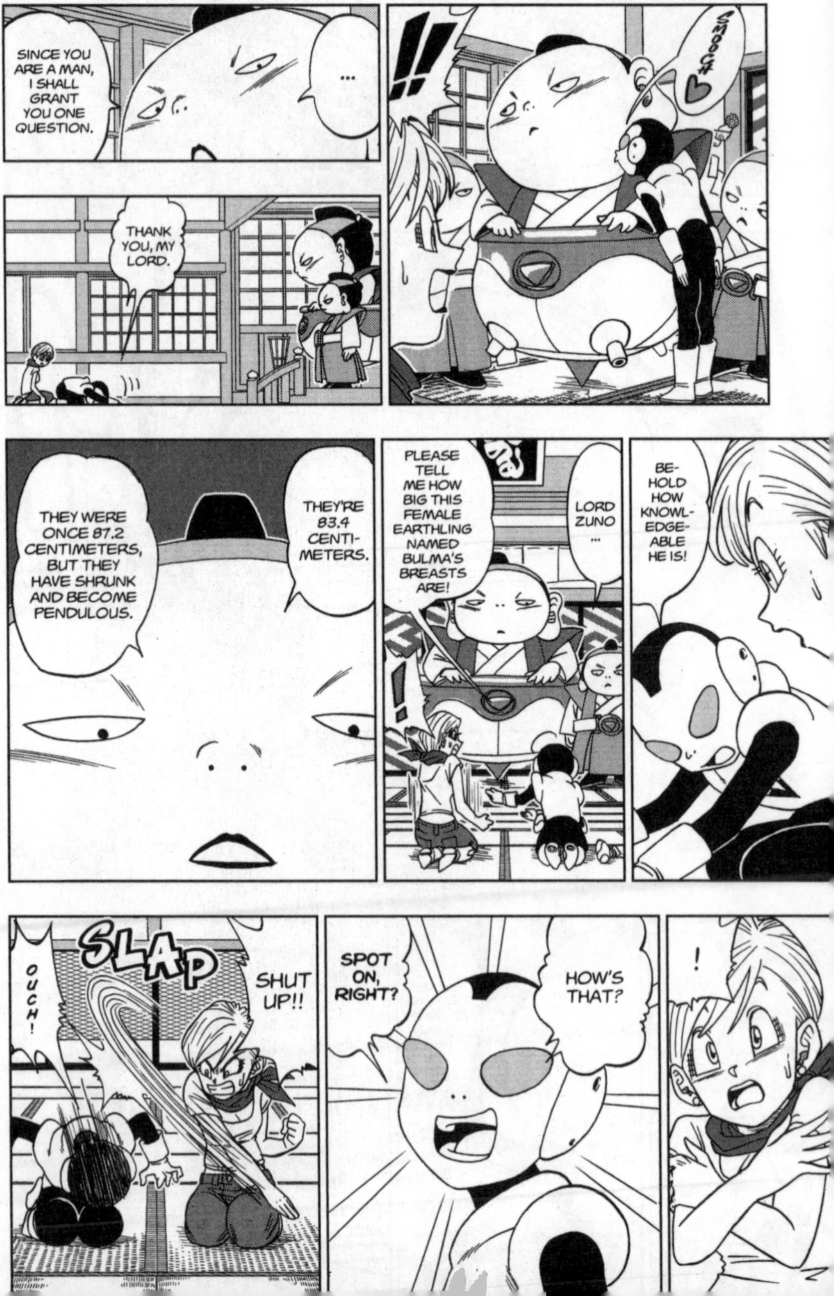
!!
SMOOCH ♥
...
SINCE YOU ARE A MAN, I SHALL GRANT YOU ONE QUESTION.
THANK YOU, MY LORD.
BE-HOLD HOW KNOWL-EDGE-ABLE HE IS!
LORD ZUNO ...
PLEASE TELL ME HOW BIG THIS FEMALE EARTHLING NAMED BULMA'S BREASTS ARE!
!
THEY'RE 83.4 CENTI-METERS.
THEY WERE ONCE 87.2 CENTIMETERS, BUT THEY HAVE SHRUNK AND BECOME PENDULOUS.
!
HOW'S THAT?
SPOT ON, RIGHT?
SHUT UP!!
SLAP
OUCH!

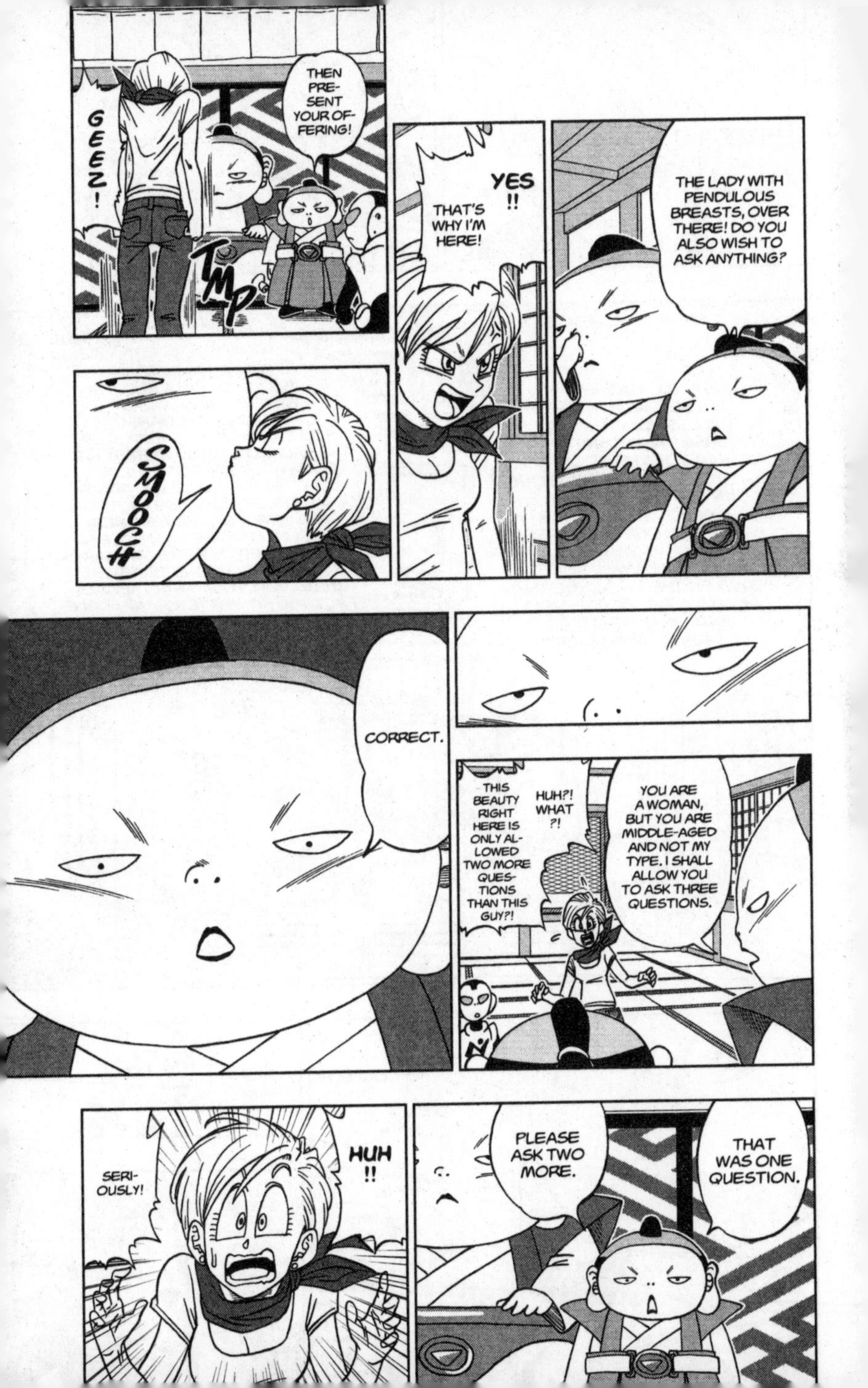
THE LADY WITH PENDULOUS BREASTS, OVER THERE! DO YOU ALSO WISH TO ASK ANYTHING?
YES!!
THAT'S WHY I'M HERE!
THEN PRE-SENT YOUR OF-FERING!
GEEZ!
TMP
SMOOCH
YOU ARE A WOMAN, BUT YOU ARE MIDDLE-AGED AND NOT MY TYPE. I SHALL ALLOW YOU TO ASK THREE QUESTIONS.
HUH?! WHAT ?!
THIS BEAUTY RIGHT HERE IS ONLY AL-LOWED TWO MORE QUES-TIONS THAN THIS GUY?!
CORRECT.
THAT WAS ONE QUESTION.
PLEASE ASK TWO MORE.
HUH!!
SERI-OUSLY!

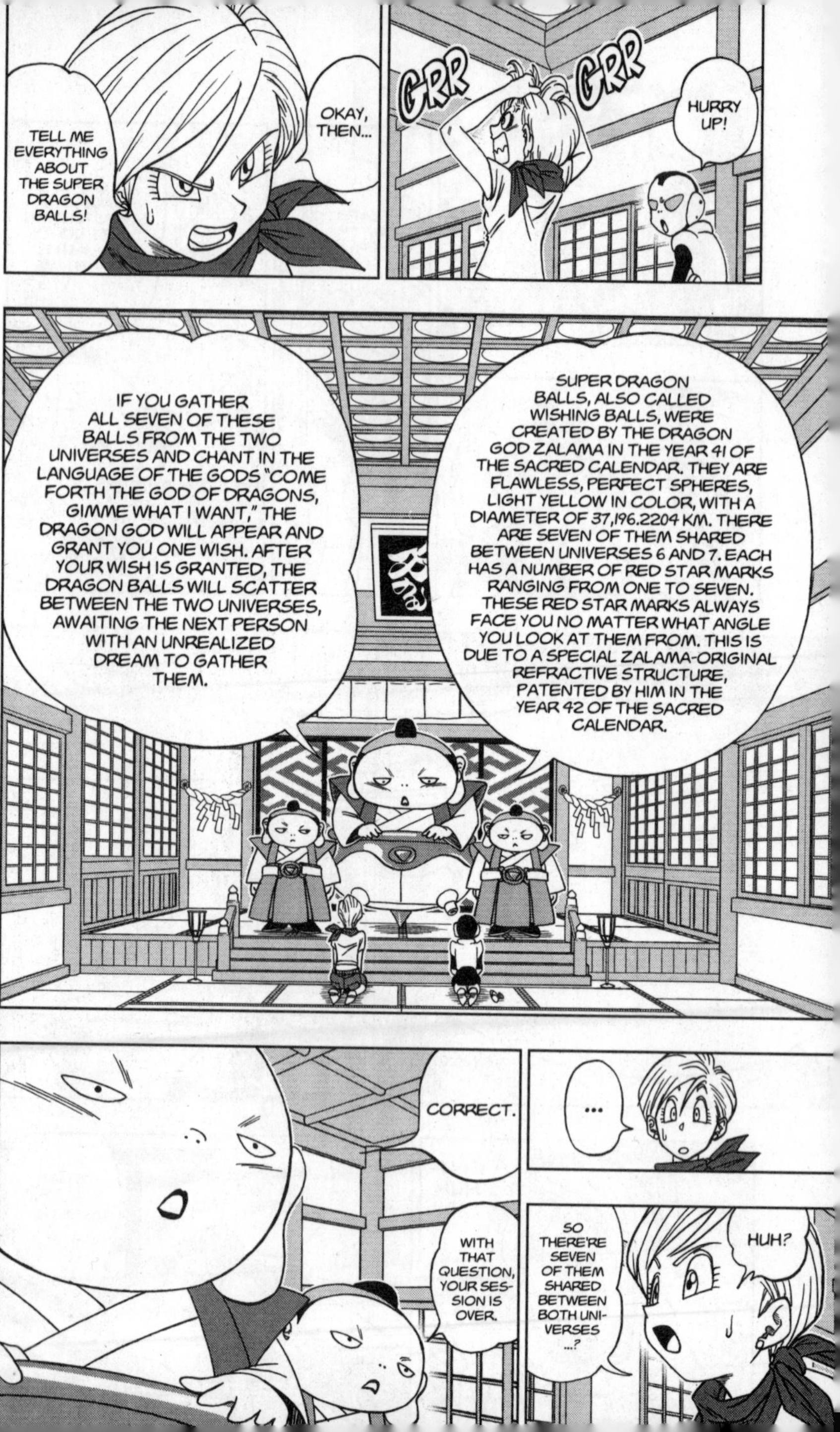
GRR GRR
HURRY UP!
OKAY, THEN...
TELL ME EVERYTHING ABOUT THE SUPER DRAGON BALLS!
SUPER DRAGON BALLS, ALSO CALLED WISHING BALLS, WERE CREATED BY THE DRAGON GOD ZALAMA IN THE YEAR 41 OF THE SACRED CALENDAR. THEY ARE FLAWLESS, PERFECT SPHERES, LIGHT YELLOW IN COLOR, WITH A DIAMETER OF 37,196.2204 KM. THERE ARE SEVEN OF THEM SHARED BETWEEN UNIVERSES 6 AND 7. EACH HAS A NUMBER OF RED STAR MARKS RANGING FROM ONE TO SEVEN. THESE RED STAR MARKS ALWAYS FACE YOU NO MATTER WHAT ANGLE YOU LOOK AT THEM FROM. THIS IS DUE TO A SPECIAL ZALAMA-ORIGINAL REFRACTIVE STRUCTURE, PATENTED BY HIM IN THE YEAR 42 OF THE SACRED CALENDAR.
IF YOU GATHER ALL SEVEN OF THESE BALLS FROM THE TWO UNIVERSES AND CHANT IN THE LANGUAGE OF THE GODS "COME FORTH THE GOD OF DRAGONS, GIMME WHAT I WANT," THE DRAGON GOD WILL APPEAR AND GRANT YOU ONE WISH. AFTER YOUR WISH IS GRANTED, THE DRAGON BALLS WILL SCATTER BETWEEN THE TWO UNIVERSES, AWAITING THE NEXT PERSON WITH AN UNREALIZED DREAM TO GATHER THEM.
CORRECT.
...
SO THERE'RE SEVEN OF THEM SHARED BETWEEN BOTH UNIVERSES ...?
WITH THAT QUESTION, YOUR SESSION IS OVER.
HUH?

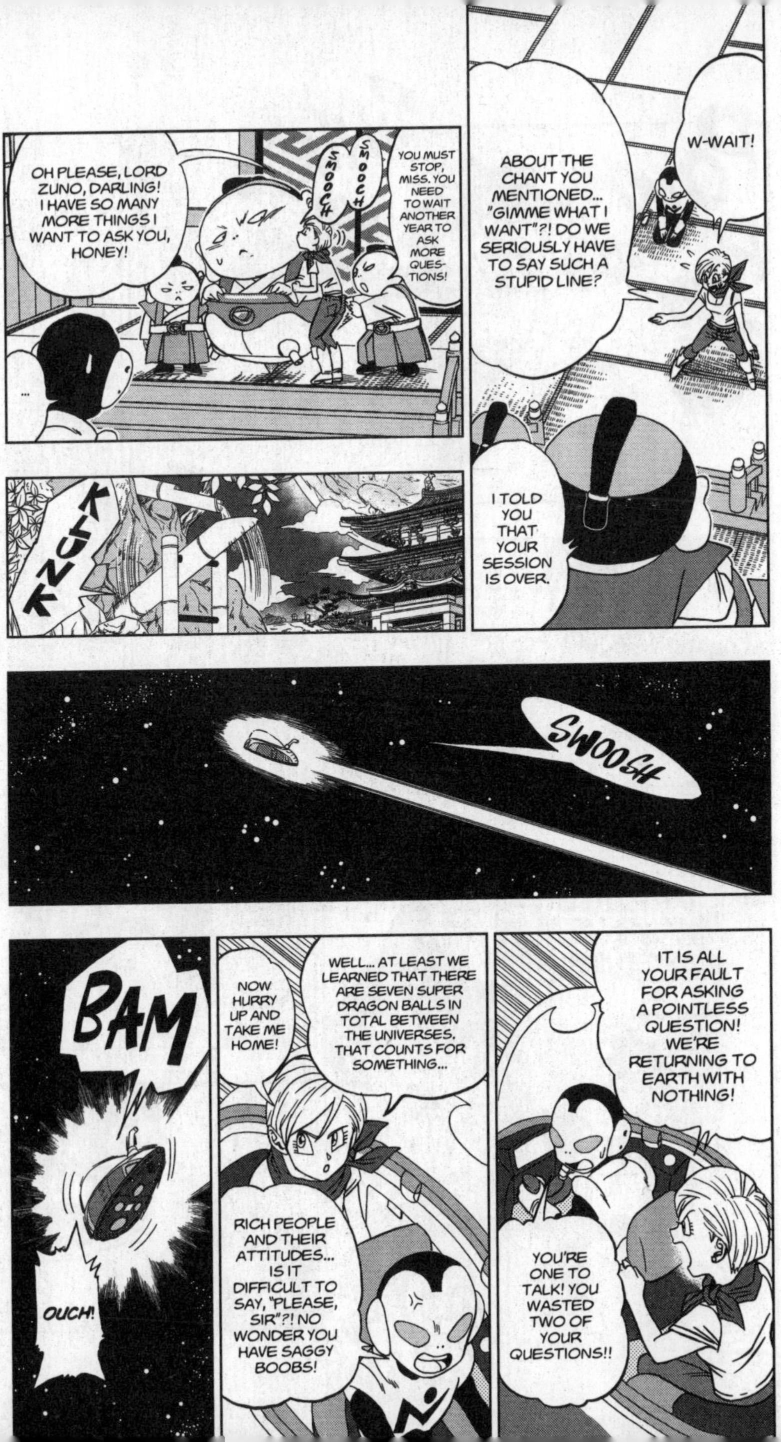
W-WAIT!
ABOUT THE CHANT YOU MENTIONED... "GIMME WHAT I WANT"?! DO WE SERIOUSLY HAVE TO SAY SUCH A STUPID LINE?
I TOLD YOU THAT YOUR SESSION IS OVER.
YOU MUST STOP, MISS. YOU NEED TO WAIT ANOTHER YEAR TO ASK MORE QUES-TIONS!
SMOOCH
SMOOCH
OH PLEASE, LORD ZUNO, DARLING! I HAVE SO MANY MORE THINGS I WANT TO ASK YOU, HONEY!
...
KLUNK
SWOOSH
IT IS ALL YOUR FAULT FOR ASKING A POINTLESS QUESTION! WE'RE RETURNING TO EARTH WITH NOTHING!
YOU'RE ONE TO TALK! YOU WASTED TWO OF YOUR QUESTIONS!!
WELL... AT LEAST WE LEARNED THAT THERE ARE SEVEN SUPER DRAGON BALLS IN TOTAL BETWEEN THE UNIVERSES. THAT COUNTS FOR SOMETHING...
NOW HURRY UP AND TAKE ME HOME!
RICH PEOPLE AND THEIR ATTITUDES... IS IT DIFFICULT TO SAY, "PLEASE, SIR"?! NO WONDER YOU HAVE SAGGY BOOBS!
BAM
OUCH!

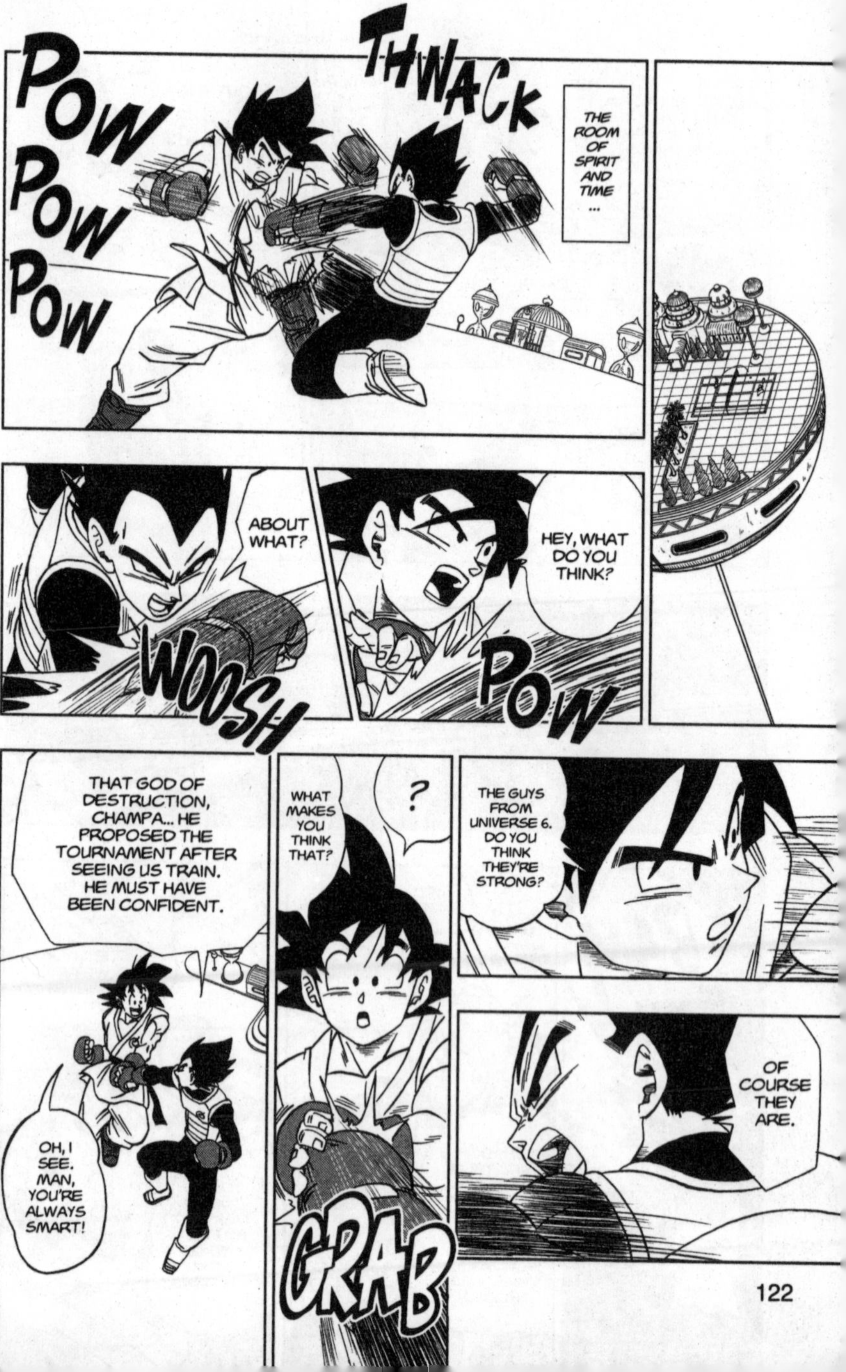
THE ROOM OF SPIRIT AND TIME...
THWACK
POW POW POW
HEY, WHAT DO YOU THINK?
POW
ABOUT WHAT?
WOOSH
THE GUYS FROM UNIVERSE 6. DO YOU THINK THEY'RE STRONG?
OF COURSE THEY ARE.
?
WHAT MAKES YOU THINK THAT?
GRAB
THAT GOD OF DESTRUCTION, CHAMPA... HE PROPOSED THE TOURNAMENT AFTER SEEING US TRAIN. HE MUST HAVE BEEN CONFIDENT.
OH, I SEE. MAN, YOU'RE ALWAYS SMART!

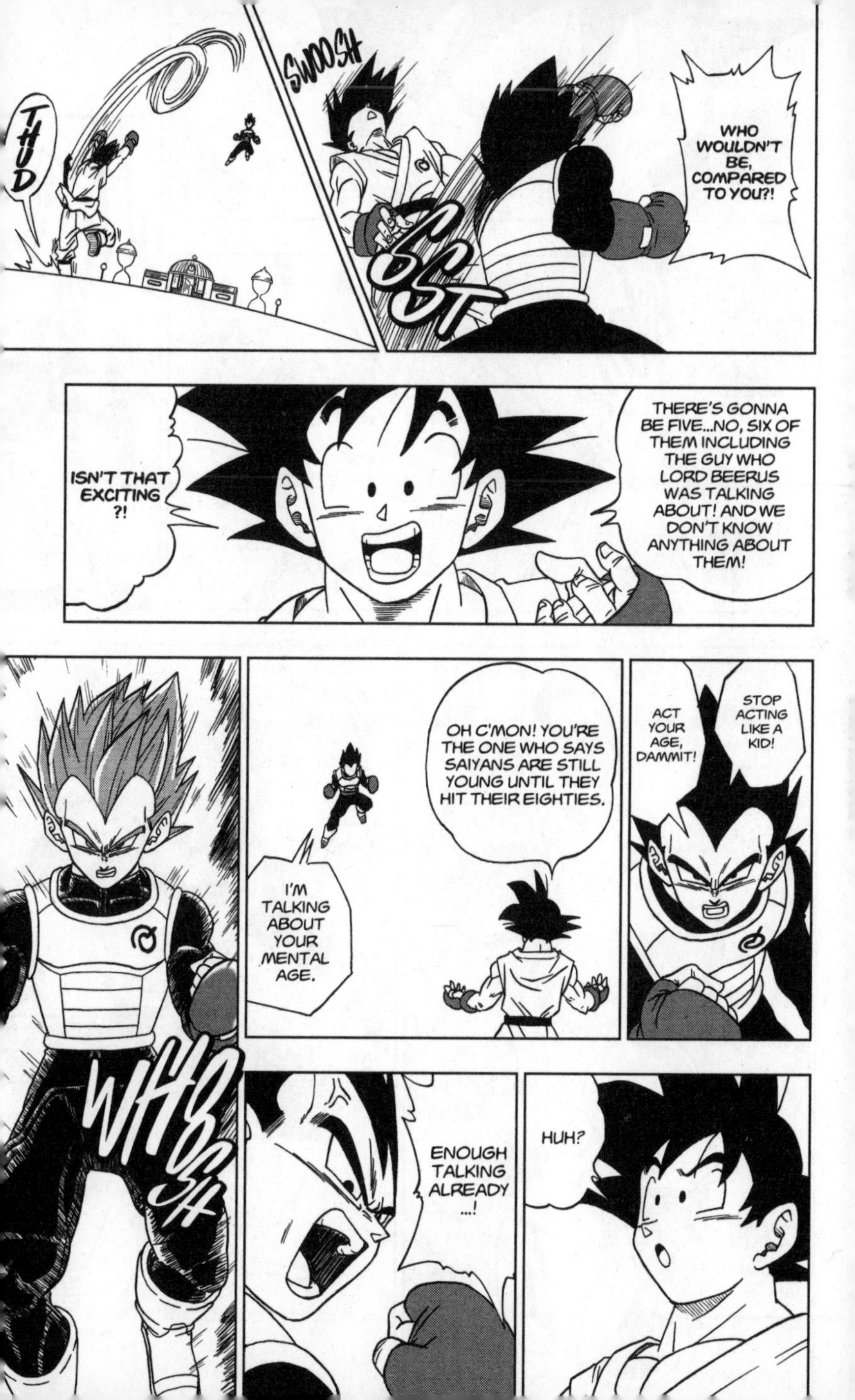
WHO WOULDN'T BE, COMPARED TO YOU?!
SWOOSH
THUD
THERE'S GONNA BE FIVE...NO, SIX OF THEM INCLUDING THE GUY WHO LORD BEERUS WAS TALKING ABOUT! AND WE DON'T KNOW ANYTHING ABOUT THEM!
ISN'T THAT EXCITING ?!
STOP ACTING LIKE A KID!
ACT YOUR AGE, DAMMIT!
OH C'MON! YOU'RE THE ONE WHO SAYS SAIYANS ARE STILL YOUNG UNTIL THEY HIT THEIR EIGHTIES.
I'M TALKING ABOUT YOUR MENTAL AGE.
HUH?
ENOUGH TALKING ALREADY ...!
WHOOSH

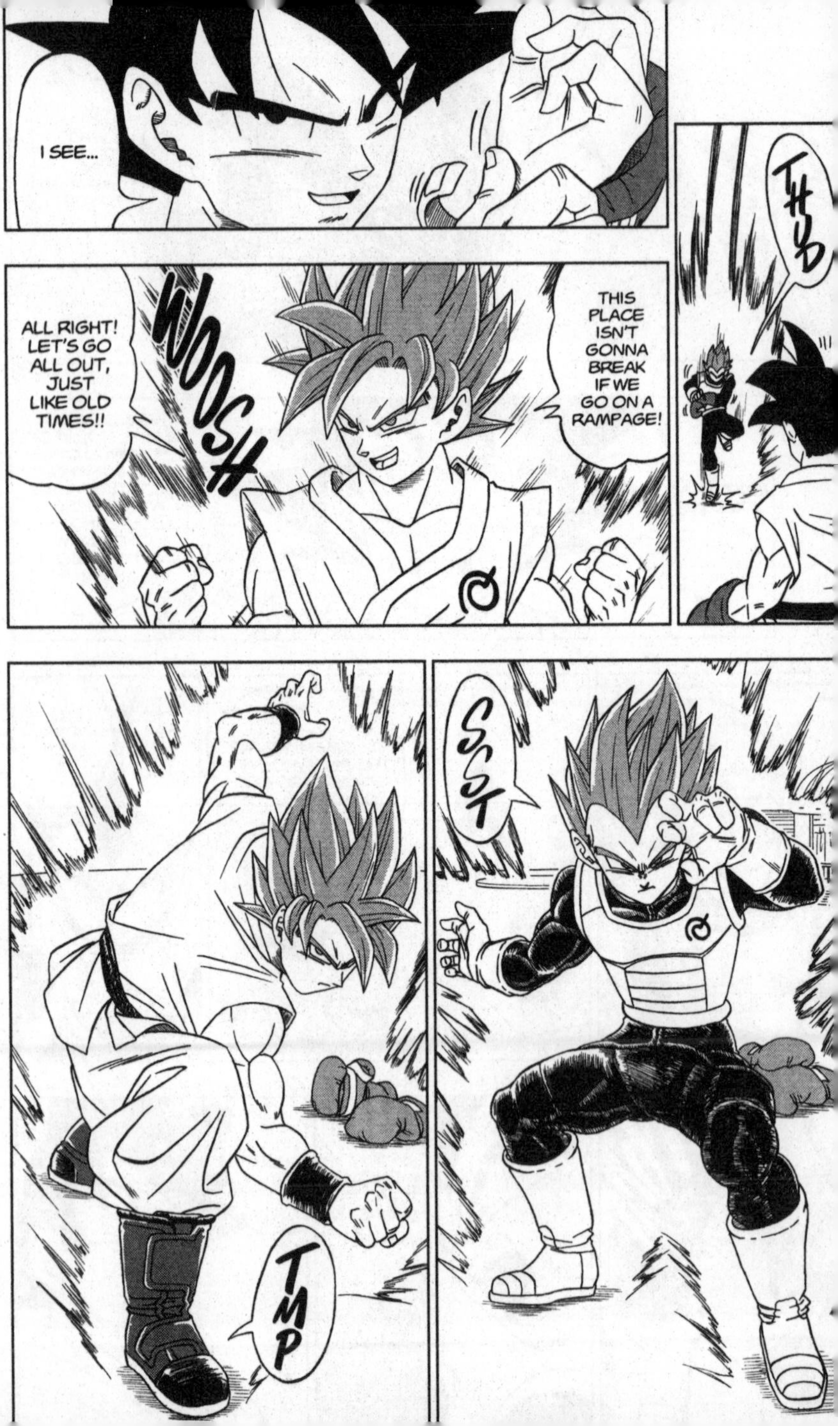
THUD
I SEE...
THIS PLACE ISN'T GONNA BREAK IF WE GO ON A RAMPAGE!
WOOSH
ALL RIGHT! LET'S GO ALL OUT, JUST LIKE OLD TIMES!!
SSSK
TMP

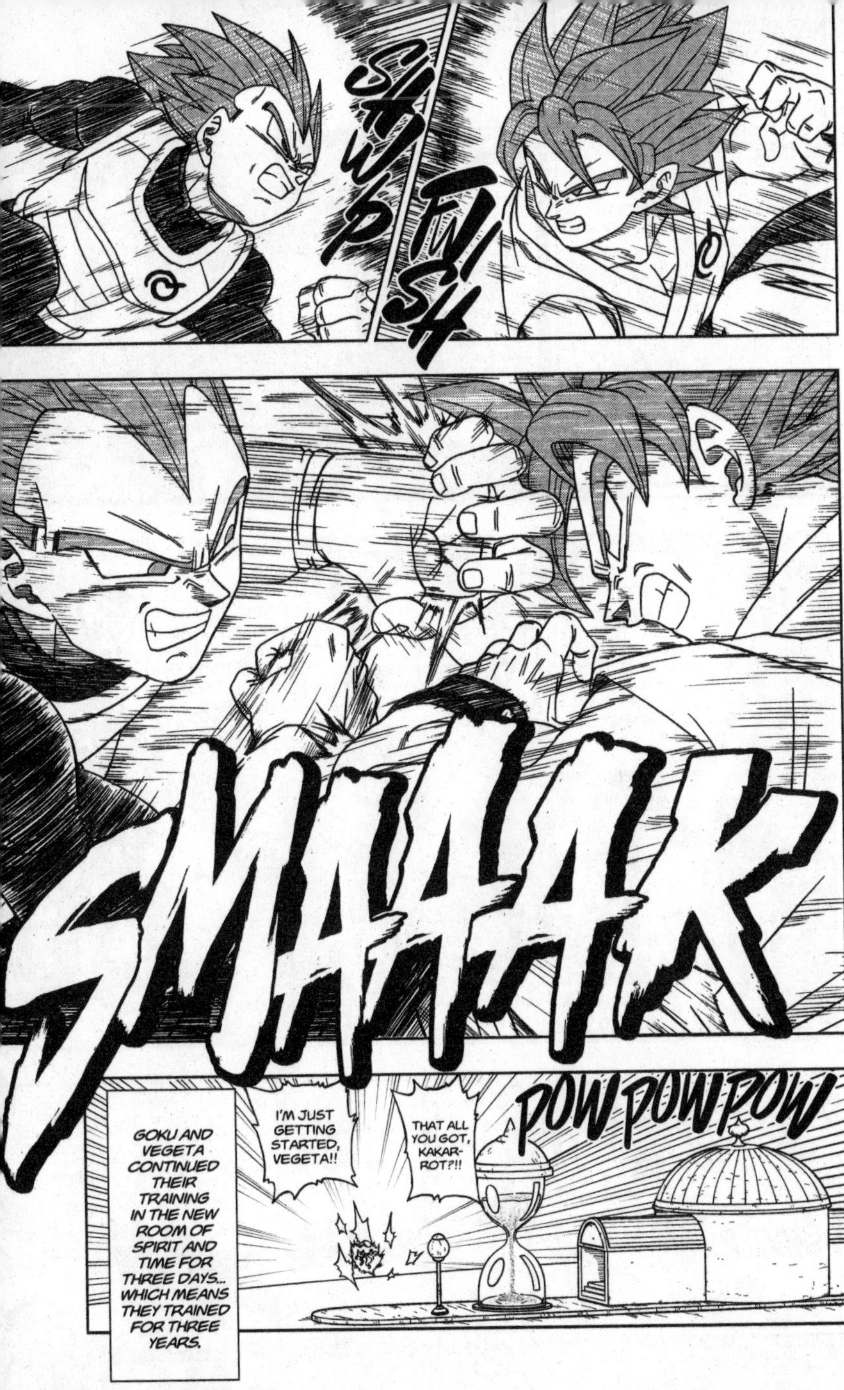
FWISH
SHWOOP
SMAAAK
POW POW POW
THAT ALL YOU GOT, KAKAR-ROT?!!
I'M JUST GETTING STARTED, VEGETA!!
GOKU AND VEGETA CONTINUED THEIR TRAINING IN THE NEW ROOM OF SPIRIT AND TIME FOR THREE DAYS... WHICH MEANS THEY TRAINED FOR THREE YEARS.

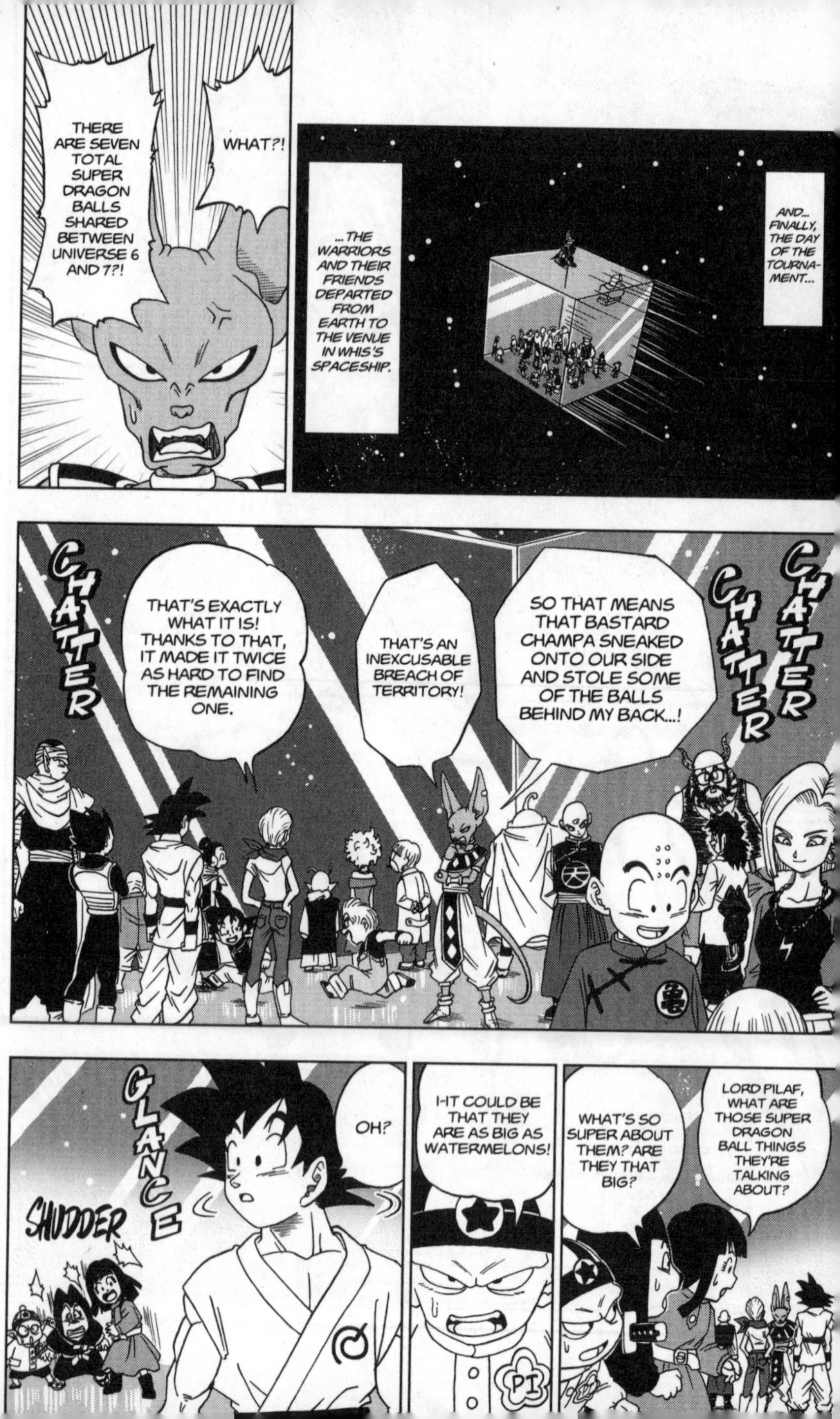
AND... FINALLY, THE DAY OF THE TOURNAMENT...
...THE WARRIORS AND THEIR FRIENDS DEPARTED FROM EARTH TO THE VENUE IN WHIS'S SPACESHIP.
WHAT?!
THERE ARE SEVEN TOTAL SUPER DRAGON BALLS SHARED BETWEEN UNIVERSE 6 AND 7?!
CHATTER CHATTER
SO THAT MEANS THAT BASTARD CHAMPA SNEAKED ONTO OUR SIDE AND STOLE SOME OF THE BALLS BEHIND MY BACK...!
THAT'S AN INEXCUSABLE BREACH OF TERRITORY!
THAT'S EXACTLY WHAT IT IS! THANKS TO THAT, IT MADE IT TWICE AS HARD TO FIND THE REMAINING ONE.
CHATTER
LORD PILAF, WHAT ARE THOSE SUPER DRAGON BALL THINGS THEY'RE TALKING ABOUT?
WHAT'S SO SUPER ABOUT THEM? ARE THEY THAT BIG?
I-IT COULD BE THAT THEY ARE AS BIG AS WATERMELONS!
PI
OH?
GLANCE
SHUDDER

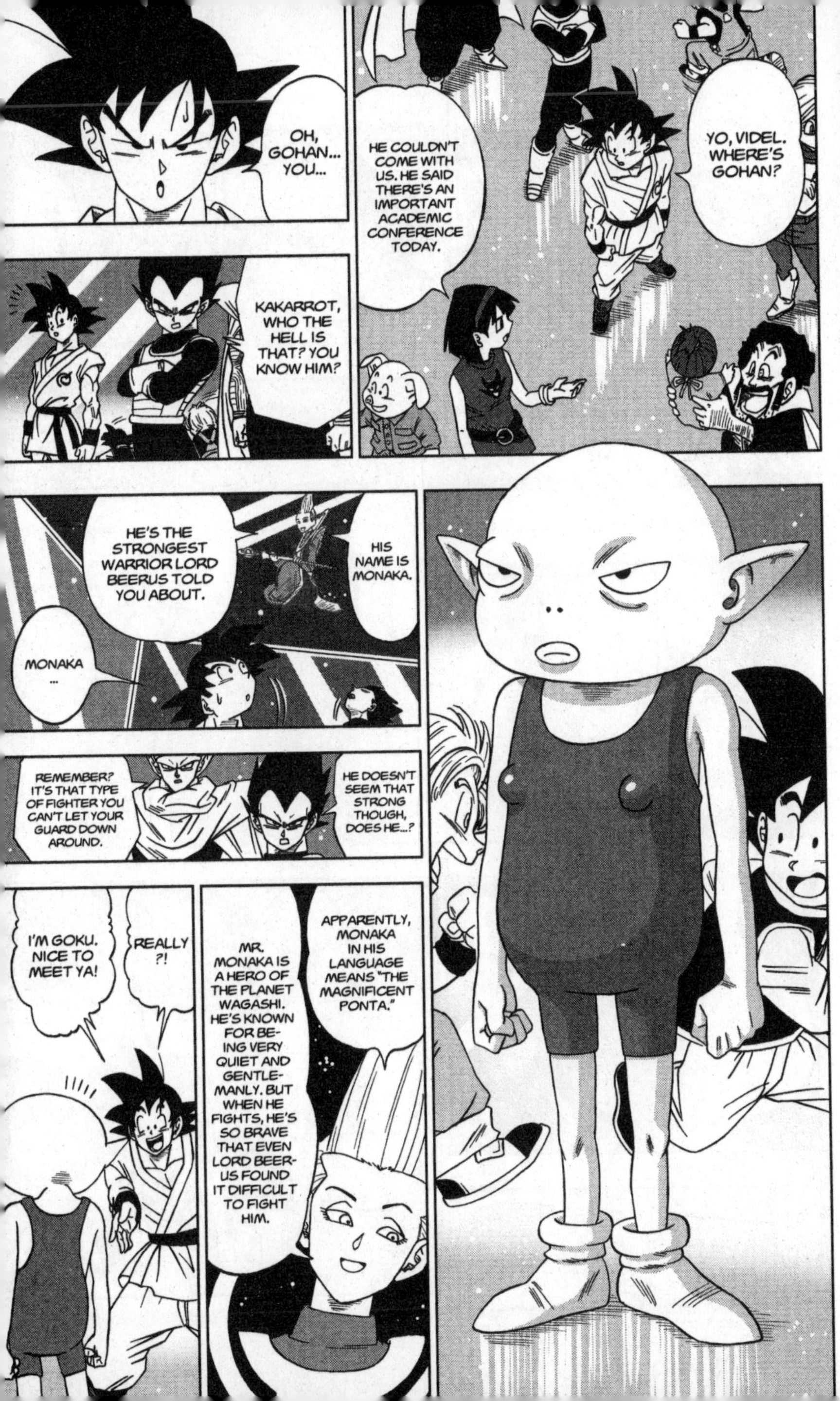
YO, VIDEL. WHERE'S GOHAN?
HE COULDN'T COME WITH US. HE SAID THERE'S AN IMPORTANT ACADEMIC CONFERENCE TODAY.
OH, GOHAN... YOU...
KAKARROT, WHO THE HELL IS THAT? YOU KNOW HIM?
HIS NAME IS MONAKA.
HE'S THE STRONGEST WARRIOR LORD BEERUS TOLD YOU ABOUT.
MONAKA ...
HE DOESN'T SEEM THAT STRONG THOUGH, DOES HE...?
REMEMBER? IT'S THAT TYPE OF FIGHTER YOU CAN'T LET YOUR GUARD DOWN AROUND.
APPARENTLY, MONAKA IN HIS LANGUAGE MEANS "THE MAGNIFICENT PONTA."
MR. MONAKA IS A HERO OF THE PLANET WAGASHI. HE'S KNOWN FOR BE-ING VERY QUIET AND GENTLE-MANLY. BUT WHEN HE FIGHTS, HE'S SO BRAVE THAT EVEN LORD BEER-US FOUND IT DIFFICULT TO FIGHT HIM.
REALLY ?!
I'M GOKU. NICE TO MEET YA!

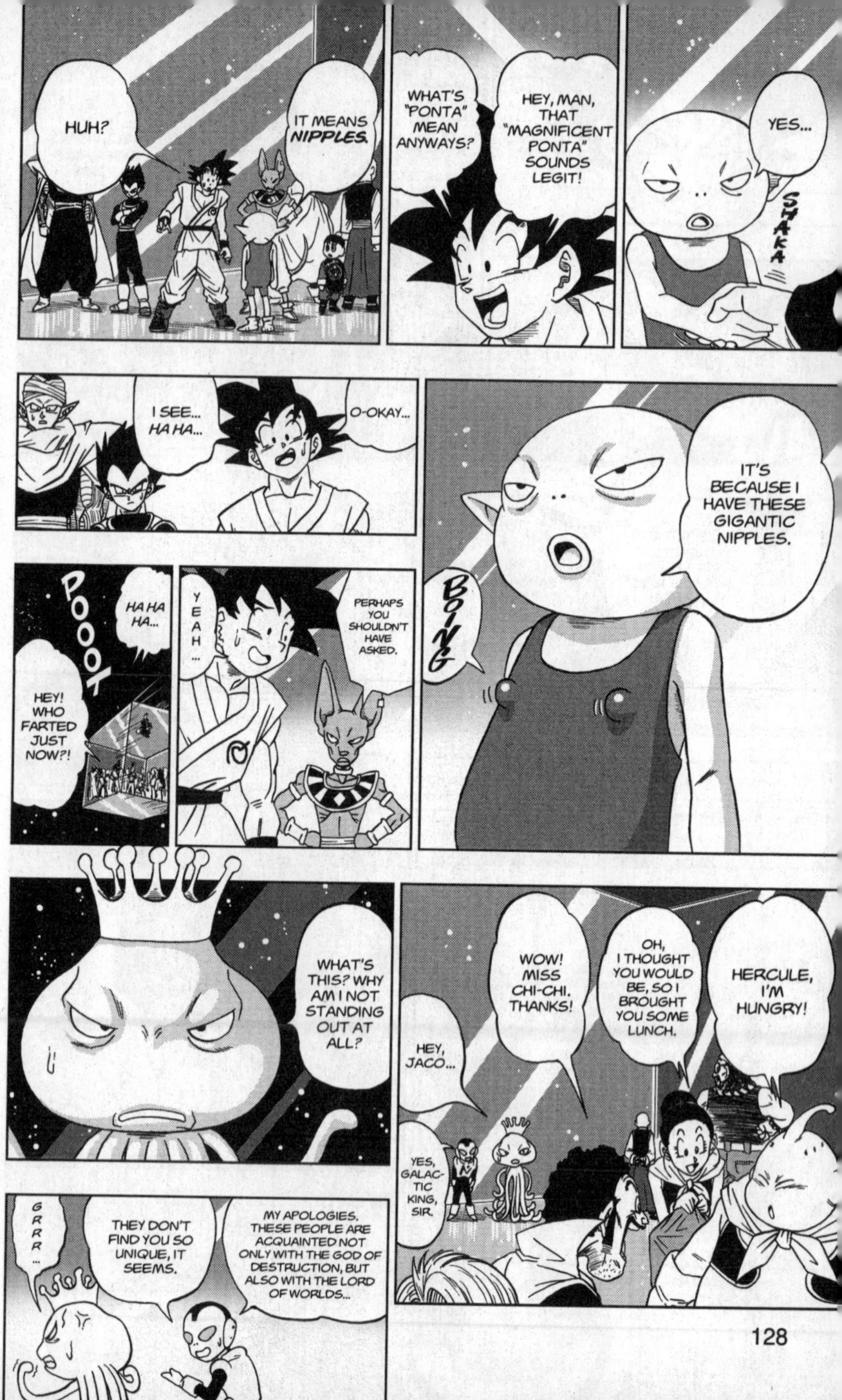

YES...
SHAKA
HEY, MAN, THAT "MAGNIFICENT PONTA" SOUNDS LEGIT!
WHAT'S "PONTA" MEAN ANYWAYS?
IT MEANS NIPPLES.
HUH?
IT'S BECAUSE I HAVE THESE GIGANTIC NIPPLES.
BOING
O-OKAY...
I SEE... HA HA...
PERHAPS YOU SHOULDN'T HAVE ASKED.
YEAH...
HA HA HA...
POOOK
HEY! WHO FARTED JUST NOW?!
HERCULE, I'M HUNGRY!
OH, I THOUGHT YOU WOULD BE, SO I BROUGHT YOU SOME LUNCH.
WOW! MISS CHI-CHI. THANKS!
HEY, JACO...
YES, GALACTIC KING, SIR.
WHAT'S THIS? WHY AM I NOT STANDING OUT AT ALL?
MY APOLOGIES. THESE PEOPLE ARE ACQUAINTED NOT ONLY WITH THE GOD OF DESTRUCTION, BUT ALSO WITH THE LORD OF WORLDS...
THEY DON'T FIND YOU SO UNIQUE, IT SEEMS.
GRRR...

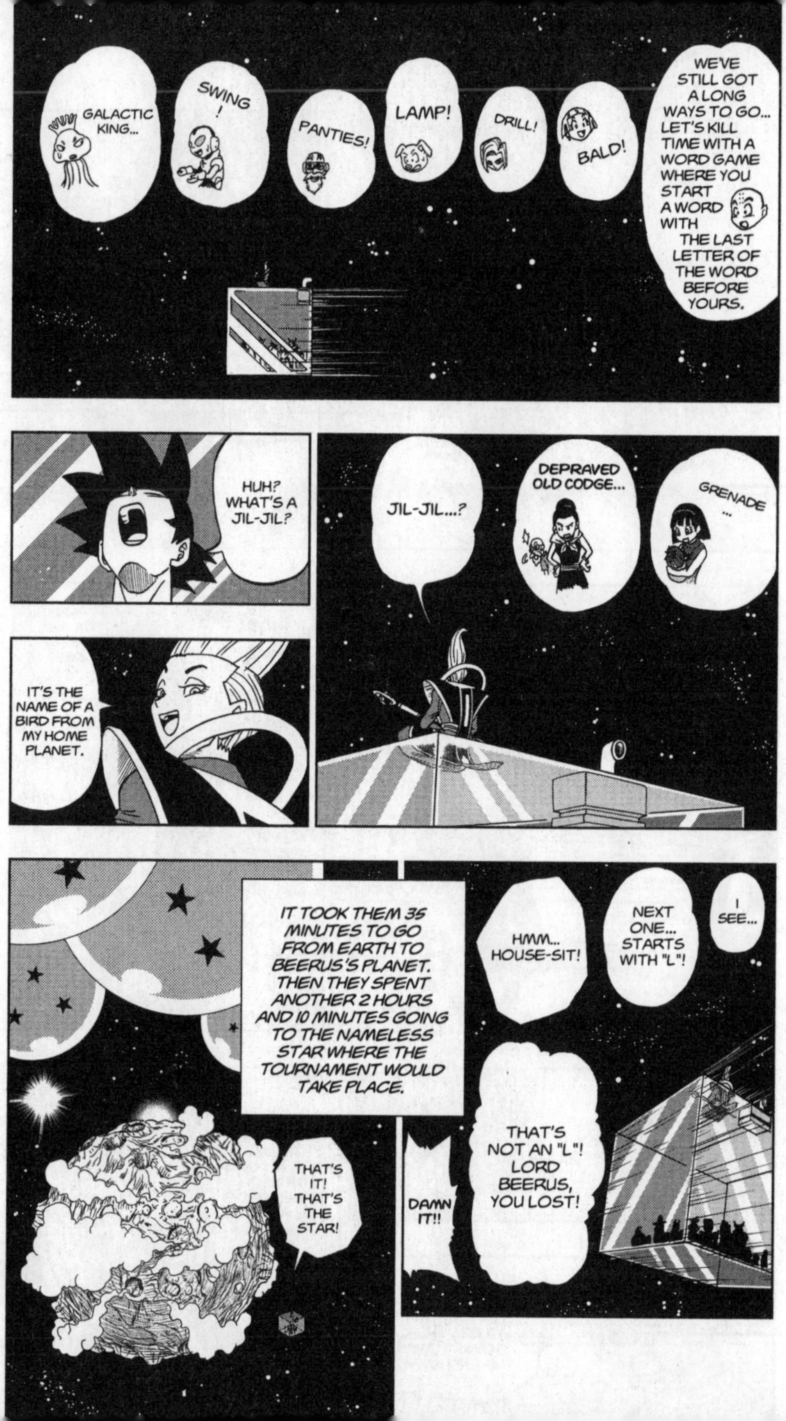

WE'VE STILL GOT A LONG WAYS TO GO... LET'S KILL TIME WITH A WORD GAME WHERE YOU START A WORD WITH THE LAST LETTER OF THE WORD BEFORE YOURS.
BALD!
DRILL!
LAMP!
PANTIES!
SWING!
GALACTIC KING...
GRENADE...
DEPRAVED OLD CODGE...
JIL-JIL...?
HUH? WHAT'S A JIL-JIL?
IT'S THE NAME OF A BIRD FROM MY HOME PLANET.
I SEE...
NEXT ONE... STARTS WITH "L"!
HMM... HOUSE-SIT!
THAT'S NOT AN "L"! LORD BEERUS, YOU LOST!
DAMN IT!!
IT TOOK THEM 35 MINUTES TO GO FROM EARTH TO BEERUS'S PLANET. THEN THEY SPENT ANOTHER 2 HOURS AND 10 MINUTES GOING TO THE NAMELESS STAR WHERE THE TOURNAMENT WOULD TAKE PLACE.
THAT'S IT! THAT'S THE STAR!

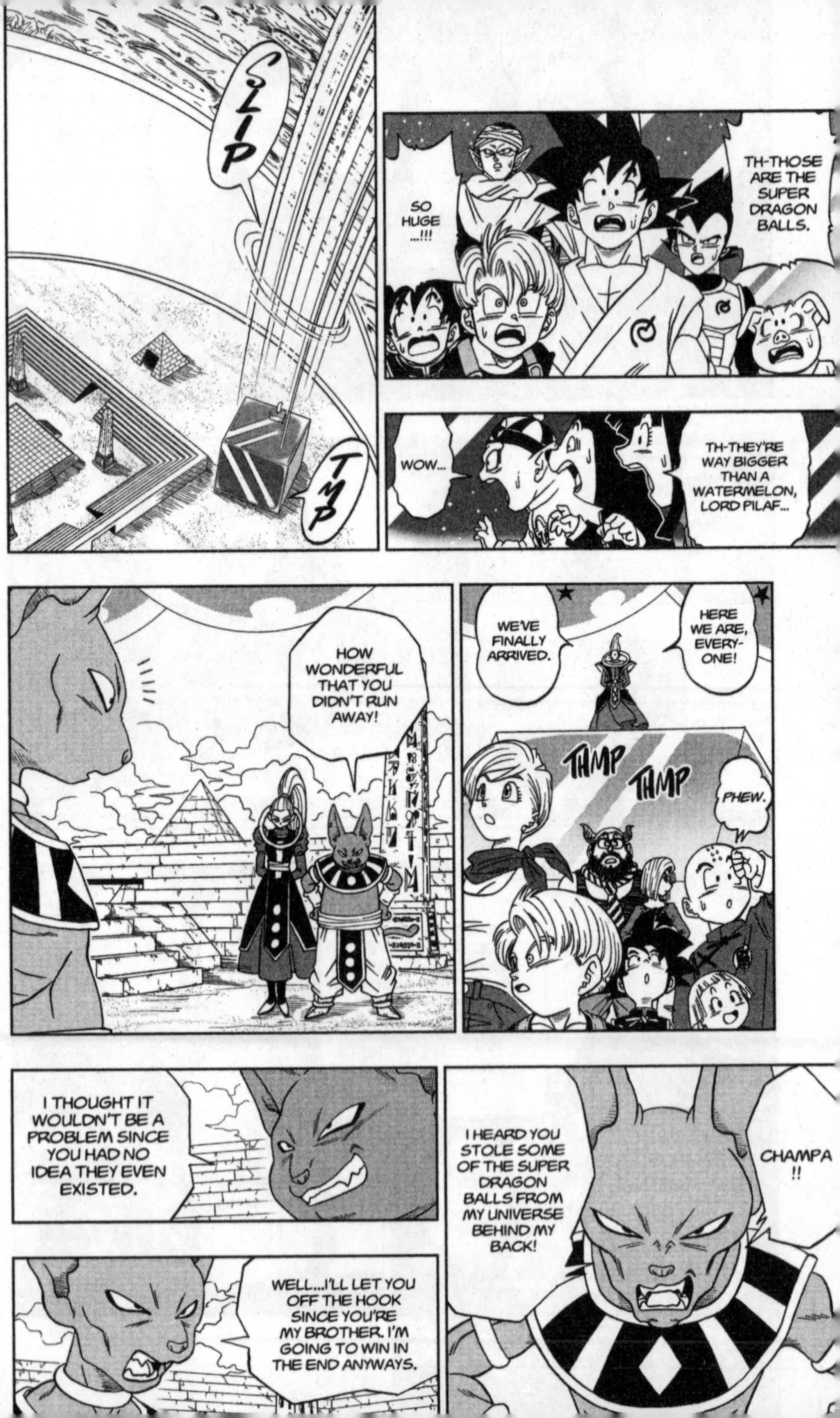
TH-THOSE ARE THE SUPER DRAGON BALLS.
SO HUGE ...!!!
TH-THEY'RE WAY BIGGER THAN A WATERMELON, LORD PILAF...
WOW...
SLIP
TMP
HERE WE ARE, EVERYONE!
WE'VE FINALLY ARRIVED.
THMP
THMP
PHEW.
HOW WONDERFUL THAT YOU DIDN'T RUN AWAY!
CHAMPA!!
I HEARD YOU STOLE SOME OF THE SUPER DRAGON BALLS FROM MY UNIVERSE BEHIND MY BACK!
I THOUGHT IT WOULDN'T BE A PROBLEM SINCE YOU HAD NO IDEA THEY EVEN EXISTED.
WELL...I'LL LET YOU OFF THE HOOK SINCE YOU'RE MY BROTHER. I'M GOING TO WIN IN THE END ANYWAYS.

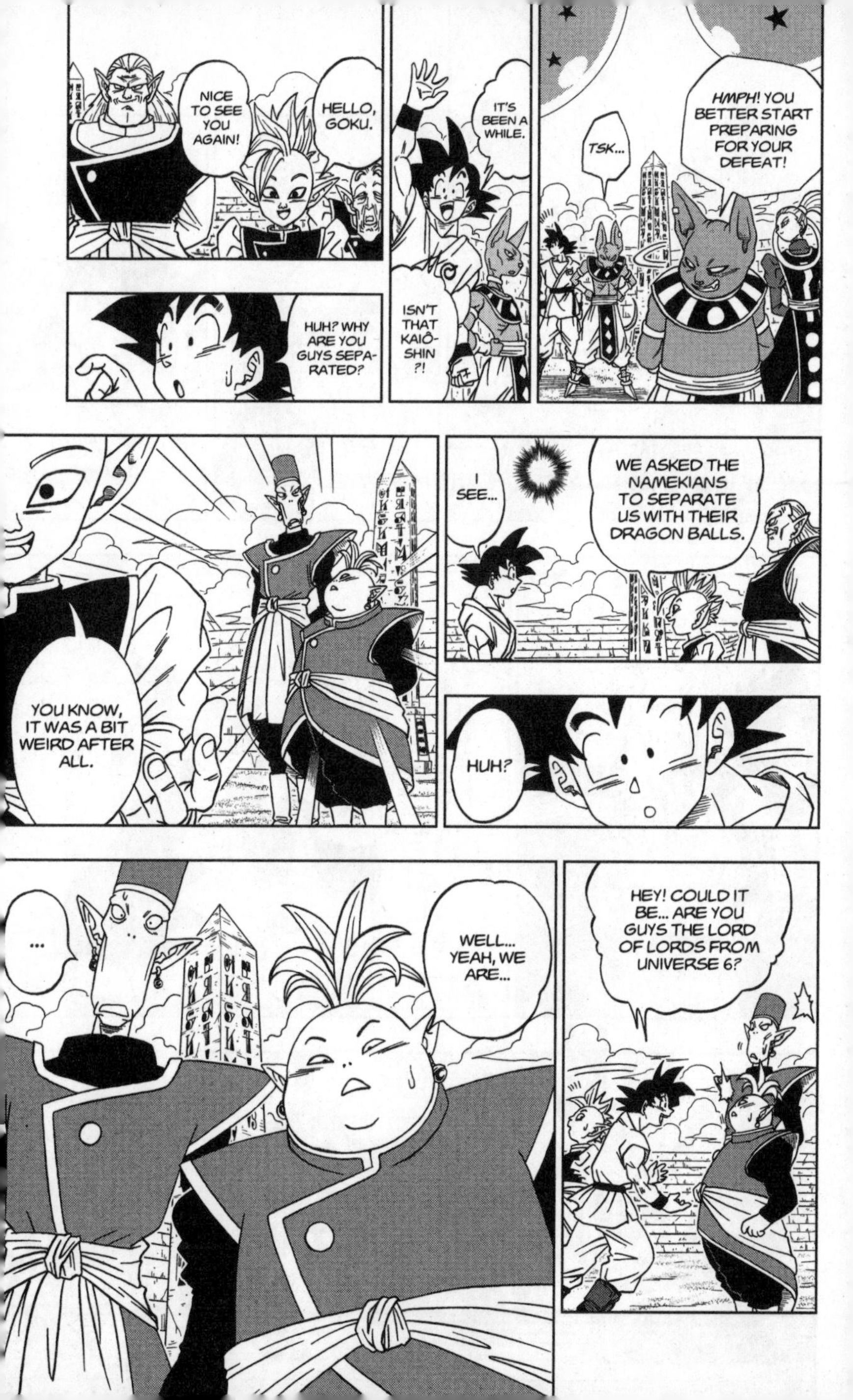
HMPH! YOU BETTER START PREPARING FOR YOUR DEFEAT!
TSK...
IT'S BEEN A WHILE.
ISN'T THAT KAIÔ-SHIN?!
HELLO, GOKU.
NICE TO SEE YOU AGAIN!
HUH? WHY ARE YOU GUYS SEPA-RATED?
WE ASKED THE NAMEKIANS TO SEPARATE US WITH THEIR DRAGON BALLS.
I SEE...
HUH?
YOU KNOW, IT WAS A BIT WEIRD AFTER ALL.
HEY! COULD IT BE... ARE YOU GUYS THE LORD OF LORDS FROM UNIVERSE 6?
WELL... YEAH, WE ARE...
...

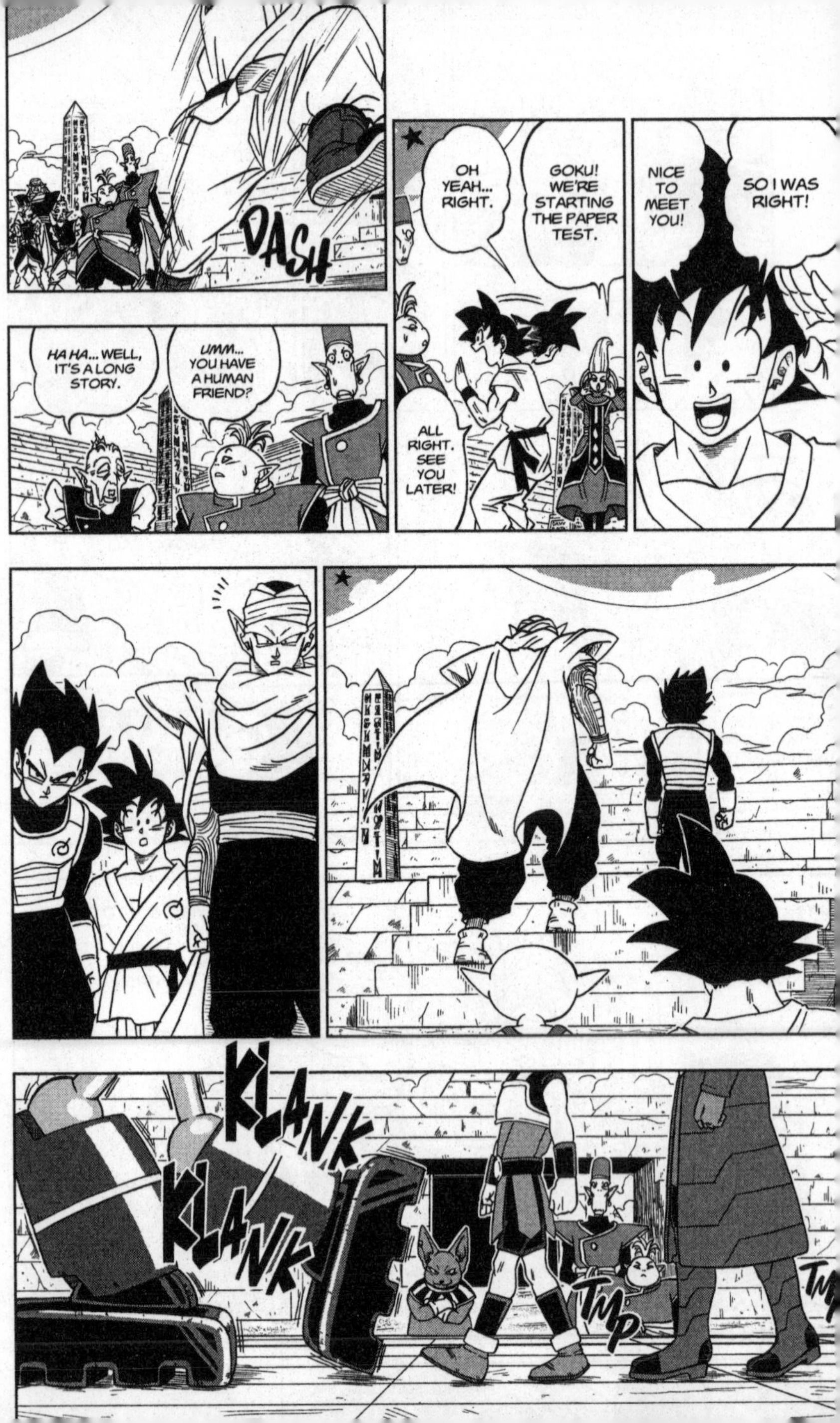
SO I WAS RIGHT!
NICE TO MEET YOU!
GOKU! WE'RE STARTING THE PAPER TEST.
OH YEAH... RIGHT.
ALL RIGHT. SEE YOU LATER!
DASH
UMM... YOU HAVE A HUMAN FRIEND?
HA HA... WELL, IT'S A LONG STORY.
KLANK
KLANK
TMP
TMP

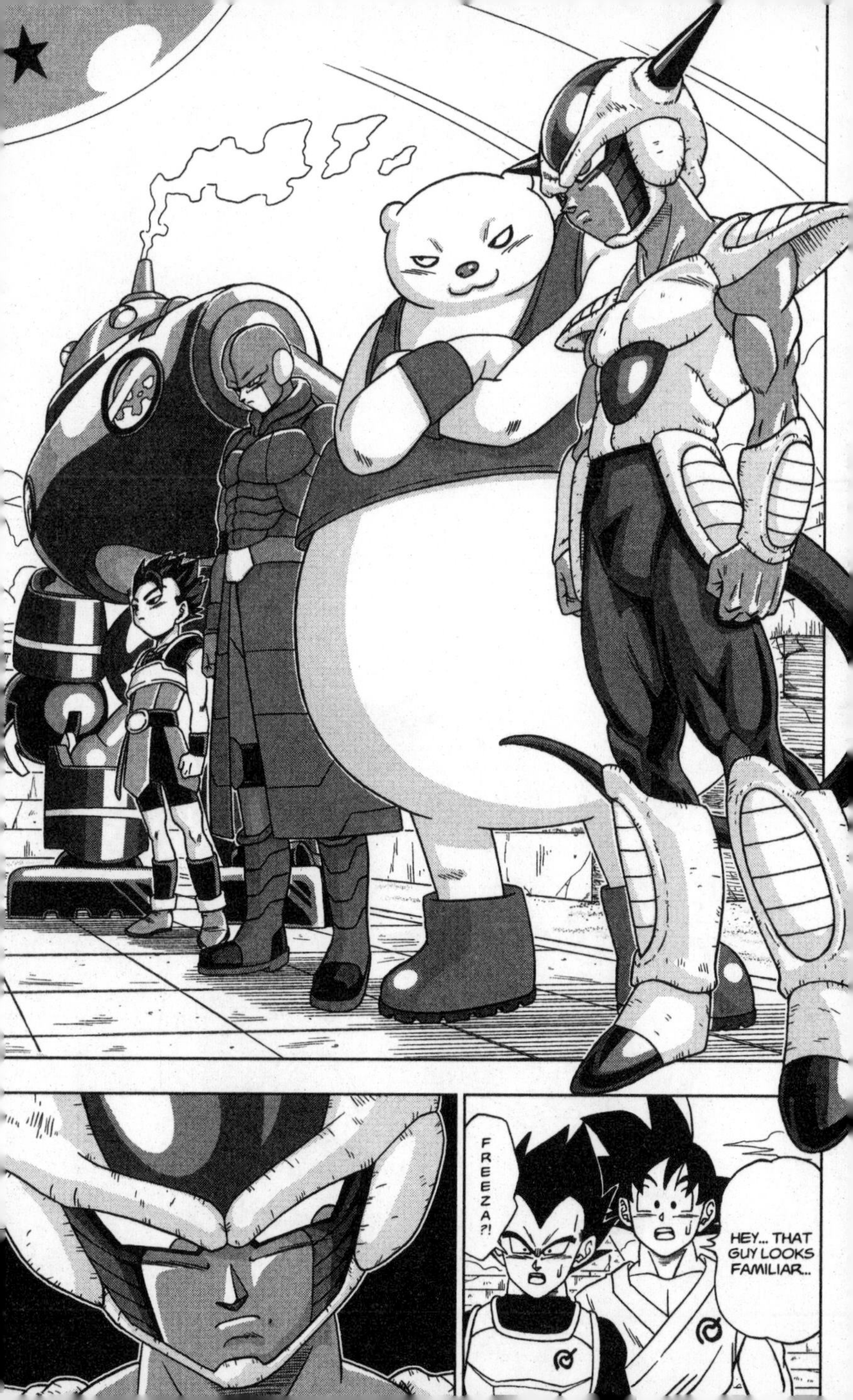
HEY... THAT GUY LOOKS FAMILIAR...
FREEZA?!

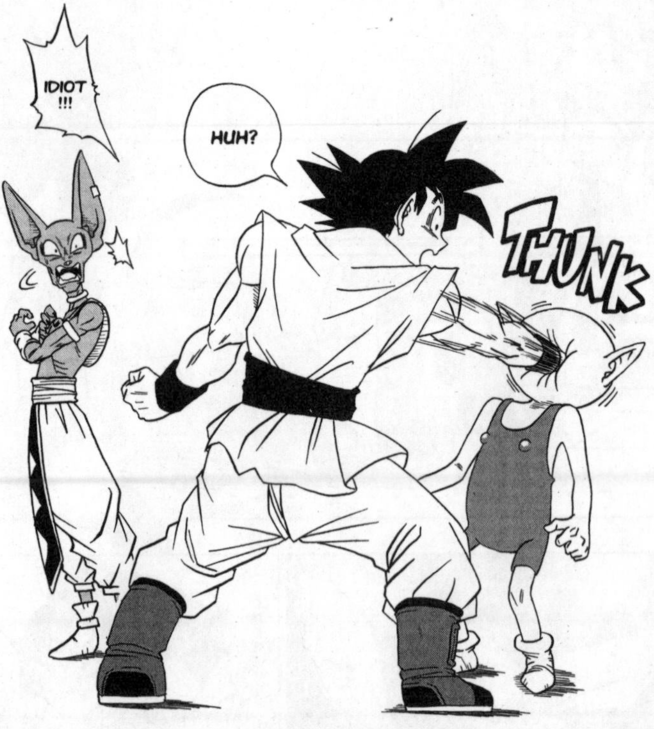
THUNK
HUH?
IDIOT !!!

DRAGON BALL SUPER

CHAPTER 8: THE BATTLE BEGINS!

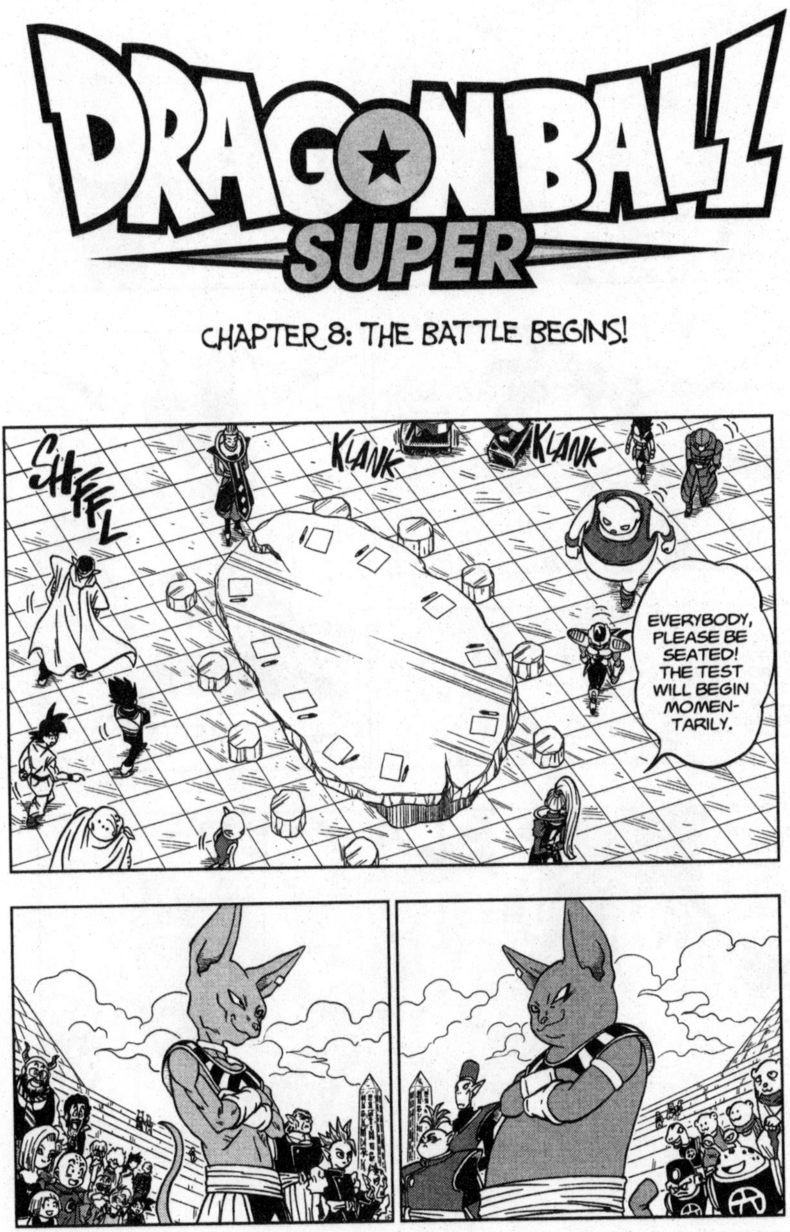
KLANK
KLANK
EVERYBODY, PLEASE BE SEATED! THE TEST WILL BEGIN MOMEN-TARILY.
SHFFL

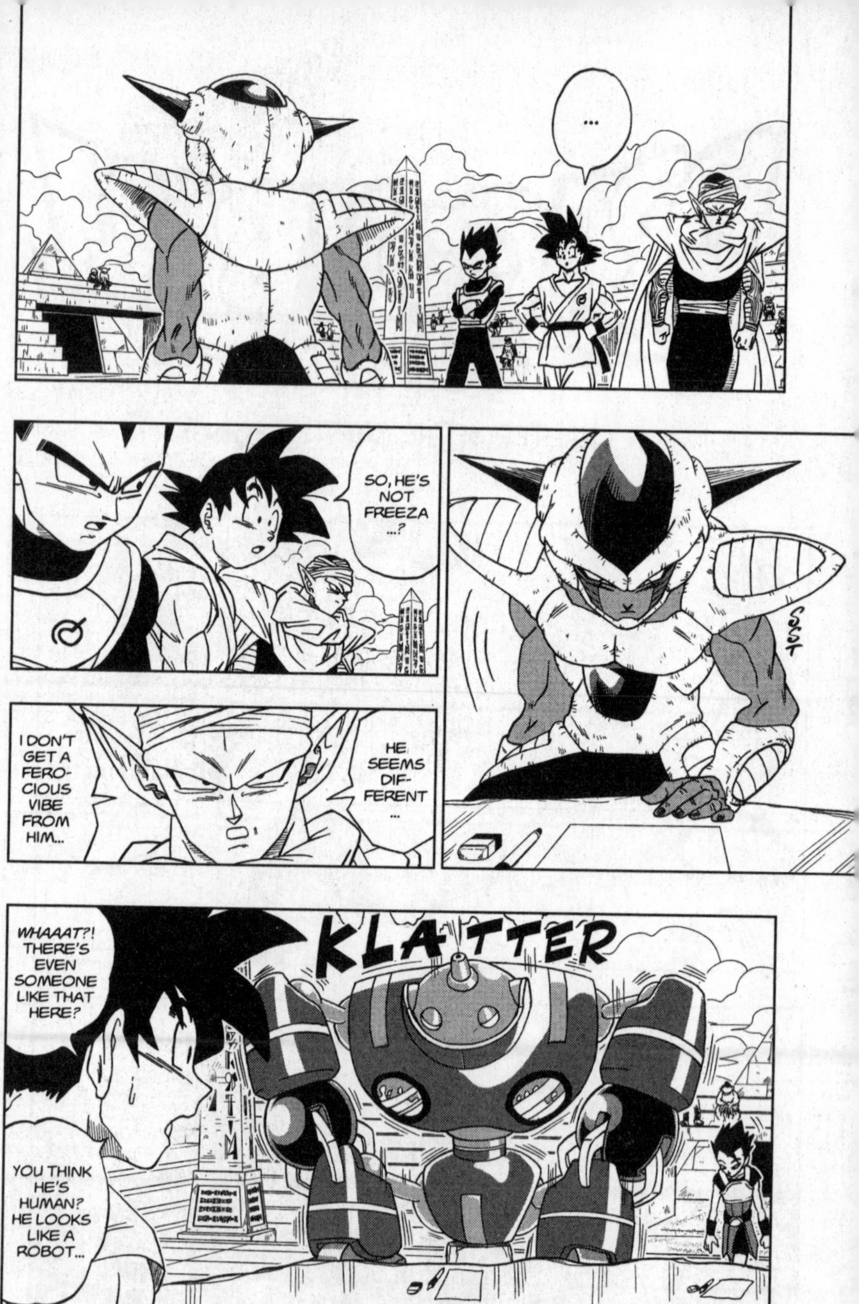
...
SSST
SO, HE'S NOT FREEZA ...?
HE SEEMS DIF-FERENT ...
I DON'T GET A FERO-CIOUS VIBE FROM HIM...
KLATTER
WHAAAT?! THERE'S EVEN SOMEONE LIKE THAT HERE?
YOU THINK HE'S HUMAN? HE LOOKS LIKE A ROBOT...

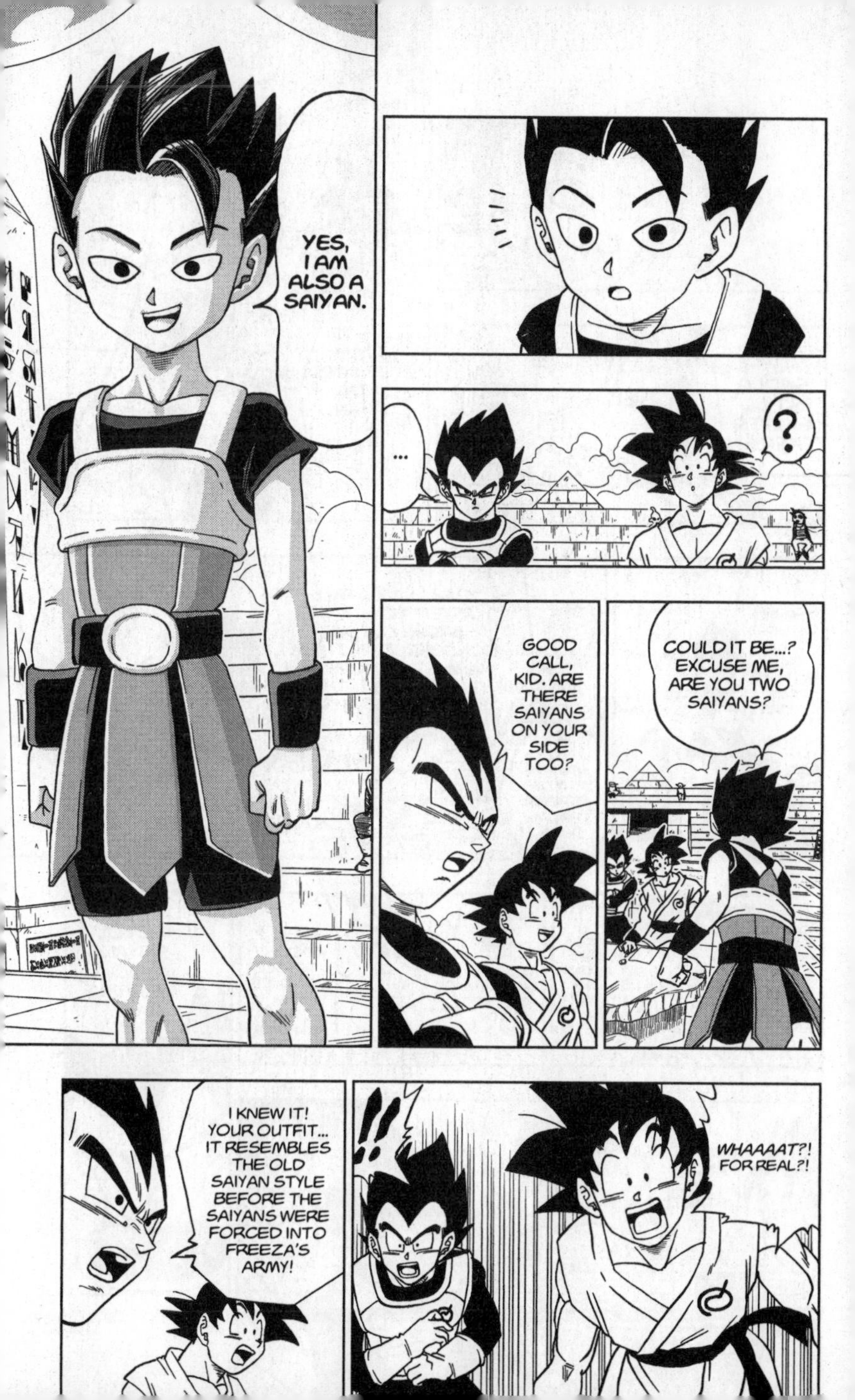
?
...
COULD IT BE...? EXCUSE ME, ARE YOU TWO SAIYANS?
GOOD CALL, KID. ARE THERE SAIYANS ON YOUR SIDE TOO?
YES, I AM ALSO A SAIYAN.
WHAAAAT?! FOR REAL?!
!!
I KNEW IT! YOUR OUTFIT... IT RESEMBLES THE OLD SAIYAN STYLE BEFORE THE SAIYANS WERE FORCED INTO FREEZA'S ARMY!

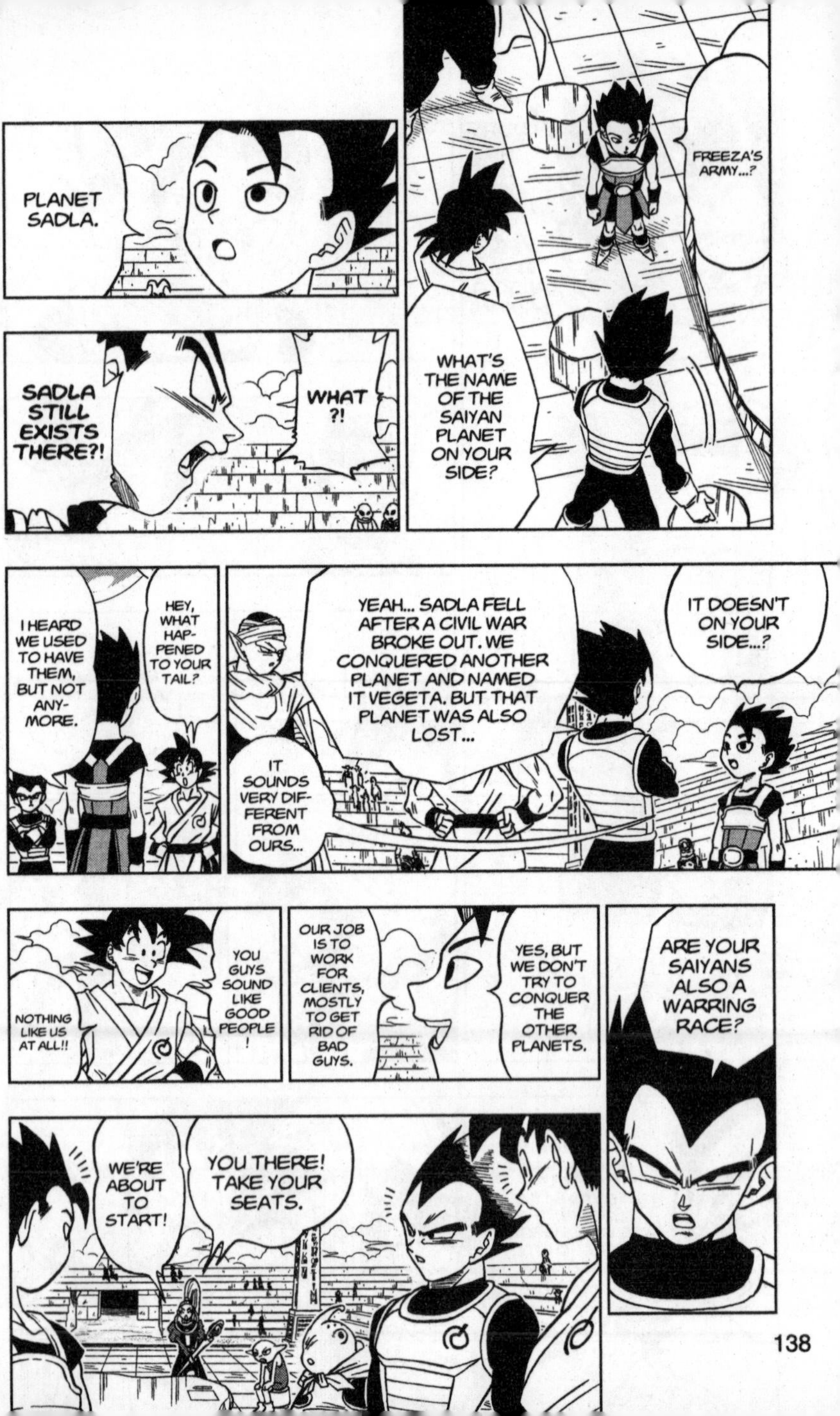
FREEZA'S ARMY...?
WHAT'S THE NAME OF THE SAIYAN PLANET ON YOUR SIDE?
PLANET SADLA.
WHAT ?!
SADLA STILL EXISTS THERE?!
IT DOESN'T ON YOUR SIDE...?
YEAH... SADLA FELL AFTER A CIVIL WAR BROKE OUT. WE CONQUERED ANOTHER PLANET AND NAMED IT VEGETA. BUT THAT PLANET WAS ALSO LOST...
IT SOUNDS VERY DIFFERENT FROM OURS...
HEY, WHAT HAPPENED TO YOUR TAIL?
I HEARD WE USED TO HAVE THEM, BUT NOT ANYMORE.
ARE YOUR SAIYANS ALSO A WARRING RACE?
YES, BUT WE DON'T TRY TO CONQUER THE OTHER PLANETS.
OUR JOB IS TO WORK FOR CLIENTS, MOSTLY TO GET RID OF BAD GUYS.
YOU GUYS SOUND LIKE GOOD PEOPLE!
NOTHING LIKE US AT ALL!!
YOU THERE! TAKE YOUR SEATS.
WE'RE ABOUT TO START!

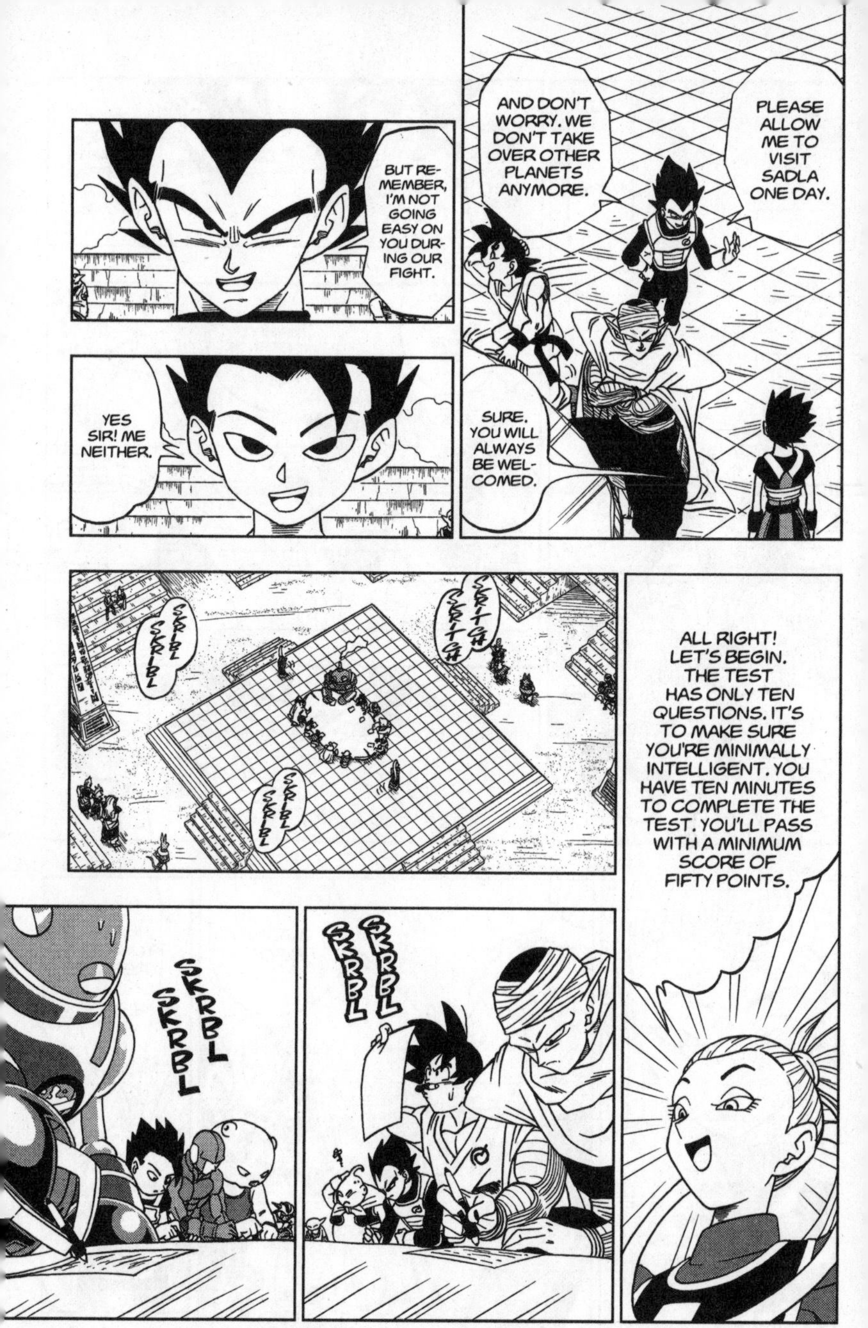
PLEASE ALLOW ME TO VISIT SADLA ONE DAY.
AND DON'T WORRY. WE DON'T TAKE OVER OTHER PLANETS ANYMORE.
SURE. YOU WILL ALWAYS BE WELCOMED.
BUT REMEMBER, I'M NOT GOING EASY ON YOU DURING OUR FIGHT.
YES SIR! ME NEITHER.
ALL RIGHT! LET'S BEGIN. THE TEST HAS ONLY TEN QUESTIONS. IT'S TO MAKE SURE YOU'RE MINIMALLY INTELLIGENT. YOU HAVE TEN MINUTES TO COMPLETE THE TEST. YOU'LL PASS WITH A MINIMUM SCORE OF FIFTY POINTS.
SKRITCH SKRITCH
SKRIBL SKRIBL
SKRIBL SKRIBL
SKRBL SKRBL
SKRBL SKRBL

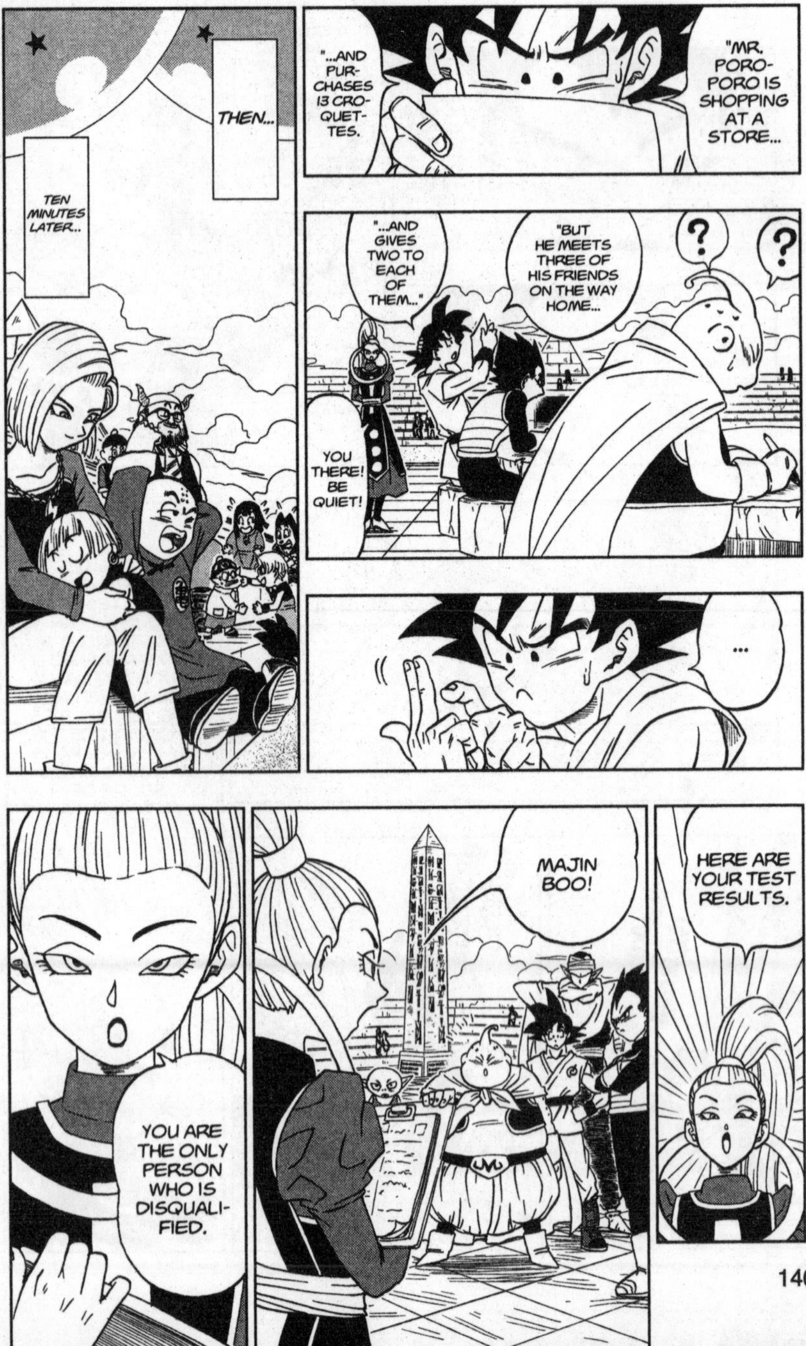
"MR. POROPORO IS SHOPPING AT A STORE...
"...AND PURCHASES 13 CROQUETTES.
"BUT HE MEETS THREE OF HIS FRIENDS ON THE WAY HOME...
"...AND GIVES TWO TO EACH OF THEM..."
?
?
YOU THERE! BE QUIET!
...
THEN...
TEN MINUTES LATER...
HERE ARE YOUR TEST RESULTS.
MAJIN BOO!
YOU ARE THE ONLY PERSON WHO IS DISQUALIFIED.

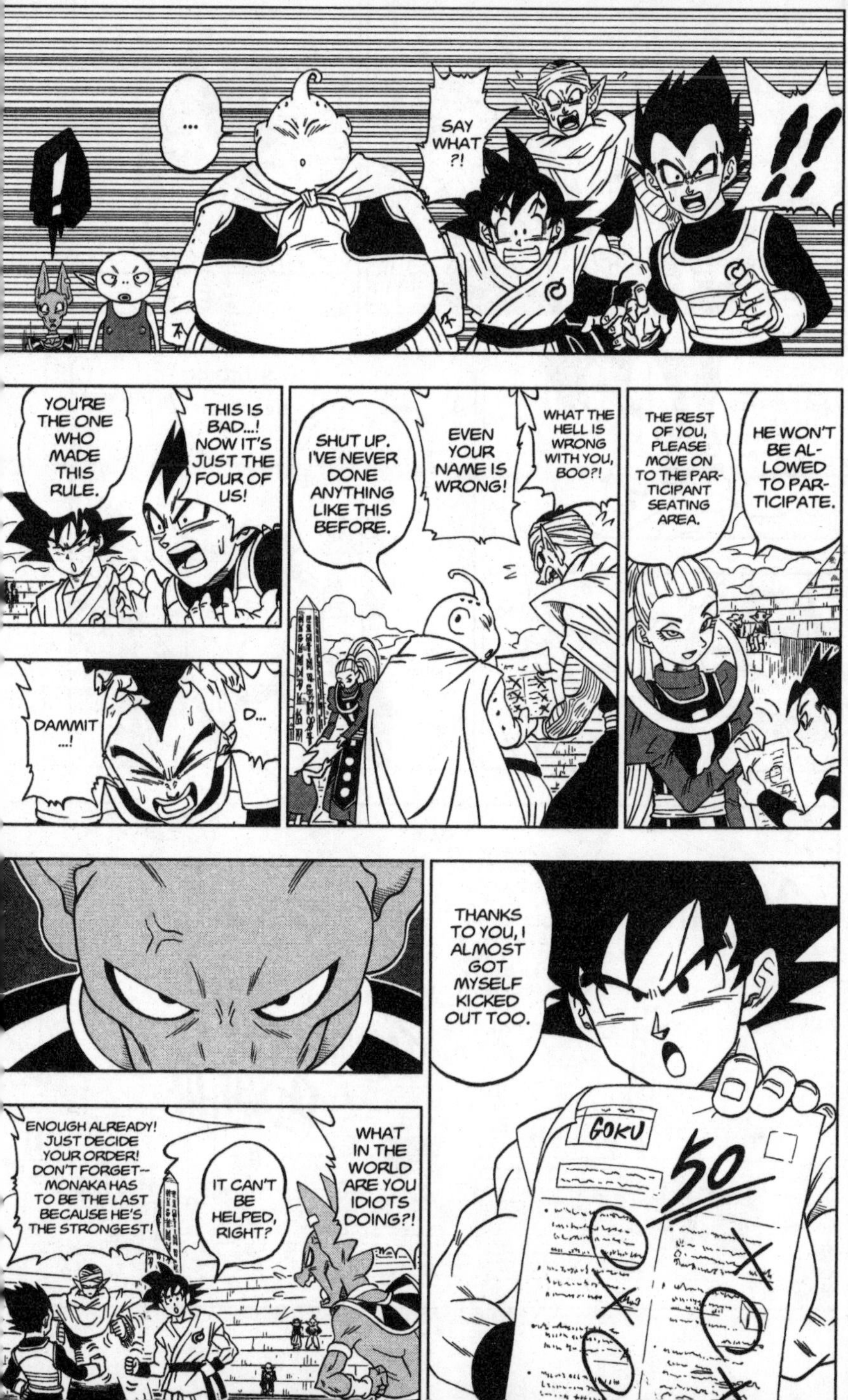
!!
SAY WHAT ?!
...
!
HE WON'T BE AL- LOWED TO PAR- TICIPATE.
THE REST OF YOU, PLEASE MOVE ON TO THE PAR- TICIPANT SEATING AREA.
WHAT THE HELL IS WRONG WITH YOU, BOO?!
EVEN YOUR NAME IS WRONG!
SHUT UP. I'VE NEVER DONE ANYTHING LIKE THIS BEFORE.
THIS IS BAD...! NOW IT'S JUST THE FOUR OF US!
YOU'RE THE ONE WHO MADE THIS RULE.
D...
DAMMIT ...!
THANKS TO YOU, I ALMOST GOT MYSELF KICKED OUT TOO.
GOKU
50
WHAT IN THE WORLD ARE YOU IDIOTS DOING?!
IT CAN'T BE HELPED, RIGHT?
ENOUGH ALREADY! JUST DECIDE YOUR ORDER! DON'T FORGET-- MONAKA HAS TO BE THE LAST BECAUSE HE'S THE STRONGEST!

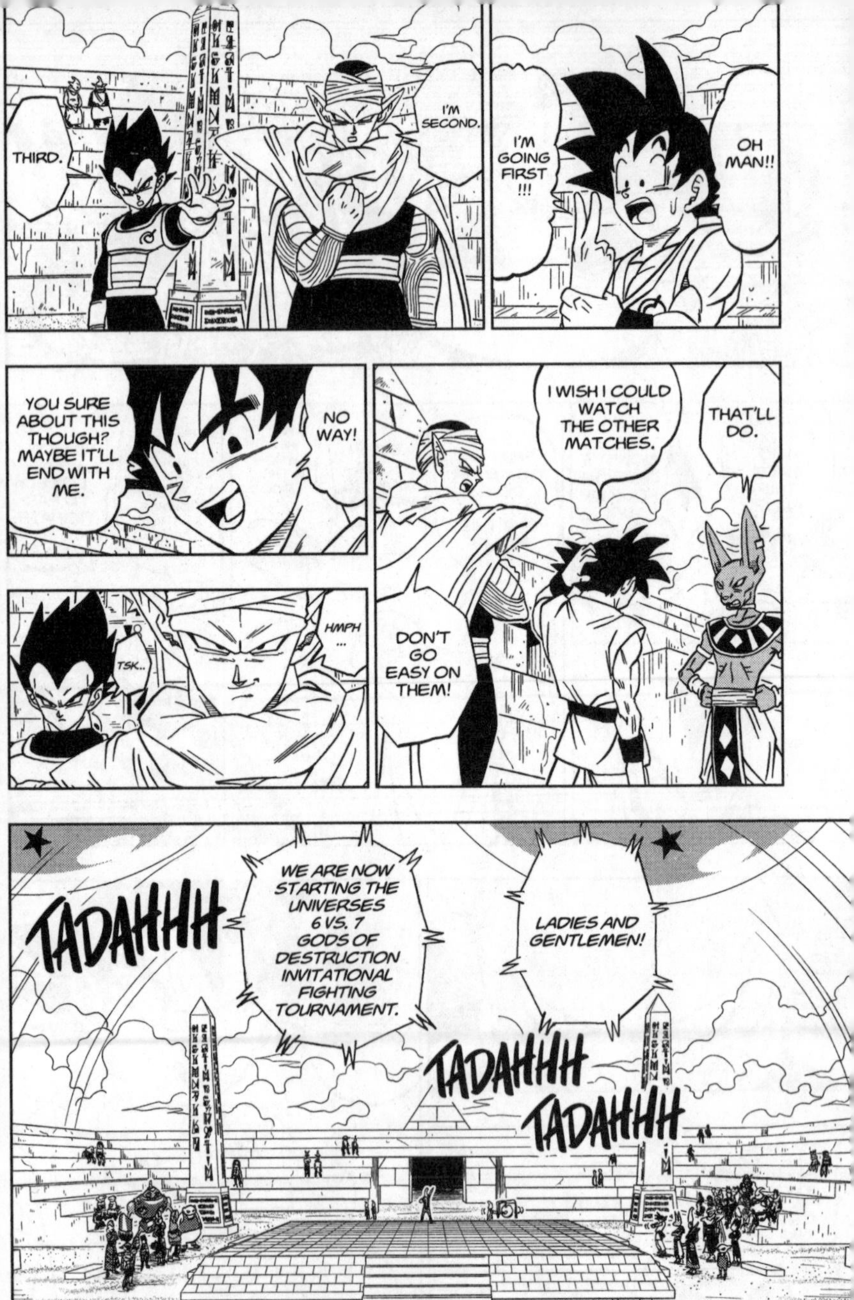
OH MAN!!
I'M GOING FIRST!!!
I'M SECOND.
THIRD.
THAT'LL DO.
I WISH I COULD WATCH THE OTHER MATCHES.
DON'T GO EASY ON THEM!
NO WAY!
YOU SURE ABOUT THIS THOUGH? MAYBE IT'LL END WITH ME.
HMPH ...
TSK..
LADIES AND GENTLEMEN!
WE ARE NOW STARTING THE UNIVERSES 6 VS. 7 GODS OF DESTRUCTION INVITATIONAL FIGHTING TOURNAMENT.
TADAHHH
TADAHHH
TADAHHH

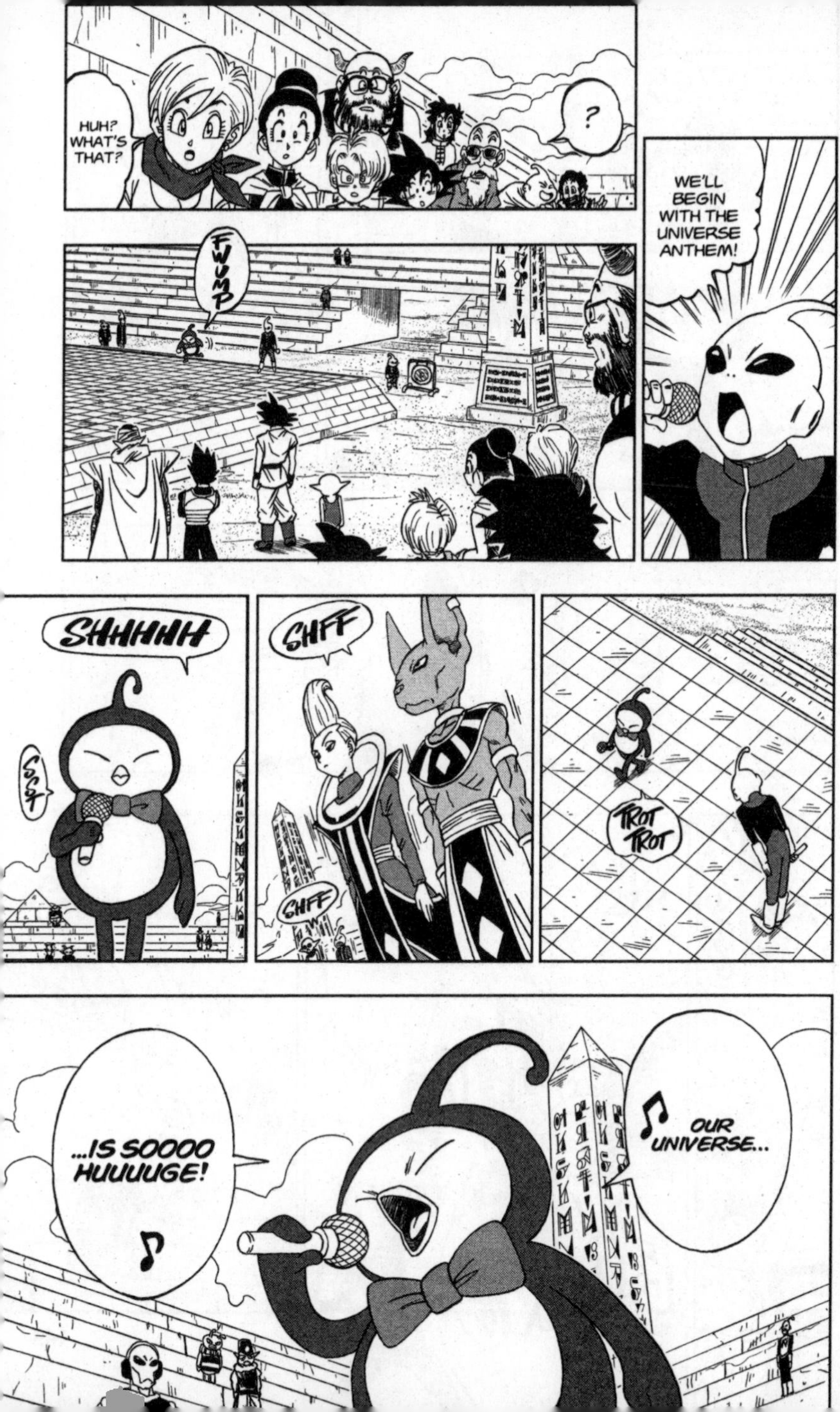
?
HUH? WHAT'S THAT?
FWUMP
WE'LL BEGIN WITH THE UNIVERSE ANTHEM!
TROT TROT
SHFF
SHFF
SHHHHH
SCK
OUR UNIVERSE...
...IS SOOOO HUUUUGE!

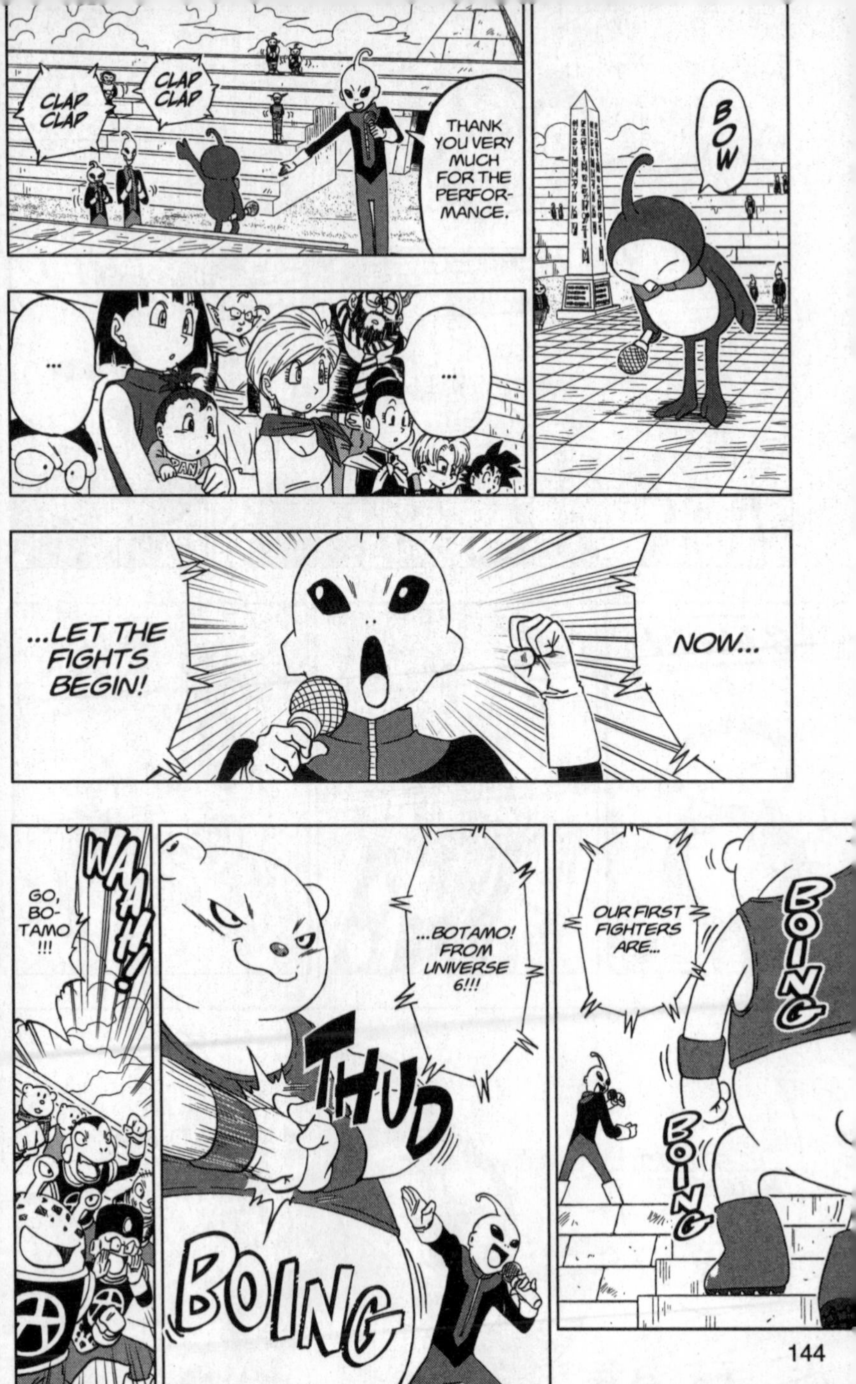
BOW
THANK YOU VERY MUCH FOR THE PERFORMANCE.
CLAP CLAP
CLAP CLAP
...
...
NOW...
...LET THE FIGHTS BEGIN!
OUR FIRST FIGHTERS ARE...
BOING
BOING
...BOTAMO! FROM UNIVERSE 6!!!
THUD
BOING
WAAH!
GO, BO-TAMO !!!

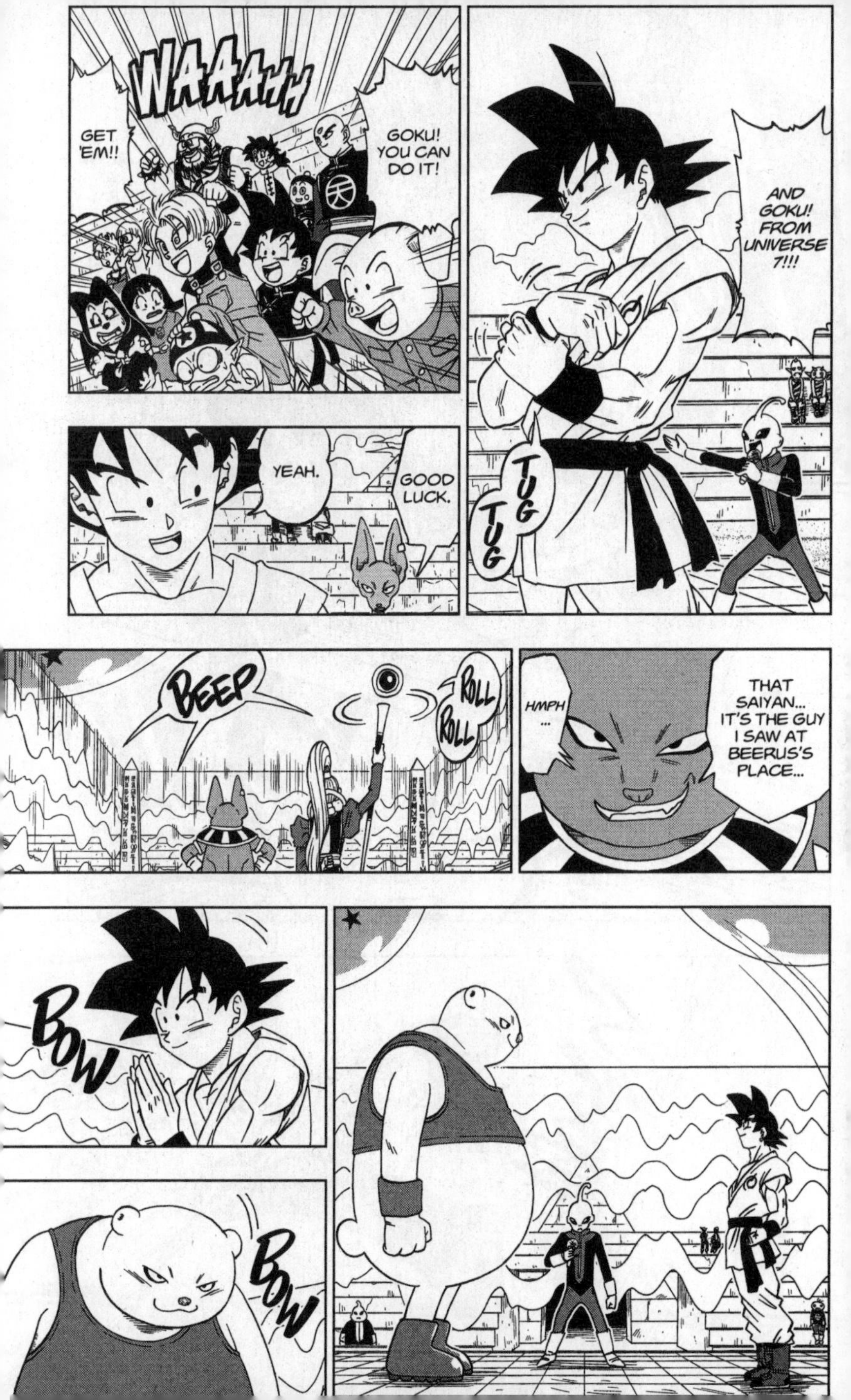
AND GOKU! FROM UNIVERSE 7!!!
TUG TUG
WAAAHH
GOKU! YOU CAN DO IT!
GET 'EM!!
GOOD LUCK.
YEAH.
THAT SAIYAN... IT'S THE GUY I SAW AT BEERUS'S PLACE...
HMPH ...
ROLL ROLL
BEEP
BOW
BOW

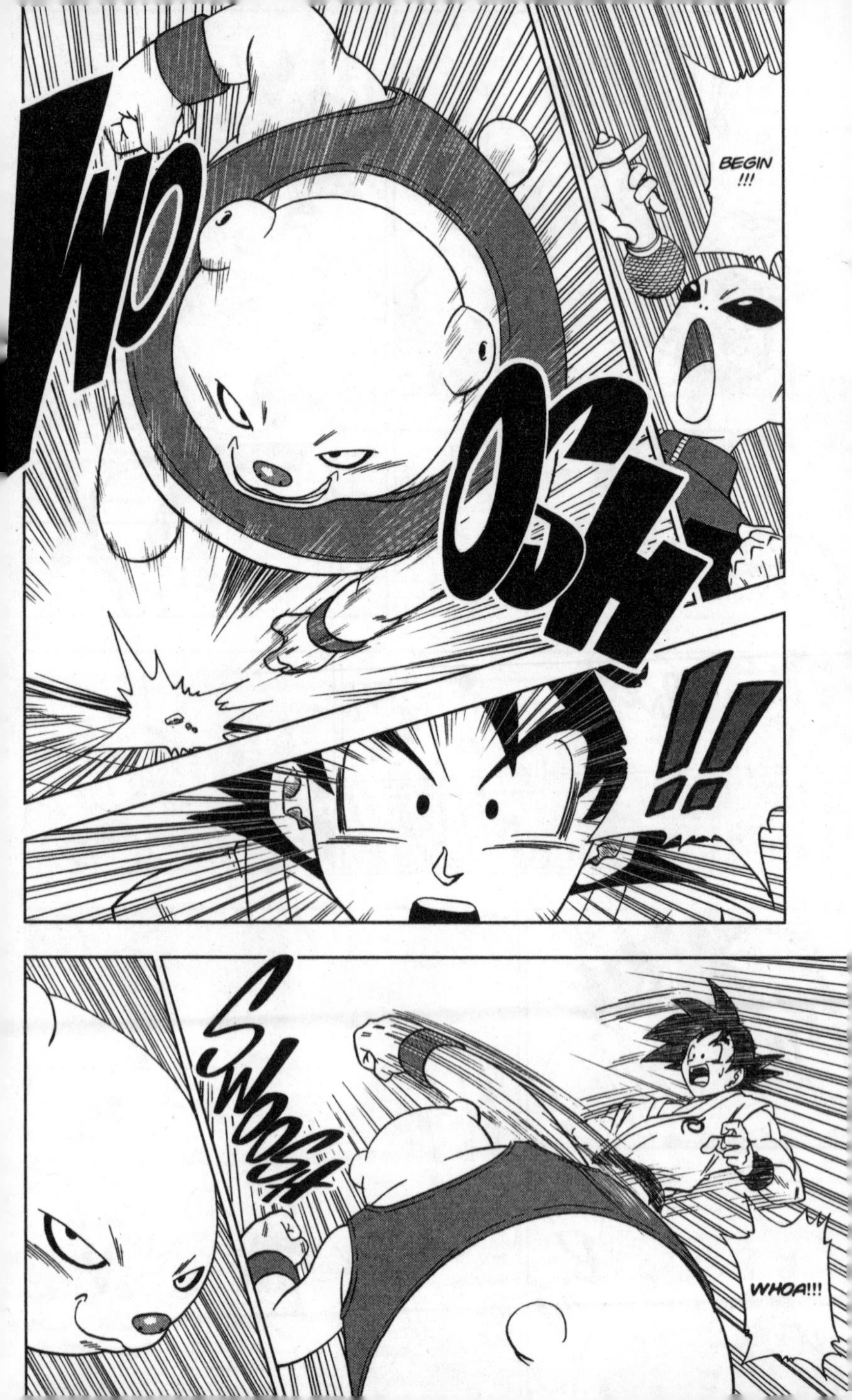

BEGIN !!!
WOOSH
!!
WHOA!!!
SWOOSH!

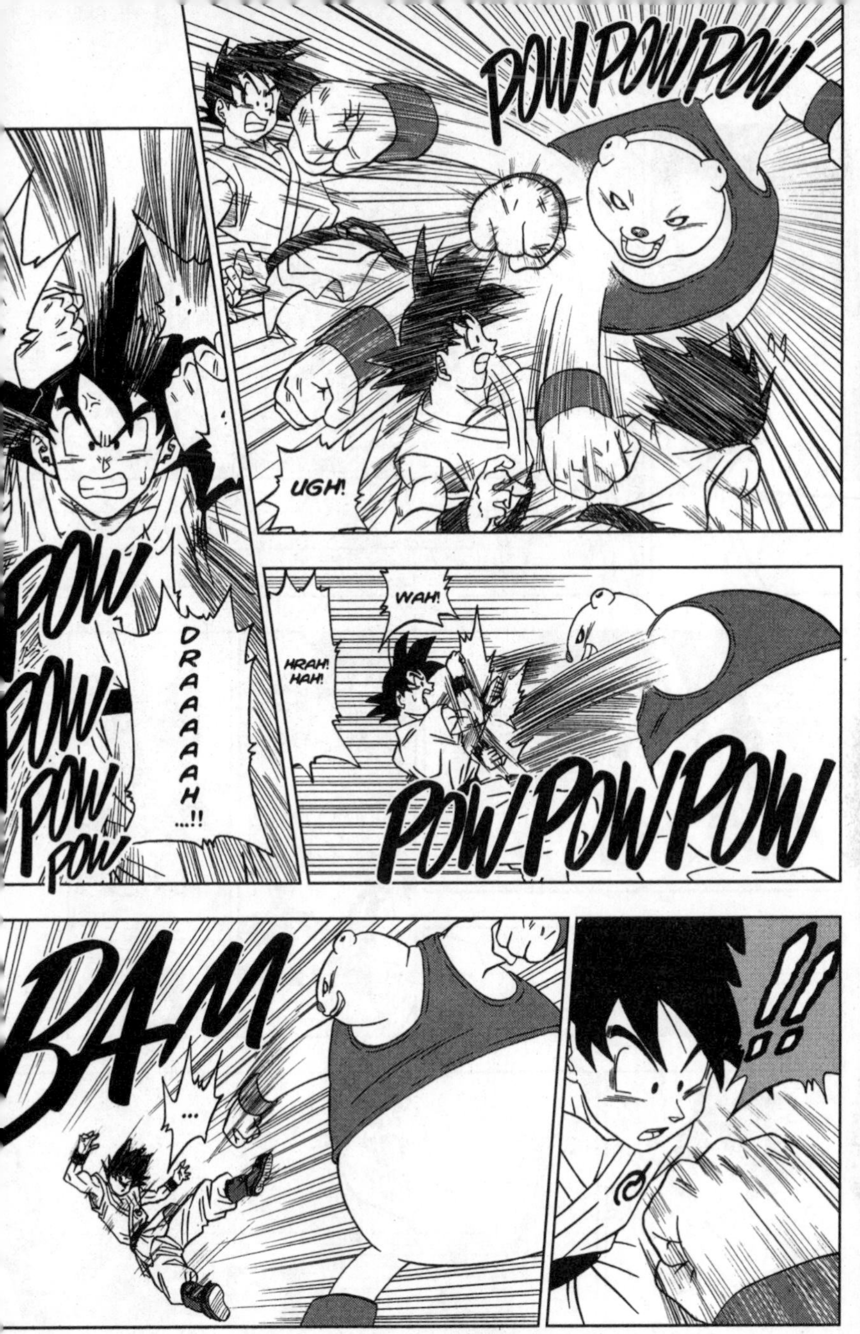

POW POW POW POW
UGH!
WAH!
HRAH! HAH!
POW POW POW
DRAAAAAAAH...!!
POW POW POW POW
!!
BAM
...

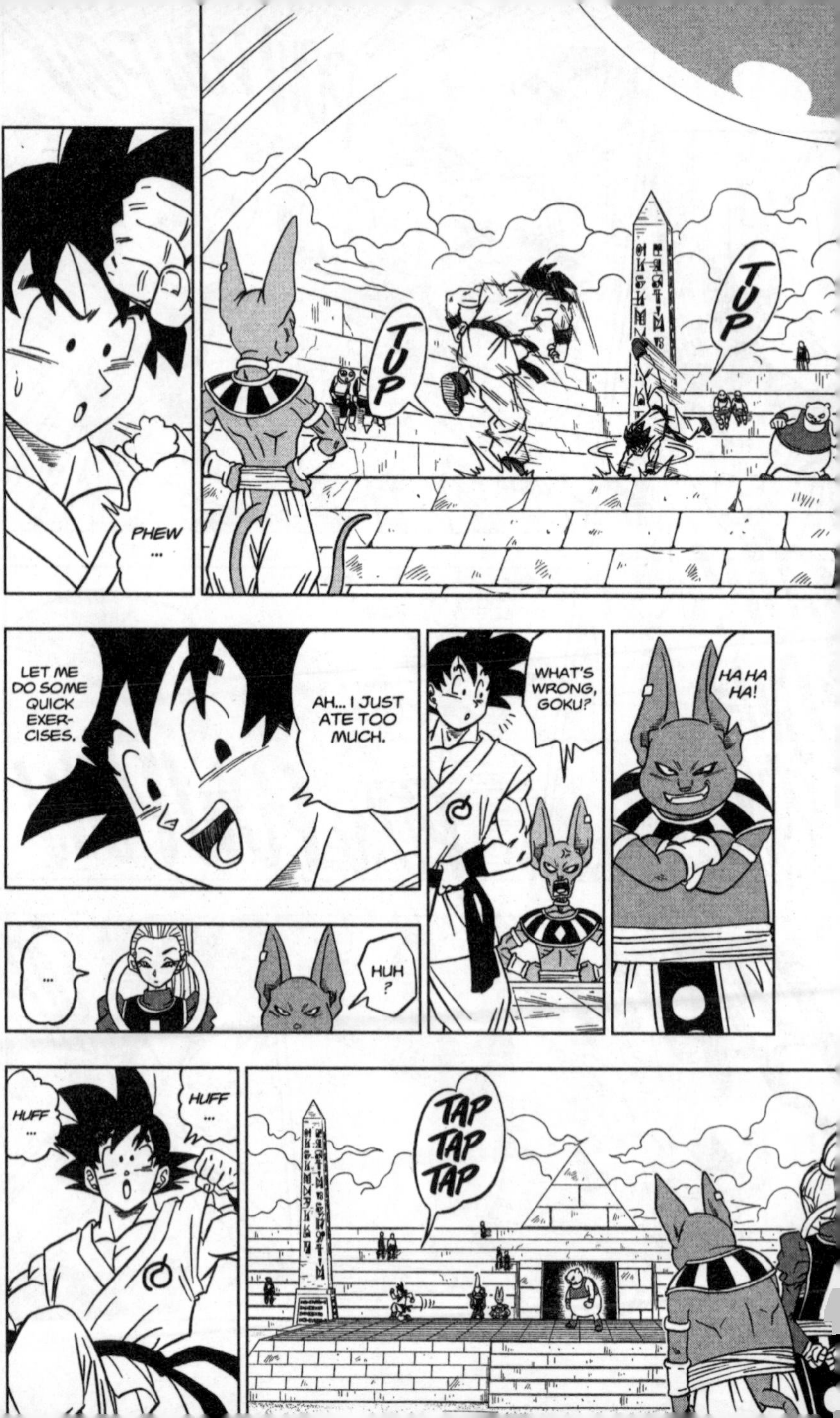
TUP
TUP
PHEW ...
HA HA HA!
WHAT'S WRONG, GOKU?
AH... I JUST ATE TOO MUCH.
LET ME DO SOME QUICK EXER-CISES.
HUH ?
...
TAP TAP TAP
HUFF ...
HUFF ...

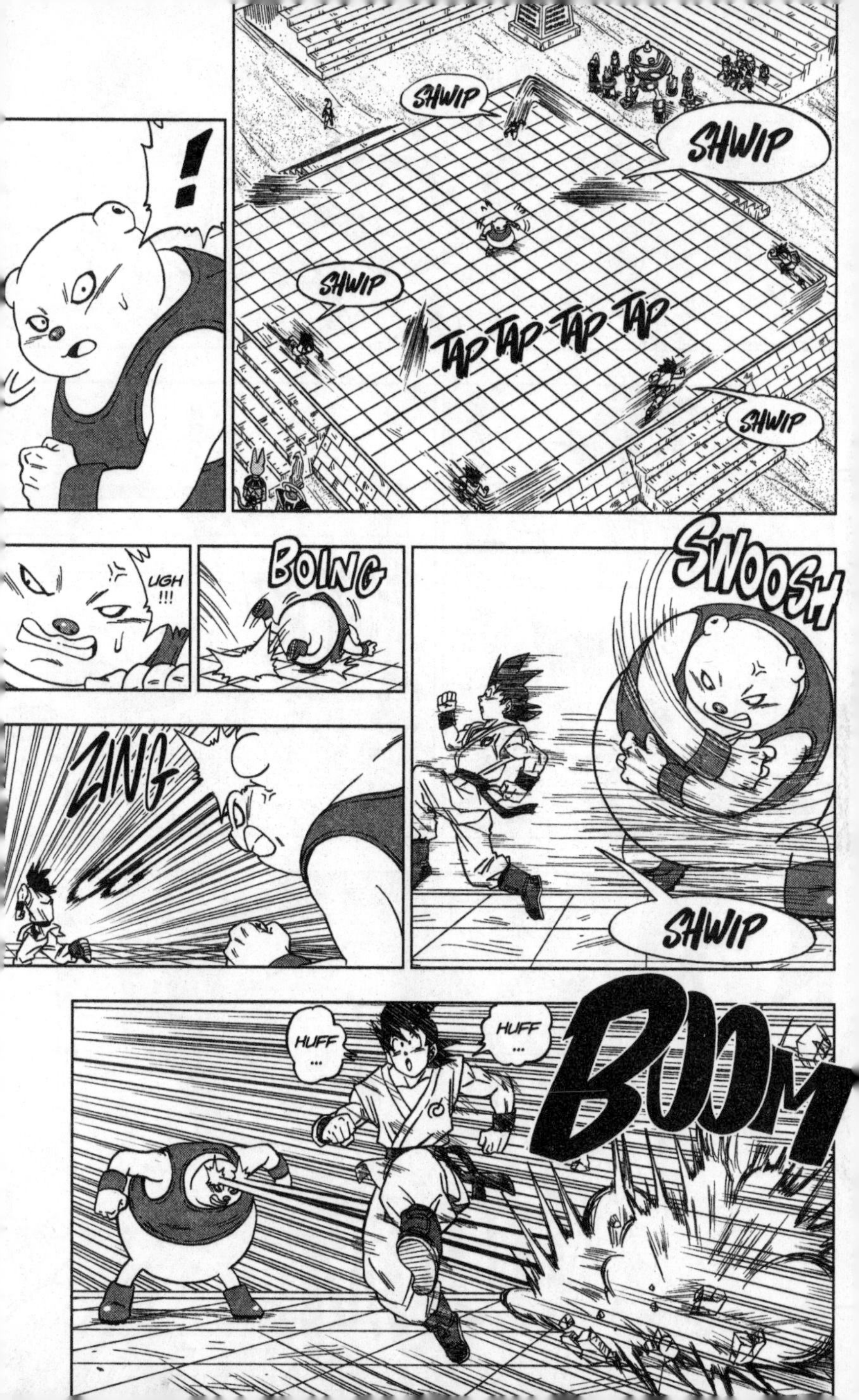
SHWIP
SHWIP
SHWIP
TAP TAP TAP TAP
SHWIP
!
SWOOSH
SHWIP
BOING
UGH !!!
ZING
BOOM
HUFF ...
HUFF ...

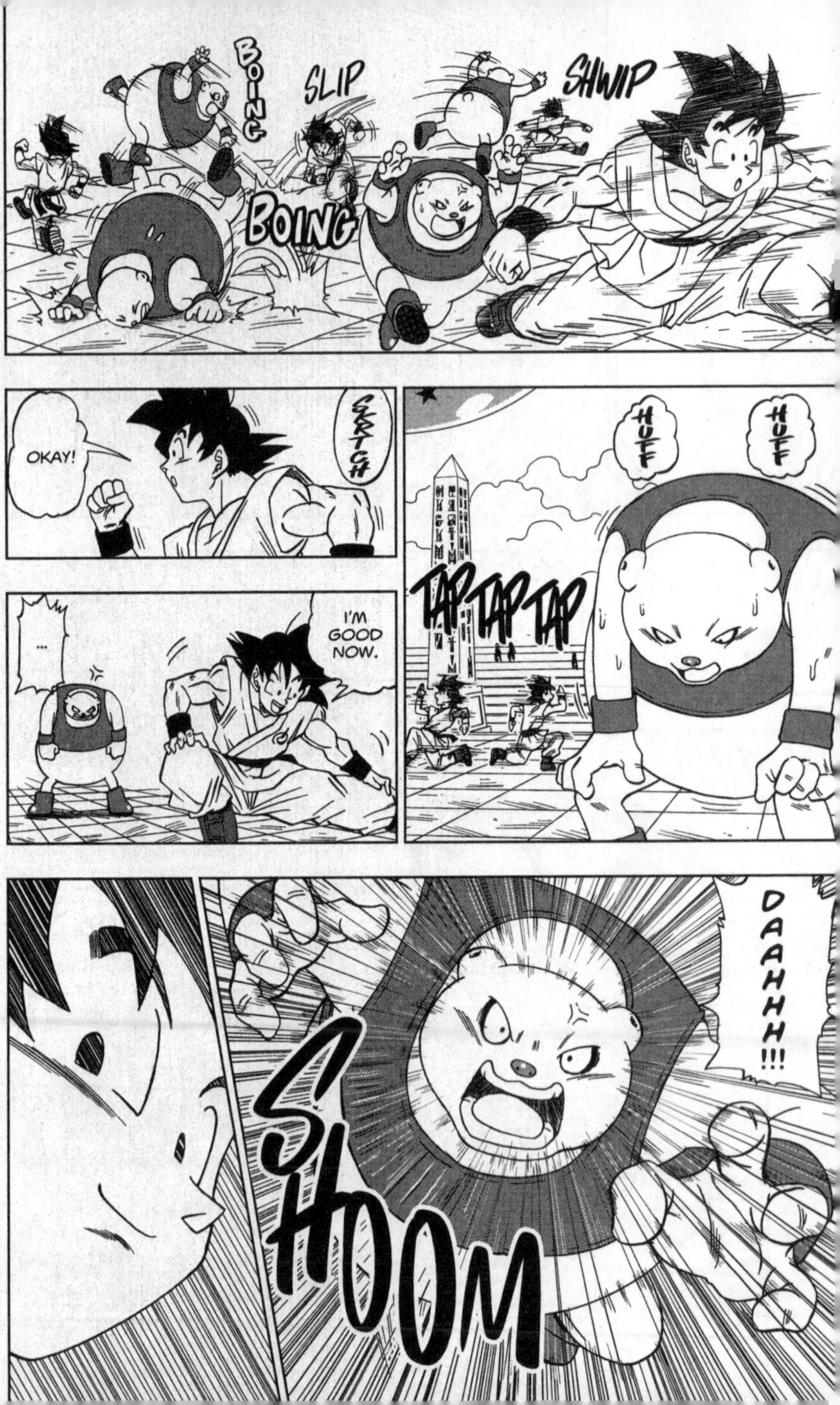
SHWIP
SLIP
BOING
BOING
HUFF
HUFF
TAP TAP TAP
SKRTCH
OKAY!
I'M GOOD NOW.
...
DAAHHHH!!!
SHOOM

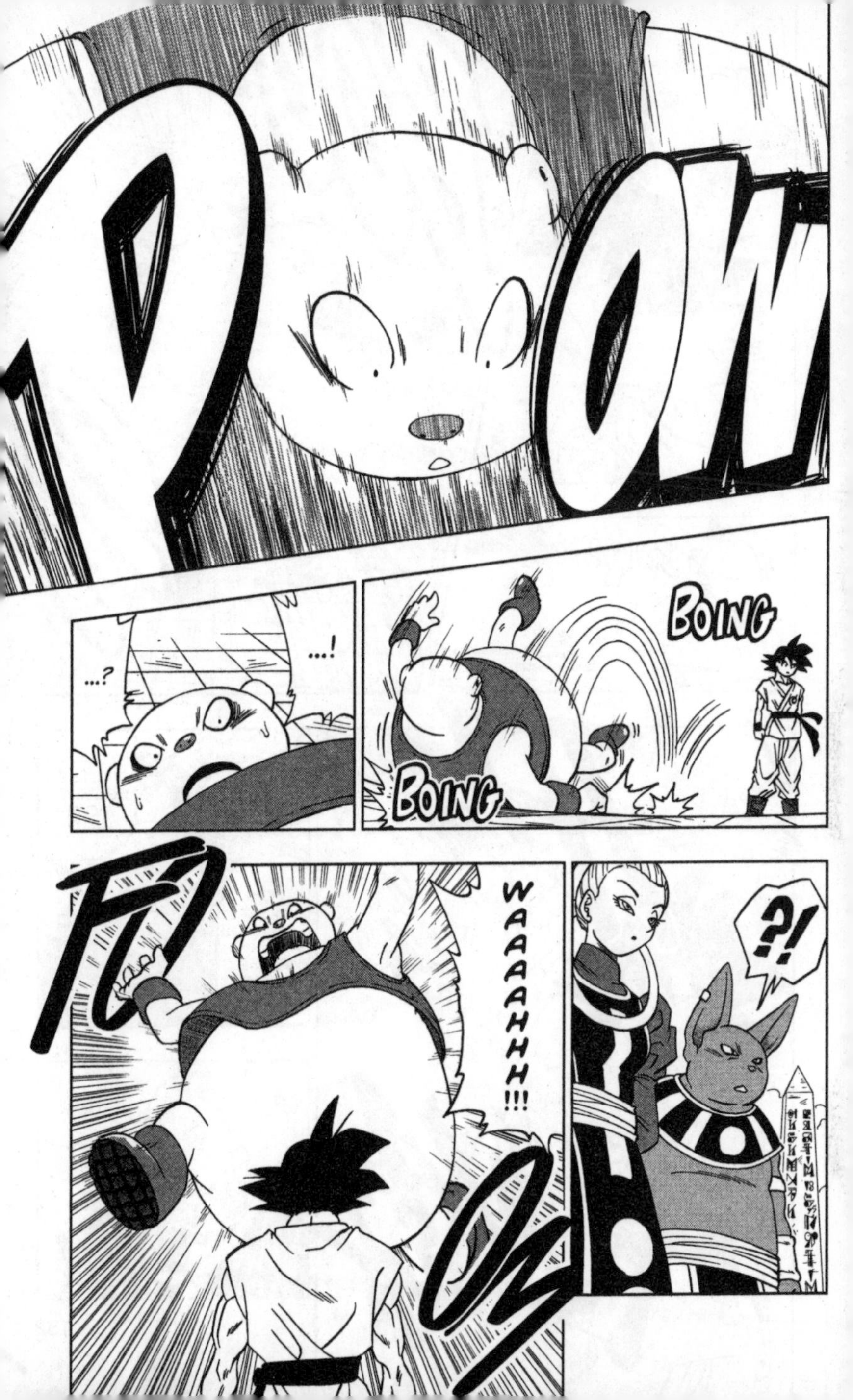
POW
BOING
BOING
...!
...?
?!
WAAAAAHHH!!!

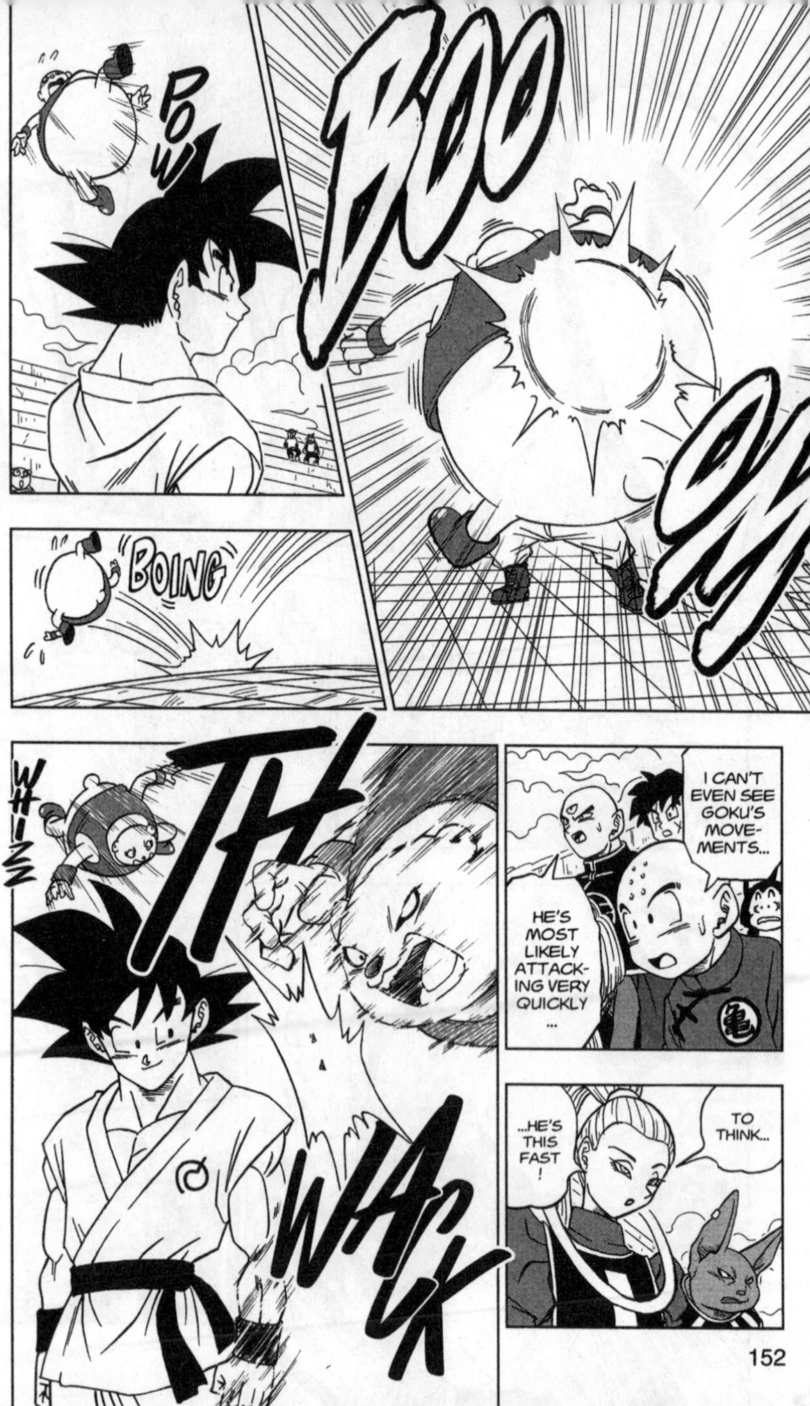
ZOO
OM
POW
BOING
I CAN'T EVEN SEE GOKU'S MOVEMENTS...
HE'S MOST LIKELY ATTACKING VERY QUICKLY ...
TO THINK...
...HE'S THIS FAST!
WHIZZ
TH
WACK

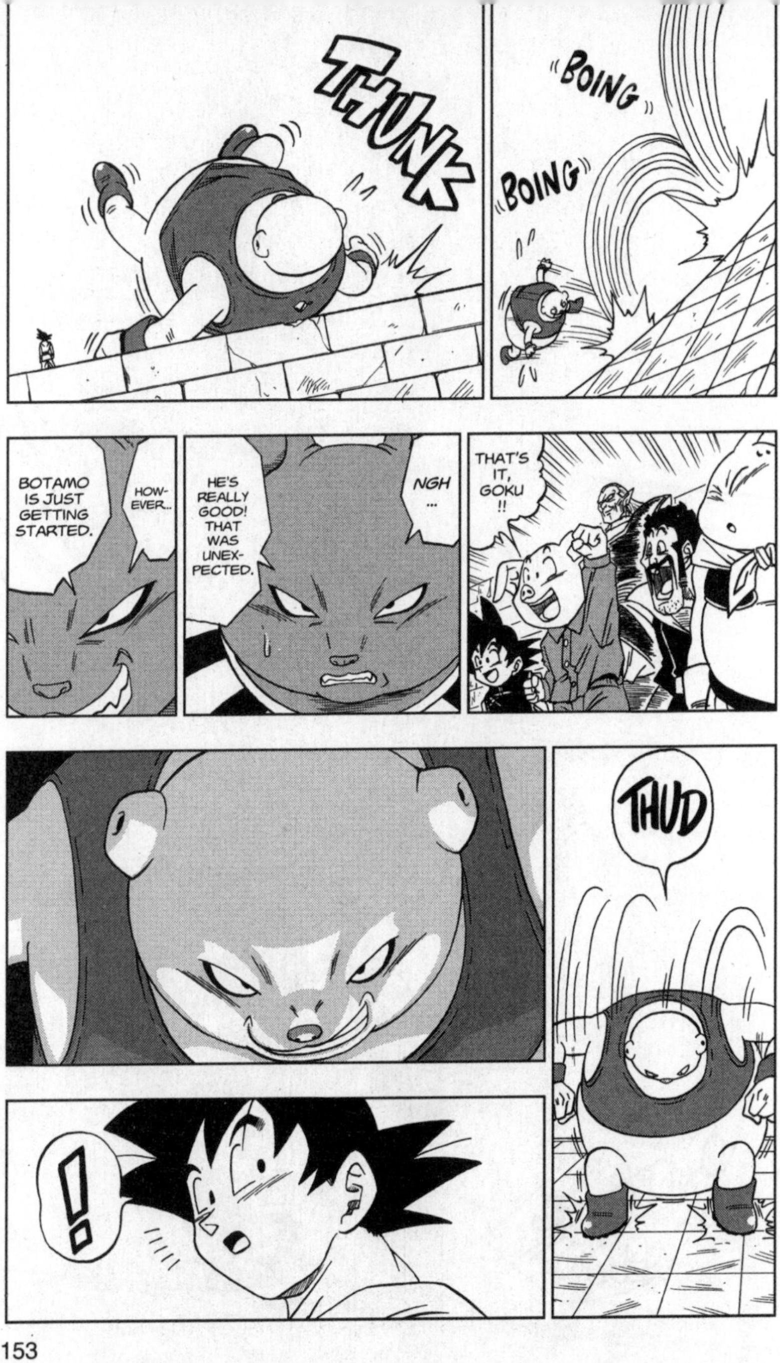
BOING
BOING
THUNK
THAT'S IT, GOKU!!
NGH...
HE'S REALLY GOOD! THAT WAS UNEXPECTED.
HOW-EVER...
BOTAMO IS JUST GETTING STARTED.
THUD
!

DRAGON BALL SUPER

CHAPTER 9: GOKU VS. BOTAMO

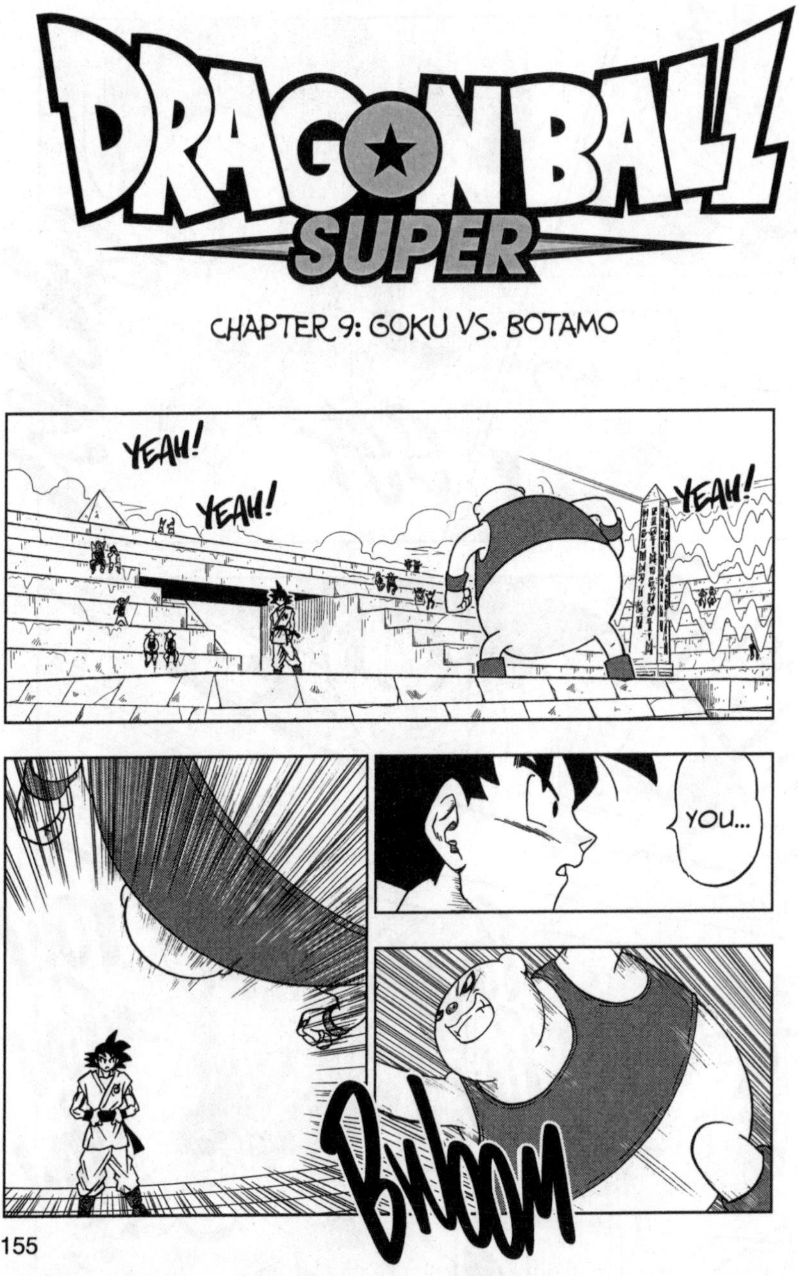
YEAH!
YEAH!
YEAH!
YOU...
BWOOM

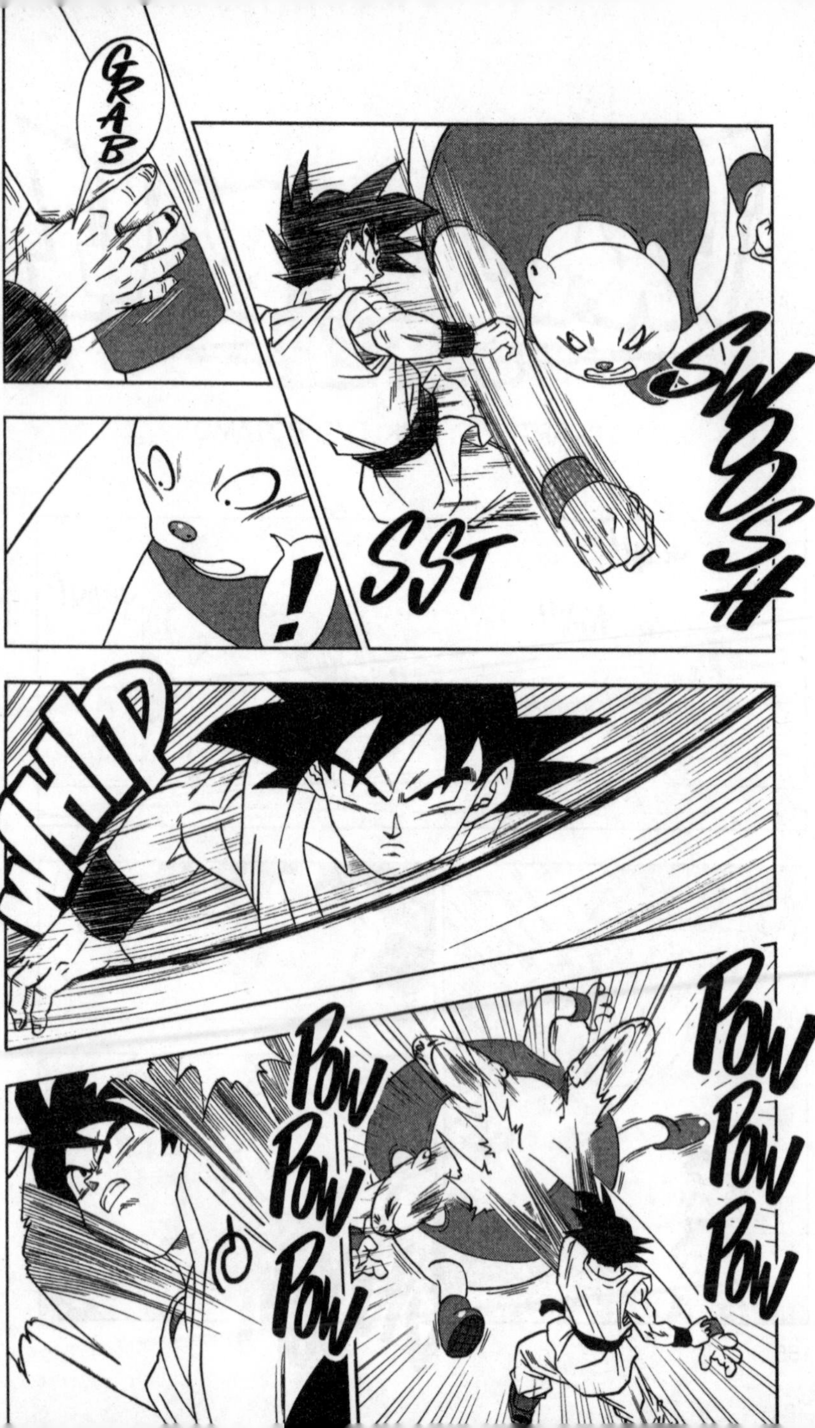
SWOOSH
SST
GRAB
!
WHIP
POW POW POW POW
POW POW POW POW

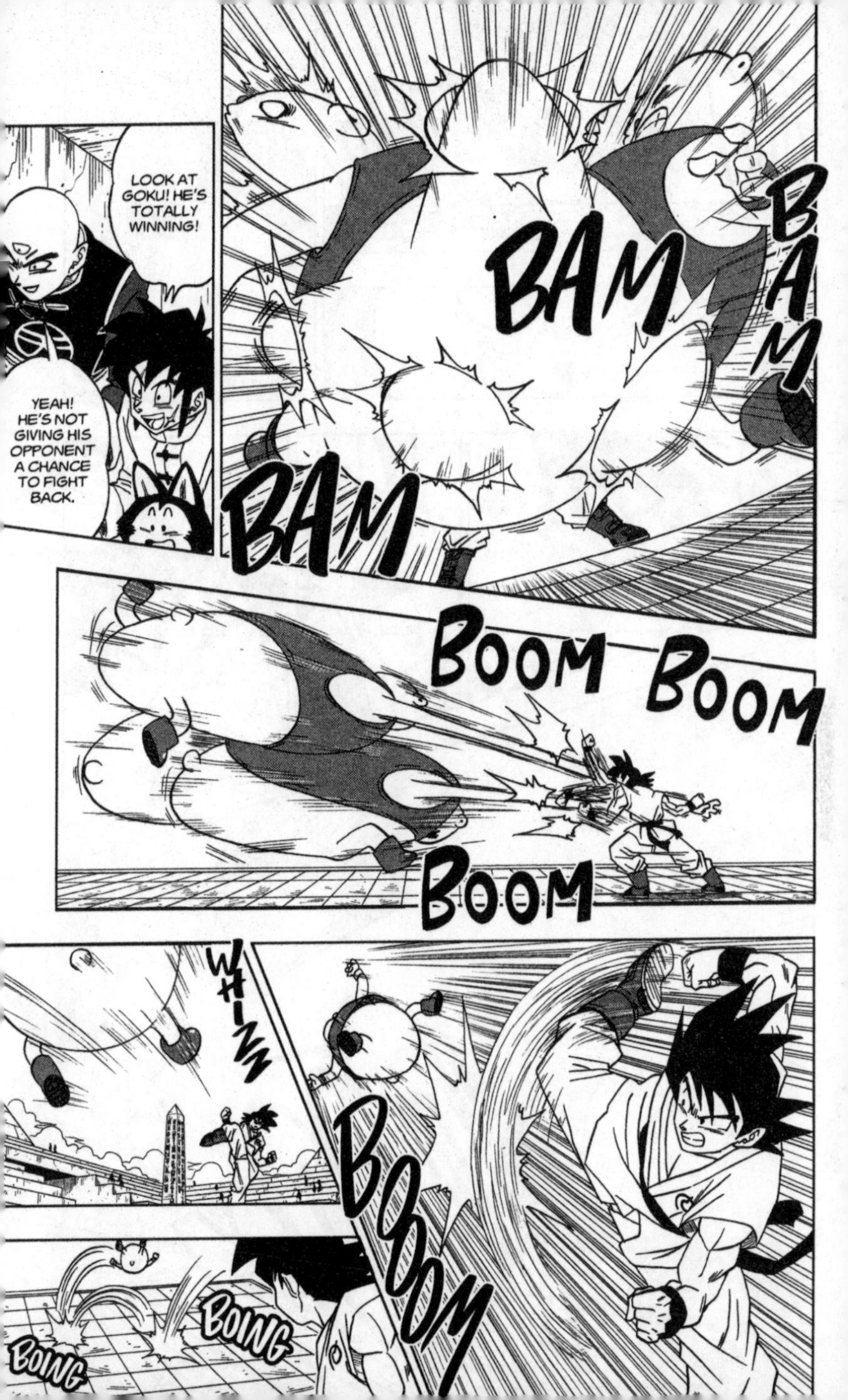
BAM
BAM
BAM
LOOK AT GOKU! HE'S TOTALLY WINNING!
YEAH! HE'S NOT GIVING HIS OPPONENT A CHANCE TO FIGHT BACK.
BOOM BOOM
BOOM
BOOOOM
WHIZZ
BOING
BOING

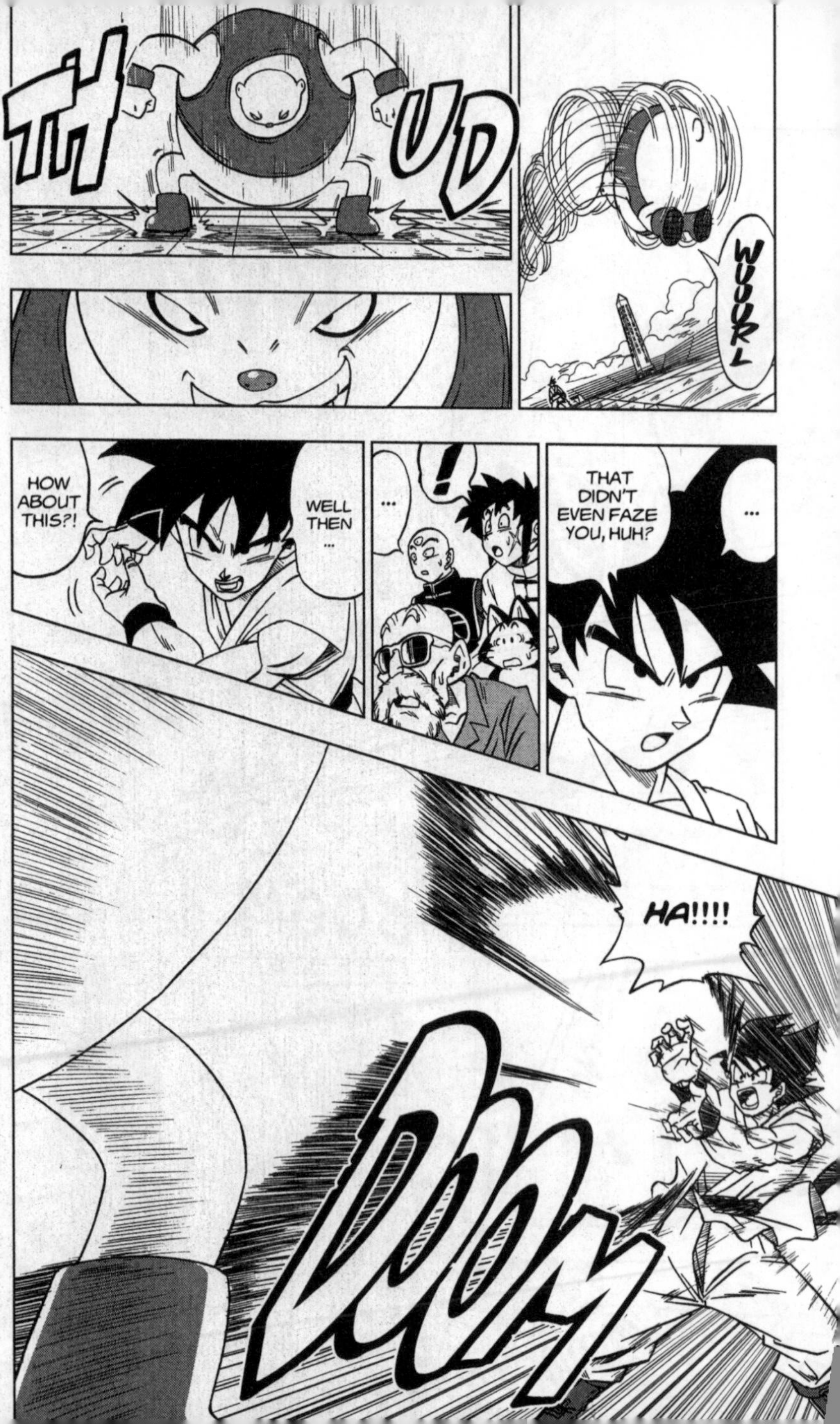
WUUURL
THUD
...
THAT DIDN'T EVEN FAZE YOU, HUH?
!
...
WELL THEN ...
HOW ABOUT THIS?!
HA!!!!
WOOM

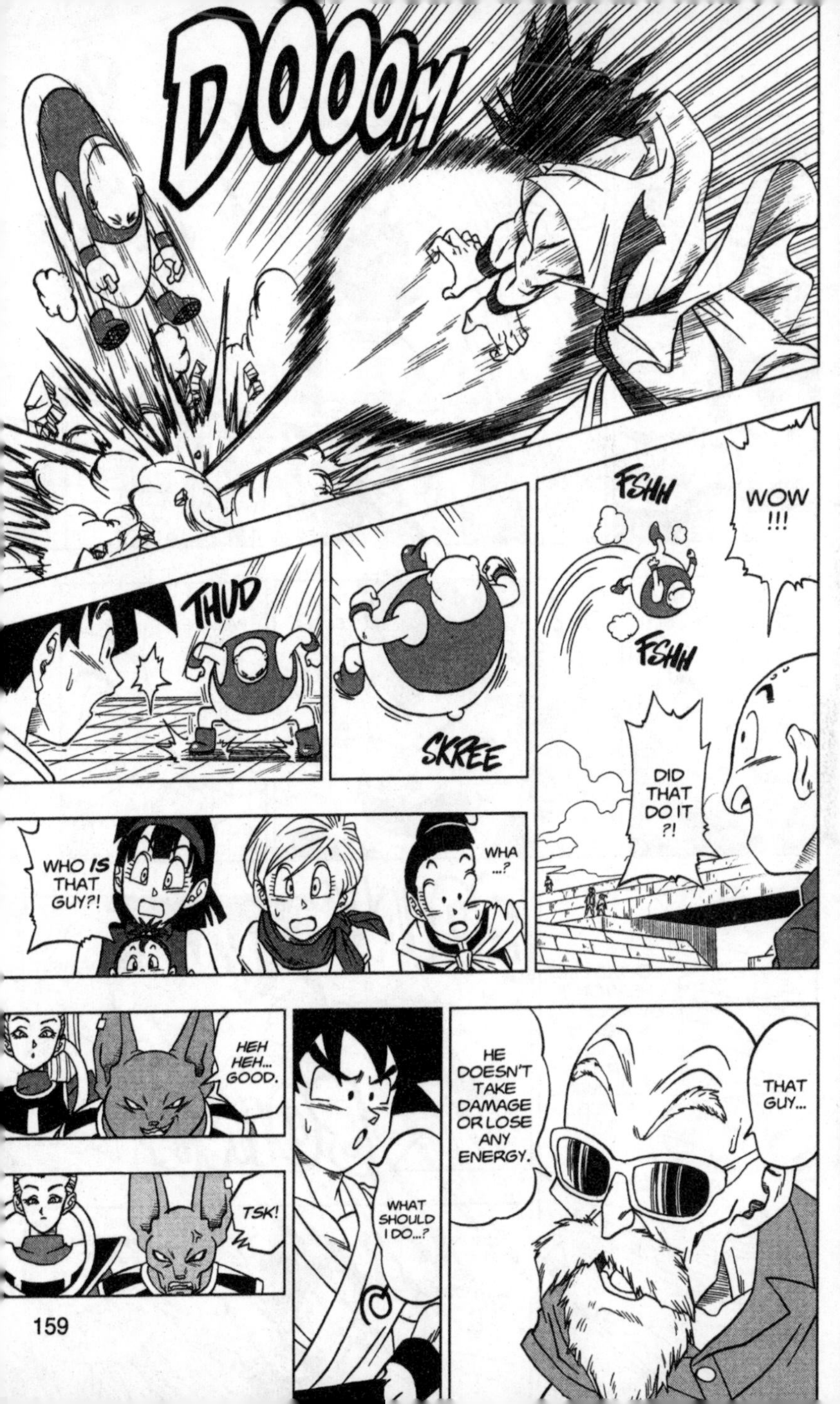
DOOOM
WOW !!!
FSHH
FSHH
DID THAT DO IT ?!
SKREE
THUD
WHA ...?
WHO IS THAT GUY?!
THAT GUY...
HE DOESN'T TAKE DAMAGE OR LOSE ANY ENERGY.
WHAT SHOULD I DO...?
HEH HEH... GOOD.
TSK!

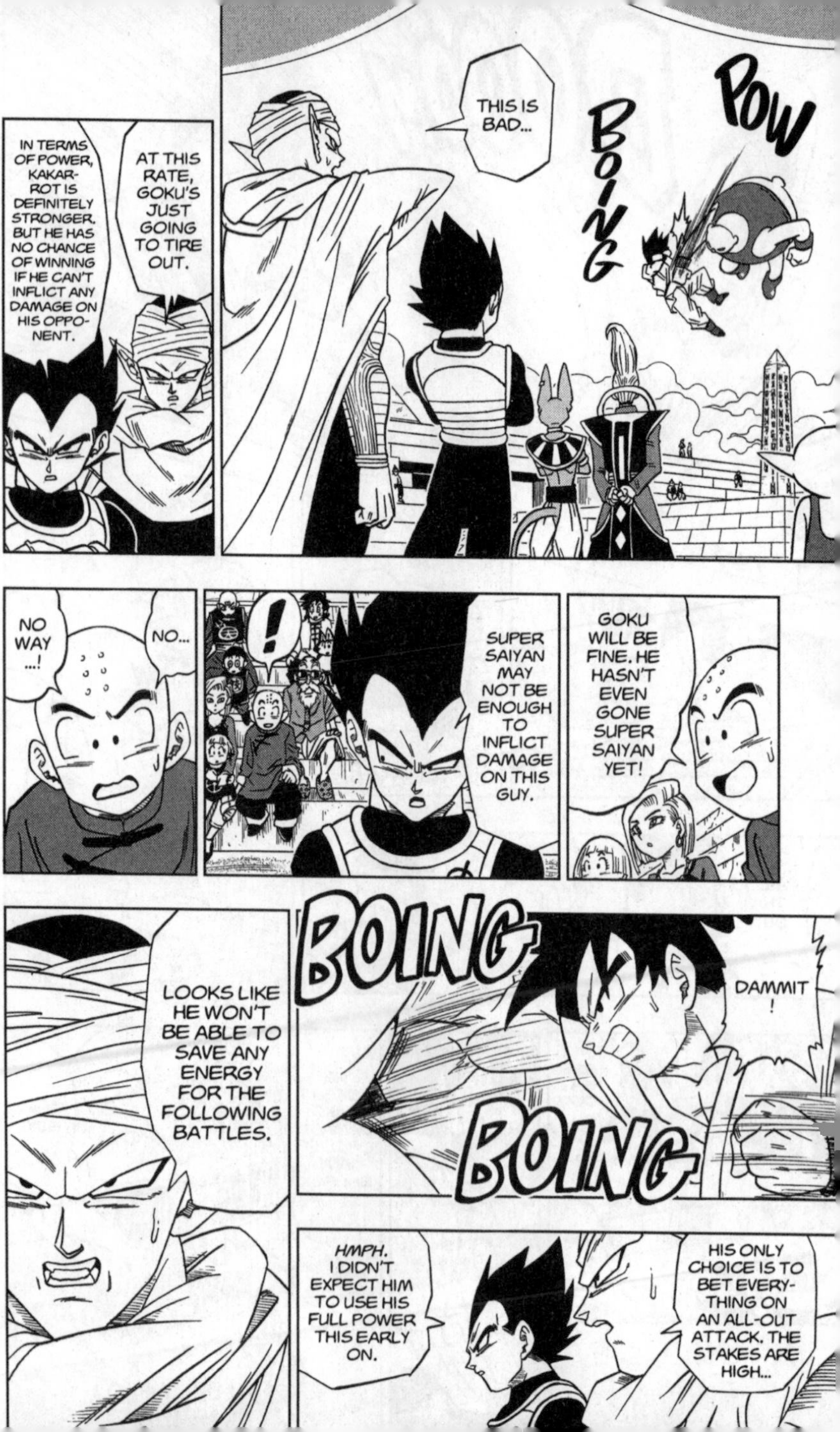
POW
BOING
THIS IS BAD...
AT THIS RATE, GOKU'S JUST GOING TO TIRE OUT.
IN TERMS OF POWER, KAKAR-ROT IS DEFINITELY STRONGER. BUT HE HAS NO CHANCE OF WINNING IF HE CAN'T INFLICT ANY DAMAGE ON HIS OPPO-NENT.
GOKU WILL BE FINE. HE HASN'T EVEN GONE SUPER SAIYAN YET!
SUPER SAIYAN MAY NOT BE ENOUGH TO INFLICT DAMAGE ON THIS GUY.
!
NO...
NO WAY ...!
BOING
DAMMIT!
BOING
HIS ONLY CHOICE IS TO BET EVERY-THING ON AN ALL-OUT ATTACK. THE STAKES ARE HIGH...
HMPH. I DIDN'T EXPECT HIM TO USE HIS FULL POWER THIS EARLY ON.
LOOKS LIKE HE WON'T BE ABLE TO SAVE ANY ENERGY FOR THE FOLLOWING BATTLES.

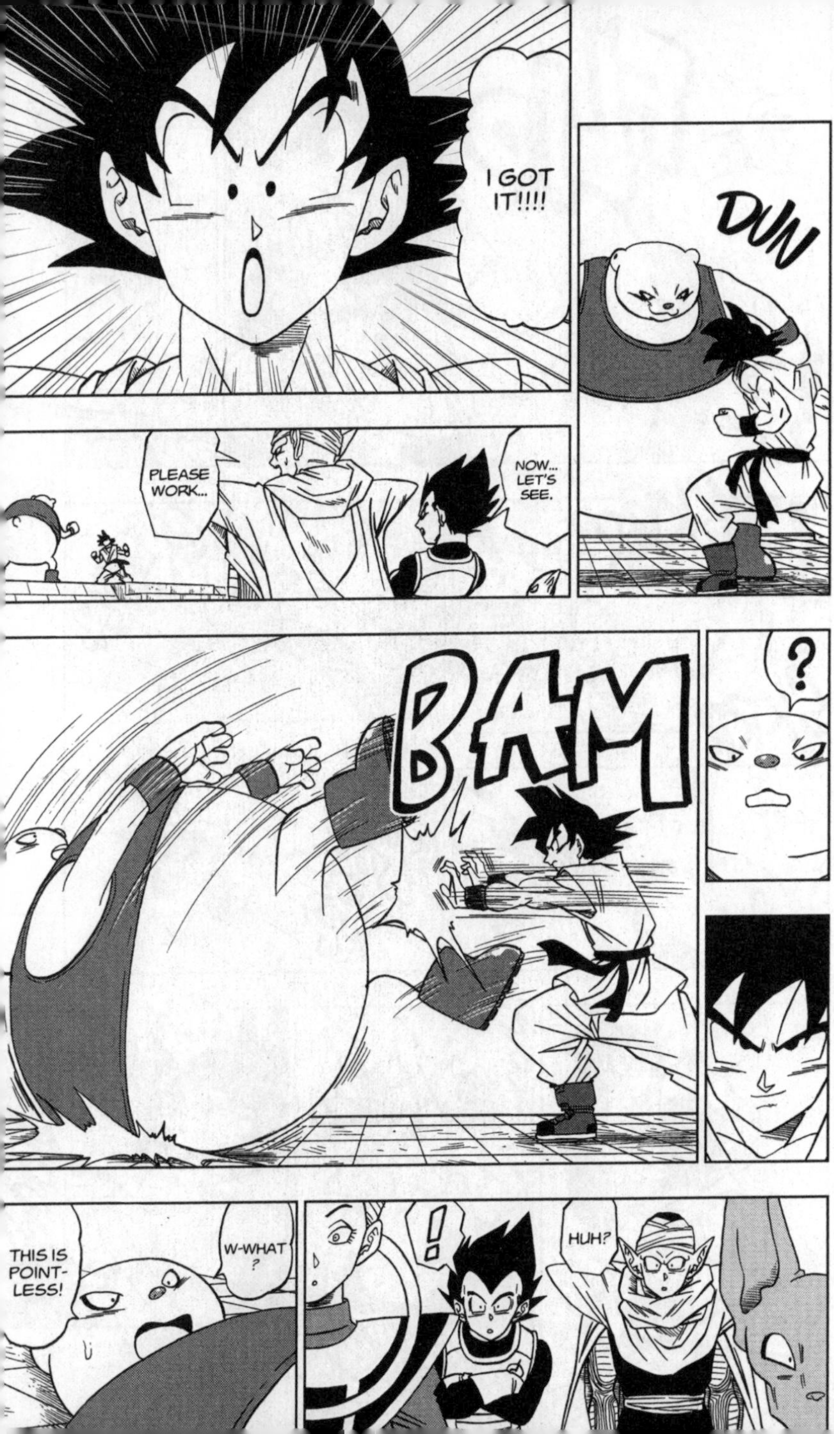
I GOT IT!!!!
DUN
NOW... LET'S SEE.
PLEASE WORK...
?
BAM
HUH?
!
W-WHAT?
THIS IS POINTLESS!

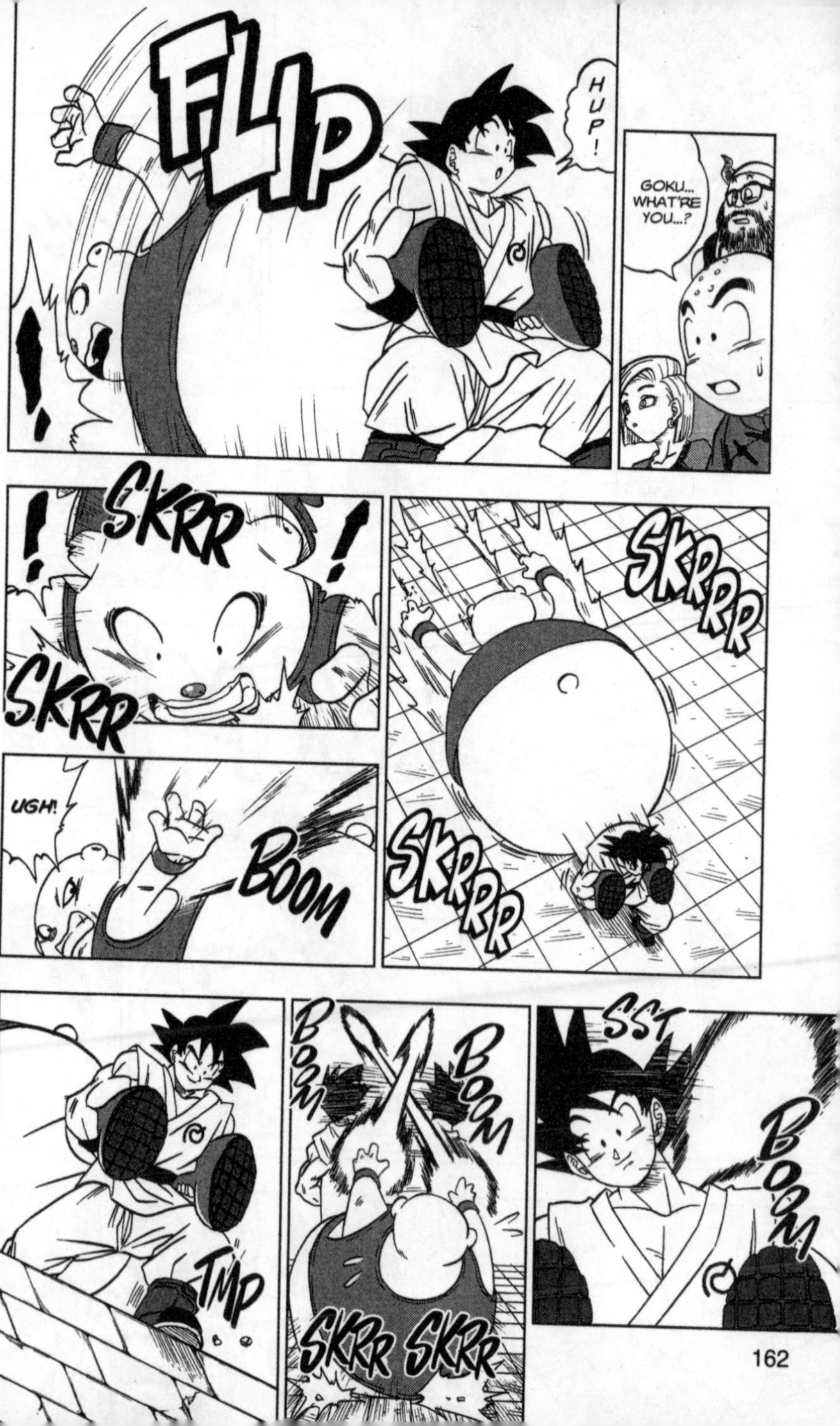
GOKU... WHAT'RE YOU...?
HUP!
FLIP
!
!
SKRR
!
SKRR
SKRRRR
SKRRRR
UGH!
BOOM
SST
BOOM
BOOM
BOOM
SKRR SKRR
TMP

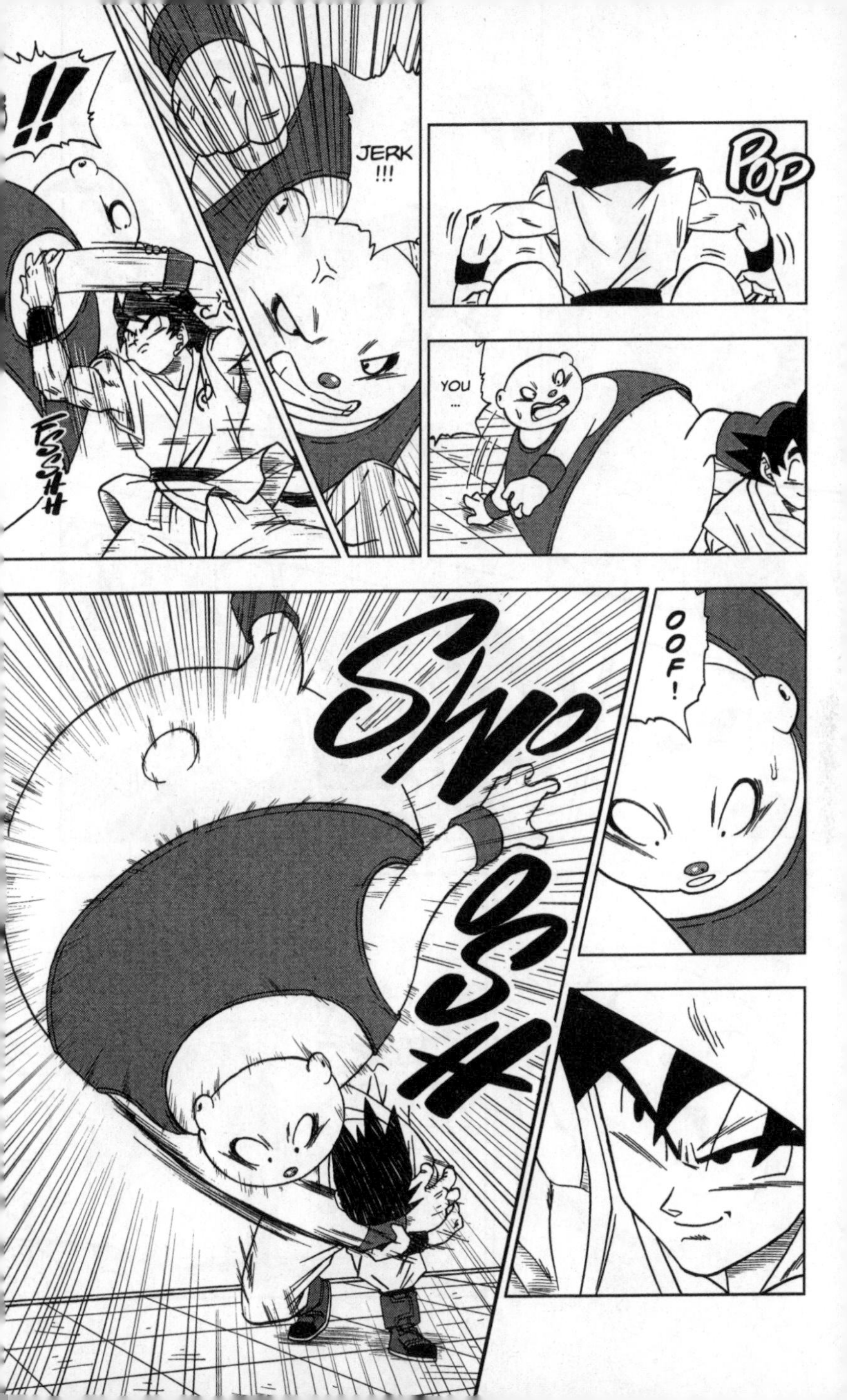
POP
YOU ...
JERK !!!
!!
FSSHH
OOF!
SWOOSH

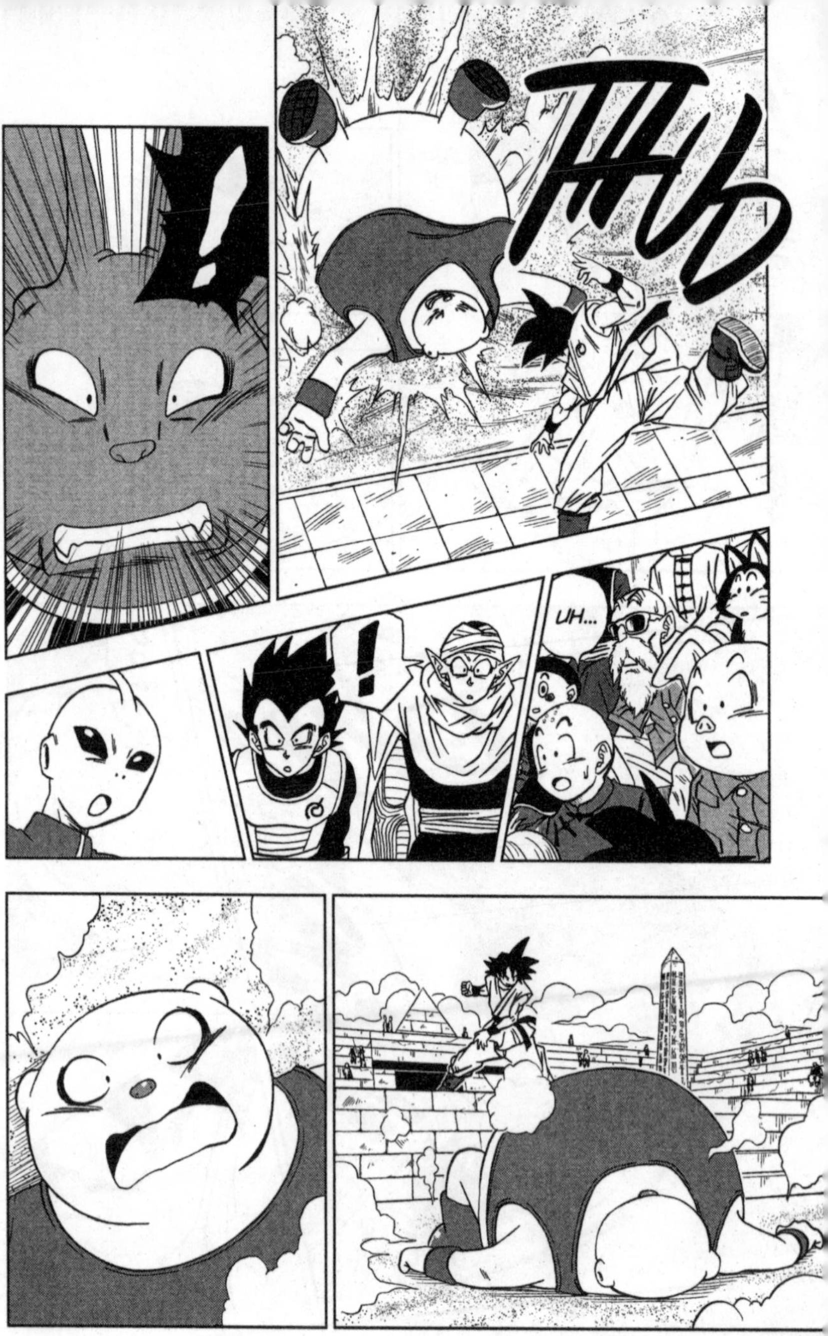
THUD
!
UH...
!

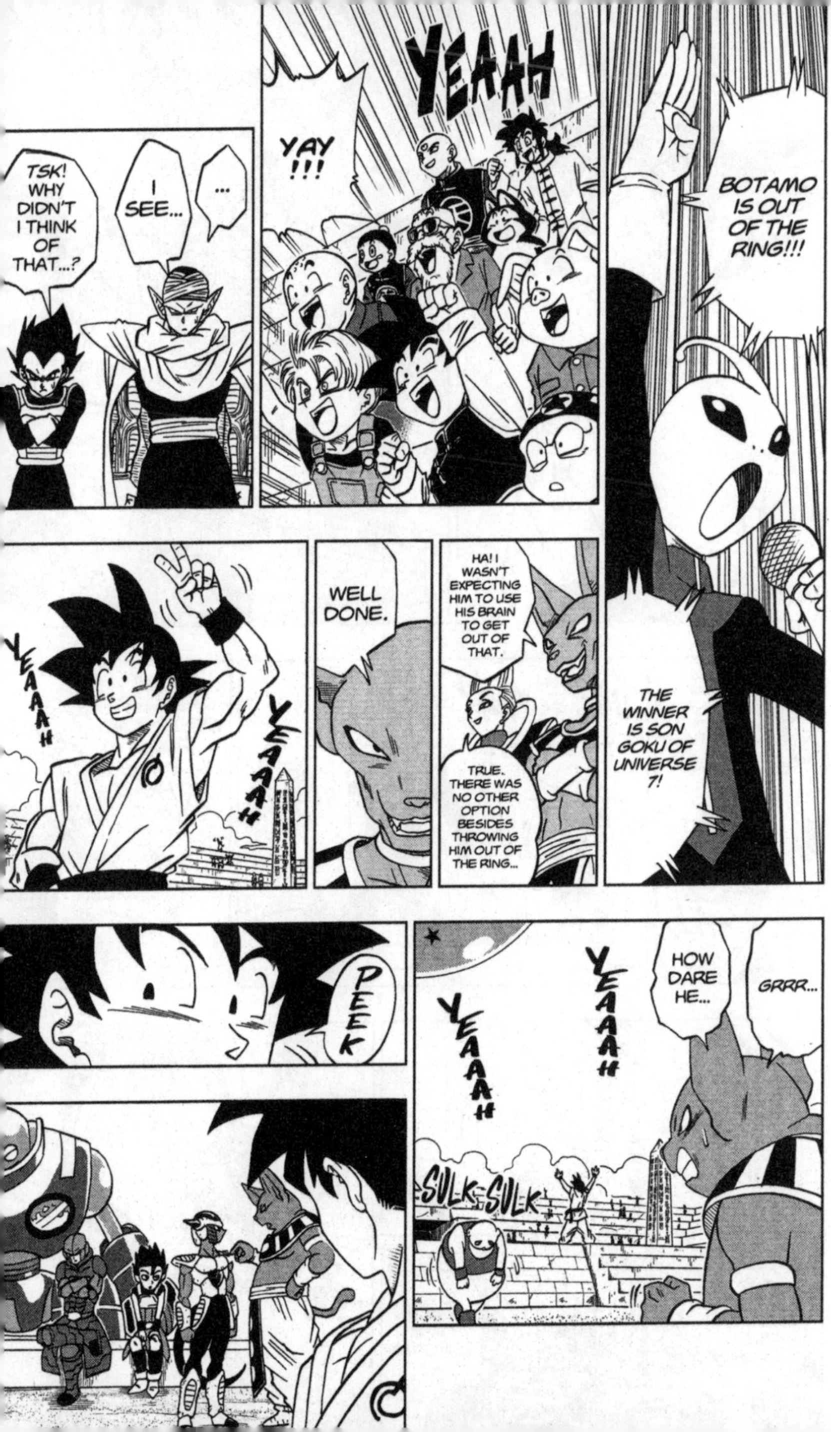
BOTAMO IS OUT OF THE RING!!!
THE WINNER IS SON GOKU OF UNIVERSE 7!
YEAAH
YAY!!!
...
I SEE...
TSK! WHY DIDN'T I THINK OF THAT...?
HA! I WASN'T EXPECTING HIM TO USE HIS BRAIN TO GET OUT OF THAT.
TRUE. THERE WAS NO OTHER OPTION BESIDES THROWING HIM OUT OF THE RING...
WELL DONE.
YEAAAAH
YEAAAAH
GRRR...
HOW DARE HE...
YEAAAAH
YEAAAAH
SULK SULK
PEEK

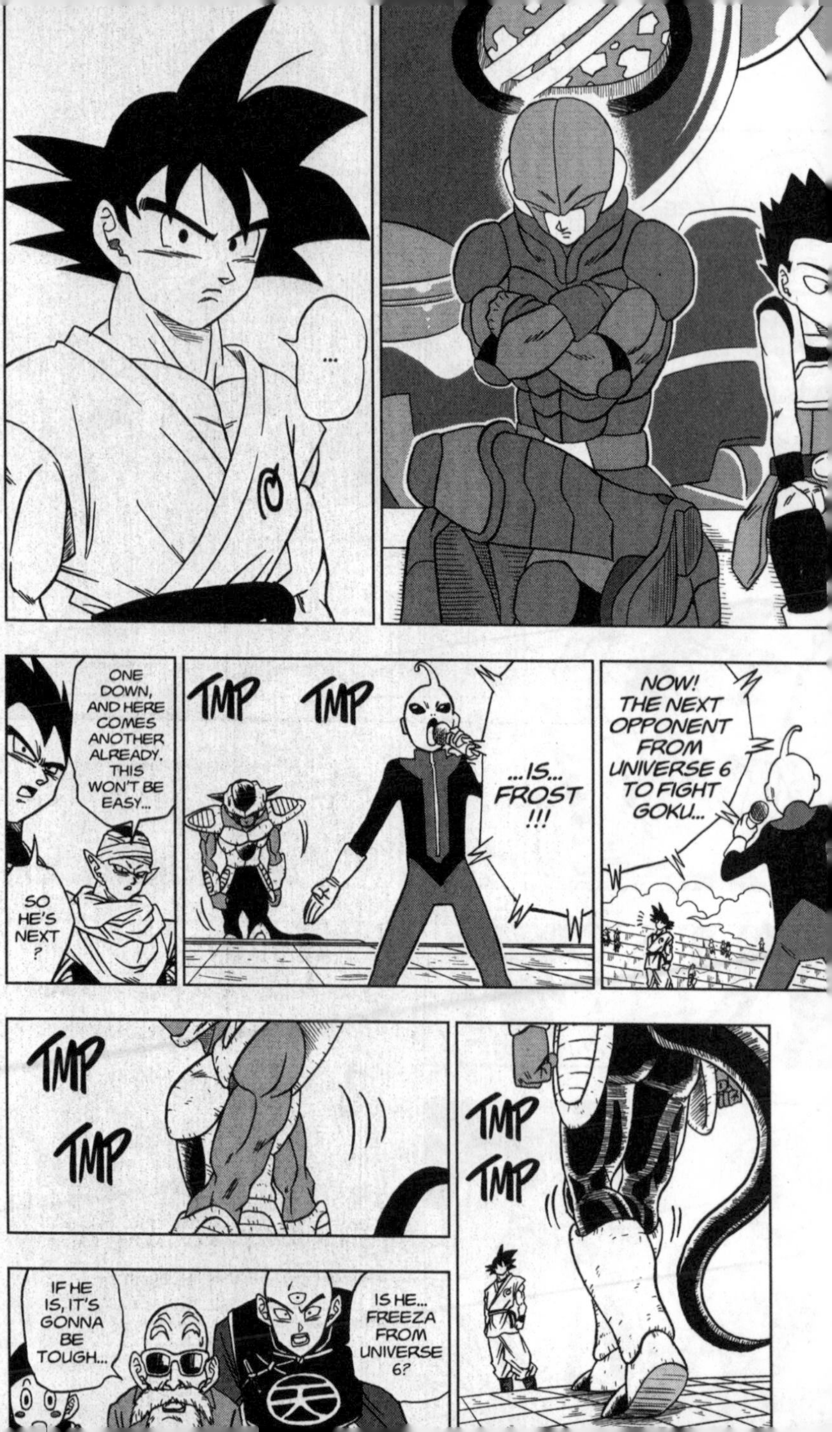
...
NOW! THE NEXT OPPONENT FROM UNIVERSE 6 TO FIGHT GOKU...
TMP TMP
...IS... FROST !!!
ONE DOWN, AND HERE COMES ANOTHER ALREADY. THIS WON'T BE EASY...
SO HE'S NEXT ?
TMP TMP
TMP TMP
IS HE... FREEZA FROM UNIVERSE 6?
IF HE IS, IT'S GONNA BE TOUGH...

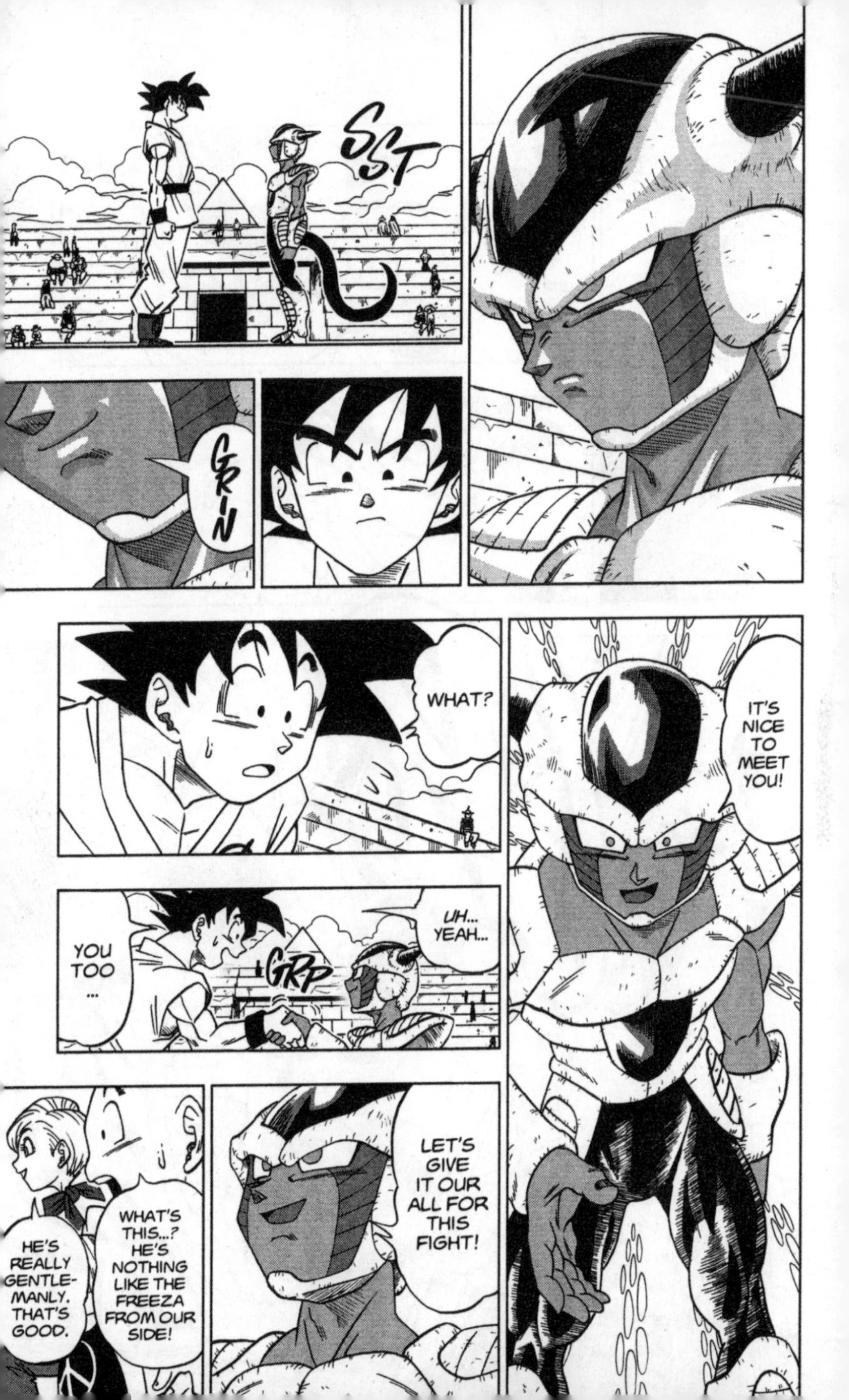
SST
GRIN
IT'S NICE TO MEET YOU!
WHAT?
UH... YEAH...
GRP
YOU TOO ...
LET'S GIVE IT OUR ALL FOR THIS FIGHT!
WHAT'S THIS...? HE'S NOTHING LIKE THE FREEZA FROM OUR SIDE!
HE'S REALLY GENTLE-MANLY. THAT'S GOOD.

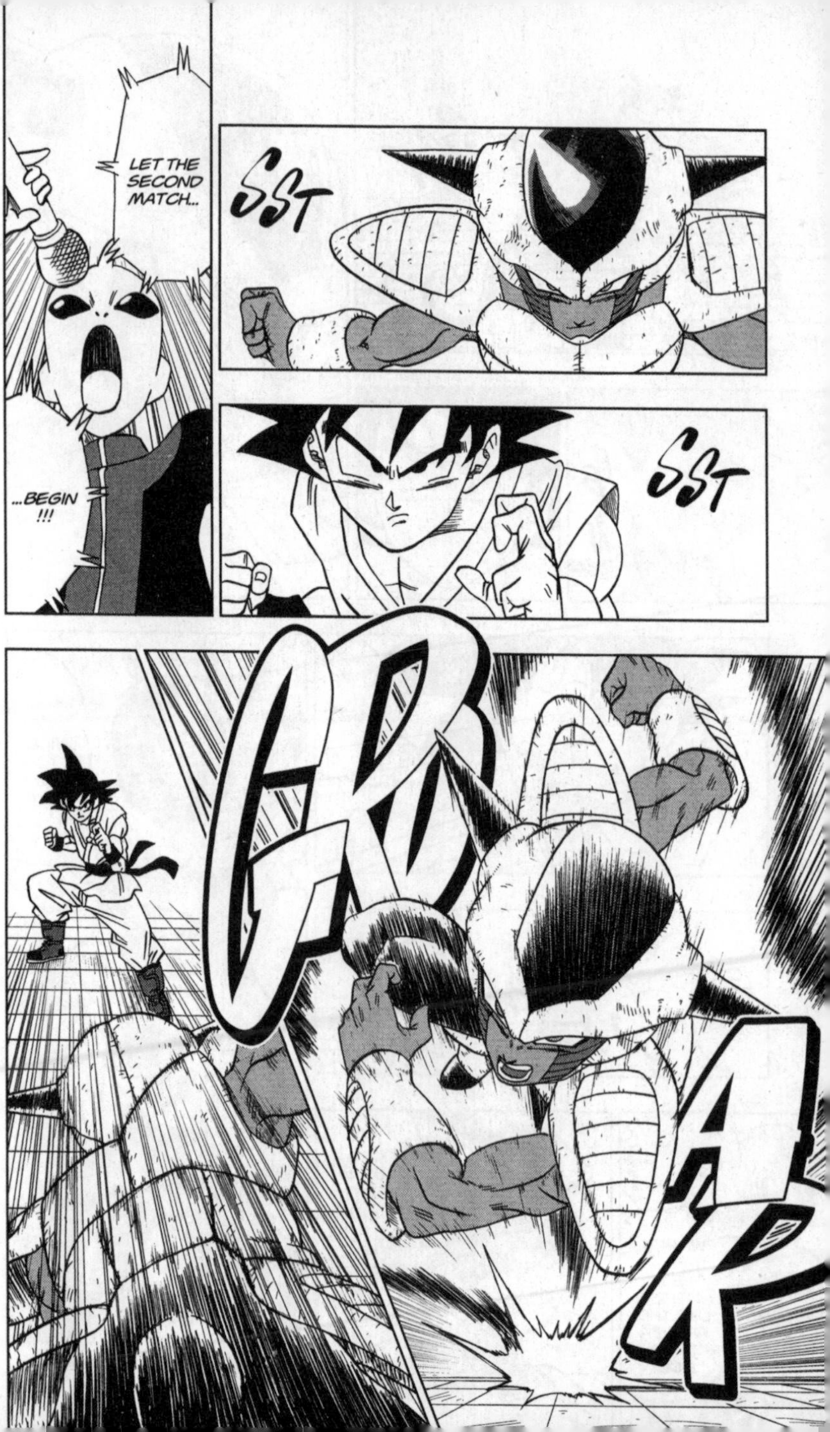
SST
SST
LET THE SECOND MATCH...
...BEGIN !!!
CRAK

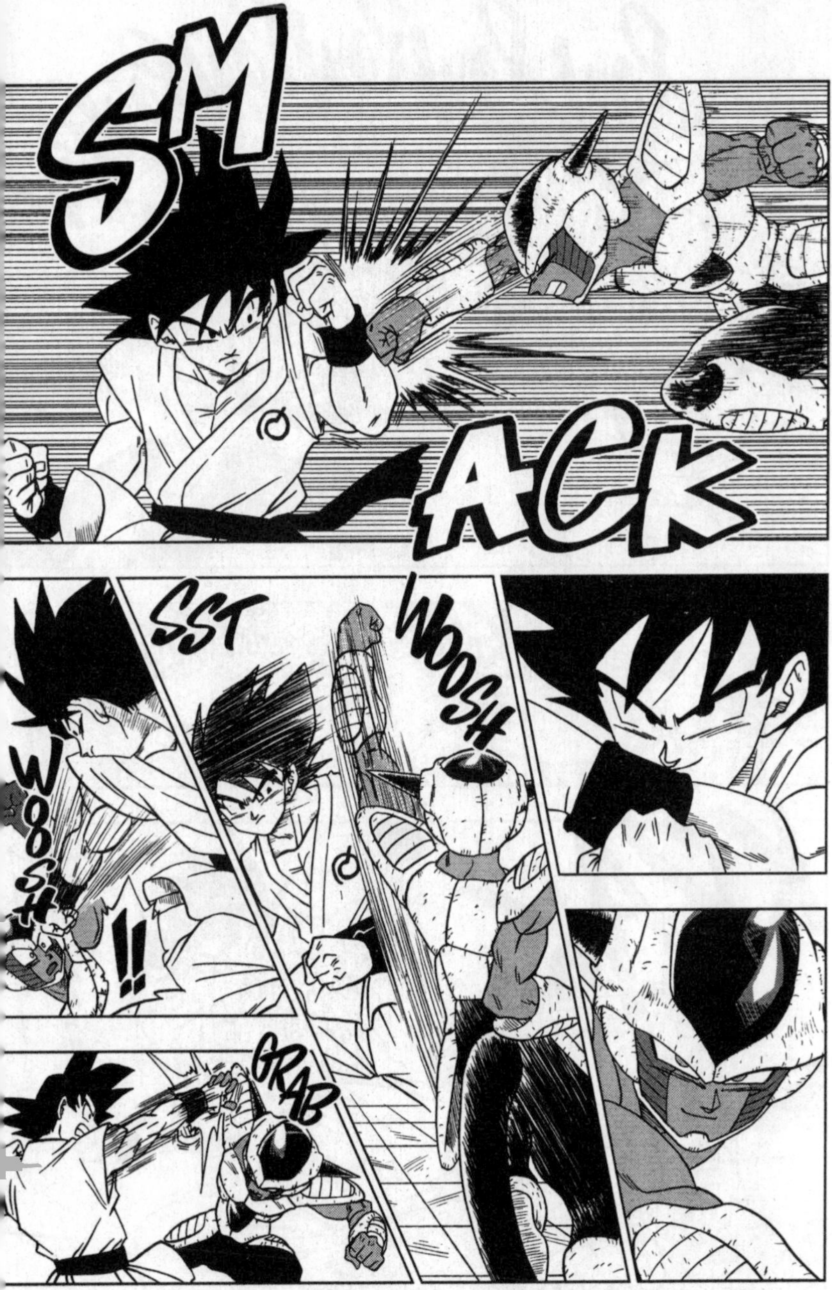
SMACK
WOOSH
SST
WOOSH
!!
GRAB

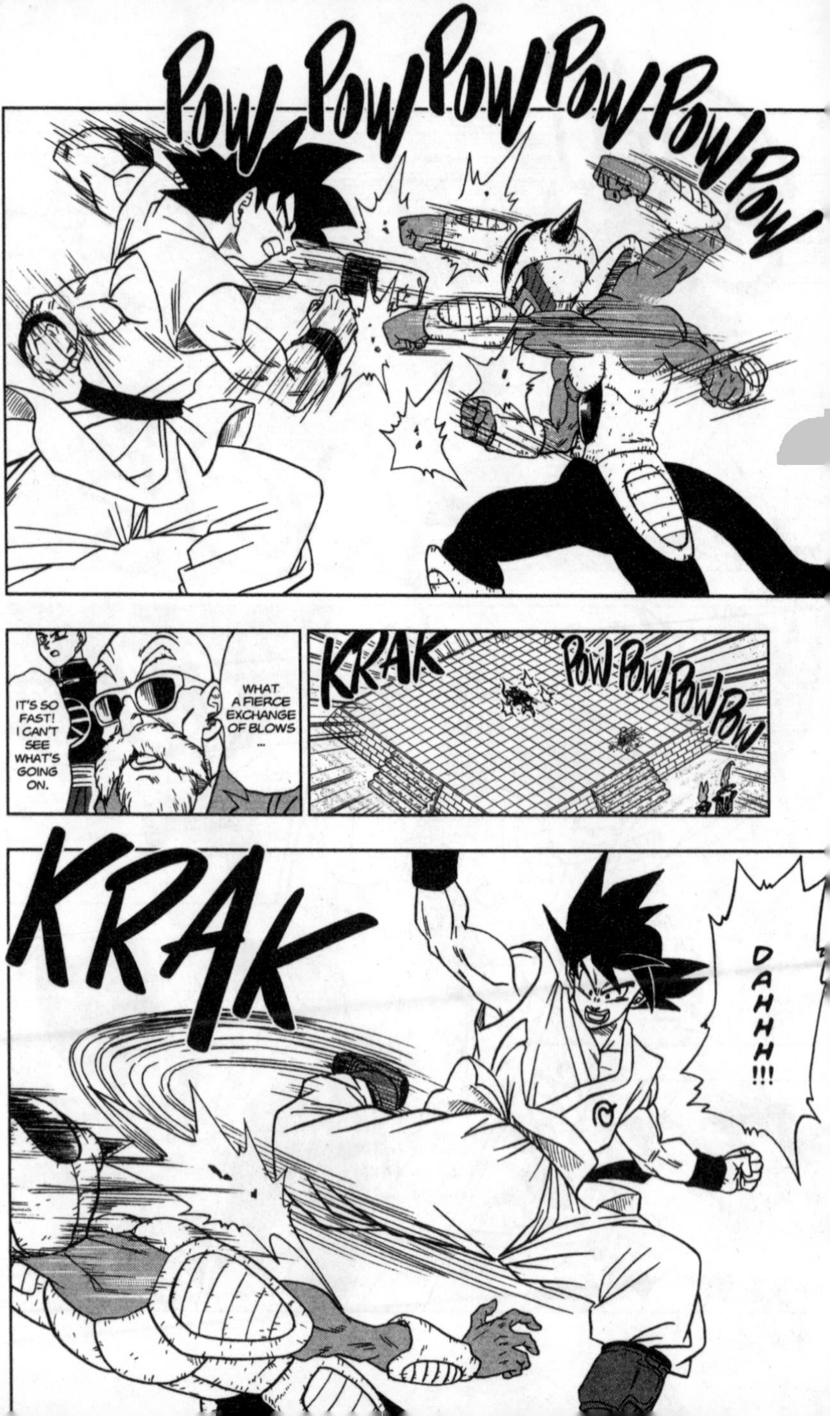
POW POW POW POW POW POW POW
KRAK
POW POW POW POW POW
WHAT A FIERCE EXCHANGE OF BLOWS ...
IT'S SO FAST! I CAN'T SEE WHAT'S GOING ON.
DAHHH!!!
KRAK

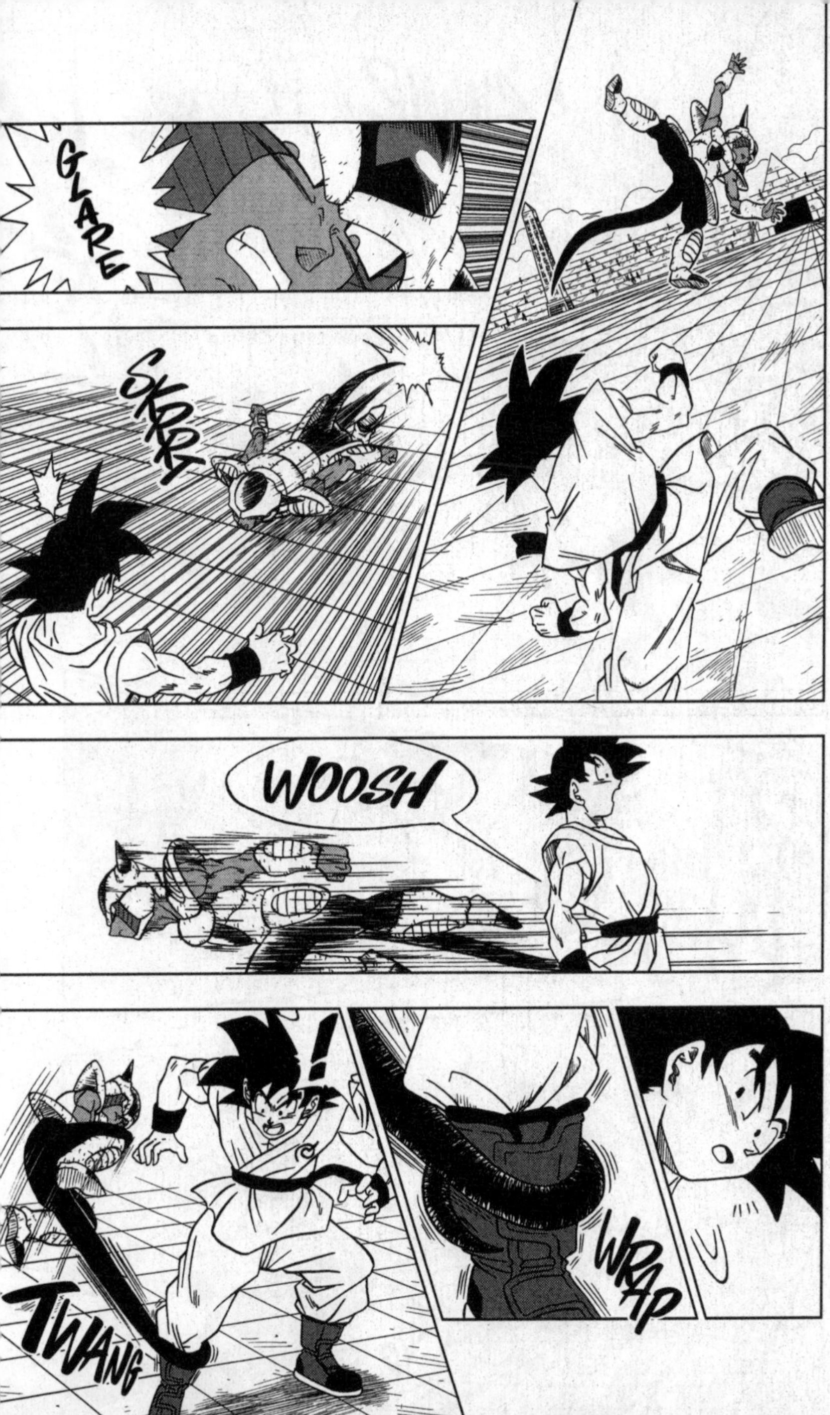
GLARE
SKRRT
WOOSH
WRAP
!
TWANG

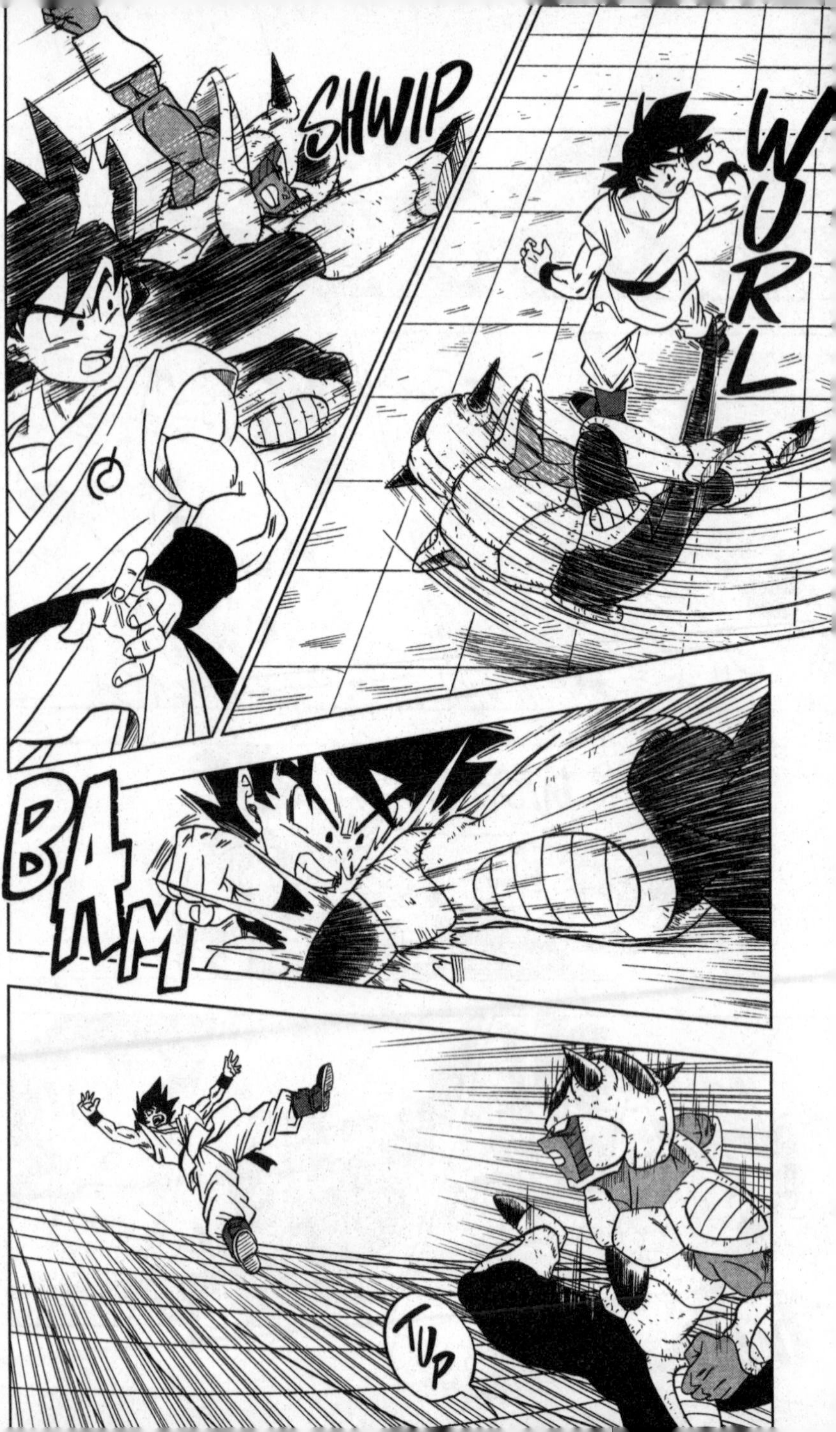
WURL
SHWIP
BAM
TUP

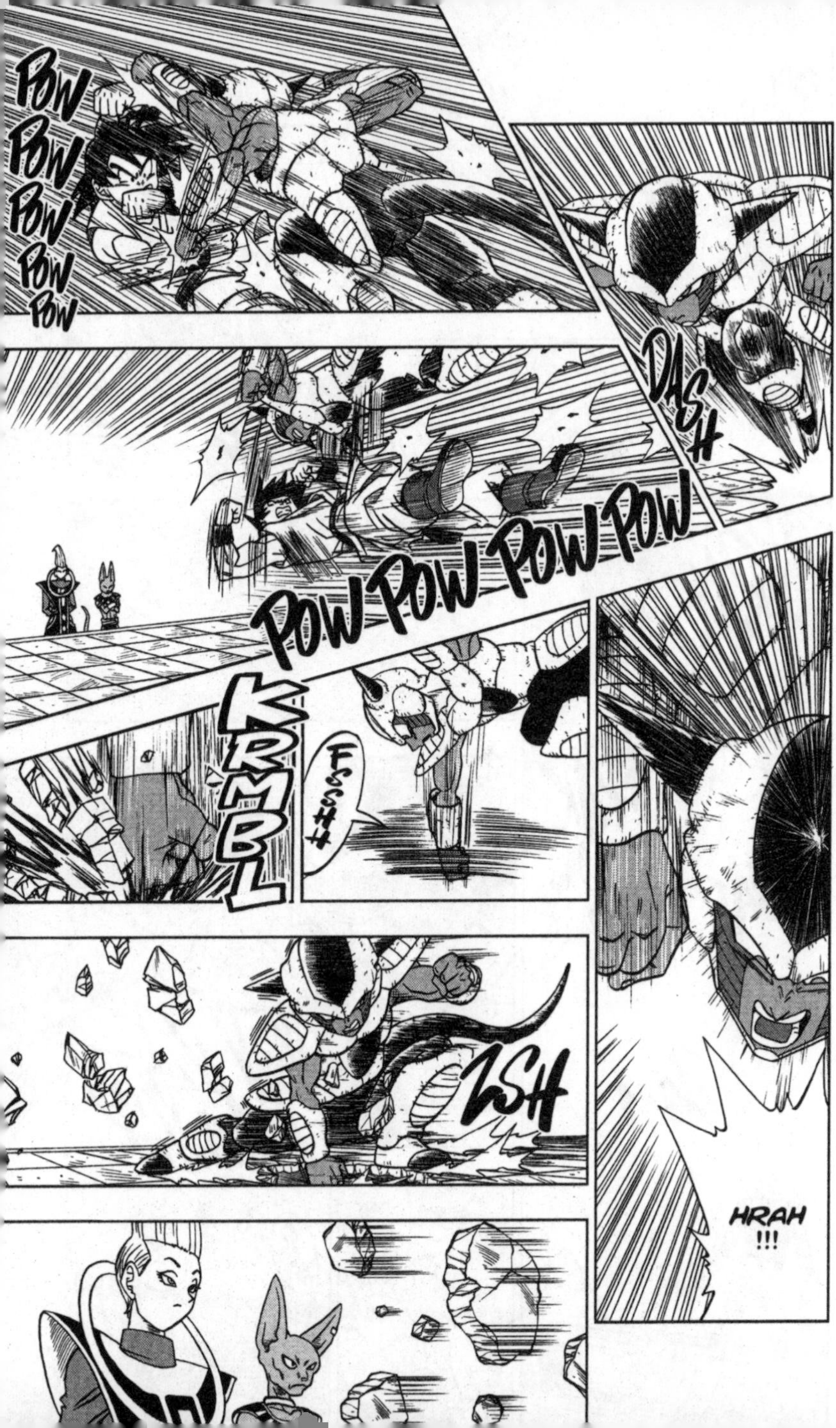
DASH
POW POW POW POW POW
POW POW POW POW
HRAH !!!
FSSHH
KRMBL
ZSH

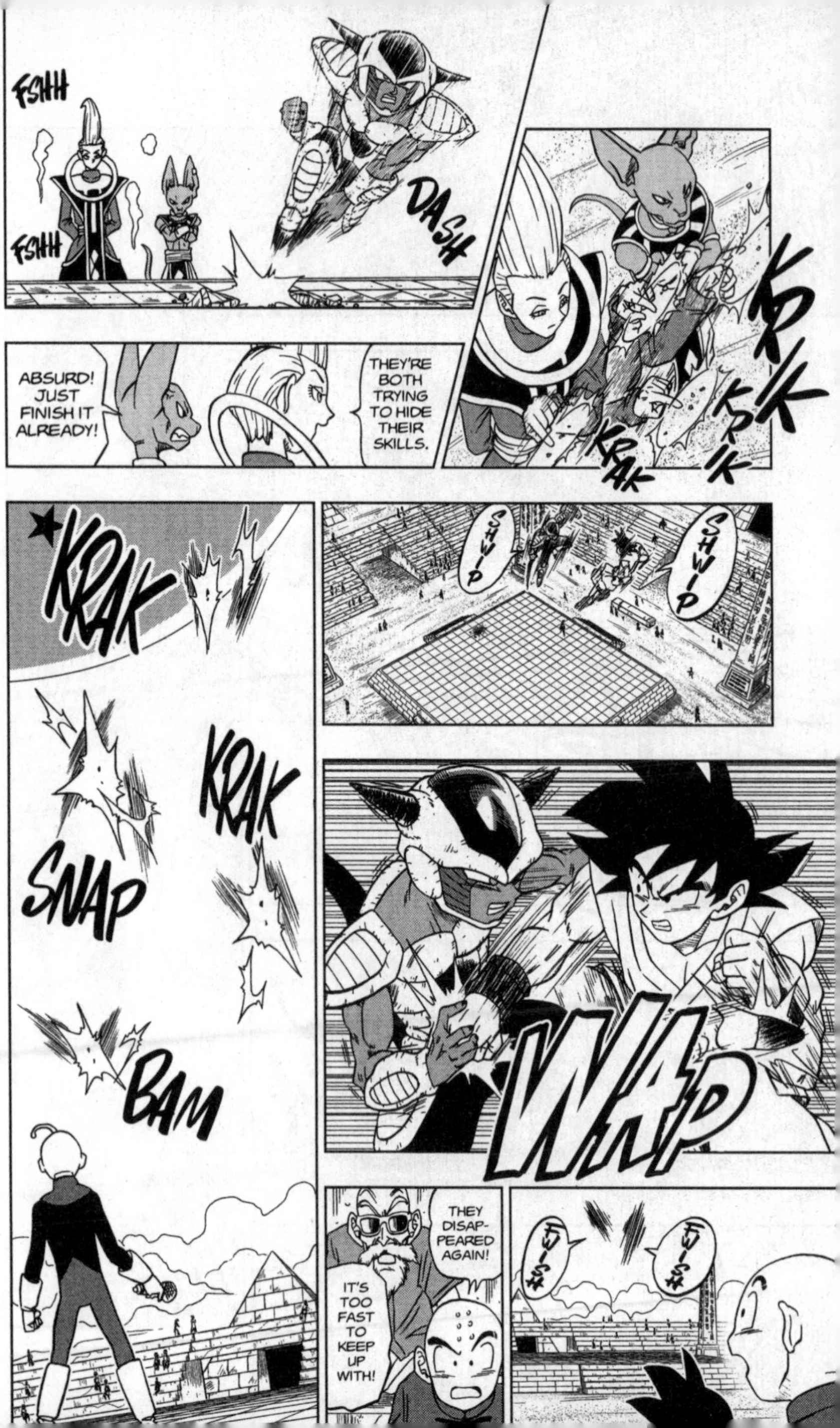
KRIK
KRIK
KRAK
FSHH
FSHH
DASH
THEY'RE BOTH TRYING TO HIDE THEIR SKILLS.
ABSURD! JUST FINISH IT ALREADY!
SHWIP
SHWIP
WAP
FWISH
FWISH
THEY DISAP-PEARED AGAIN!
IT'S TOO FAST TO KEEP UP WITH!
KRAK
KRAK
SNAP
BAM

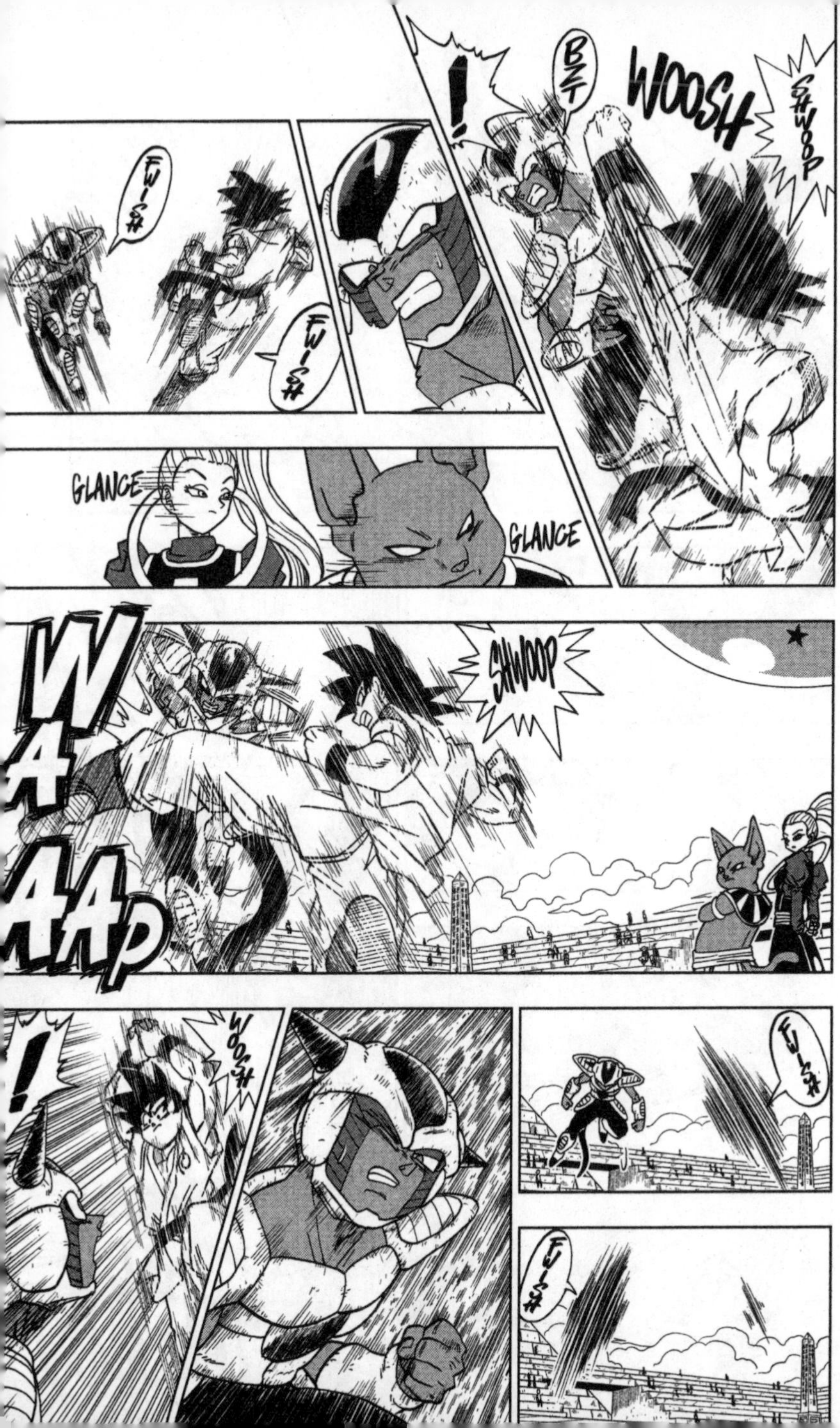
SHWOOP
WOOSH
BZT
!
FWISH
FWISH
GLANCE
GLANCE
SHWOOP
WAAAAP
FWISH
FWISH
WOOSH
!

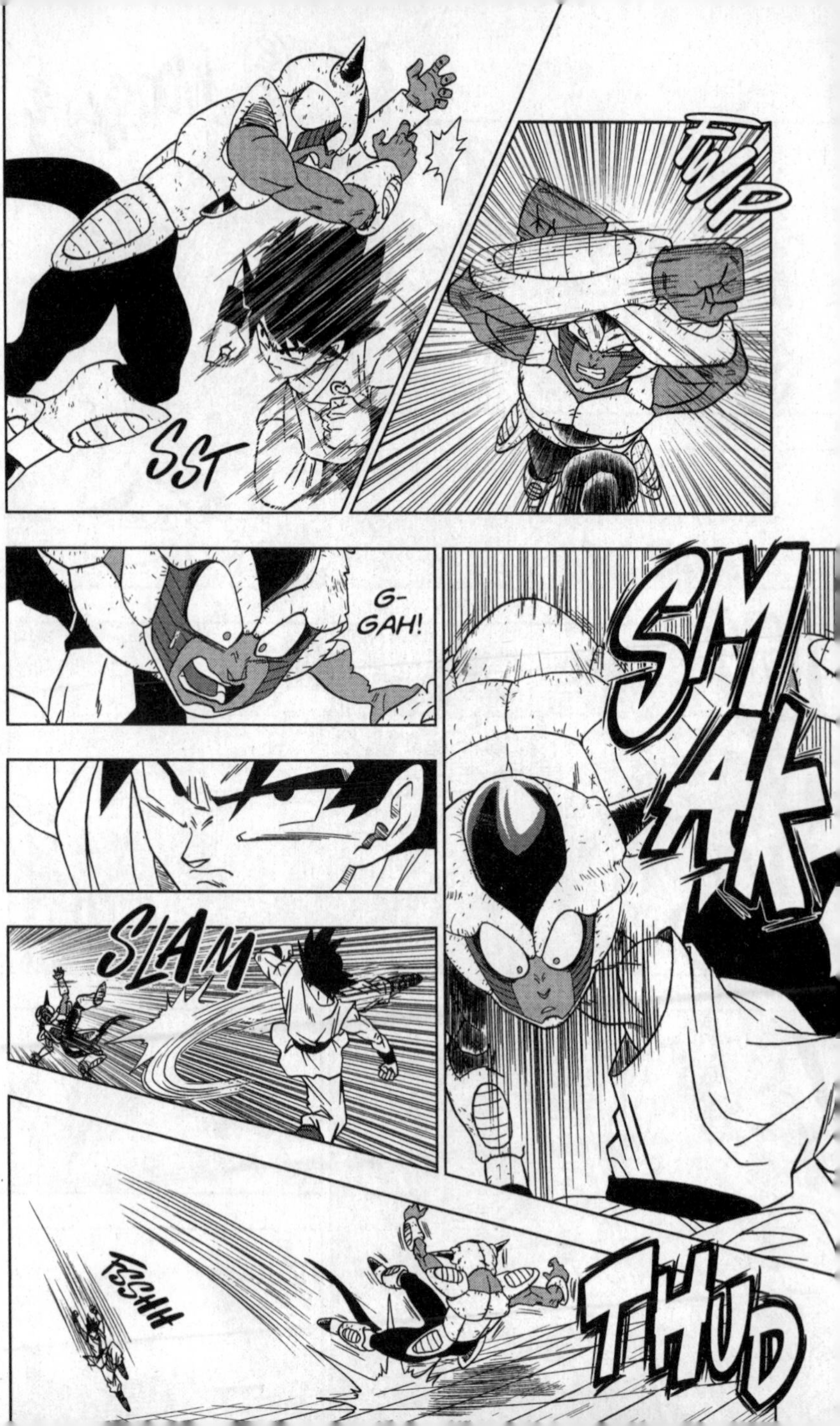
FWIP
SST
SMAK
G-GAH!
SLAM
THUD
FSSHH

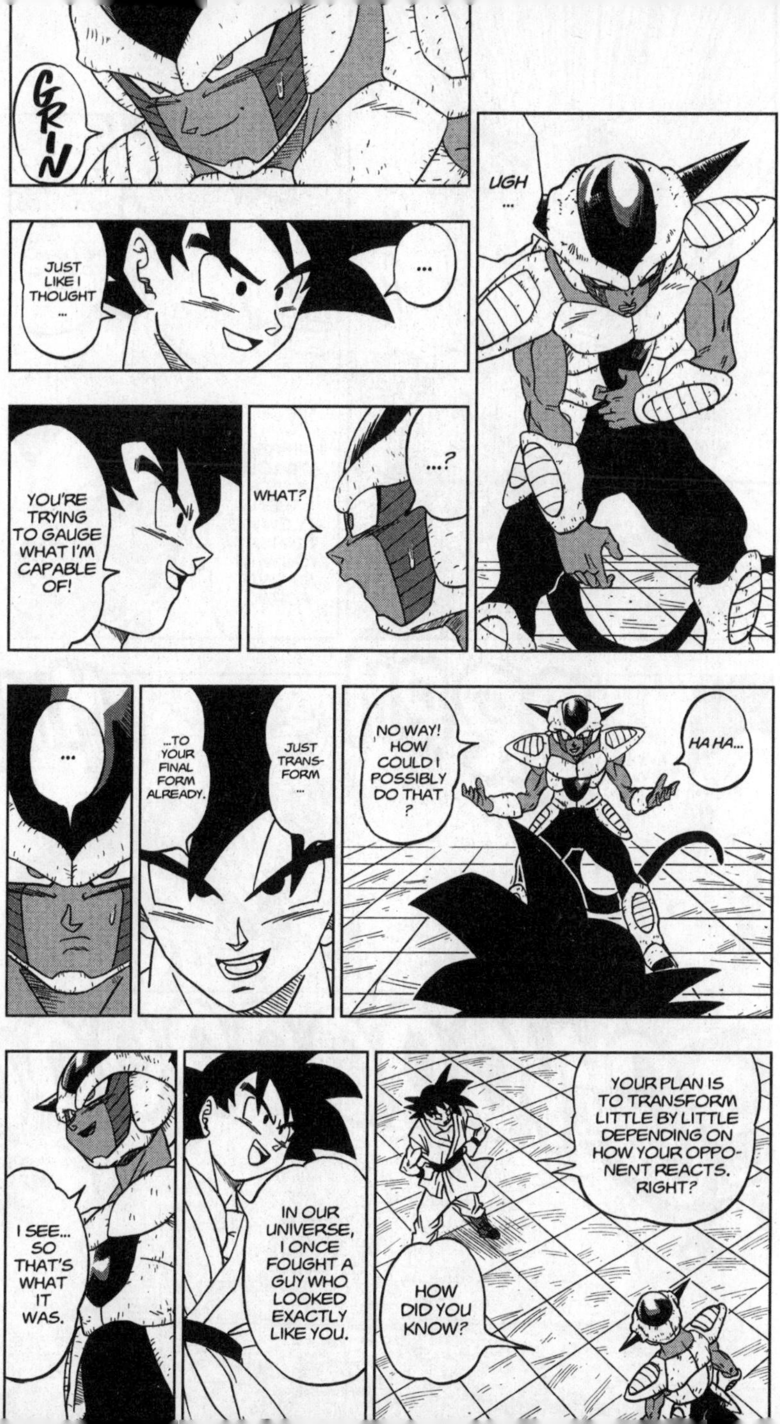
UGH ...
GRIN
...
JUST LIKE I THOUGHT ...
...?
WHAT?
YOU'RE TRYING TO GAUGE WHAT I'M CAPABLE OF!
HA HA...
NO WAY! HOW COULD I POSSIBLY DO THAT?
JUST TRANS-FORM ...
...TO YOUR FINAL FORM ALREADY.
...
YOUR PLAN IS TO TRANSFORM LITTLE BY LITTLE DEPENDING ON HOW YOUR OPPO-NENT REACTS. RIGHT?
HOW DID YOU KNOW?
IN OUR UNIVERSE, I ONCE FOUGHT A GUY WHO LOOKED EXACTLY LIKE YOU.
I SEE... SO THAT'S WHAT IT WAS.

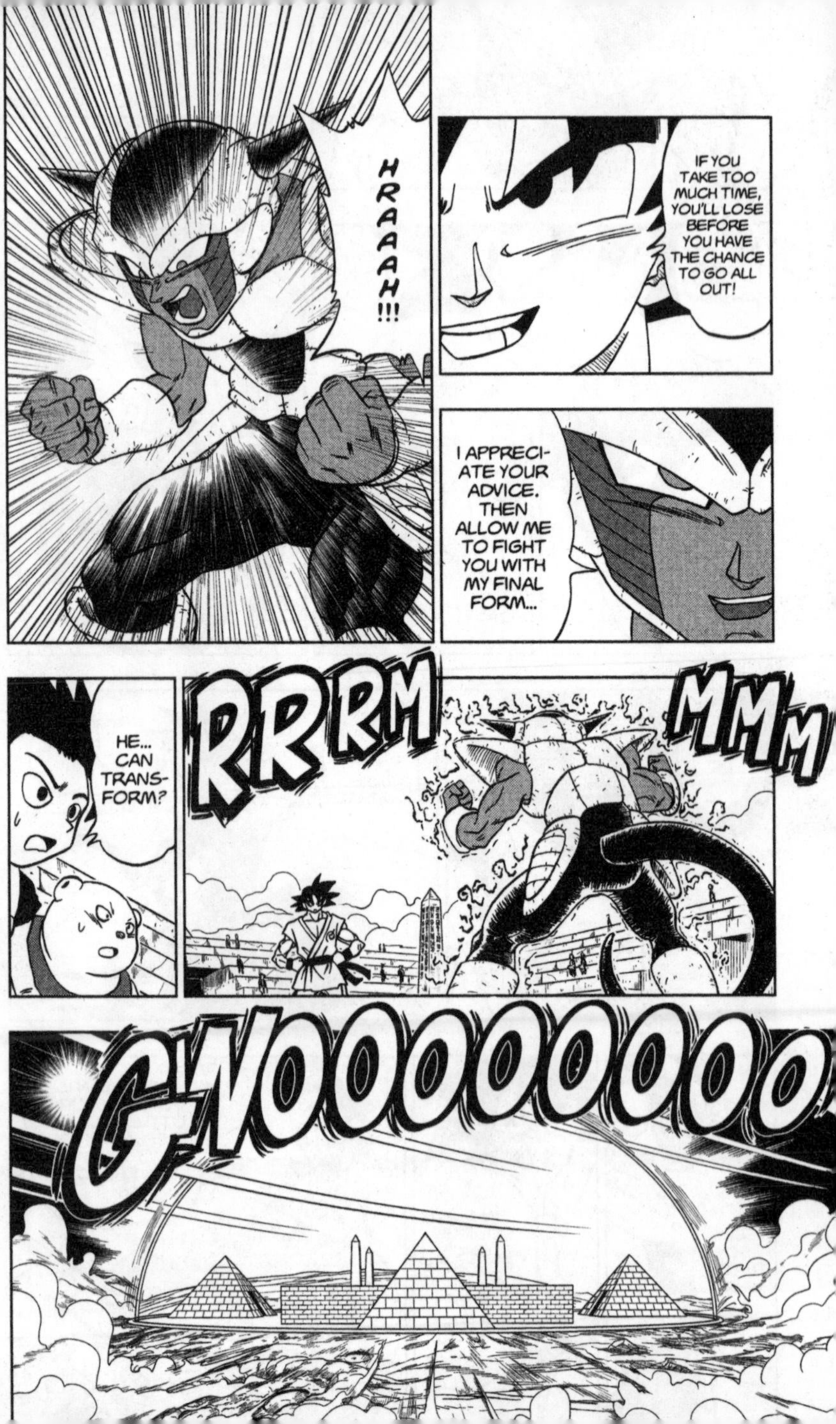
IF YOU TAKE TOO MUCH TIME, YOU'LL LOSE BEFORE YOU HAVE THE CHANCE TO GO ALL OUT!
I APPRECIATE YOUR ADVICE. THEN ALLOW ME TO FIGHT YOU WITH MY FINAL FORM...
HRAAAAH!!!
RRRM MMM
HE... CAN TRANSFORM?
GNOOOOOOO

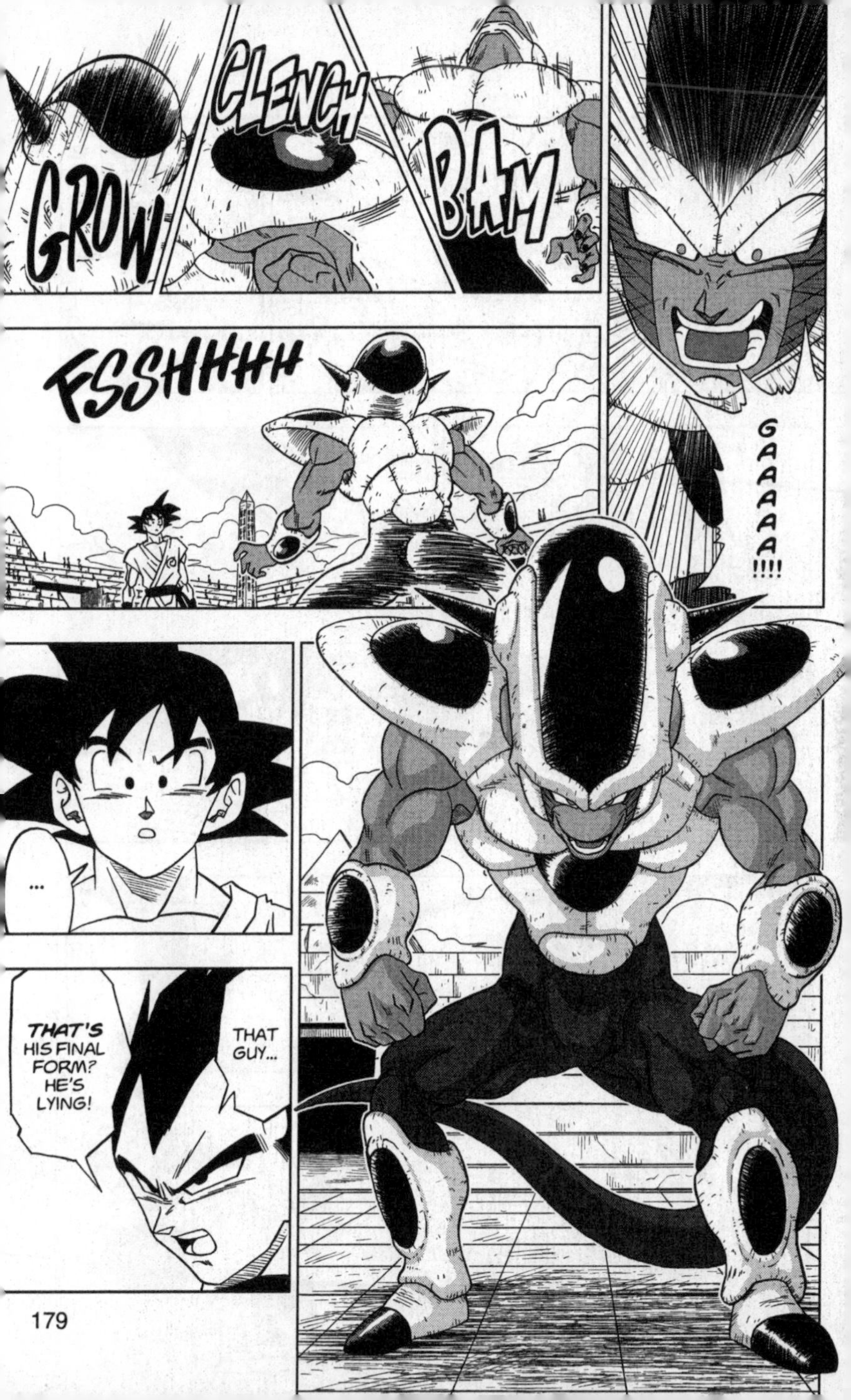
GAAAAAA!!!!
BAM
CLENCH
GROW
FSSHHHH
...
THAT GUY...
THAT'S HIS FINAL FORM? HE'S LYING!

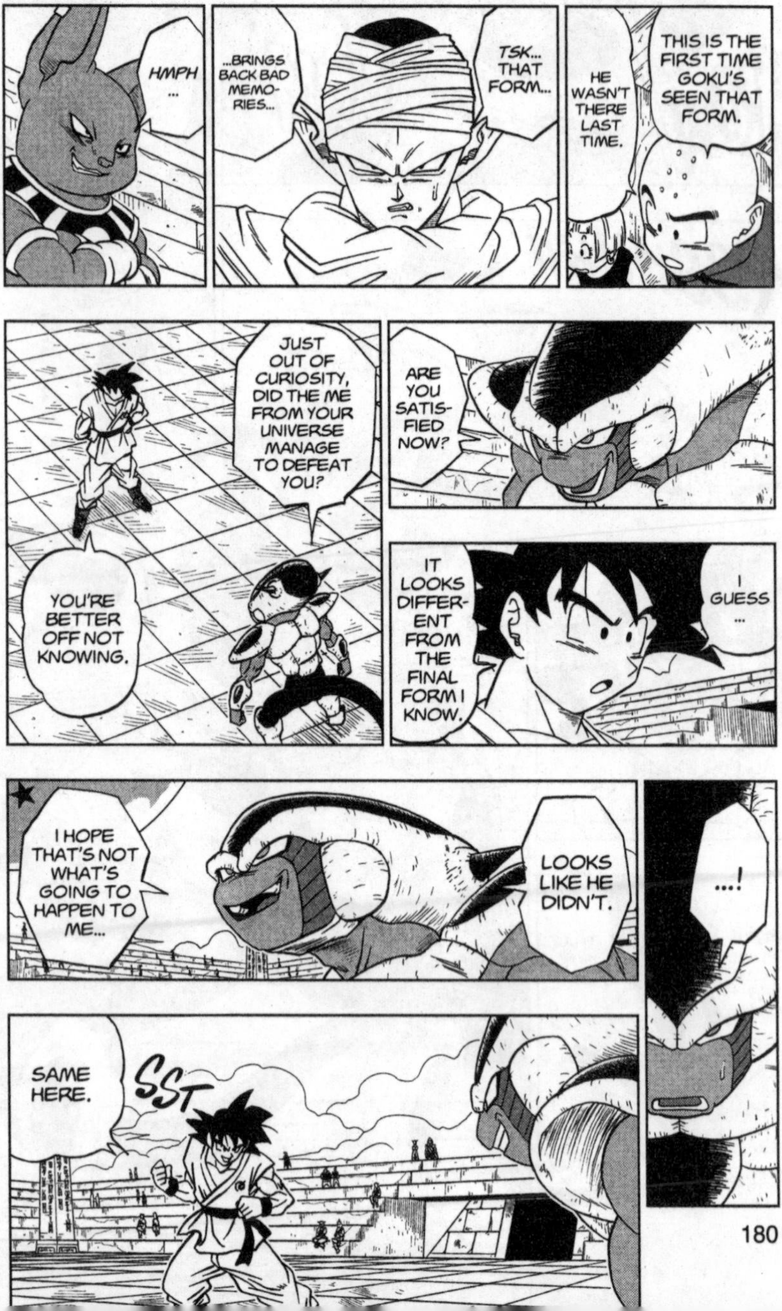
THIS IS THE FIRST TIME GOKU'S SEEN THAT FORM.
HE WASN'T THERE LAST TIME.
TSK... THAT FORM...
...BRINGS BACK BAD MEMORIES...
HMPH ...
ARE YOU SATISFIED NOW?
I GUESS ...
IT LOOKS DIFFERENT FROM THE FINAL FORM I KNOW.
JUST OUT OF CURIOSITY, DID THE ME FROM YOUR UNIVERSE MANAGE TO DEFEAT YOU?
YOU'RE BETTER OFF NOT KNOWING.
...!
LOOKS LIKE HE DIDN'T.
I HOPE THAT'S NOT WHAT'S GOING TO HAPPEN TO ME...
SAME HERE.
SST

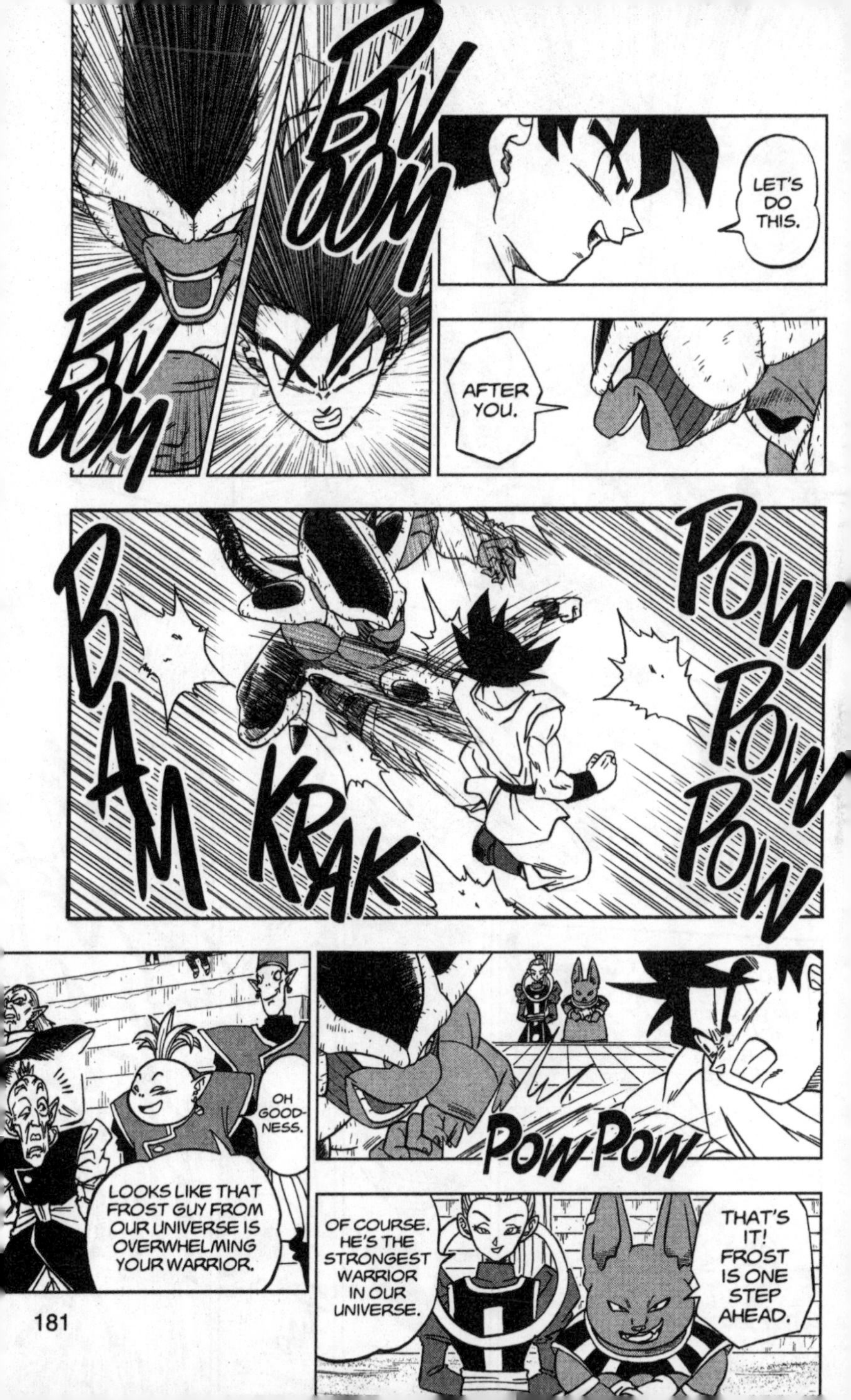
LET'S DO THIS.
AFTER YOU.
BWOOM
BWOOM
POW POW POW POW
KRAK
BAM
POW POW
OH GOODNESS.
LOOKS LIKE THAT FROST GUY FROM OUR UNIVERSE IS OVERWHELMING YOUR WARRIOR.
THAT'S IT! FROST IS ONE STEP AHEAD.
OF COURSE. HE'S THE STRONGEST WARRIOR IN OUR UNIVERSE.

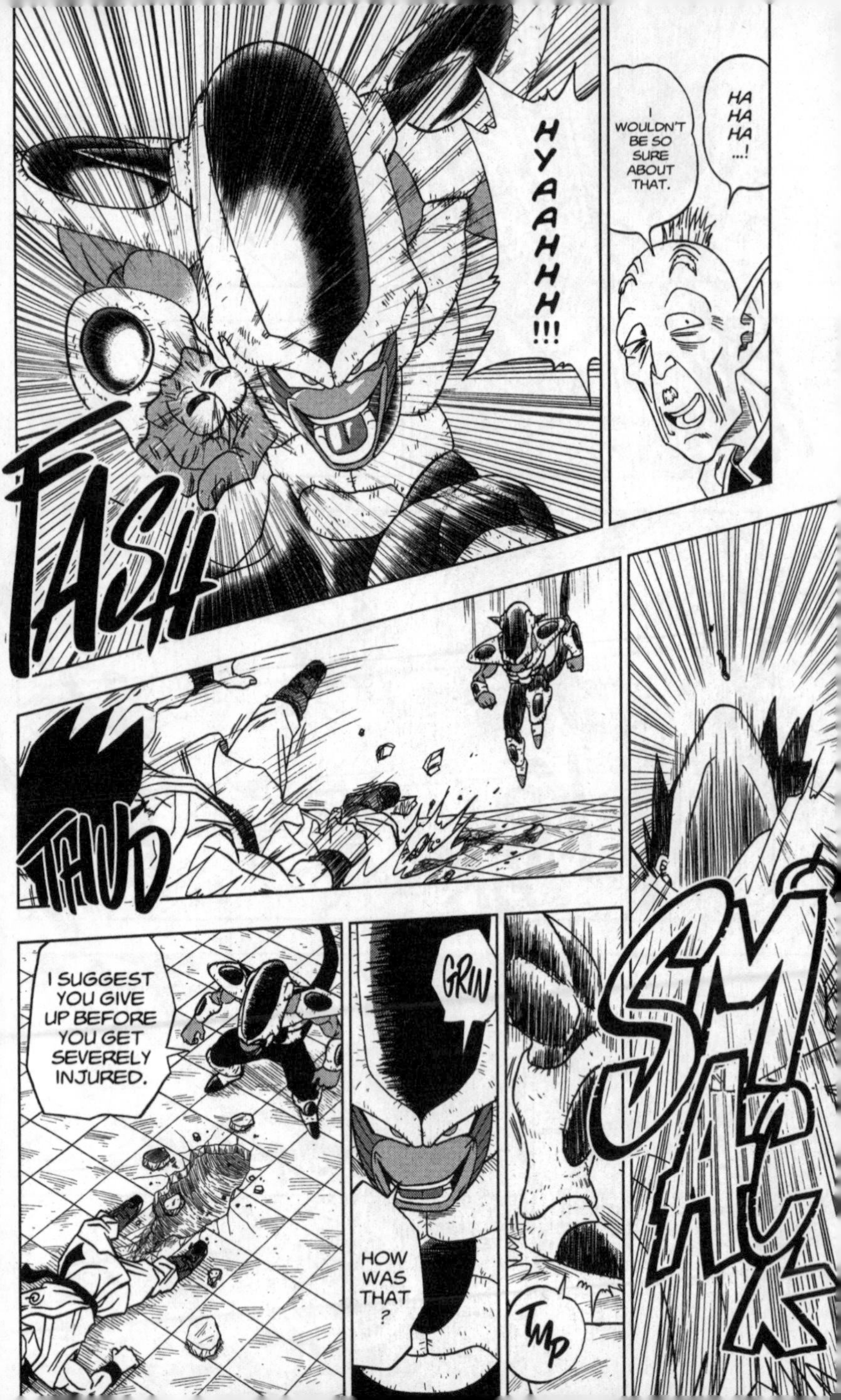

HA HA HA ...!
I WOULDN'T BE SO SURE ABOUT THAT.
HYAAHHH!!!
FASH
SMACK
THUD
TMP
GRIN
HOW WAS THAT?
I SUGGEST YOU GIVE UP BEFORE YOU GET SEVERELY INJURED.

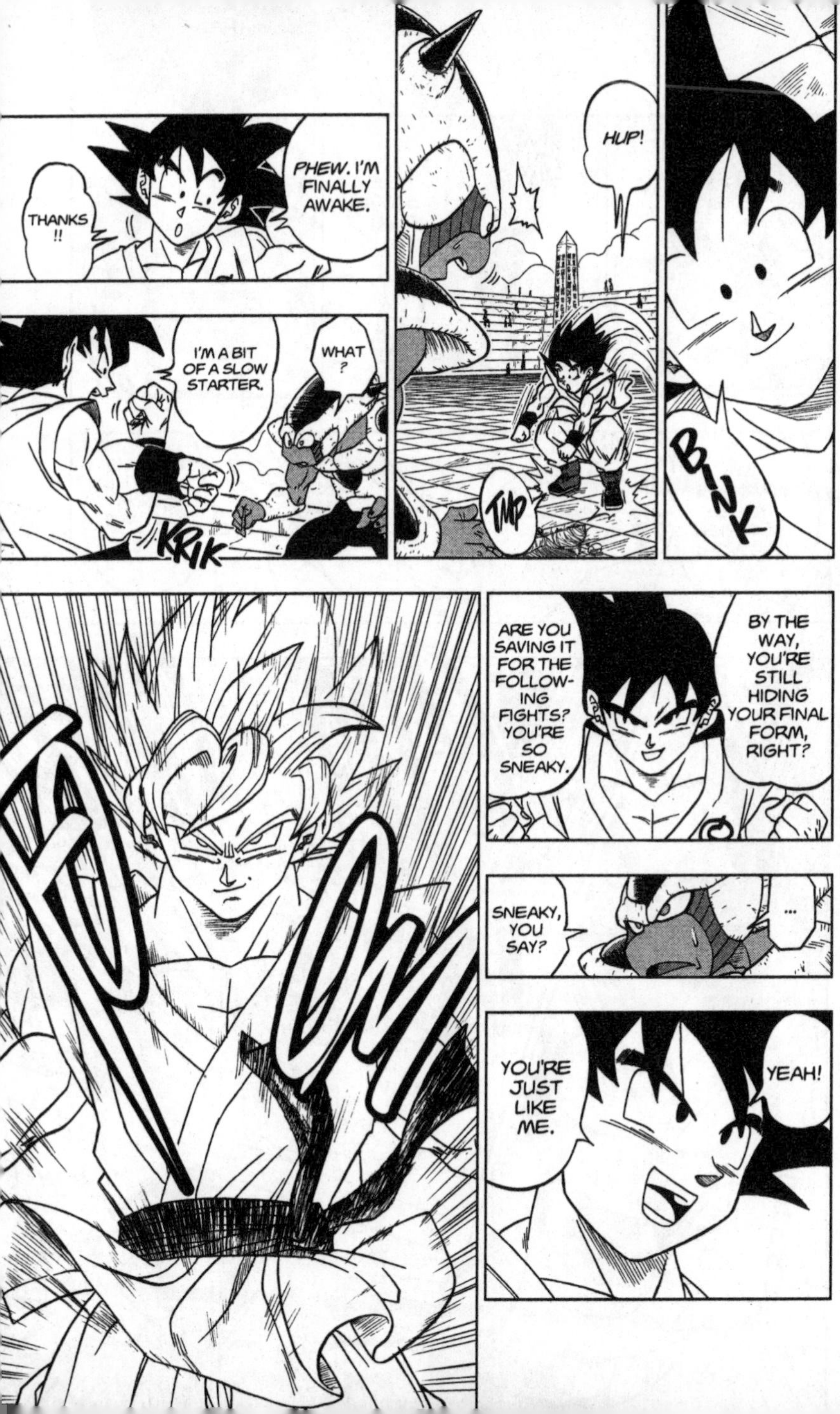
BINK
HUP!
TMP
PHEW. I'M FINALLY AWAKE.
THANKS!!
WHAT?
I'M A BIT OF A SLOW STARTER.
KRIK
BY THE WAY, YOU'RE STILL HIDING YOUR FINAL FORM, RIGHT?
ARE YOU SAVING IT FOR THE FOLLOWING FIGHTS? YOU'RE SO SNEAKY.
...
SNEAKY, YOU SAY?
YEAH!
YOU'RE JUST LIKE ME.
FOOM

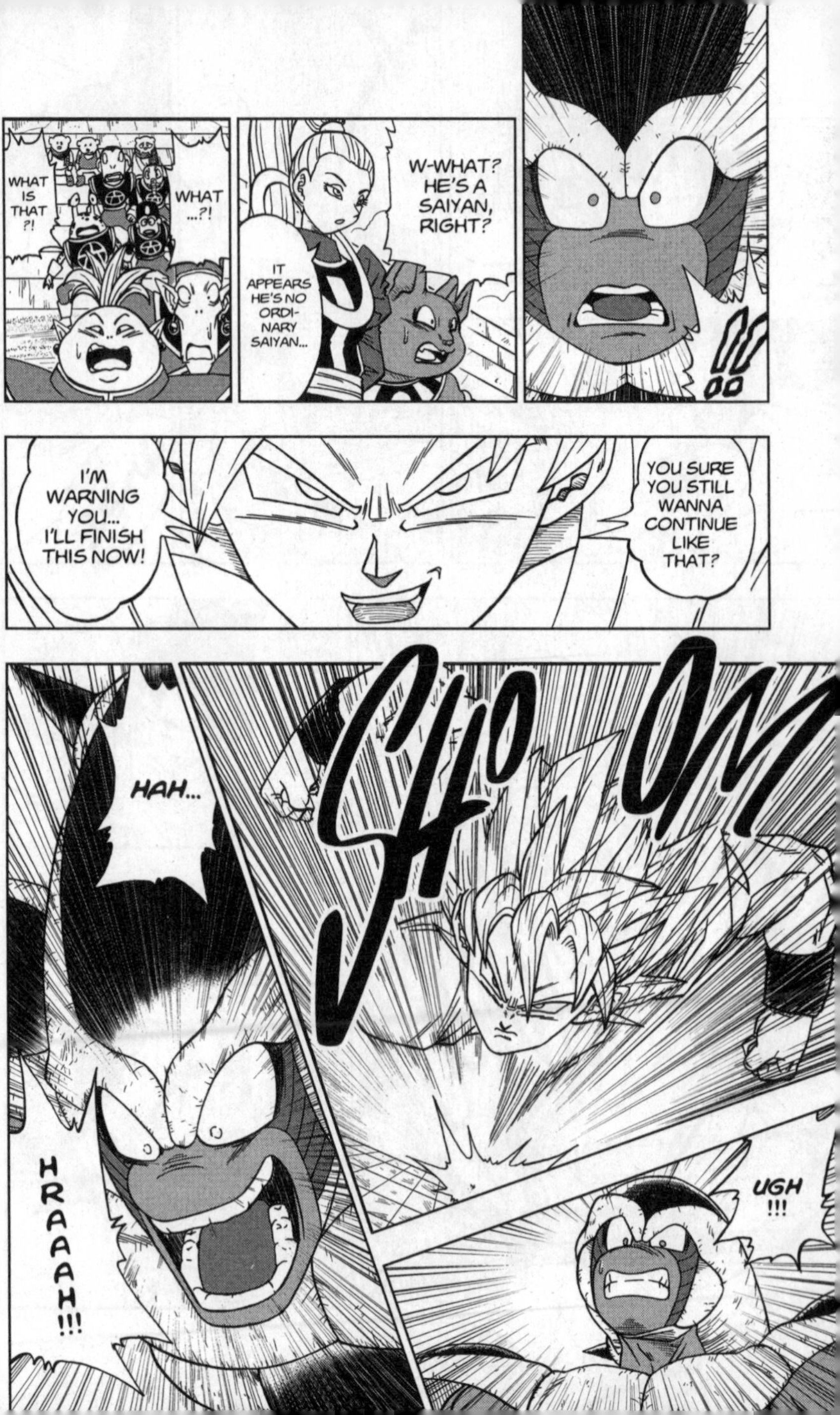
!!
W-WHAT? HE'S A SAIYAN, RIGHT?
IT APPEARS HE'S NO ORDINARY SAIYAN...
WHAT ...?!
WHAT IS THAT ?!
YOU SURE YOU STILL WANNA CONTINUE LIKE THAT?
I'M WARNING YOU... I'LL FINISH THIS NOW!
SHOOM
UGH !!!
HAH...
HRAAAAH!!!

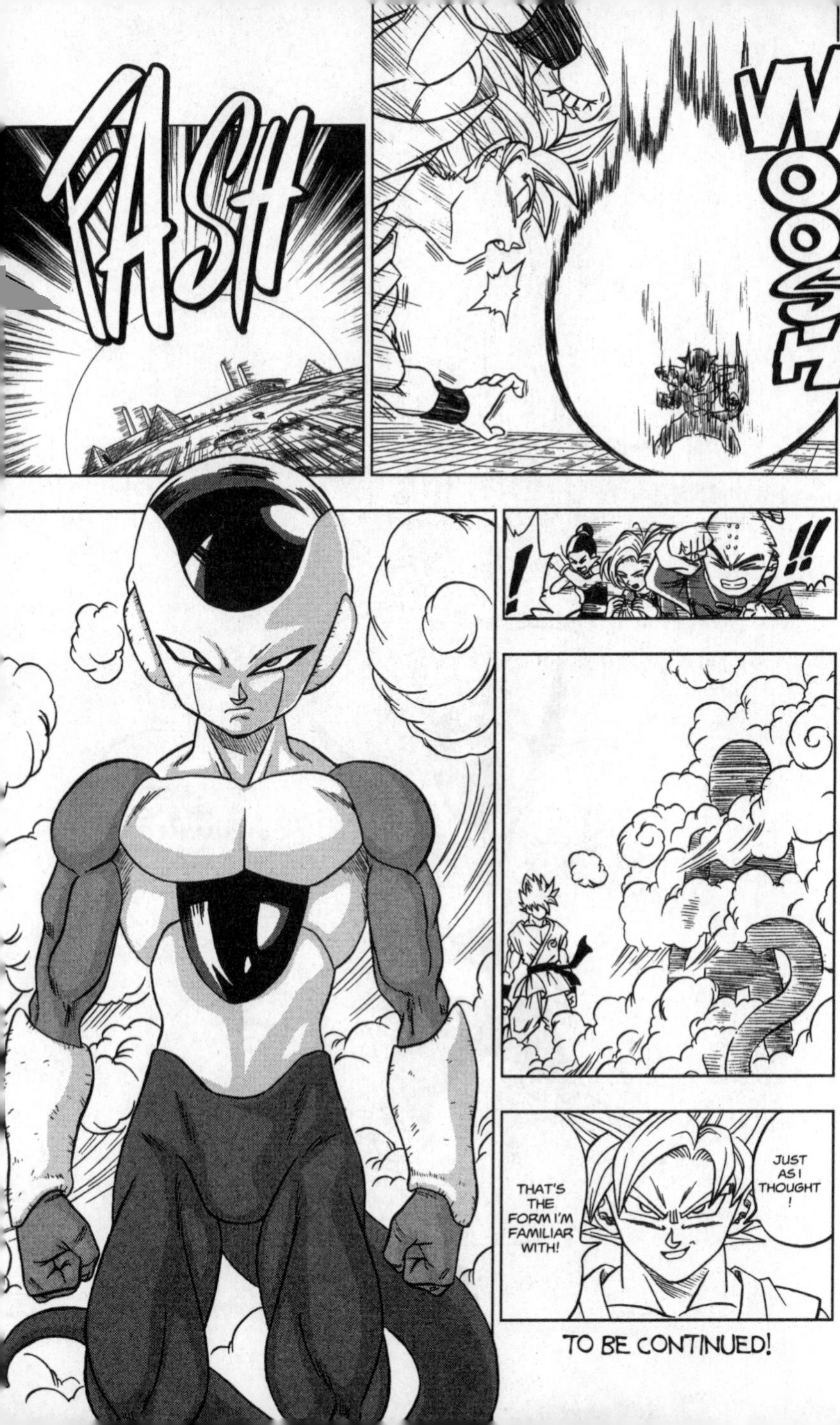
WOOSH
FASH
!!
!
JUST AS I THOUGHT!
THAT'S THE FORM I'M FAMILIAR WITH!
TO BE CONTINUED!

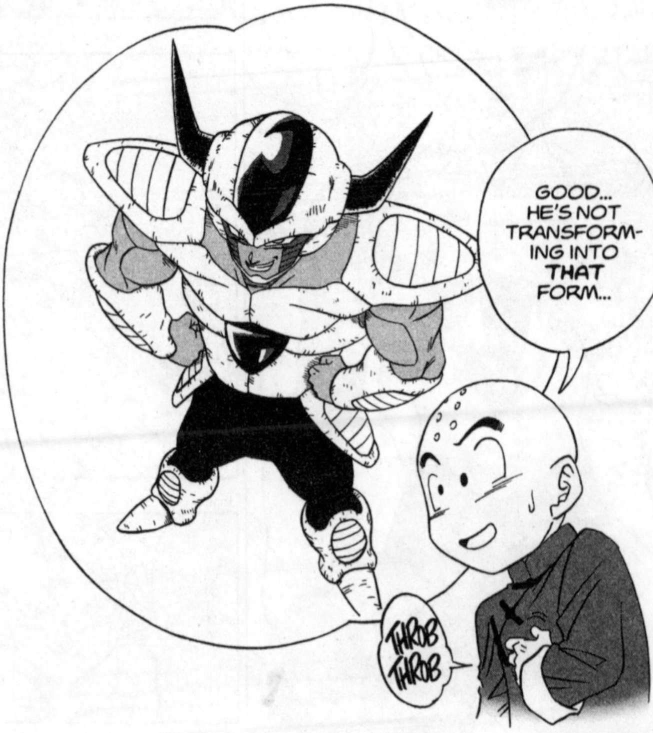
GOOD... HE'S NOT TRANSFORMING INTO THAT FORM...
THROB THROB

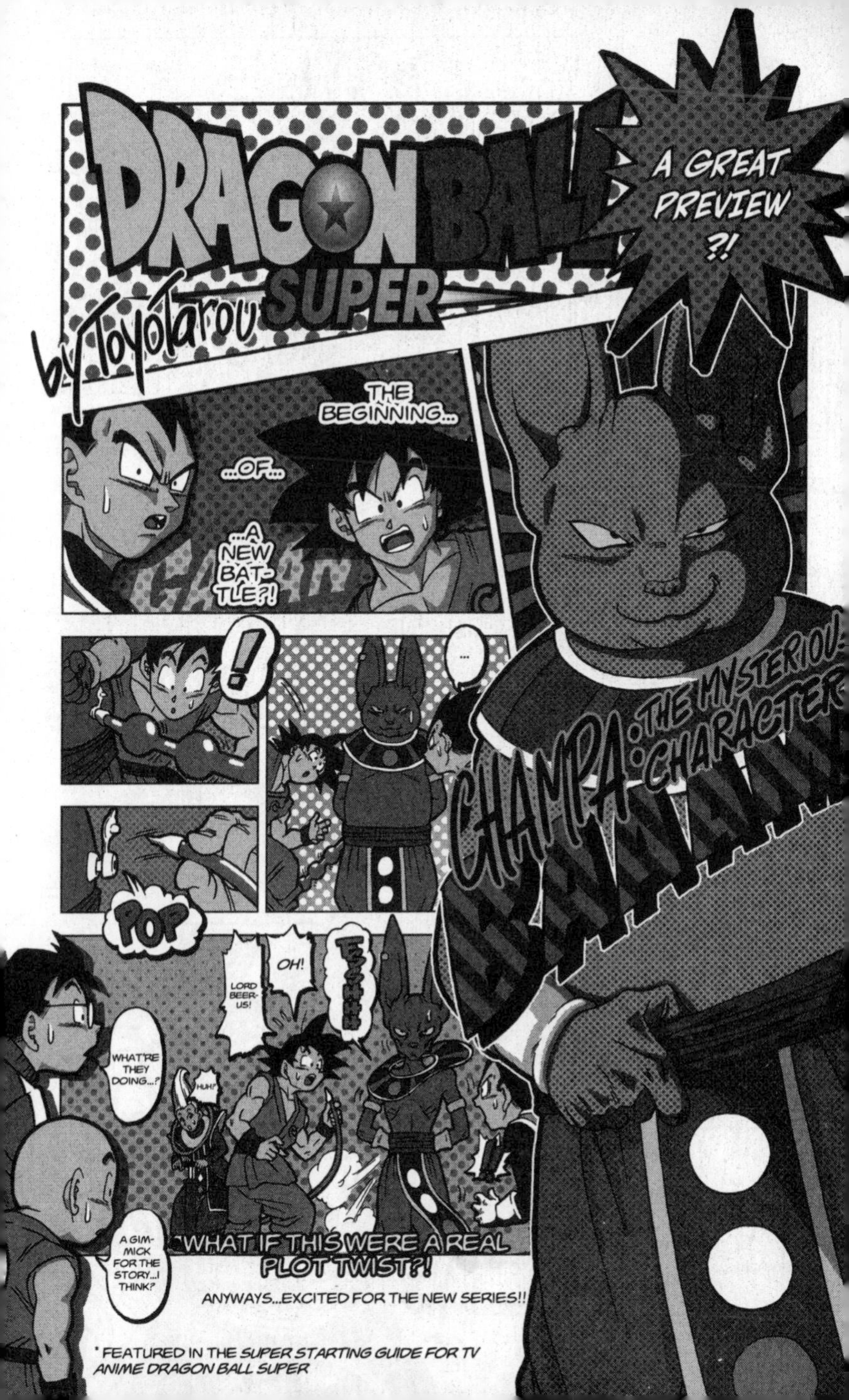
A GREAT PREVIEW ?!
DRAGON BALL SUPER
by Toyotarou
CHAMPA: THE MYSTERIOUS CHARACTER
THE BEGINNING...
...OF...
...A NEW BATTLE?!
!
...
POP
OH!
LORD BEERUS!
HUH?
WHAT'RE THEY DOING...?
A GIMMICK FOR THE STORY...I THINK?
*WHAT IF THIS WERE A REAL PLOT TWIST?!
ANYWAYS...EXCITED FOR THE NEW SERIES!!
* FEATURED IN THE *SUPER STARTING GUIDE FOR TV ANIME DRAGON BALL SUPER*

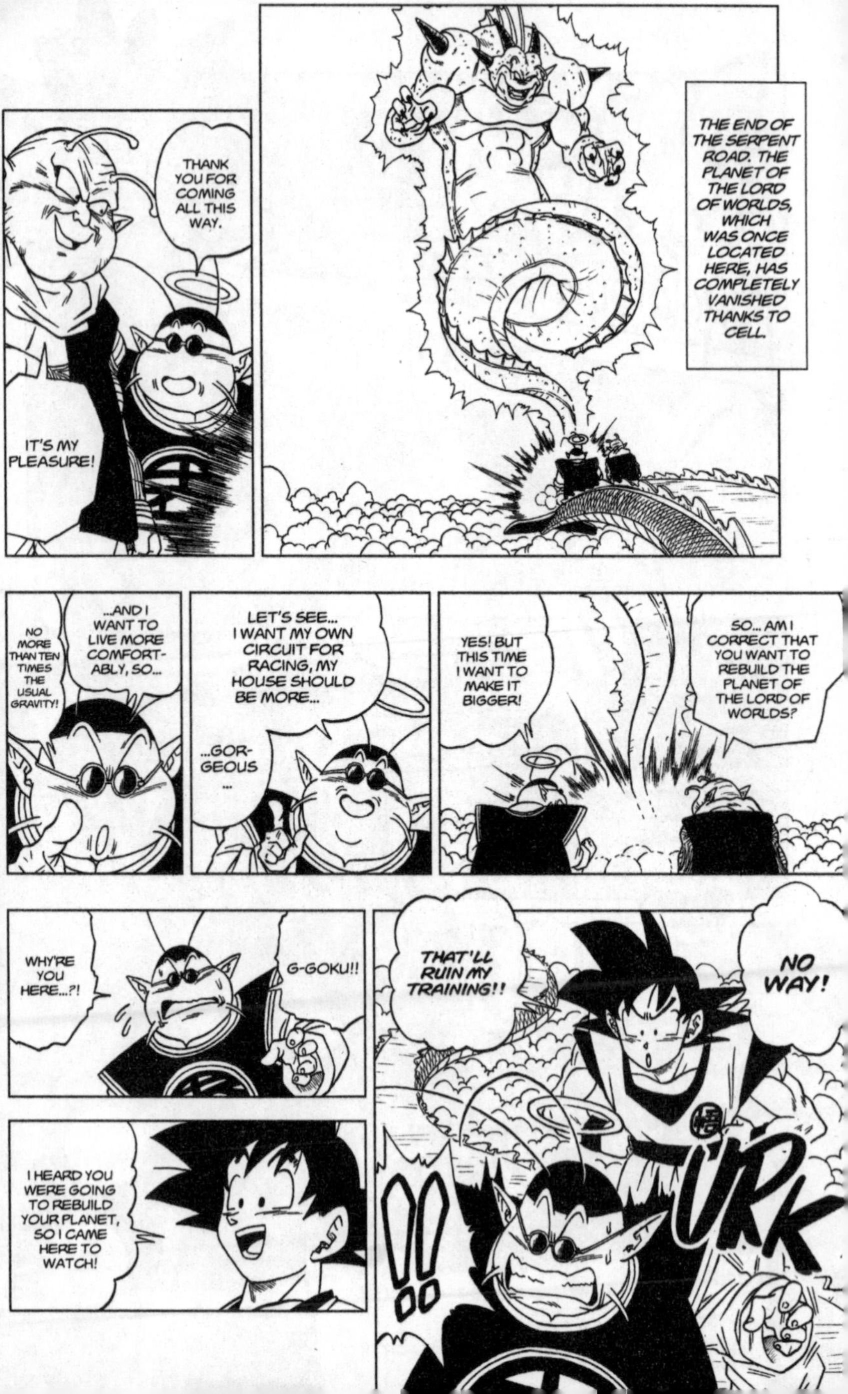
THE END OF THE SERPENT ROAD. THE PLANET OF THE LORD OF WORLDS, WHICH WAS ONCE LOCATED HERE, HAS COMPLETELY VANISHED THANKS TO CELL.
THANK YOU FOR COMING ALL THIS WAY.
IT'S MY PLEASURE!
SO... AM I CORRECT THAT YOU WANT TO REBUILD THE PLANET OF THE LORD OF WORLDS?
YES! BUT THIS TIME I WANT TO MAKE IT BIGGER!
LET'S SEE... I WANT MY OWN CIRCUIT FOR RACING, MY HOUSE SHOULD BE MORE...
...GOR-GEOUS ...
...AND I WANT TO LIVE MORE COMFORT-ABLY, SO...
NO MORE THAN TEN TIMES THE USUAL GRAVITY!
NO WAY!
THAT'LL RUIN MY TRAINING!!
URK
!!
G-GOKU!!
WHY'RE YOU HERE...?!
I HEARD YOU WERE GOING TO REBUILD YOUR PLANET, SO I CAME HERE TO WATCH!

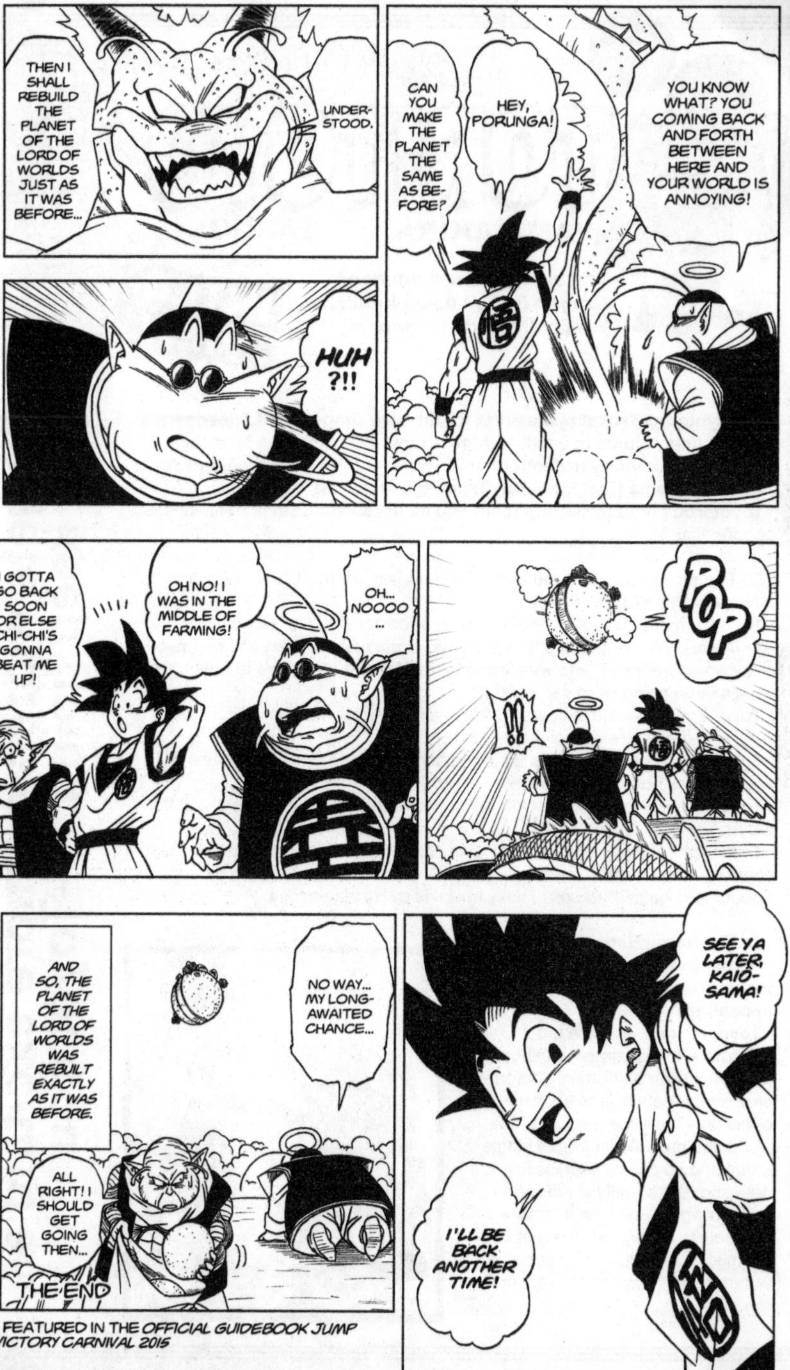

HEY, PORUNGA!
CAN YOU MAKE THE PLANET THE SAME AS BE-FORE?
YOU KNOW WHAT? YOU COMING BACK AND FORTH BETWEEN HERE AND YOUR WORLD IS ANNOYING!
UNDER-STOOD.
THEN I SHALL REBUILD THE PLANET OF THE LORD OF WORLDS JUST AS IT WAS BEFORE...
HUH ?!!
POP
!!
OH... NOOOO ...
OH NO! I WAS IN THE MIDDLE OF FARMING!
I GOTTA GO BACK SOON OR ELSE CHI-CHI'S GONNA BEAT ME UP!
SEE YA LATER, KAIO-SAMA!
I'LL BE BACK ANOTHER TIME!
NO WAY... MY LONG-AWAITED CHANCE...
AND SO, THE PLANET OF THE LORD OF WORLDS WAS REBUILT EXACTLY AS IT WAS BEFORE.
ALL RIGHT! I SHOULD GET GOING THEN...
THE END

*FEATURED IN THE *OFFICIAL GUIDEBOOK JUMP VICTORY CARNIVAL 2015*

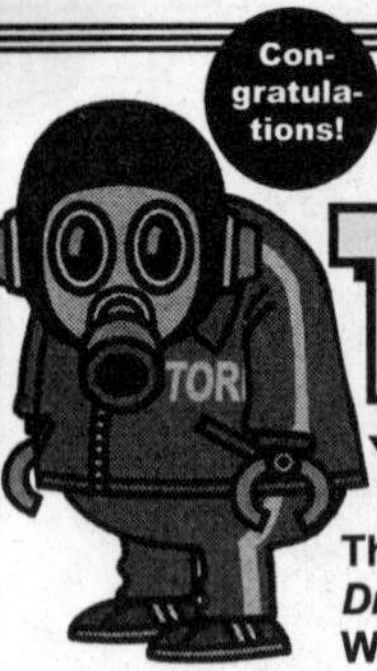
Con-
gratula-
tions!
TORI

DRAGON BALL SUPER 1 In Stores Now!!

TORIYAMA AKIRA TOYOTAROU

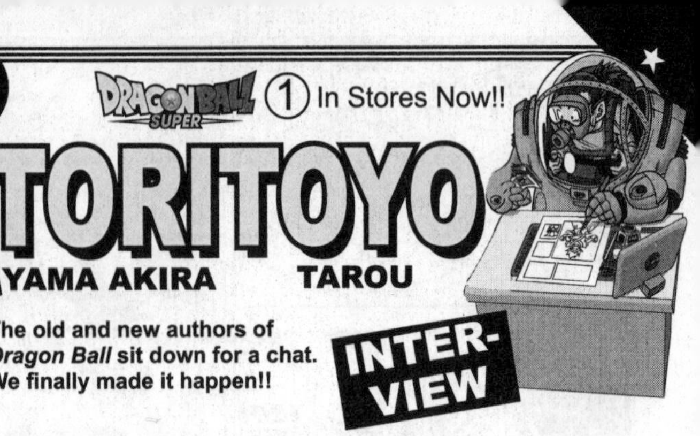

The old and new authors of *Dragon Ball* sit down for a chat. We finally made it happen!!

INTERVIEW

"It gets more and more exciting as you keep going." —Toyotarou

Q: Toyotarou Sensei is the artist for the new *Dragon Ball Super* series and the first volume is finally in stores now! We wanted to take this opportunity to interview both of you. Thank you for your time today.

Akira Toriyama (Tori for short):Thank you for having me.

Toyotarou (Toyo for short):Thank you for the support. I'm grateful for this opportunity.

Q: The plot in this volume is focused mainly on the Universe 6 Arc. How was this storyline created?

Tori: We made two very intense arcs in a row for *Battle of Gods* and *Resurrection F*. We thought that this time, a relatively simpler and brighter story would be better, and we started there. We sort of wanted to balance out what's been going on in the world.

Toyo: You know, the Universe 6 Arc is a fighting tournament and it's been a very long time since one of those has happened!

Tori: I worked on one a little bit at the beginning and end of the Majin Boo Arc, but they both went unfinished! (*laugh*)

Toyo: Yeah! Goku left with Oob in the first round at the last moment of the series.

Tori: Right! (*laugh*) I checked my own copies later and every time I try to come up with something new, I'm just like, "Wow…just how much did I forget about these guys?!" (*laugh*) That's how it is every single time.

Q: Toyotarou Sensei, from your perspective, what do you think makes Toriyama Sensei's work so appealing?

Toyo: I think words are too superficial to explain such things… Elements such as perfectly deformed characters, details in every aspect of his drawings, the amount of the world you can take in from a single panel and so on are especially amazing. But it really is difficult to put into words just how it makes me feel. Truthfully, there is just this inexplicable excitement that surges within me all "*Bwoosh*!!" every time I read his work.

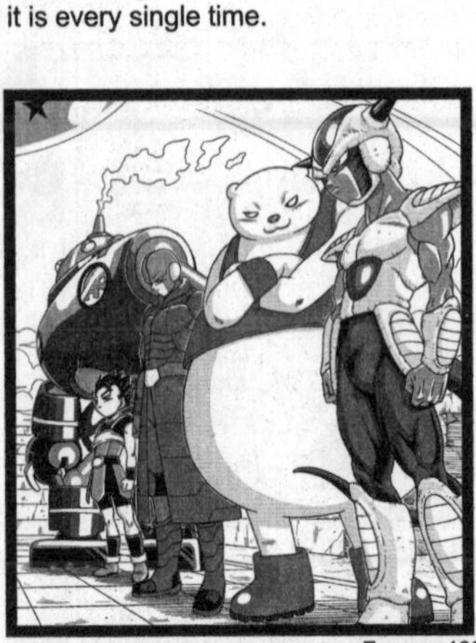

From p. 133

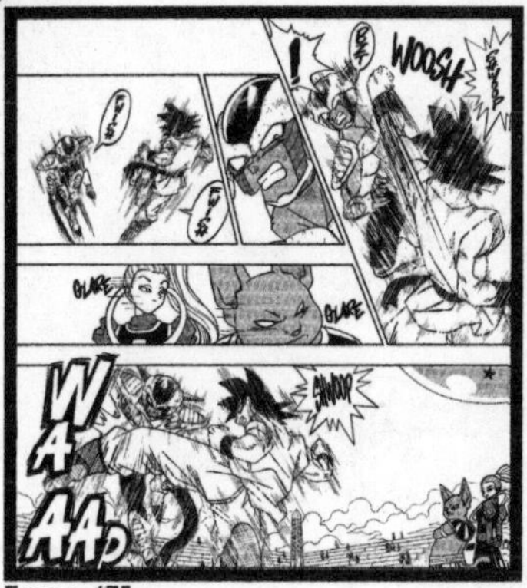
WOOSH
!
FWISH
FWISH
GLARE
GLARE
SWOOP
WAAAAD
From p. 175

Q: *Dragon Ball* is the series that's inspired you the most since you were a child. How do you feel about the fact that you are drawing it yourself?

Toyo: Oh, please! It's more like...as I keep drawing and drawing, the more it becomes obvious that I'm far so behind him. (*sweating*)

Tori: That's not true at all! I think of everyone who works on *Dragon Ball*, including the animators, your work is the closest to my own!

Toyo: No way!

Tori: You are so good at composition! It's really cool. Right now, I don't think I could make such lively drawings. When I supervise other people's work, including anime and other media, I always find some part that I'm not happy with. When that happens, I definitely ask them to fix it. But when I see your name on it, I know I can be at ease. I can quickly just say, "It's all good!" and that helps me a lot. (*laugh*)

Toyo: Oh wow...I'm always scared that Toriyama Sensei is getting more and more frustrated with me. He gives me the scripts for this series. So, normally when I draw, I always have Sensei's original manga next to me for reference. This is so that readers won't think, "This isn't *Dragon Ball!*" But I also feel that I should try to expand my imagination and draw more things like my own original movements or various facial expressions and stuff like that.

Tori: I don't mind if you let loose! Not at all!! (*laugh*).

Q: Toriyama Sensei, is there any advice you'd like to give to Toyotarou Sensei?

Tori: Me? I'm pretty much...happy with how he's doing already. (*laugh*)

Toyo: Umm, you know...anything I need to fix or something else...I'd be really grateful if you were stricter about what I'm bad at. (*sweat*)

Tori: HA HA HA! (*laughing hard*) Nothing in particular... (*thinks for a few seconds*) Seriously, there's nothing! Let me see...if I do have to say anything, I think you'll get even closer to perfection if you vary perspective more across a page's composition. Other than that...if you can add your own originality, I would probably think, "This is amazing!" Seriously, I'm *that* grateful for all your work. I finally get to see a successor who can create such a perfect continuation of my work!

Q: Lastly, could you tell us a little bit about the upcoming story in *Dragon Ball Super*?

Tori: I have this idea about the future of a certain person...and I'm thinking about combining it with this new universe. I'm going to make this story simple so that kids can enjoy it too. That's at least what I hope will happen. (*laugh*)

Toyo: A "certain person"? That's something that I'm interested in! I'm looking forward to it!

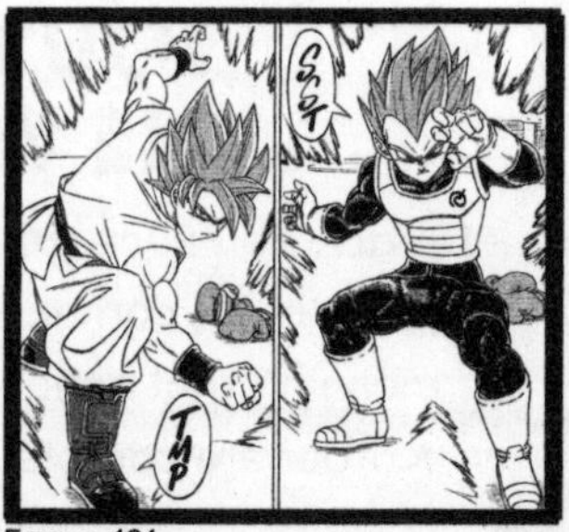
SKSH
TMP
From p. 124

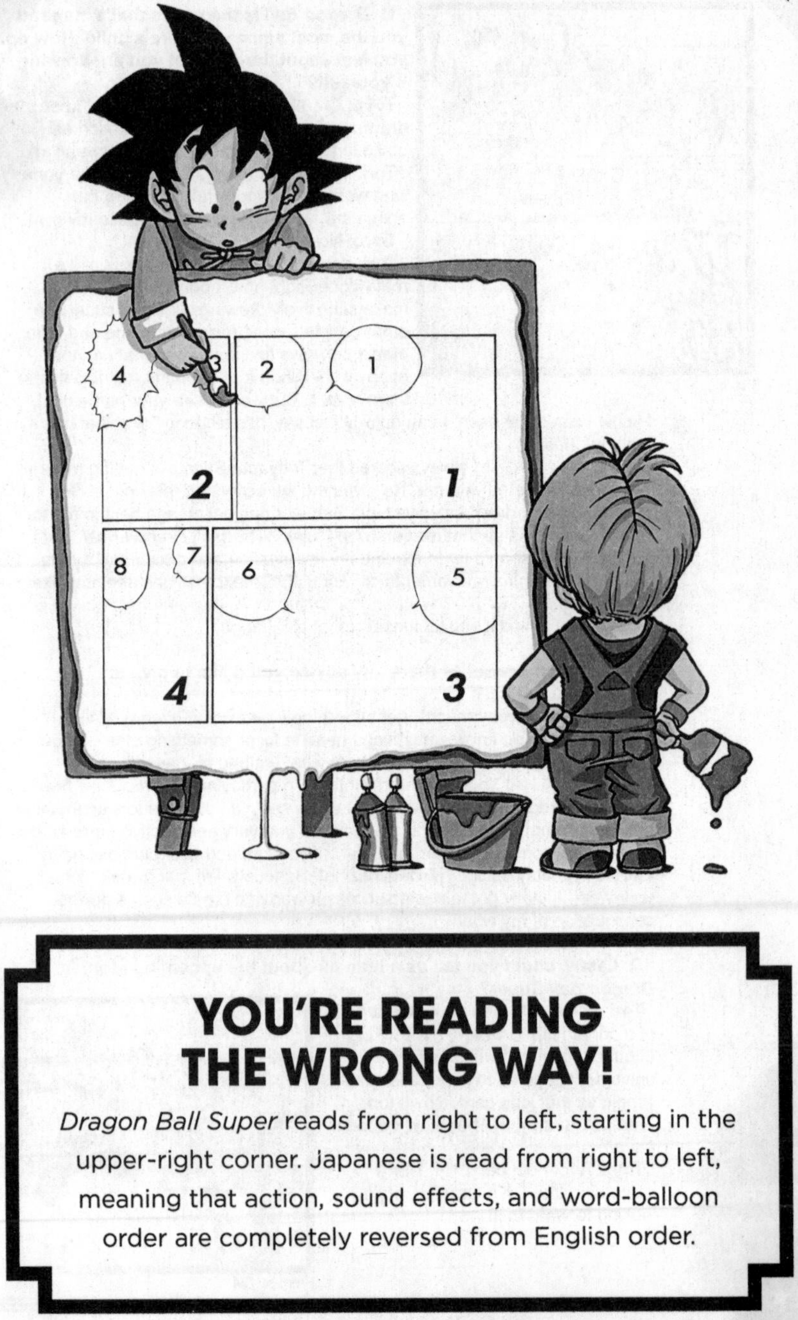

1
2
3
4
1
2
5
6
7
8
3
4

YOU'RE READING THE WRONG WAY!

Dragon Ball Super reads from right to left, starting in the upper-right corner. Japanese is read from right to left, meaning that action, sound effects, and word-balloon order are completely reversed from English order.